PREVIOUS CONVICTIONS

By the Same Author

THE ROCK POOL
ENEMIES OF PROMISE
THE UNQUIET GRAVE
THE CONDEMNED PLAYGROUND
THE MISSING DIPLOMATS
IDEAS AND PLACES

LES PAVILLONS
(*co-author*)

PREVIOUS CONVICTIONS

BY

CYRIL CONNOLLY

HAMISH HAMILTON

LONDON

First Published in Great Britain, 1963
by Hamish Hamilton Ltd.
90 Great Russell Street London WC 1

Printed in Great Britain by
T. & A. Constable Ltd.
Hopetoun Street Edinburgh

To B.S.

Oak before ash, look out for a splash

CONTENTS

PART TWO
THE GRAND POSSESSORS

PART THREE

THE MODERN MOVEMENT

PART FOUR

PAGING MR SMARTIBOOTS

INTRODUCTION

The problem of the literary journalist who feels inhibited from completing larger projects is how to make a book. In the old days critics used to write very long articles and no one noticed that Macaulay's essays were book reviews or that Sainte-Beuve's 'Causeries du Lundi' were what we call Sunday journalism. Now articles are much shorter and therefore more monotonous. The naked bones of reviewing cannot be concealed.

Why a book? Because we like to get the best of our ephemeral criticism between hard covers where it may be perpetuated a little longer and even refresh those to whom it is familiar besides influencing those who do not know it already. If I have a gift it is that of being able to communicate my enthusiasm for literature and throw a little light on my favourite authors—and there are a great many. My last two books of collected essays are both out of print: I really don't know why one goes on. But a year or two's further circulation may still preserve many of these articles from the certain oblivion which would otherwise attend them and perhaps help to kindle a more fertile enthusiasm in new readers. And this book is so arranged that it builds up to a picture of the author; an ageing Narcissus complete with pool.

The plan is simple. It consists of four sections: the first, the visible world ('I am one of those for whom the visible world exists.' Gautier) consists of travel pieces, articles on the Rococo, on underwater fishing while there were still some fish, on animals before they became smart. I wanted to communicate my love of travel and also of works of art and the urgent necessity of preserving them and the beauties of nature above and below sea-level together with the threatened world of animals for which we now have a British rallying-point.[1] The next section, 'The Grand

[1] The World Wildlife Fund.

Possessors' (from the preface to Shakespeare's *Troilus and Cressida*) takes us into literature proper and we slalom down the sacred mountain from Petronius to Big Meaulnes. I have omitted writers who do not awaken in me the appropriate kinship reaction (e.g. Victor Hugo) even if I think I have written well about them and I have selected what I consider to be the best article out of several on favourites like Flaubert and Baudelaire. Readers may notice an attachment to the English eighteenth century and the French nineteenth and perhaps too much about Horace Walpole who links up with the Rococo again. Of all periods not my own I have been most deeply moved and formed by the French nineteenth century, by Baudelaire, Flaubert, Rimbaud, Mallarmé, Nerval, Huysmans, Villiers and the Goncourt Journals. But one cannot always shelter in the past and so the next section—also literary—is confined to the modern movement, especially in England and America. (Thus Gide, Valéry and Surrealism are omitted in favour of Fitzgerald and Hemingway.) Here there are some gaps. I was not satisfied with anything I had written in the last ten years about Wilson, Waugh or Auden or younger writers whom I had reviewed without really getting to know. In these two literary sections I have not tried to expand reviews but rather to combine them in such a way that they produce a flowing line, a chronological montage which atones for their brevity. They are rich in cross-references. I have included an earlier piece on Joyce which has never been reprinted to show how differently one felt in war-time London about his death (1941). The last section consists of some satires and parodies, and concludes with three less frivolous statements to complete the self-portrait. 'The Downfall of Jonathan Edax' was written for the *Sunday Times* 'Seven Deadly Sins' as a study in covetousness; I had in mind the character (or one aspect of it) of the late T. J. Wise who, unlike Edax, did not accidentally murder his father (Alberich-Hagen). The article on book-collecting, however, does express my own feelings. 'Bond Strikes Camp' was written before the spy trials of 1963 and was intended as pure farce.

One of the sadnesses of bringing out a book is that till then a reviewer enjoys a certain immunity which he forfeits through realising his ambition whereupon all the other critics fall upon him. He is like those creatures which in the mating season throw caution to the winds and are immediately devoured by the predators whom they would normally escape. And yet it has to be done. Secretly I am convinced that there is no happiness outside my prose and I want the world to know it. 'In that case why not take more trouble?' 'How can I take more trouble when I am still writing reviews all the time this is coming out?' 'Well, couldn't you get another job?' 'Such as?' 'Oh, I don't know—teaching, lecturing, broadcasting—'

Vainglorious desiccation! No, writing for a Sunday paper has tempered my improvidence and widened my knowledge; it has respected my solitude and prevented *rigor mentis* setting in. Without the weekly stint I might have written longer and better—or dissipated my powers in false starts and frustration

> 'convict by flight, rebel to every law,
> conviction to the serpent none belongs'.

1

THE GRAND TOUR

I HAVE always been fascinated by the Grand Tour. In how many biographies over the last three centuries does it not form the pleasantest chapter? The hero's first encounter with the wonder of Europe, the sense of the past, the attraction of foreign minds, the acquaintance with love, and then the belated return from the little foreign courts with their polished manners to the crudities of the pocket borough, the club and the gaming table....

It redeems adolescence and breathes some fresh air into the political fiery furnace. But is there an age limit? And what survives in the present day from that enchanted circuit? I have just been given the chance to find out.

What are the essentials of the Grand Tour? A visit to Italy, in particular to Florence, Rome and Naples (which in those days was a capital with a glittering court). These could be approached by Paris, Lyon and Turin (another court) or by the South of France (Montpellier was a favoured resort) or by the republic of Geneva, Lausanne and the Simplon. Voltaire at Ferney was a 'must', and Milan and Venice were capitals of pleasure.

I broke all the rules and took my wife, who had never been to Italy, thus falling into the old Grand Tour role of bear-leader. We concentrated on the essentials, which were Florence and Rome, and substituted Palermo for Naples, now shorn of so much of its glory.

The Grand Tour is a mood and a state of mind. There must be no worries about money; one must be able to buy a book or a tie or give somebody dinner; one must feel like an heir coming into his inheritance who has nothing to do every day but live it from morning to midnight, without anxiety or remorse. One must be consumed with curiosity and permit no misgivings about the leaky receptacle where all the new information (much of it forgotten from previous visits) will be stored. Our duty is to learn and feel, not to reason why.

On the Grand Tour we owe something to ourselves, a little relaxation of an evening. The Englishman of the eighteenth century was not guilt-ridden; he brought a mask and a domino, he did not crawl through museums as if preparing for an examination.

I suppose in our time the Grand Tour should be undertaken by car or by making use of the new special car-and-sleeper services, but there seemed no point in motoring to Sicily. Flying, on the other hand, would deny the benefit of the slow plunge southward and set us down in Rome before Florence, which is inartistic. We chose the Simplon Express, and so sleepers were booked and one cloudy morning we set off with reserved Pullman seats and meal tickets on the Golden Arrow.

I am partial to trains; I belong to a generation which grew up to worship flight for flight's sake; I was an original member of the Oxford Railway Club. I also have a weakness for good hotels and experience a satisfaction at going to ground in one of them with the pack at my heels.

The Golden Arrow, especially with a cabin on the boat, is still the most luxurious and therefore the most exhilarating way of getting out of the country. It provides a good breakfast on the English side and an excellent luncheon on the other. On both train and boat there still survives that perfect attentive service from an assortment of mellow Jeeveses that one is accorded nowhere else.

At the Gare du Nord one must take the first decision. 'How gaily I used to jump into a taxi and visit the bars while the train crawled round the *Ceinture*. Nowadays . . . I sit glumly in my compartment.' When I read this sentence of Evelyn Waugh two years ago I felt rather sorry for him. Now I, too, sat on in the *Ceinture*, thinking of the money saved on tips and taxis, and sipping champagne.

How Parisian is the *Ceinture*! And how Parisian one would be if one could recognise its landmarks. Even following it with a map we got lost. A glimpse of the Sacré Coeur, of razor-sharp corner houses, of leafy boulevards which we trundled over, then some splendid inland waterway with locks and harbours, some woods and precipices—could they be the Buttes Chaumont? A cemetery —was it Père la Chaise? A forest—the Bois de Vincennes? And then we seemed to be returning again to the heart of the city in the slanting sunset—somewhere very near the Seine.

Here at the Gare de Lyon the magic ended; we ceased to be Grand Tourists; crowds of sinister little people milled about; something seemed vaguely wrong. Our sleeping car attendant wore no uniform and was having a row with a porter-like creature, the kind who so pointedly explains that he does not go any farther. 'Je connais mes droits,' he screamed. 'Je vous *emmerde*!' Our attendant (an Italian) bellowed back and seemed rather tipsy. We left them and went to get our tickets for the *wagon-restaurant*.

Should we choose the first or the second service—dine as we left, at half-past eight, or let appetite simmer till nine forty-five? A nice problem. But all the tickets for the first service were already booked by Vampire's Tours. The second then, but all the tickets for that had been reserved by the Locust Agency. Monsieur would have to wait and see if there were any cancellations.

Well, there are always cancellations. The Simplon Express slid off into the dusk with packed carriages to Venice and Trieste, Florence and Rome. As we moved out, the fifty members of the first party filed by us. There were no vacancies, only some rather good smells.

When it was time for the second service we tried again. The corridors were now jammed with waiting couples and impatient business men. Once more a party of fifty Nordic harpies pushed past. There were indignant murmurs.

Then the word went round. There would be a third service, the wagon-restaurant would not be disconnected at Dôle. Till then it remained locked, and by Dôle the whole corridor was packed with hungry people. The diners left; the train stopped—and the wagon was disconnected with a dreadful clink. We had been betrayed.

A woman screamed, 'At least give us some bread', and was handed a biscuit. A business man thundered, 'If there were a journalist here he would write that in France there was not enough to eat'—'I am a journalist,' I rumbled, 'and I shall write precisely that.'

*

Few sights are more beautiful than the Lombard plain in the thick morning mist from the lower berth of a wagon-lit, with the leather curtain slightly raised and the blue *veilleuse* still gleaming. With a net full of guide-books and the little reading-light, the enclosed wash-basin and one's clothes swinging on the hanger, one is snug as a Pharaoh. Now we leave the poplar alleys and quiet waterways and take to the mountains with a tunnel nearly as long as the Simplon, until the acacia scrub on the hills gives way to olives, a stream tumbles southwards and we descend by Prato to the sunlit valley.

Amid those cypress-wooded hills that mount
Beyond Vinciliata and quarried Ceceri
To where by San Clemente we so often have seen
Tuscany spread its grave and gracious landscape out
From Vallombrosa to the far Carraran peaks;
A vision of enchantment, a delight more deep
Than ever elsewhere spirit or sense may hope to know.

I used to dislike Florence, its inadequate river, its medieval bankers' machicolated fortresses miscalled palaces, its inadequately Mediterranean climate and rainy *rentier* reminders of Bath and Cheltenham, its pale priggish culture-stricken *pensionnaires*—and now it is Ferney without Voltaire, for this is the first time I have been here without visiting Berenson. When first taken to stay with him I was young and rebellious, I kicked against the prigs, read Joyce, and stole out looking for night-life. I never imagined I would one day quote from his old friend Bob Trevelyan's poem to him. It took the last war to make me see he was right, that culture, as he used to say, was precarious, like a match lit in the surrounding darkness that everyone is trying to blow out.

To some extent my attitude had been due to B. B. himself. He felt an ambivalence to the city of his election which seemed provincial to him now that the Russians had gone, and he didn't much like his guests going into the town. Sightseeing in the Val d'Arno was something they were supposed to have got over long ago; one could do it better in his library. Up the hill came the world of fashion and the American professors and art students, while down below lurked people whose talent he admired but whose 'bohemianism' he deplored—Norman Douglas inseparable from Orioli, Reggie Turner, the friend of Wilde, and the Lawrences, then at work on 'Lady Chatterley'; the *trattoria* set whom 'one couldn't possibly know if one lived in the place'. I wish I had tried harder to meet them.

Afterwards I came to love B. B., the sage who enjoyed every happiness except that of artistic creation, the only kind he truly wanted, and now I found myself returning to Florence haunted by his silken voice yet also deeply curious about that more gifted and yet forbidden society which too had passed away.

There was also the Florence of Uncle Eustace in Huxley's *Time Must have a Stop*, Florence considered above all as a pleasure city. With this in mind we made for the Grand Hotel (the modern equivalent of staying with Walpole's friend, Sir Horace Mann) and were never for a moment disappointed.

About ten days' extravagance is enough before the *cafard de grand luxe* sets in and there emerges the point of tension which will become intolerable; the pianist in the bar who projects his personality, the electric clock that suppresses a click before not striking, the staring lift-boy, the concierge who seems to know too much about us. But on this first morning, with the sun shining on a breakfast of hot chocolate and saffron scrambled eggs, nothing could be more friendly.

There is a message from Harold Acton and an invitation from Osbert Sitwell, both of whom hold through the present the keys to the past. Later in the afternoon Harold calls, a grave Florentine patrician who is also an English aesthete, and takes us out to dinner at Pratolino, where we question him about the *Côté de chez Norman.*

Alas, even the *trattorie* which he haunted, 'half king and half cabbie', have disappeared, the light-hearted world so minutely described by him in *Looking Back* and *D. H. Lawrence and Maurice Magnus* and in Osbert Sitwell's *On the Continent* is gone for ever.

And now the Florentine week begins in earnest, a round of rain and sun, of churches and villas, work and play. For sightseeing is work and one clocks into a museum like an office, arriving fresh and leaving with jangled nerves and a furious hunger, still several rooms behind schedule, yet with a satisfaction comparable only to that felt in wartime by those 'engaged in work of national importance'. In a city like Florence, all along our route in fact, one is conscious of a host of predecessors all busy passing judgment until it seems quite impossible to find anything new to say.

'One grows to feel the collections of pictures at the Pitti Palace splendid rather than interesting.' (Henry James was here.) 'None of the works of the uncompromising period, nothing from the half-groping geniuses of the early time . . . a princely creed I should roughly call it—the creed of people who believed in things presenting a fine face to society.' I gave one star to Raphael's 'Fornarina', another to the little Flemish pictures in the corridor with Breughel's magical 'Orphée aux enfers'. The Pitti remains one of the few examples of what a royal collection was actually like in its original surroundings, but we have grown used to the more simplified presentation of works of art.

For this we must go to the Uffizi, after pausing to give these royal palaces credit for one feature so pleasing to Medicis and Hapsburgs—the jewel room. I have always loved the chill of rock crystal, the blue of Lapis, the combination of gold with ivory, small sea-monsters in the shape of baroque pearls or bearing elaborate salt-cellars, agate loving-cups, sapphire and emerald mermaids, satyrs in sardonyx—all the devices by which the princes of the high Renaissance and their goldsmiths sought to carve a chain of hand-holds back to antiquity.

The only 'three stars' for Florence we awarded to the Botticelli room in the Uffizi, as far as contents are concerned perhaps the most beautiful room in the world. We can have reservations about him, we can read volumes explaining the symbolism, the techniques, the doctrinaire significance of these two paintings, the 'Birth of Venus' and the 'Primavera', but nothing can prepare us for the shock when we are confronted by this flowering of the human spirit, the conjunction of an artist whose powers are at their highest, whose erotic sensibility is at full flood, with the moment historically ripe for him, when, after mortifying the flesh for a thousand years, the mind of man is avid for a religion of beauty.

Even without Savonarola to maim Botticelli, even without the sack of Rome to end the 'middle summer's spring' of humanism, the room is instinct with sadness; one weeps first and analyses after; there is something in the breaking water, the whorl of pale wavelets under Venus' whorled shell, or in the pose of the youth examining a fruit with outstretched arm, which confers a benediction on man's search for knowledge and eases the weariness of living. A goddess is present and by believing in her the painter has revealed to us for ever the divinity within himself.

There is another small roomful of Botticellis with the mysterious 'Calumny', there are Flemish rooms (always my favourite), Leonardos, Guardis and Longhis; the Uffizi is perhaps the most perfect picture-gallery in the world and the least tiring. In Florence the Renaissance began a hundred years before anywhere else. This accounts for its fortress-like civic architecture but also gave rise to Giotto and the major breakthrough of Masaccio's frescoes in the Carmine. The Tombs of the Medici close the cycle. Michelangelo is independent of place, the Duke seated in meditation, the figures of Day and Night belong to a timeless world of the imagination, frighteningly adult. Like the Laocoön or 'Paradise Lost' they exist outside the cage of history.

There is nothing like the contemplation of works of art above one's head to provide an appetite; we rush out to find our level. . . .

Florentine cooking is delicious, digestible without being monotonous; besides the tender steaks, the enormous asparagus, the wild strawberries and the fish stew from Leghorn, there are one or two agreeable dishes one can find everywhere, the artichoke omelette (yet it is not really an omelette), *tortino di carciofi* and *fagioli all' ucceletto*, white beans simmered with oil, garlic, sage and tomato in a big earthenware pot until they are impregnated with the aroma and deliciously tender.

Villa-visiting took us out into the country, first to Mrs. Trefusis, who at the Ombrellino owns one of the most civilised views in the world and a terrace which might be the setting for the big scene in one of James's novels. Then farther afield to La Pietra with its renaissance garden, an arrangement of grass and gravel, bay and myrtle, light and shade created by Arthur Acton to absorb the unique collection of statues which he went on making through the first half of the century, salvaging them from abandoned gardens and dilapidated palaces of the North, a work of art in its own right.

Still farther away in the cheerful chianti country Sir Osbert Sitwell directs from his hill-top castle the production of his excellent vermouth, flinty-fragrant as his wit. We saw these houses with roses and wistaria in bloom, when the lemon trees in their huge tubs were emerging from their winter quarters.

The sun shone for us at Montegufoni but when we revisited I Tatti, Berenson's humanist sanctuary, it was pouring with rain. The great buff house with its magnificent library is now the property of the University of Harvard, to which he bequeathed it as a centre for the study of Italian art. The villa remains exactly as he left it, and I wandered through the empty rooms with their familiar objects, the Sienese paintings, the Chinese porphyry lion 'that had listened', he once said, 'to so much good conversation', even the array of thin gilded glasses that were used at his dinner parties, while I puzzled over the nature of existence.

A man who lives to a great age and who acquires both fame and wisdom in the process, remaining for upwards of sixty years in the house which he has built, comes to seem more permanent and indestructible than many a landmark beside which we grew up. And suddenly he is there no longer; the order and ceremony with which he was surrounded prove an illusion and all the affectionate encouragement which he gave to others, that too has vanished. However lovingly the home may be preserved, the personality evaporates with its discrimination and mischief; the perfect house becomes like a dead tooth; unswept, the cypress avenue grows older than its planter.

How many ghosts gallop round with us on our journey like riderless horses! It is time to move on.

*

There is no pope in Florence, no pagan monuments, scarcely any baroque, no *dolce vita*. Rome has them all; we deal stars thick and fast. Two for the Piazza di Spagna at azalea time, the steps all the way up a forest of blossom, two more for the Piazza Navona where one can dine quietly in the open while tracing the lines of Domitian's stadium for Greek foot-races in this loveliest of Roman squares.

Round the stadium were grouped the brothels where Saint Agnes won her martyrdom under Diocletian, and her church by Borromini combines with the Bernini fountain of the four rivers to complete the sumptuous baroque ensemble. There are two good restaurants and a café on the square, and the youthful co-proprietor of one of them was during our visit involved in a killing. He had pursued and unfortunately contrived to shoot a teenage gangster who was stealing a transistor set from a client's parked car.

The hotel we had chosen was an old favourite. A hundred years ago the King of Portugal had stayed there and its furnishings and pictures have remained in keeping with his visit. Some of the rooms are palatial, and ours was a converted salon with four long windows and three beds. There is a rumour that furring of the pipes has long prevented hot water ever rising above the first floor, but this I consider unfounded.

The hotel is really very comfortable, it leaves us to our own devices, and it converges on one of the most attractive quarters of Rome, the Via Condotti with its beautiful shops, and such resorts of ancient elegance as the Caffè Greco and Ranieri's, the Spanish Steps, and all the narrow streets leading towards the Piazza del Popolo or the Piazza Colonna.

Another road slants uphill to the Pincio Gardens and Valadier's, still the best place from which to view at sunset the whole tawny prospect of old Rome with its bridges and cupolas. The hotel is a favourite with people like ourselves and so old friends keep popping up which saves us the uncertainties of waiting on letters of introduction and frees the whole day for sightseeing. This life within the hotel becomes part of the Roman day, like the *Rome Daily American* which inaugurates it and which soon seems to contain all one ever wants to know of the world.

The walk from the hotel to the foot of the Spanish Steps, where husbands cross over for the American Express and wives turn right for the hairdresser, to meet again on the red plush seats of the Caffè Greco for chocolate or Negronis, is a daily ritual, when all the hotel habitués are encountered.

One hears of other hotels in Rome: the Edwardian magnificence of the Grand, the papal charm of the Nazionale and the Minerva, the view from the top rooms of the Hôtel de la Ville, the chic of the Hassler, the gaiety of the Flora, the august obscurity of the Croix de Malte; but none of us ever dream of moving to them. The Inghilterra is in our bones.

There are three sights which I always revisit on the first day: the Pantheon, the Piazza Campidoglio and the National Museum (delle Terme). The Pantheon is one of the seven wonders of my world; it is certainly the oldest roof in Europe whose bronze dome delighted Rutilius Namatianus when he sailed away to France in 416, the last poet of the Roman Empire. All the credit for it is now given to the Emperor Hadrian, who incidentally borrowed the idea of a circular opening to admit the light from Nero's Golden House.

The bronze doors are original, so is the pavement; the vast

octagonal temple is as broad as it is high. The Barberini Pope removed the bronze from the roof for the Baldacchino of St. Peter's, but the gilt-bronze of the interior dome was taken to Byzantium in the seventh century. Both should be restored.

One can climb to the top of the Pantheon and look down through the hole (thirty feet across), but I have never dared. It is enough to stand by the tomb of Raphael and look up. 'The game is to describe a sphere in a cylinder: if the curve of the dome were projected beyond the point where it meets the vertical walls of the drum, the bottom of the curve would be just tangent with the floor.'

If the Pantheon is a building which did away with the monotony of the rectangular Greek temple, the Piazza Campidoglio is a space—but what a space! It was designed by Michelangelo, flanked on three sides by palaces, two of which are museums, while in the centre is the equestrian statue of Marcus Aurelius, surely the most perfect evocation of power tempered by wisdom, even by compassion. 'Extending its arm with a command which is in itself a benediction,' as Hawthorne put it. 'I doubt if any statue of King or captain in the public places of the world has more to commend it to the general heart,' wrote Henry James. 'Irrecoverable simplicity—residing so in irrecoverable style . . . in the capital of Christendom the portrait most suggestive of a Christian conscience is that of a pagan emperor.'

It is a certain wistfulness of expression that captivates us and which is found also in the portraits of the philosopher-emperor on the reliefs in the adjoining museum. For both the flanking palaces, renaissance masterpieces in their own right house magnificent collections more or less as they were seen by the Grand Tourists of old.

In the Capitoline museum are Hawthorne's Marble Faun and the 'Dying Gladiator [or Gaul]', and the extraordinary room of Roman portrait busts: soldiers, emperors and sages—cagey Augustus, beatnik Heliogabalus, bull-necked Nero, Socrates looking like Verlaine, and a lady who is the image of Virginia Woolf. What a wealth of information about personality, a typologist's casebook.

The museum of the Conservators, opposite, is even richer. I think of a friend of mine who arrived in Rome in the small hours after a long day's journey and drove his car round and round Aurelius's statue (a perfect turning circle) for half an hour in a state of ecstasy. The fourth side of Michelangelo's square (where once the Sibylline books were kept) is open to the Capitoline steps by the statues of Castor and Pollux and here Horace, in the poem which was also his farewell, pictured priest and silent vestal for ever ascending

> dum Capitolium
> Scandet cum tacita virgine pontifex.

The National Museum is opposite the station, inside the Baths of Diocletian where it is always cool. It contains some beautifully laid out modern rooms and I make my way first to the top where the garden frescoes from the Empress Livia's villa occupy four walls of an otherwise empty room. An apparently monotonous design of fruit-trees and flowering shrubs meanders round the wall across a low painted trellis which invites one to step over. But the effect is magical for we are seeing nature through the eyes of the first Roman empress.

This was how the world looked, this was what a garden meant to her . . . or rather, it had only just begun to look like that, owing to the painter Ludius, 'noted for having been the first to introduce in this kind of pictorial composition views of buildings and ports, and famous for the freshness, the vivacity and the sense of reality that he knew how to bring out in his landscapes . . . in the rendering of the continuous garden the artist obtains, by means of light and shade, atonal gradations of colour, the desired spatial effects' (Rizzo).

One can almost touch them in this misty orchard, bursting pomegranates, golden quinces and the illusory fruit of the strawberry tree. Roses bloom underneath, oleanders are in flower and cypresses with birds perching wherever they can while quail or a tame pigeon waddle by the low railing. Irrecoverable simplicity!

'The distance remains magically imprenetrable,' wrote the ninety-year-old Berenson, 'veiled as it was in the gardens of Lithuania where I lived when I first came to awareness.'

Quite as remarkable are the finds from the Roman villa of the Farnesina, where in 1879 were discovered 'the most beautiful mural paintings that had ever been admired in Rome'. These frescoes (another triumph of preservation) are among the most vivid and haunting to be seen outside Naples, and yet they are inferior to the exquisite stuccoes which adorned the ceilings of three of the rooms. These are light and airy *chinoiserie*: delicate bridges span ravines or link gossamer temples where poets meditate and goatherds sacrifice, a boy is led up to an old Silenus, a satyr raises a leather bottle, a sentry Priapus salutes from the hip.

A museum of such perfectionism is a powder-magazine where the imagination can suddenly be blown sky-high. Perhaps the mosaics will set off the train—for whereas a few years ago I found Pompeian painting the supreme art, now I give mosaic the palm—its colours are fresher, it is less blurred and also less conventional. What we all need is another Berenson to give us a great work on Greek and Roman painting and mosaics which will make correct attributions and identify certain painters as Sir John Beazley has done for Greek vases. Then Ludius (or Studius) and lofty Fabullus and Dioscorides of Samos, or Seleucus (whose signature is found in the Farnesina), will come into their own.

Somehow every Roman evening is different while the days, clotted with sightseeing, are all the same. Except when one gets out in the country—where more museums, more neck-stretching await us. One day it is an open car to Tivoli and Palestrina and a morning at Hadrian's villa with its broad canal lined with statues and its marine theatre where the manic-depressive emperor could haul up the drawbridge and dine on his tiny island.

On the way we stopped at the tomb of the Plautii, with its superb lettering, and then went on to the permanent aquatic strip-tease of the Villa d'Este where water spurts and foams and billows to take the shape of every known fountain. Compared to

Hadrian's villa or the Temple of the Sibyl it is insubstantial, superficial almost, yet nothing is more satisfying than its impressive water-organ or the looping cascades that run along the Alley of the Hundred Fountains. Only the Nile mosaic in the museum at Palestrina, a floating paradise islanded with temples and enlivened by crocodile and ibis, religious processions, soldiers, duck-hunts, hippopotamus chases, houseboats peddling lotus seeds, can compete with the Cardinal d'Este's caprice in homage to wetness.

Alas for Palestrina and Hadrian's villa, I never understood them till yesterday, when I read Mr. Mackendrick's excellent *The Mute Stones Speak*. Then I learnt how much the bombing of Palestrina had revealed of Sulla's Temple of Fortune: 'a turning point in the history of architecture, perhaps the most seminal architectural complex in the whole Roman World'. We saw nothing of this, and climbed up and down in vain—any more than we saw (with informed eye) Hadrian's palace-block in the Piazza d'Oro: 'Here the vastness, sweep and richness comes to a climax in a design which has been called lyrical, feminine and even Mozartian.' So much curiosity; and so little discovered!

We were a little better prepared—by Georgina Masson's *Italian Gardens*—for Caprarola and the Villa Lante, another formal water-paradise where a stream is made to evolve through the phases of a river, an Anna Livia in miniature, from a basin down a series of terraces to a square 'sea' with stone boats and a sculptured island.

The Villa Lante, like the Villa d'Este, was the design of a Cardinal (Gambara). The gardens were begun by Vignola—his masterpiece—in 1566. Montaigne admired them in 1581 and Sacheverell Sitwell has written, 'Were I to choose the most lovely place of the physical beauty of nature in all Italy or in all the world that I have seen with my own eyes, I would name the gardens of the Villa Lante.'

Only eight miles away in the same Viterban foothills is the Villa Orsini at Bomarzo with its abandoned valley of monsters. Giants held an appeal for Vicino Orsini, who (around 1564 perhaps) made use of extraordinary outcrops of stone which could be carved into threatening shapes, a dragon or a giantess or an elephant—there is even a giant tortoise. They have been ignored for centuries, and we still know nothing of owner or sculptor. The whole suggests the workings of a bizarre but highly erudite and congenial imagination.

All this appreciation and Christian Rome still untouched! Where can one start? With the vine mosaic of Santa Costanza? Or with a sophisticated baroque gem like the oval San Andrea del Quirinale? The Grand Tourist would begin with St. Peter's and brush the rest aside. Fortunate hidalgos—they didn't have to write about it.

Here in Rome one would wish Christianity to be radiant with happiness and promise as befits the seat of the head of the Church and on a Sunday afternoon we found the Basilica hung with banners and crowded with pilgrims for a saint had just been canonised.

Here in St. Peter's, as in the earliest and most primitive of churches, we are reminded that Christianity is a religion of joy. One certainly does not feel it in the Sistine Chapel where the personality of Michelangelo (five stars, I am afraid) seems obsessed with crime and punishment. The beardless almost florid Christ of the Last Judgment is a truly terrifying arbiter whose patience with our wickedness is (in one furious gesture) exhausted. Yet this same artist could depict the heart-rending figure of Remorse or the impersonal lonely wisdom of the Sibyls or the sublime creation of Adam and then insert himself only as a grimacing mask on a flayed skin. Whenever we encounter Michelangelo we are baffled and humiliated in our littleness even while we marvel.

Nothing is more reassuring than Bramante's Tempietto prototype of so many enchanting pavilions, which we visited next, or more poignant than the tombs in San Pietro in Montoro of the two Irish exiles, Tyrone and Tyrconnel who ended their days here after the 'flight of the Earls' in 1607. From the Janiculum, with its tranquil panorama, we went on to the Aventine, nearer to the Rome of the last century than any other part I know, with the lovely early church of Santa Sabina and then came back by the little temples of Vesta and Fortune.

*

And now the pace quickens. Aqueducts of the Appian Way flash past us between the tunnels, the hills seem brighter and greener; a glimpse of sea-girt Gaeta and then the fertile gardens of the *Terra di Lavoro* whose tall poplars are garlanded with vines.

Three stars for the Naples museum pulsating with life from the Campanian cities. Once again that tremor before the small still-lives, the peaches with a jug of water, the glow of Pompeian red in architectural *trompe-l'oeil*, the 'genre' scenes of Dioscorides, the exquisite mosaic of marine life with squid and octopus, crawfish and John Dory (art forms that were to disappear for the next 1,500 years).

Shall we give up everything to the study of these flickering foreshortened landscapes and harbours? Not just yet, for we are taking the night boat to Sicily. It is most comfortable and we dine well and watch Italian television as the silhouette of Capri slides by, hung with lights like a cruise-boat and we enter the freshening Tyrrhenian.

It is many years since I was in Palermo, and I was distressed to see so much bomb damage still unrepaired along the waterfront, and behind it all such slums and overcrowding. Several travellers returned from Sicily had told us of the sinister atmosphere they found there; we may have been suggestible but it did seem as if the gaiety and welcome of the mainland was clouded with apprehension and as if there was much truth in the stories of the 'honourable society', the Mafia, which was now being modernised on American lines and spreading its rackets everywhere. One had the impression of well-organised exploitation in every petty detail increasingly threatening towards the west and centre of the island.

Hitherto the tour had confined us to cities but here our hotel stood somewhat outside in a large garden by the sea and we breakfasted under the palms. The Villa Igiea is a very good hotel indeed and noise-free, and possesses a beautiful *art nouveau* salon of 1908, left as a memorial to its architect, Basile. As most of the company filming *The Leopard*, including Visconti and Burt Lancaster, were installed there, it proved an almost too absorbing spectacle and caused us to miss several chapels by Serpotta, the late baroque sculptor whose plaster compositions of saints are so moving.

Huge crowds and building programmes make sightseeing in Palermo a torment, a new 'West End' is draining the elegance away from the old centre of the *Quattro Canti*; the baroque palaces along the Via Alloro are coming down, the Arab *Khalsa*, once the most picturesque quarter of fisherfolk and fine buildings will soon be a thing of the past. The Arabs are represented by one or two small palaces, the Hohenstaufen Emperors by their superb tombs in the cathedral where that unhappy family seems to brood in Byzantine aloofness.

Nearly everything that wins a star is the work of the Normans; especially the happy little botanically-minded cloister of San Giovanni degli Eremiti whose domes rise out of a former mosque, the Capella Palatina which merits two stars and Monreale which deserves three. The general effect is overpowering and enhanced by the grandeur, dignity and brightness of the interior with not an inch left bare. I found the mosaics here warmer and bolder, better conceived and more original than those in the much smaller Capella Palatina which seemed a rehearsal for them, though others prefer its more miniature scale and subtler lighting.

Monreale alone makes a visit to Sicily essential, even if it were without its view and Norman-Arab cloister. I have seen these Norman wonders of Palermo four times now and I find that memory has completely obliterated my other visits. Just precisely what is the point of sightseeing if everything goes in at one eye and out the other so that after ten years the whole of Europe has to be mugged up again? But hush! This is the Grand Tour.

And now we come on something seen for the first time—Sicilian Rococo. I remember vividly the glass furniture—coloured glass with brocade covers—that Mr. John Richardson had installed in Mr. Douglas Cooper's château near the Pont du Gard, and which had come via the auction room from the Villa Rosebery at Naples where it had been acquired from the Villa Palagonia outside Palermo; the prettiest furniture I had ever seen.

And I remembered Goethe's description of meeting in the street a distinguished elderly gentleman in Court dress followed by liveried servants holding out dishes for alms. It was the Prince of Palagonia, creator and owner of the villa, collecting money to free Christian slaves. This does not tally with other reports of him as a lecherous hunchback, 'a poor miserable lean figure shivering at every breeze'. This was the Prince Ferdinando who was responsible for the fantastic decoration; the villa itself was begun by an earlier Ferdinando in 1715.

A curved open staircase leads up from the outside and the main façade is also curved which lends it an enchantment not marred by the circular garden with its ubiquitous evidences of decay. It is otherwise with the interior. What was a highly original, even surrealist décor has almost entirely disappeared including, besides the glass furniture, ornaments composed of fragments of broken mirror, old picture frames, barometer tubes, brocaded sofas with iron spikes concealed in them, rusty iron mobiles and chandeliers, columns and pyramids of broken china encrusted with tea-pots. . . . Now all is derelict and though help is supposedly on its way, it may arrive too late.

There is a large domed room with a looking-glass ceiling and rococo decoration, with polychrome portrait-busts of the family, and a long dining-room in bad repair. These rooms are faced both with marble and with glass to look like marble. A sculptured frieze of musical dwarfs survives on the coach-house. 'It is eccentric surely; it is amusing; it may even be pretty,' writes Mr. Lees-Milne. It would do very nicely for me.

Bagheria, except for its eighteenth-century villas, is like a straggling town in Andalusia but a little way up the hill the Villa Valguarana boasts a superb façade and an enchanted view.

The next day, after bidding farewell to our resourceful and patient mentor, Mr. Archibald Colquhoun, we left at crack of dawn by bus, the most practical way to see the island. There is much to be said for the touring bus, especially in a not wholly developed region. A polyglot hostess describes what we are about to visit in three languages so that we will never forget it. Although each spot can be reached by train or car, only a maniac could get to all of them and when hotels are so indifferent the bus enforces a certain standard. We all become coach-proud. And sometimes our hostess tells us in three languages there is nothing to see and we can go to sleep and then we drop off obediently. What I liked best was calling at the different hotels to set down passengers so that we could make our choice for the next time.

We leave Palermo past the Favorita palace (said to equal the Brighton Pavilion) and then along the lovely north coast to Segesta—three stars, and for the last time. It is in a romantic position on an isolated hill-top, a large unfinished Doric temple (the columns are unfluted) perhaps abandoned because of fire or invasion but of the perfect period. For temples must not be judged by how complete they are but by the moment when they were built, and after the fifth century (Segesta is safe by forty or fifty years) some virtue goes out of them.

We went on to lunch at Erice, a high mountain plateau covered with grass and pine-woods where a medieval village and castle perch on the site of the great temple of Venus (attributed to Aeneas), a landmark to sailors of the ancient world. Late in the afternoon we came by Trapani and Marsala to Selinunte, still unspoilt, its colossal columns and chaos of ruins abutting on to rushy sand dunes by the loneliest of seas and then to coffee in cheerful Sciacca (the poor man's Nerja) before being squirted out for the night in Agrigento, a booming and most *mafioso* town.

The next day was begun with the temples which are in wonderfully preserved condition, but later in date than Segesta and somewhat lacking in inspiration, except for the scanty remains of the colossal temple of Zeus and the early temple of Hercules. A broad new asphalt road with petrol station winds round the temples that I once approached on foot over the fields and adds bitumen to their numen. We are now in the far south; it is already very hot by breakfast; we drive round Licata through a pale empty heat-haze with scattered new settlements in cube-shaped houses and a landscape of strange crops—early tomatoes and ground-nuts.

Gela with its oil-derricks, like a boom town on the Texan gulf, and Caltanisetta (inland) mark the easternmost limits of the Mafia. It is a relief to take to the hills and ascend the lovely green valley with its hazel orchards to Piazza Armerina. This was what we had come to Sicily to see for the greater part of the excavations are only ten years old.

The Palace of the Emperor Maximian (A.D. 286 to 305), the colleague of Diocletian, is as ambitious as any from Nero's Golden House to Diocletian's Spalato. It is an enormous agglomeration which has been enclosed in perspex to preserve the mosaics until it looks like some *avant-garde* prizewinner at an international exhibition. The site, 2,000 feet up a wooded green valley with a high mountain protecting it to the north, is one of the pleasantest on the island. The Emperor was identified by Gentili through the portraits of a small boy who is twice represented with a squint. (The Byzantine chronicler John Malalas described Maximian's son Maxentius as cross-eyed.)

The huge area of mosaics was the work of hundreds of craftsmen imported in a hurry from North Africa. Most scenes have to do with the chase or the bringing back alive of large animals for the circus. There are also some gruesome studies of agonising giants and the famous Bikini girls of later and more delicate workmanship. The Imperial latrines must be the envy of tourists from all over the island.

Although the father-in-law of Constantine, Maximian seems to have been aggressively pagan; a ruddy well-pomaded Hemingwayesque tycoon mad on big game and bloodsports, deplorably square, with a bevy of daughters all taking after him. Or are they more probably a Windmill cabaret of water girls?

Syracuse, in spite of the new approach past chemical factories, is still a sacred island. It is the only place in Sicily where one could settle; the air, the light, the sea breeze, the baroque squares, the promenades round the sea-wall contribute, but above all it is a city where the isolated outposts of the world of antiquity of which we have seen so many are concentrated and constitute the place where we live. 'What one feels here,' wrote Gregorovius beside the fountain Arethusa, 'is love for Hellas, the fatherland of every thinking soul.'

Our hotel is about to be taken over but the view across the Great Harbour redeems it and there is a good sea-food restaurant round the corner. The cathedral combines some great columns of a temple to Athena with a dazzling rococo façade.

In the museum is an archaic *ephebus* of the early sixth century and the Venus of Syracuse. According to Maupassant 'C'est la femme telle qu'elle est, telle qu'on l'aime telle qu'on la désire.' I thought the guardian seemed unduly watchful. Bathing had already begun by the Anapus. There was an American yacht in the harbour with special equipment for locating statues under water and hauling them up. Summer was as tempting as Venus.

On our last day we reached Noto, one of the most southerly towns in Europe with its baroque palaces and blue-green araucarias, the lightly swaying Norfolk island pines which guarantee a mild winter. And now begins the long, lovely, exciting, exhausting journey home, at first under the lee of Etna by Catania, Acireale and other cities, past the little tempting islets below Taormina and many unspoilt beaches and then by the train ferry to the mainland with the Sicilian coastal range bidding us an oblique farewell. If I were a rich man looking for a property I would be tempted by the Calabrian coast between Palmi and Tropea with its groves of huge olives and the many lovely strands and coves far from the main road which cluster round Cape Vaticano.

We had allowed for a day and a half in Rome, just enough, as it happened, to see the end of the fine weather. One morning we spent at the Etruscan museum in the Villa Giulia, finding the Apollo of Veii slightly repellent by comparison with the archaic Apollo of Tiber in the Terme, but enraptured by the jovial couple on the Caere sarcophagus carved in what looks like orange-pink blancmange, by the thin Giacometti figurines and by the bronze cauldron over the edge of which alternate figures of men and dogs peer to see what's cooking.

On our last morning, a Sunday, we stopped on the way to the station to hear some Gregorian singing at Sant' Anselmo. The modern church, which belongs to the international Benedictine College, is spacious and austerely elegant. The monks file in and sing unaccompanied, a balm to the soul and the ceremony proceeded with a clear-cut distinction and suavity, with visiting priests and nuns and even a cardinal in the congregation.

No railway addict could have contrived a brighter homeward journey. Our tickets permitted a choice of Alpine routes. We decided to go by Zurich. Leaving Rome at 10.20, the streamlined Settebello (one of the beautiful trains of the world) with unhurrying anapaests (and only three stops) set us down from our armchair seats at Milan in time to catch the Gottardo, of the network of Trans-Europe expresses, which stops only twice before Zurich.

The Settebello is American style with not very good food but enormous wash-rooms. The Gottardo is beautifully Swiss like the lakes and waterfalls and spruce-woods past which it thunders. A young *maître d'hôtel* in morning coat announces dinner which is served by uniformed waitresses from a vast *à la carte* menu. And in Zurich later that night we sipped our Fendant underneath the photograph of Joyce in what is my favourite old-fashioned restaurant.

Grey houses, green hills, a lake and two blue rivers, arcaded quays where one can still recapture the charm and exhilaration of pre-1914 Central Europe—Zurich was the perfect place to return to the North while we cashed the last of those coloured slips which had brought us all that sunshine and San Pellegrino, which had unlocked so many doors and rolled back so many centuries. After this we were able by means of another brilliant Trans-Europe (the Arbalète) to breakfast in Zurich and dine in London thirteen hours later, muttering with Maecenas 'Lubricos quate dentes' (shake out our last tooth) 'vita dum superest bene est' (while one's alive all is well).

2

REVISITING GREECE

AFTER examining a clutch of well-made travel books, I have sometimes wondered for how many pages one could keep it up by setting out to tell the truth, not only about places but about the inadequacy of our feelings. (I have known the Acropolis to resemble a set of false teeth in a broken palate.) When at last we take our long-wished-for holiday what really happens?

There is, first, the period of preparation (in a sense the only time we are abroad); guide-books are compared; experts are consulted; a mirage of a brown, lean summer-self descending on an obese island dances before our eyes and we are convincingly importuned by the wrong clothes, the wrong books, the wrong introductions. 'Of course you will need a white dinner-jacket and a cummerbund'; 'you must take the *whole* of Pausanias'; 'an ultra-violet filter'; 'stout walking shoes'; 'the rubber flippers should be made to measure'.

At twenty we travel to discover ourselves, at thirty for love, at forty out of greed and curiosity, at fifty for a revelation. Irresponsible, illiterate, shedding all ties and cares, we await the visitation, the rebirth. Gradually the present dissolves, England becomes totally unreal; we have in fact already left, not yet air-borne but anxiety-cradled; 'if the flippers are not ready, they cannot possibly be sent on'; 'you quite understand that these traveller's cheques are not negotiable on Mount Athos'; 'don't go to the new hotel but the other one'; 'don't go to the old hotel'; 'there are three new hotels'; 'Corfu is the place for you: it has everything'; 'yes, if you like a green island. I prefer Mikonos'; 'it's never too hot on Corfu'; 'you would hate Corfu'.

D-Day. Running in the new dark glasses in the car to the airport. Livid clouds, infra-red buses, a lurid day-of-judgment air about the hoardings along the clotted avenue. Signs of panic, cleverly concealed, as I board the plane, where I suffer from a private phobia, dispelled only by champagne, that the signal 'Fasten your safety-belts' is staying on for the whole voyage.

Paris: the heat advances across the tarmac, our gaoler for the next six weeks. 'Thick brown overcoat, stout walking shoes, whole of Pausanias,' it mumbles; 'Mr. Connolly? I think we can take care of all that.' Inevitable contrast between London and Paris, the one muffled under its summer cloud-cap, all Wimbledon and roses, the other with a migraine of politics, bleached and persilled in the heat. The bookstall at London Airport for a nation of magazine-readers—if that; at Le Bourget full of expensive works on art and philosophy. The paralysis of suburbia contrasted with the animation of the *banlieue* where a fair is in progress and a horse-drawn dray of children jingles under the catalpas.

How much of a holiday is spent lying gasping on one's back, in planes, trains, cabins, beaches and hotel bedrooms, the guide-book held aloft like an awning? We really travel twice—as a physical object resembling a mummy or small wardrobe-trunk which is shuttled about at considerable expense; and as a mind married to a 'Guide Bleu', always reading about the last place or the next one.

It is suddenly apparent that the heat permits no reading of any kind; whole areas of consciousness must be evacuated, the perimeter of sensation shortened; no past, no future. Only the guide-book survives and the other books we have brought sneak to the bottom of the suitcase. And now the Seven Indispensables perform their ghostly jig from pocket to pocket. The passport, the traveller's cheques, the tickets, the dark glasses, the reading glasses, the pen, the comb. Where are they? I could have sworn I had them a moment ago.

A flying visit to Versailles to see the *petits appartements* rendered famous by the Pompadour, the Dubarry and Madame de Mitford. Intense disappointment; so much redecoration, and everywhere the milling multitudes, locusts of the post-war summer. Illumination: *The human eye deteriorates all it looks at.* Why is the decoration of the House of the Vettii at Pompeii so much less exciting than the new excavations? Because the human eye has faded the colours, vulgarised the painting. The camera also enfeebles its subject, and being photographed too often I believe to cause cancer of the soul.

And now, Venice, city of sore throats, frayed tempers and leaking wallets; alas, never the same for me since I reviewed Hemingway's last novel but one. Much as I disliked the book I remain obsessed by his terrible colonel. I drink Valpolicella and take the fatal stroll to Harry's Bar, stopping on the little bridge where the colonel had a heart-attack on his way from his wine to his martinis. How he would have hated the Biennale! So much painting that should never have come South of the Alps, North of the Po, West of Suez or East of Saint Louis, all maltreated by the heat, the humidity and the merciless light—except the paintings which have some secret poster-quality, Delvaux's clustering cow-like nudes or Bacon's agonising tycoons. Art is bottled sunshine and should never be exposed to it.

And everywhere art-critics, never a painter; symbol of the age of culture-diffusion when publishers and village-explainers travel while authors have to stay at home, when painters in Maida Vale hear from their dealers in Mozambique or Mogador, when Byron would have received a postcard: 'Dear B. London must be very hot. Just off to Ravenna to join the Galignanis and then to meet some Greek publishers at Missolonghi. Hope to be able to do something for you. How goes the Canto?—Yrs., John Murray.'

Revisit the equestrian statue of Colleone in its dingy square. The base is too high. Better in a photograph. Failure to experience any emotion over Tintoretto. Horror of Surrealist masters in Biennale. Moved by nothing later than Pompeii. Great paintings should be kept under lock and key and shown as seldom as wonder-working images. The real connoisseurs of art were the Pharaohs; they took it with them. Intoxication with Venetian gardens, the oleander drooping over the canal at some scabrous corner, the ubiquitous freshwater sea-smell and the best drink in Europe, a tumbler of ice-cold peach-juice in the colonel's bar. More hordes of milling tourists, squeaking *lederhosen*; Clapham Junction of the mechanised masses in the Piazza. Everybody is somebody. Nobody is anybody. Everyone is everywhere.

At last the boat: survival of an earlier form of travel, obeying the strange psychology of 'on board ship'. Whom we hate on the first day we shall love on the last, whom we greet on the first we shall not bid farewell; boredom will become its own reward and change suddenly to ecstasy. The *Achilleus* is a charmed vessel, trim, white, gay, its inmates friendly and delightful. The islands of the lagoon bob at their moorings as we churn through the warm night and the next blue day past Monte Gargano and Brindisi, with its lemon ices and Roman column, and across to Corfu where we stay for three hours instead of a week, just time to see the famous view at Canoni, so called because the tourist is fired at it like a cannon-ball.

That evening we are streaking through the Corinth Canal like mercury rising in a thermometer. The *Achilleus* has now gone completely Greek. The food is interesting and local, the crew sings, the married couples no longer flash their signals of distress, 'save me, rescue me'. The passengers crane over the rail to where the distant corona of Athens glows above the dark bulk of Salamis. We enter the sooty bustle of Piraeus as the last evening steamers beetle forth to fertilise the expectant islands and are extracted from our carefree cabin like ticks from a dog's ear. Nothing on shore will quite come up to it, even as Nice is never worthy of the Blue Train or New York of the *Queen Mary*. *Arriver, c'est déjà partir un peu.*

*

Great heat, like a smart doctor, begins every sentence 'You'll have to cut out. . . .' With the temperature always around ninety, generalities alone can be appreciated, details and detours must be ignored; we are but fit for the simplest forms of sightseeing.

Air throbs, marble hisses, the sea glistens with malice, the exhausted landscape closes at lunch-time and does not reopen before six o'clock when the sun ceases its daily interrogation. We stagger across the grilled slabs of the Propylaea with only one idea—which is both idea and sensation—the juice of a lemon and an orange in equal proportions poured again and again over cubes of ice. After this post-war duty visit we flee the Parthenon and rush to take the first boat at the Piraeus. It is crowded and unbelievably noisy but there is a cool breeze as we round Sunium.

Bathed in lemon-yellow light like Rabat or Casablanca, Rhodes has some claim to be the perfect island. Neither too large nor too small, too hot nor too cold, fertile, hilly, legendary and exotic, it lives in the present as well as the past. The medieval city of the knights has been so perfectly restored by the Italians as to outdo Carcassonne; it is a golden flypaper for tourists who are led to it like bombers to a dummy target, leaving the real town uninjured. Between the austerity of the medieval fortress and the flamboyant Fascist concrete outside the walls the old Turkish quarter sprawls in exquisite decay.

The few simple elements required by the Moslem conception of beauty, the dome and minaret, fountain, plane-tree and arcaded courtyard are here combined into a dozen similar but never monotonous patterns . . . we are in a tiny Stamboul, a sixteenth- and seventeenth-century quarter of dignified exiles with their Persian tiles and Arabic inscriptions, their memories of fallen grandeur. No farther from the comfortable but hideous Hôtel des Roses than you can spit a pomegranate seed stands the little mosque of Murad-Reïz, its cemetery planted with mulberry and oleander. Few places are more soothing than a Turkish graveyard, where the turbaned tombs are jumbled like spillikins around the boles of cypresses and the cicadas zizz above the silent koubbas.

Here sleeps the commander who captured Tripoli, and probably the administrators who lost it, heroes and footlers together, the generals and admirals, the Beys and Pashas of that cruel, clean, pious, frugal horticultural community. The great admiral's grave is well kept-up and hung with Mecca-green cloth; otherwise the nodding conversation pieces are abandoned to shade and sun, each stone turban proudly proclaiming its owner's status or bearing a verse from the Koran by which we linger in bewilderment —even as one day in some far-flung graveyard a passing Chinese may halt, baffled by the enumeration of our meagre virtues.

Mikonos by contrast is a rude stone altar erected to the stern god of summer. The town is a white African sneer arching brightly round the bay where a row of little restaurants vie with each other in disappointments. The heat swaggers through the spotless alleys where bearded Danish painters seal every exit with their easels.

To swim one must bump across the bay to some blinding cove or trudge the iron-hot mountain path, paved with mule-dung and brown thistle. The sun needles the brain cavity, desiccates the lung and obtains a garnishee upon the liver. Doors bang, nerves jangle, little waves bristle and buffet through the afternoon and in our sleep fashionable voices cry 'Mikonos for me', 'il y a toujours du vent à Mikonos'.

After this stony sanatorium its humble neighbour seems to flower with statues, tremendous in its exuberant and irretrievable collapse. Whereas Delphi's mountain womb remains one of the holy places of the human spirit, Delos is complex and baffling, irreverent even in its piety. With its swans and geese and cafeteria, the sacred lake where Apollo was born must have been not unlike the Round Pond in Kensington Gardens; the commercial Roman town survives in better shape than the Greek; the shrines of Isis and the phalloi of Dionysus have stood up better than Apollo's altars. In this centre of the ancient slave trade, this eclectic battener on the world's religions whose moneylending priesthood were the Rothschilds of antiquity, the god of man's fulfilment in this world, the wielder of the lyre and the bow, is noticeably absent.

Yet Delos is magical. According to the admirable Greek usage, no fence surrounds the ruins nor is there an entrance fee; black with tourists and lizards, prostrate in the sunshine, the ancient stones are part of the world's daily life. Among the Roman pavements is the mysteriously haunting mosaic of anchor and dolphin which was found on the seals of the wine-jars on the Greek ship salvaged outside Marseilles by M. Cousteau, and which aided him to identify his Sextius, owner of the vessel, with the proprietor of this sumptuous villa. By such means are we enabled to creep backwards into time, liberated by significant detail such as the hand, in the museum, from that colossal archaic Apollo which was broken off by the fall of the sculptor Nikias's fabulous bronze palm-tree.

Delphi remains sacred to Apollo while Delos had permission to exploit him; both became enormously rich, both tottered to destruction after Julian's reign in A.D. 363 with full treasuries, gold ceilings and colonnades of marble statues (Delos had 3,000 intact under the opprobrium of the Christians). Abandoned to pirates through the Dark Ages, Delos must still have been one of the wonders of the world, a desert island carpeted with temples and matchless private buildings, a thousand years of sanctity still clinging to the shrines and avenues while Delphi, pillaged by Byzantium, issued its despairing last oracle and the bronze horses of St. Mark's, as I like to think, were reft from the impassive Charioteer.

We may walk across the sacred lake or stand on Apollo's temple at Delphi where the earth-dragon fumed and fretted and the priestess gave out incoherent moans for the priest to polish into the double meanings which answered our desire. But it is difficult to feel aware of the terrible god of youthful strength and intellectual beauty. He exists only in museums. For though Greek architecture has barely survived, and Greek music and painting not at all, we have at last learnt how to display sculpture at its best.

In the new museum at Athens we no longer need to pretend to ourselves; here the chain of masterpieces signal to each other down the ages. This is how Greece was; this is what man can do. Apollo is manifest at last with his smile which seems instantly to annihilate all time and all suffering. Joy is under everything and if we feel pain it is our fault because we are not divine enough. Death has an appropriateness which transcends sorrow; the world belongs to the beautiful charm; is welded to courage, thought to action—even the serpent is a friend.

But humanity could not grow up without a religion of the mother; the world could not always belong to the graceful tactless hearties with red curls, bulging eyeballs, stocky behinds, a try-anything-once look below their waving helmets. Can one think of any archaic sculpture which takes even Zeus beyond early middle age? In this art 'Hippocleides doesn't care' triumphs over the maxims of the seven sages. Irresponsible perfection went out about 475 B.C.; yet is it my imagination or are not the contemporary Greeks one of the happiest as well as the most friendly nations in the world?

3

IMPRESSIONS OF EGYPT (1955)

'FLIGHT 159 for Rome, Cairo, Khartoum and Nairobi'; from the early morning London drizzle we are shepherded into our plastic no-man's-land. Our emblem is the air hostess: she smiles and life is good; our pastor is the Captain who broadens in the doorway and tells us where we are, and where we are is right. Sunshine above the cloud-carpet, 'nothing but well and fair'. The Alps scatter beneath us; surprised Elba blushes and we descend from euphoria to luncheon, sealed off from wintry Rome. A glimpse of Capri, of Cape Palinuro, a lingering sunset over Etna, 'visibility about two hundred miles' and night is served with a good dinner. The hours slip by and suddenly we are circling concentric boulevards, neon-lighted avenues and a large sign 'Welcome to Egypt'. No greatcoats; much khaki; a mild luminous dusk and a loudspeaker blaring Arab music. I recognise that voice like broken toffee, it is indeed the celebrated Om Khalsoun and I learn that she appears on this first Thursday of every month in a Cairo music hall. Through Southern streets, past silent villas, I rush there in a taxi, but—my first disappointment—am offered only a black-market seat at two pounds for the end of her performance.

The first view of Cairo is another. The streets resemble downtown Athens; we are in one of those numerous cities whose commonest vista is of a big block of flats in bilious concrete, a patch of blue sky, some very poor people and a hoarding. The Nile at first sight bewilders, in colour not unlike the Thames in summer, yet its opposite shore is fringed with palm-trees and the skyscrapers and warehouses down the river remind one of New

Orleans. But lime replaces lemon in long drinks, first hint of the tropics.

The great museum is a further disappointment for the 'new look' of modern showmanship has hardly reached it; there is a basement feeling and the marvellous statues are ill-lit and overcrowded. To spare him the contrast with the austerity of the Old Kingdom I go straight to Tutankhamen. Here the arrangement is more spacious and worthy of the greatest treasure trove of modern times. One soon develops an affection for the sleepy Valentino who died at eighteen in an atmosphere of religious conflict which recalls our own Edward VI; one needs also the beetle's-eye view for minor objects—gold sandals or gold toe-caps—and a respect for mere quantity. Regalia with innumerable spare parts, boats, beds, thrones, games, dolls, crowns, amulets, jewelry of all kinds, huge gold chambers, gesso ceilings, life-size guardians with golden spears lead one up to the two great coffins, the larger somewhat ungainly, the next more lifelike and finally to the deeply moving death mask with its withdrawn pearly eyes and full young lips, its striated headdress of gold and lapis lazuli. The colours of blue, green, beige and gold seem ideally suited for this highly finished art where bird or insect or flower have settled down into rigid winged forms which cram the maximum of dogma into their conventional roles as necklace, diadem or earring.

The museum states the problem which remains with us all the way: here is a civilisation which is both the parent of humanism and its worst enemy, creator of personality yet concerned only with permanence. Brought up in Greece and Rome, how can we manage to like it? 'The Egyptians by their study of astronomy discovered the solar year and were the first to divide it into twelve parts. . . . They were the first to bring into use the names of the Twelve Gods which the Greeks took over from them, and were the first to assign altars and images and temples to the Gods, and to carve figures in stone.' But what figures, Herodotus, and what Gods! The academic monotony of this endless parade of animal dignitaries and bird-headed chamberlains! Not an inch of surface on wall or column without its maze of compulsive clichés, no place for originality or intelligence, no feeling for artistic invention, only magic run to seed and man reduced to an avenue of 'spinggies' as the guides call them. 'Like an Egyptian temple, magnificent to look at, and inside a priest singing a hymn to a cat or a crocodile,' as the later Greeks put it. To which the museum answers: '(1) Patience. (2) No art is the worse for a breath of Permanence. (3) You cannot apply the standard of 500 B.C. to a civilisation a thousand, even two thousand years earlier. Go to Saqqara. And if you find a religion dull, there is always a remedy. Believe in it.'

Saqqara is reached by Memphis, where we first meet ancient Egypt in its true surroundings (the open air) in the form of a sphinx of rose alabaster and a fallen colossus outstretched among the palms. The step Pyramid of Zoser is the world's oldest building. It looks like the top of a mountain but a little more deliberate and by this deliberation is unmistakably human. The great Imhotep was its architect and recently courtyards and colonnades have been unearthed, with every kind of column, even proto-Doric. Near by M. Zacchary Goneim is at work on his own newly-found pyramid whose base peeps tantalisingly out of the sand. One chamber has proved empty and he is now tunnelling underneath it to find the true burial chamber. Unless the robbers have anticipated him. They nearly always do and every necropolis is the scene of an insectlike conflict between the Pharaoh who begins his tomb on the day of his accession and is compelled to take his treasure with him that his jaws may function in a future life, and the tomb robbers, crammed with cunning and unbelief. The God-King mines and countermines, constructs false doors, blind shafts, labyrinths of dummy passages, retires deeper into his pyramid as into an oak gall. The probing antennae pursue him, for however many builders he immolate, his own priests are not always to be trusted. The nobles put up less resistance, their tombs are robbed but contain fewer valuables while those at Saqqara introduce us to bas-relief (the most exquisite of Egyptian art forms) and present that unfailing theme of hunting in the Delta swamps among the wild duck and the hippo, of gliding on tiny boats through the papyrus while wife and daughter applaud as the harpoon falls or the goose-stick whistles through the air which constituted the good life for a thousand years.

After Saqqara, what can one say of the Pyramids? That the great Pyramid covers thirteen acres and is four hundred and fifty feet high, earliest of the Seven Wonders of the World and alone to outlivet he other six? That the length of one side divided by half the height gives the number Pi correct to five places of decimals? Or that, surrounded by honking cars and Sunday crowds, they are more like two indestructible film stars signing autographs? If only one could get them alone!

*

Meanwhile another Cairo awaits us, immensely dusky, dingy, noisy, devoid apparently of all domestic architecture but possessing some of the oldest buildings of the Moslem world, the ninth-century mosque of Ibn Tulun, severe and vast, the stretch of city wall (now cleared) dating from the year one thousand, a Viking and Byzantine shield carved on the gate, and the twelfth-century mosque and seminary of El Azhar. This is a dream of cloistered wisdom: the mosque includes a forest of columns like an unspoilt Cordova surrounded by swirling Arabesques and cufic inscriptions. The great floor was carpeted in red by the late king, and, grouped all over it, the candidates for law and priesthood squat around their teachers. They wear white turbans over a small tarboosh and come from every corner of the Moslem world and in every colour from *eau de Nil* to *noir de Balliol*. It is a place to which one is irresistibly drawn. Old Cairo has none of the magical white alleys, the spicy scents and splendid costumes of Morocco; it is built of grey brick or yellow stucco and long distances must be covered between each pleasure. The days are warm, the nights still treacherous and after four of them I took a train of all-white wagon-lits to Luxor. Here one must sightsee or perish; the hotel empties from breakfast to dusk as if set on a ski-run and there is indeed talk of a *téleférique* to the Valley of Kings. Light meters dangling, guide-book in one hand, fly whisk in other, our noses smarting from mummy-dust, we troop into meals obedient to the gong, while like patient elephants the temples wait for us among the sugar cane. Luxor, Karnak, Medinet Habu, Dahr el Bahari. . . . 'Egyptian architects wanted to erect the tallest, broadest, most solid structures the world would ever see: and they succeeded. The monuments of the Nile valley were projected as symbols of triumphant power. . . . They are the marks inflicted on nature by a race of giants, on the scale of stupendous entities brought into existence by nature herself.' (*Ancient Egypt* by J. Manchip White.) And yet they are not too heavy. The impression in the great hypostyle hall of the temple of Amon at Karnak is of one of the most awe-inspiring sights in the world, especially when the stonework is etched out by moonlight. There is restraint and agility yet the huge pylons with their holes where the pennons floated, the avenues and courtyards, the sacred lake, the soaring painted capitals, the host of side chapels form a whole which reduces most Greek temples to skeletal insignificance. In such a place at such a moment Egypt pulverises all objections. I begin to see that one must try to believe, to appreciate the supreme wager, the foredoomed bet on the immortality of the body by which the ancient Egyptians expressed their passionate love of life. Even Howard Carter admitted to shedding a tear on finding the little tutelary Goddesses whose gold wings met to protect the sarcophagus of Tutankhamen, an emotion which perhaps saved his life (for if one can believe anything, one can believe that), and with a grain of reverence one begins to notice the many small exceptions to the dull conformity of Egyptian art.

*

The last year witnessed four outstanding discoveries; the 'solar' boat at Giza, the buried pyramid at Saqqara, the Hyksos Stele at Karnak and the First Dynasty Tombs at Saqqara North. What are the prospects for this year? M. Zacchary Goneim is convinced that at any moment he will come on the unplundered burial chamber of his new pyramid, he may also discover the system of ramps by which the pyramids were built; the two boats will be extracted, chemically treated, and put together. It remains to be seen whether anything is inside them. At Karnak the discoverer of the new stele, M. Lashib Hababti, is just about to uncover the whole processional avenue of sphinxes, two kilometres long, from the temple of Luxor to the great temple of Karnak, now buried under thirty feet of mud and rubble. At Saqqara North, Professor Emery of London University, 'last of the great excavators', has located two more tombs of the First Dynasty, of Horaha and Udaimu (or, more probably, of his Queen). This last tomb will not be excavated till December but may prove the most interesting for these great underground chambers and storehouses have revealed a perfection of architectural detail which indicates that the first rulers of united Egypt, *circa* 3500 B.C., were already a master-race beside whose skills the pyramid-builders seem a mere end-product. Where did this 'dynastic' or 'master-race' spring from? According to Dr. Derby their skulls were of a different shape from those of the long-suffering roundheads of the Delta. They arise in all their glory straight out of the night of prehistory —from the deep South? the bracing North? the Yemen or Sumeria? or from some intermediate zone of acclimatisation on the shore of the Red Sea? One unrobbed tomb in the great necropolis of northern Saqqara (where the early dynasty Serapeion also lies hidden) may yield the secret.

But the year is not to be judged by excavation only; in other fields the Past shows its gains and losses. An example of each: One of the most disappointing 'musts' in the guide-book I found to be the temple of Luxor, urban, straggling, dun-coloured, a mosque bestrides its entrance whence the grave Wagnerian motiv of the noonday muezzin sounds over the baked mud to stimulate a vague appetite for luncheon and a sense of duty done. Yet in this temple has originated a new school of archaeological mysticism which provides a burning topic for the visitor and a welcome insurgence of intellectual values in this world of Baedeker and 'international' cooking, of mewing kite and bubbling hoopoe. Here for ten years from 1940, working by night and sleeping by day, M. Schwaller de Lubicz, an esoteric Alsatian philosopher, aided by his wife and stepdaughter, toiled away measuring stones and angles or recording inscriptions to evolve theories which were simultaneously generated by a brilliant French Egyptologist, M. Varye and his collaborating architect, M. Robichon. According to this little group the great Egyptian temples are not merely the dwelling-places of the Gods, their priests and stores and altars, dwellings frequently destroyed or enlarged by egomaniac conquerors to suit their pride and prosperity—but 'constructions in evolution', symbolical of the whole relationship of the universe to man in this sacred country which was held to be a pattern of the sky. The plans were laid down in ages of transition by great sages like Imhotep (2950 B.C.) and Amenhotep to prefigure future astronomical changes as when the sun entered a new house of the zodiac after 2500 years. Then the reigning Pharaoh would have to pull down the existing temples, re-erect them on a 'secret library' of old foundations, reorientate them to new axes, new materials, further courts. Thus the temple of Luxor contains the ancient idea of the Microcosm, of man's body as an image of the universe with every organ corresponding; it is shaped like a walking skeleton, the separated feet on a slant at the entrance, the knees by the colossi in the forecourt, and so right up to the skull in the Inner Sanctuary, with even the gland represented. Esoteric messages to those worthy of them are conveyed by a number of subtle suggestions; we must read each stone as carefully as a page of *Finnegans Wake* for every crack and seeming imperfection has a meaning. In the 'knee court' the break in the blocks runs through the knees of the Pharaoh in relief; the legs of the colossi are exaggerated and distorted while other reliefs suggest a young prince sacrificing at the age of twelve, even as Jesus went at that age to the temple. Some stones are to be regarded as transparent, a blank space on one side being filled in by a corresponding drawing on the other, some inscriptions on one wall of a shrine correspond with drawings on the wall opposite. It becomes therefore the height of vandalism to remove even the smallest stone without detailed measurement and careful photography for even unfinished sketches or lapidary lacunae intentionally illustrate imperfect or transitory aspects of the soul.

The patterns of flagstones in ramp or courtyard are particularly full of meaning and sometimes include whole mosaics where can be seen, in the case of Luxor, the same wise tutelary head. These theories are put forward in M. de Lubicz's unobtainable *Le Temple dans L'Homme* and in even rarer and earlier pamphlets by M. Varye while M. Robichon (who still works at Karnak) confines himself to collecting architectural evidence in models, photographs and drawings. The movement was greeted with a storm of abuse ('where's your proof') when it broke ground in the French reviews *Critique* and *Mercure de France*. The older generation of Egyptologists, especially M. Drioton, were appalled while M. Saint-Fare Garnot wrote, 'Le débat ouvert dans les colonnes de votre périodique a été institué par un incompétent, devant un tribunal d'incompétents.' Alas, M. Varye, the best qualified of the three, was killed in a motor accident in 1951, but his ideas have been admirably developed. 'Egyptology was born and developed in an age of extreme rationalism. The ancient Egyptians have been regarded as a materialist people, yet is it possible that so great a people could have been so dully materialist, so devoid of philosophy, of speculation?' (Smart.) These new theories at once found support among poets like Jean Cocteau yet continue to be fiercely attacked by specialists who find M. de Lubicz's numerological arcana particularly provoking. 'Man in antiquity progressed only in proportion as he turned his back on myths of every origin in the light of Hellenic rationalism,' roundly declared M. Papadopoulo, editor of *La Revue de Caire*.

I should like to assist my readers to a conclusion. One must bear in mind that a materialist two thousand years hence could live for a very long time with a Japanese garden without appreciating the symbolism of its design; on the other hand 'seek and ye shall find' has dangerous consequences. M. de Lubicz both baffles and stimulates, like a Baconian, and when I visited the temple with his book, the 'golden number' eluded me and wall and column seemed as incoherent and uncommunicative as ever. Yet when I am with M. Robichon light breaks in and one is inspired by the minutiae of his own inspiration. Take the statue of Sekhmet. M.

Robichon claims that it exudes a mineral magic which causes compasses to deviate and diviners' rods and needles to go haywire; one part of the statue vibrates, another is warmer than the rest; the crook of her tall wand, covering the solar plexus, is particularly radioactive. Yet the same statue, like the Portland Vase, has been smashed to pieces by an Arab guardian who was convinced that it was bewitching him and this time the dread Lion-Goddess could offer no protection. Many of the measurements seem fanciful but M. Varye's principle remains correct, that we must revalue the great discoveries of nineteenth-century archaeologists by the humbler light of our present understanding of psychology and mystery-religions. M. Robichon's contribution to the monumental *Karnak* which has just appeared and M. de Lubicz's new and weightier volume (not yet published) should bring fresh evidence. Equally exciting should be the new work on the inscriptions and texts from the tombs of Tutankhamen by a philologist, M. Piankhov. 'Le temps va ramener l'ordre des anciens jours.'

*

I mentioned also a loss; a better word would be disaster. The scheme which is dearest to the new government is that of the High Dam above Assuan with thirty times the capacity of the present one, which at a cost of two hundred million pounds is to bring enormous advantages to the country. It will increase electric power and permit heavy industry, make Egypt independent of the reservoirs in Equatoria, add 700,000 feddans for the cultivation of rice, be 300 feet high, 'and bring prosperity for 500 years'. It will take ten years to complete but the waters will be rising after two. The whole Nile above Assuan will become more of a lake than it is already, hideous as only a reservoir can be, and stretching for 150 kilometres into the Sudanese province of Dongola. Korosko, Derr and Wadi Halfa will be submerged with all the Nubian temples including Abu Simbel which rises within the tropic, near the Sudan frontier.

I decided I must go there, braving the three-day journey on the Sudanese river-steamer, with its fiendish parody of English cooking and 'life on board ship'. It was worth it. The steamer, by now festooned with small brown flies, reached Abu Simbel in the late afternoon; a sickle of sandy beach with a squatting mimosa in flower, desert everywhere, and the cliffs of pale scintillating powdered brick, orange into rose, from which the four colossi of Ramses II, each sixty-six feet high, beam in tremendous welcome. As we climb up, the thighs tower above us and the smaller colossi of his graceful daughters: someone has scribbled impertinently on one of the legs; it is in archaic Greek. At eye-level the usual frieze of pinioned captives stagger by, loose-lipped Negroes on the one side (a frontier courtesy), and intellectual Semites on the other, for this is a supreme assertion of Egyptian power, the outpost of her grandeur, dominating the Blemmyes and the dusky imitation pharaohs of Meroe and Napata. Within are two more rows of colossi and the receding vaults of the temple proper, all painted and decorated in what was then permanent darkness, hollowed out of the solid rock. The aspect is both radiant and mysterious, magnificent yet full of grace; the designs are somewhat coarse but often brightly coloured and illustrate the oft-repeated battle of Kadesh like a staff-college lecture. In the Cairo museum are two delightful small obelisks from the little outside temple to Ra and, carved in the same glistening sandstone, a row of baboons whose hands were upraised to the rising sun, a giant scarab and the King baboon as leaders. Now falls the brief unpaintable twilight, the green glow forsakes the towering figures and the frieze of cobras above, glitters and disappears as two rows of Nubians and Sudanese form on the sand for evening prayer, butting the earth as in Egyptian paintings. The gangplank lifts, the paddles grind and carry us on beneath the Southern Cross to the fleshpots of Wadi Halfa. (Excellent hotel.) After a glimpse of the second cataract, northern limit of crocodiles, realising that if I go any further I shall have to buy a hat, I grab a plane for the return journey.

Abu Simbel is unique: it is in the same class as the Pyramids, Lascaux, the Pantheon, the Double Cube at Wilton and the Temperate House at Kew, and so I advise all those who love what will certainly perish to make the journey. Although some shake their heads and say the dam will never be finished—'Egypt is Egypt', or 'The Sudanese will object',—and others talk of the UNESCO mission, of a dam within a dam or a large-scale replica to be made for a museum, even of the good to Philae which will result, I would count on none of it. What chance has one temple against 700,000 feddans of rice and some munition factories?

So let the pilgrimage be organised that the world may file past in the next two years and say goodbye. . . .

*

From Wadi Halfa to Cairo one flies for eight hundred miles over a desert which pales gradually from orange to off-white. Not a bush, not a blade, except when we cross the green ribbon of the Nile or the liquid blob of the Fayum. In many places the desert comes right down to the river, in others the oxen toil at the water-wheels under the palms as from time immemorial.

This valley represents a civilisation which in times of strength expands like a stomach to engulf Syria in the north, the Sudan to the south. When it is weak the organism dissolves into small separate kingdoms, which ultimately reunite and begin a new process of northward and southward expansion. Such is Egyptian history. The present is a moment of expansion, but it remains to be seen whether the strength is there. The Sudan is welcomed as a long-lost brother, the Arab League brings in the north, Cairo is to become the moral capital of Islam and of Africa.

The rulers of this freak of geography which is Egypt have always to face the same problems, arising from overcrowding in the fertile strip and from centuries of foreign domination: poverty, ignorance, ill-health, corruption, and inertia. The present regime is a military-socialist movement which has grown out of a league of eight hundred young officers who vowed to end corruption and restore the dignity of the Army. They kept their secret for four years, a miracle in the East, and seized power without bloodshed. Effective power resides in three members of the Council of the Revolution, which has attacked corruption and inertia by enforcing reforms long promised but never carried out. Since agreeing to leave Suez and the Sudan, the British are treated as warm friends though American capital is much in evidence and many Germans are employed. The real losers are the Turkish land-owning class whose power and prestige are gone for ever; for almost every Egyptian is now conscious that the country belongs to him, and the measures accomplished could not conceivably be reversed.

The improvement in education, social services, medicine, land, housing, and irrigation must gladden all who use their eyes. It is difficult to see how any other group in the country could have provided the drive and energy to set all this in motion. There is certainly a faint smell of Fascism (the slogan is 'Unity, Work, Discipline'), but it is mitigated by peaceable intentions, by a desire to retain the maximum of good will and a tendency to proceed cautiously by careful planning, trial and error. The rulers intend to go out of uniform, re-establish the Army (carefully purged) as a non-political body, and set up two new parties, Republican and Socialist, to safeguard the revolution and return to democratic ways. Turkey is the model, and Turkey has certainly progressed from an enlightened military dictatorship to a democracy in a very few years. Egypt is now almost normal for tourists, while foreigners who live here claim that they have not felt so safe for four years. However, the effects of anti-imperialist propaganda are still felt, and it is not advisable to venture into the villages or poorer quarters without a dragoman or member of the Tourist Police.

The personal popularity of the Prime Minister is astonishing: 'The best ruler Egypt has had for a thousand years,' my dragoman told me. 'Sixty per cent. good, forty per cent. bad' was a more liberal admission. . . . Too much censorship, too much military impatience, distrust of the middle class, ignorance of administration, too many heavy sentences summarily imposed by the courts, an increasing anti-Semitism, and a tendency to postpone indefinitely the drafting of the new Constitution. Yet on the whole an atmosphere very like England in wartime, of puritanism and moral fervour, Beveridge and brigadiers, together with an English feeling that such a state of things is not permanent, that no one—not even the ruler—wants it to last, that, the revolution won, humour, charm and tolerance will again predominate.

Yet how much good is being done! Consider the Nile, vibrating with sunlight, flecked with tall feluccas, hazily blue against the sugar cane and palms. But the whole river cries 'Hands off', the *Guide Bleu* advises us not even to trail a finger, for here and in all the neighbouring canals and water holes reigns the *bilharzia*, one of the most ingenious maggots devised by nature for the undoing of man. In some delta villages up to ninety per cent. of the population suffer from the debilitating intestinal disease (found even in mummies) which it inflicts, and hookworm is nearly as common. Typhoid, tuberculosis, malaria, elephantiasis, and purulent ophthalmia also take their toll; and as for past treatment of them, it must be remembered that sixty per cent. of the population is illiterate, that few doctors would practise in the villages, and that hospital beds number two per 1,000 as against sixteen per 1,000 in Switzerland.

The 'simple fellah' believes, like his ancestors in the days of Herodotus, that Nile water is good, a sovereign remedy, while filtered water causes impotence. He does not associate malaria with mosquitoes, nor mosquitoes with their free-swimming larvae. Insecticides have to be thrust upon him, but they are becoming more and more popular, while a religious campaign to enforce the Koranic precept against polluting water helps to eliminate *bilharzia*, even as a better disposal of sewage and garbage helps with ophthalmia and typhoid, or slum-clearance with the ravages of tuberculosis.

Combined medical and welfare centres are being set up in more and more towns and villages, bringing midwives and information officers, medicine and loudspeakers, and new schools are being built out of the fortune from the confiscated royal estates. The acceleration in all these essential forms of progress has advanced under the revolution from, as it were, ten to thirty miles an hour, and at last the money and the will-power are forthcoming in co-operation with the peasant, who is beginning to own his wonderful land.

For the traveller how unique is Egypt! Where else can the tourist be offered such perpetual winter sunshine, such huge and extraordinary monuments or such a collection of beautiful buildings as are to be found in medieval Cairo? Yet there is something sad about it; the gulf between the traveller and the native—the gulf of language, of habits, of religion—is too wide; and the hotels, with the exception of the Semiramis in Cairo, have a melancholy all their own. There is a sunset *cafard* which the evening's amenities can hardly dissipate; after the long, heavy dinner nothing to do but contemplate the list of prohibited gambling games—Harakiri, Zoukov, Ascenseur—and creep to bed. The main stream of tourism still flows from Cairo to Beirut rather than down to Luxor and Assuan.

When I look back I think with most joy of my second visit to the Cairo Museum, of the Mosque El Azhar, older than Cordoba, and of the theological students squatting on the royal red carpets beside their teachers under a forest of columns, of many charming talks in Cairo, of Taha Hussein, the blind writer, whose ambition it is to edit a really good Arabic translation of the complete works of Shakespeare, of my delightful mentor from the Ministry of Information, a leading authority on Oscar Wilde and flying saucers, of the giant shrimps and fresh limes, of the oasis of the Coptic Museum.

Yet always I return to Assuan, one of the most beautiful places I have ever seen, to the tombs on the brick-red slab of desert, the sailing-boat depositing one, at the violet hour, on Kitchener's Island, most lovely of tropical gardens, where every tree is new and must be learnt from labels, the bulbous emerald trunk of *Chorisia Speciosa*, the yellow-flowering *Markhamia* from Uganda, the *Belmoriana* from Lord Howe Island, the Indian 'Butter Tree', and the hoary mimosa to which all the white ibises of the river come skimming home to roost with joyous croak and clatter in the green and ashen twilight.

Kitchener's Island, the perfect garden, Assuan Dam, the largest and loveliest of waterworks . . . they are relics of our art and altruism for which we receive scant credit. One day they will go the way of the lines of Suez or El Alamein or of the Edwardian novels and proconsular memoirs which sleep like papyri behind the locked grilles of the hotel library.

4

IN QUEST OF ROCOCO

ONE can describe a passion only in terms of passion. Many years ago I noticed that certain works of art brought tears to my eyes. Lines of Horace, Dryden, Rochester, Pope, the last paintings of Watteau, Mozart's *Voi che sapete* while in the summer of 1938 two small buildings—Palladio's Roman theatre at Vicenza and the Amalienberg pavilion outside Munich—were added to my list. What had they in common? Perfection or the ideal of perfection—a lyrical conception of humanity, a response to all that is transitory and fugacious, a calligraphy of farewell. I have, of course, been more deeply moved by that art which springs from the tragic sense of life, I have been fissured by romanticism, spell-bound by Baudelaire or Wagner yet I have come to believe that there exist also an unselfconscious gaiety, an acceptance of human limitation quite as significant as the romantic protest and no less congenial an incubator of works of art. The Amalienberg, a royal huntman's bagatelle which Mr. Sacheverell Sitwell calls 'a supreme monument of the period', was the first rococo I had seen, for of my youthful visits to Potsdam and Dresden I have no clear recollection. Here in that round room of blue and silver with its long mirrors and hanging chandelier was a poetry of living, a revelation of intimacy and delight that I had not thought possible.

Ci-gît, dans une paix profonde,
Cette dame de volupté
Qui pour plus grand sûreté
Fit son paradis en ce monde.

So familiar are we today with the rococo that it comes as a surprise to learn that the cult is very recent. To love and understand the first half of the eighteenth century would seem a prerogative of the present.

'Rococo is a term applied specifically to a type of ornament, style or design belonging to the reign of Louis XV and the beginning of the reign of Louis XVI. In general, it applies to everything that is old and out of fashion in the arts, literature, costume, manners, etc. "To like the rococo", "to fall into the rococo", "that is very rococo".'—*Dictionary of the Académie Française*, 1842.

'Rococo. A debased variety of the Louis XIV style of ornament proceeding from it through the degeneracy of the Louis XV. It is generally a meaningless assemblage of scrolls and crimped conventional shell-work wrought into all sorts of irregular and indescribable forms, without individuality and without expression. The term is also sometimes applied in contempt to anything bad or tasteless in decorative art.'—*Chambers*, 1882.

The first allusions to the new style referred to it as '*goût moderne*' or '*goût du siècle*' (Blondel, 1738). The expressions 'Pompadour', 'Rococo', came from the studios and were first used by Maurice Quai in 1796-97. In 1828 Stendhal writes: 'Bernini was the father of that bad taste called in the studios by the somewhat vulgar term Rococo.' Victor Hugo is the first to admire it: 'The belfries of the Cathedral [in Nancy] are Pompadour pepper pots . . . the square of the Town Hall is one of the gayest, prettiest and most complete of any rococo square I have ever seen . . . it is a marquise of a square' (1839).

In 1836, the word appeared in English, in 1843 Burckhardt uses the term in Germany whose art historians have slowly succeeded in stripping it of its pejorative meaning. Since it is now international I am in favour of keeping it, not of bringing forward the French *rocaille* which is apt to create a false distinction, being used by French apologists in order to disassociate their country from the extreme consequences of its own invention. *Le style Louis XV* is more familiar but imposes an artificial chronology.

We must now face the problem of what rococo is and where it came from. Mr. Fiske Kimball of Philadelphia has settled this question in his monumental *Creation of Rococo* (1943). He proves, I think, conclusively, that the movement begins as a breaking up of the massive baroque of Louis XIV into contrasting asymmetrical curvilinear forms, an invasion of architecture by decoration until (as in some German churches) decoration creates its own architecture. He is thus at variance with the German theory that rococo is but another name for late baroque, which came as an organic development from Italy to Vienna and Vienna to Germany. Nor does he believe that it was evolved by the Nordic 'will-to-form' nor by direct observation from nature nor from the properties of new materials such as stucco and porcelain. Its genesis is in the arabesques of Bérain which Lepautre translated into decoration and which were carved in hard oak panelling around Versailles about 1699, the artists being stimulated by demands for the new Palaces of Marly and Meudon, for the King's *oeil-de-boeuf* room and chapel and for the night nursery of the young Duke of Burgundy. By close study of the original drawings and builders' accounts Mr. Kimball has sorted out the possessors of inventive genius from the hierarchy of official craftsmen: the great precursors Bérain and Lepautre who soften up the heavy baroque, Oppenordt and Vassé who lead the first attack under the Regent, Audran and Watteau with their arabesques, Pineau, Meissonier and Lajoue, the brilliant general staff of *le style pittoresque* in the victorious years 1730-35, and finally Babel and Cuvilliès. We watch the somewhat finicky *Régence* line struggling with the heavy shapes of doors and windows, furniture and panelling and gradually controlling the shape of the object itself until by the late 1730's every article in use; view and vista, palace or summer house, temple or tomb begin to be subjugated to the line of ebb and flow, to the convolutions which govern both water and the shells and rocks which are formed by it and the sprays and tendrils which drink it in.

The reaction begins after 1750 when the younger Cochin, the antiquarian Caylus and the Abbé Leblanc take up the cudgels in the name of French good taste, when the youthful Marigny sets out on his Italian journey and returns with all Pompeii, when Servandoni's St. Sulpice and Soufflot's Panthéon arise, when Gabriel replaces Boffrand and, above all, when England is victorious in the Seven Years War (1759). Pedantic England, led by Burlington and William Kent, had side-stepped the rococo and gone straight from classical Palladio to neo-classical Adam (who returned from his Dalmatian trip in 1759)—with Horace Walpole's neo-gothic as the only deviation! The rococo was not a movement to outstay its welcome, there was no decadence, its latest achievements are among its best; rather was it displaced by the overwhelming reality of the new vision of the classical world which had materialised in all its simplicity and strength in Herculaneum, Spalato, Greece and Asia Minor before the eyes of eighteenth-century travellers. The magic of the rococo is in that it is a European movement of spontaneous originality, a true *style moderne* arising between two backward-looking periods, the grandiose baroque and the academic neo-classical.

Mr. Kimball builds his case on correct dating and the personality of artists; for him it is the last years of Louis XIV (Bérain, Lepautre) and the *Régence* (Oppenordt) together with the decorative wood-carving of Pineau after his return from Russia (1727) and the genius of the architect and goldsmith Meissonier that are truly important. The hôtels de Toquelaure, de Touilly, de Soubise and some rooms at Rambouillet (all before 1740) form what he considers the peak. The soft paste of Vincennes and Sèvres, St. Cloud and Mennecy, the faïences of Strasbourg and Marseille, the tapestries of Boucher, the lacquers of Martin, the engravings of Gravelot and Eisen, the bindings of Pasdeloup, the silver of Thomas Germain, the snuff-boxes, knick-knacks and even the whole gamut of Louis XV furniture he sees as secondary artefacts of the architect's creation.

He also minimises political and economic influences although it is clear that the rococo was an explosive affirmation of the private life, an escape from Versailles; its great phase opens with the stage of the reign of Louis XV referred to as *les premières infidélités*. In fact, the whole of Europe needed liberation from heroics and the rococo is an art sponsored by leading personalities; the Regent Orléans, Louis XV, Stanislas of Lorraine, Frederick the Great, Maria Teresa, Madame de Pompadour ('*Reine et Marraine du rococo*', Goncourt), Count Brühl, the Schönborns, the Wittelsbachs and Spanish Bourbons, the Margraves of Bayreuth and Ansbach which caught on immediately with the humblest of their subjects and united all in a masquerade of gaiety and pleasure terminated (as is every European aesthetic movement) by an internecine war.

Let us suppose that the imagination of some studious American is kindled by the Bouchers in the Frick collection (formerly in Madame de Pompadour's collection at Crécy) or his tapestries in Philadelphia from the oval room of the hôtel de Soubise and that he decides on a journey to learn more about the civilisation that produced them. Where should he go?

He might stop off at London's Wallace collection where he can study the basic rhythms among some of the finest furniture, china and paintings of the period. England was to the fore in three minor examples of the rococo: the so-called Chippendale furniture, Lamerie's silver and the china of Chelsea and Bow, so luxurious, fresh and countrified. London's masterpiece was the interior of Ware's Chesterfield House decorated by the best French workmen (1749) and demolished in 1934. There is however a surprising amount of stucco, often by Italian workmen.

In France he would visit the *petits appartements* at Versailles, now in course of restoration, the hotels already mentioned (especially Soubise) and various rooms, doorways and staircases of the Faubourg St. Germain and the Place Vendôme. But Paris, despite the Place de la Concorde, is not the capital of rococo; the opposition to the style there was strong and constant. Mr. Kimball quotes from Cochin's secret memoirs: 'At that time there were any number of makers of bad ornaments who enjoyed the most brilliant reputation; like Pineau who ruined all the architecture of the period with his sculpture, like La Joue, who was a rather mediocre painter of architecture and who designed some miserable ornaments which sold with the greatest rapidity. It was M. Openor, the architect, who began the flight from the good taste of Louis XIV's reign . . . and things went from excess to excess reaching the height of absurdity which we know only too well.'

This attitude persists two hundred years later when in his *Architecture Française* (1951) M. Hautecœur writes of the creators of the *style pittoresque* in words which might easily be applied to cubists or surrealists: 'When we find some form of exaggeration in France, we must discover its perpetrators and these perpetrators are Oppenordt, son of a Dutchman, Meissonier, born in Turin, Pineau, who returned after a long stay in Russia, Cuvilliès, born in Hainault or Lajoue, who was not an architect, but a painter.'

If, then, there is so little left, it is not entirely due to the *guerre aux châteaux* of the Revolution but because the style was itself revolutionary, abandoned later by the fashionable and the conservatives through a mistaken worship of straight lines and moderation. Only in Nancy, fief of Louis XV's Polish father-in-law Stanislas, is there a rococo architectural ensemble, one of the loveliest agglomerations north of the Alps, where Heré's planning is enriched by Lamour's exquisite ironwork. The situation there and in Germany was quite different from France; the country was proud of its rococo and the princelings were seldom in a position to re-decorate, while their descendants regarded the splendid rooms which they inherited as a symbol of a golden age. Here the devastation is entirely due to the last war and irreparable damage has been done in the three capitals of the rococo, Würzburg, Munich and Berlin. Those who find Cuvilliès' surviving work in Munich cloying or overcrowded should study the vanished decoration of the golden hall of Charlottenburg and Voltaire's rooms in Sans-Souci, the work of the more sober yet no less gifted Johann August Nahl. Of Hoppenhaupt's silver room in the Potsdam Neue Schloss (removed in its entirety by the Russians), Mr. Sitwell writes, 'the boiseried rooms decorated in silver are quite inconceivable in their loveliness; many of the doors have a wave-like waterfall treatment which is again echoed in some of the wall panels in two shades of gold, or with a greenish silver that gives variety to that more conventional shade of moonlight. Pictures by Watteau can surely have never found a more congenial environment.'

I do not think that the ecclesiastical rococo of southern Germany can be attributed entirely to French sources. There would seem to have been some instantaneous fusion around the lake of Constance of French, Italian and Austrian influences among the deeply religious yet pageant-loving master-craftsmen and wood-carvers of Württemberg and Bavaria. The impulse to build or renovate large monasteries spread westward from baroque Vienna along the Danube and the Inn while the stucco-workers came up from the Ticino and the court architects returned from Paris with new books of ornament and design.

In central Germany the position is clearer. Here the great family of Schönborn, Prince Bishops who traded and mediated between Vienna and the West, controlled Würzburg, Bamberg, Mainz, Speyer and Trèves. In 1719 Johann Philip Franz, succeeding to his estates, announced to the alarm of his Chapter that the building bug (*Bau-Wurm*) had got him. He chose as his architect a young captain of engineers who had just returned from the Turkish wars where he had visited Vienna and Belgrade. This specialist in fortifications and cannon foundries became one of the great architects of the eighteenth century, a large, generous, serene and triumphant personality. Johann Baltazar Neumann's first plans for the Residence of Würzburg were made in 1719, and in 1723 he was in Paris consulting Boffrand and Robert de Cotte. The Palace took shape from 1720-44 and included much exquisite decoration by Bossi, a card room in green lacquer, a mirror room with Chinese ceiling in gold, grey-blue and white with a black marble chimneypiece, all destroyed by incendiaries in the raid of March 16th, 1945. The great staircase hall and three other sumptuous rooms remain. The Tiepolo ceiling in which Jupiter's envoys carry the good news of the establishment of Apollo's reign to the four continents almost makes one forget the war damage by their airy serenity. For Tiepolo (as can be seen from his 'rooms' in the 'Ca' Rezzonico') is the quintessence of the spirit of the rococo in painting. (It is misleading to talk about 'a rococo painter' but there are clearly some artists such as Boucher, Huet, Pillement, Longhi, Devis and Laroon who abandon themselves to the movement as wholeheartedly as the great porcelain modellers Kändler and Bustelli.)

Besides work on seventy churches, Neumann was also in charge of artillery, fortifications, waterworks, roads, bridges, factories in all the Schönborn dominions; he even held a scientific chair at the university and left behind an unfinished theoretical textbook. He also built Schloss Werneck outside Würzburg and the lovely staircase hall at Bruchsal near Karlsruhe, an apricot palace once full of exquisite rococo work by Feichtmayer, now badly damaged. Two chapels for the Schönborns in the Würzburg Residence, and attached to the cathedral, lead on to his other masterpiece, the pilgrimage church of Vierzehnheiligen (1743 onwards) between Bamberg and Bayreuth. Every aspect of this church is grand, warm, welcoming and lovely. Twin towers of golden stone rise above the fields and woods while all within is light and harmony. Like Wies (though much larger), it is a church in which every square foot is exquisitely decorated.

Feichtmayer's confessionals suggest sedan chairs or boxes at the opera and (as at Wies) the main feature is an oval shrine with a colonnade of coloured marbles built in the oval centre of the church and removing emphasis from the altar at the end of the nave. This feature distinguishes those churches which are built in the eighteenth century from those which are merely renovated, for the oval form satisfies an aesthetic need of the age. Neumann is thus a link between French rococo and south German church interiors though in Tiepolo's fresco (1753) it is neither as a pilgrim nor as a court architect that he chooses to be represented but as a full colonel of artillery meditating beside his cannon.

The Goethean genius of Neumann subdivides into two in the brothers Zimmermann who came from a family of craftsmen in Wessobrunn. Johann Baptist (1680-1758) went forward in court circles as a painter and decorator and drove back from Paris to

Munich in a golden coach while Domenico (1685-1766) became an architect for the humbler monasteries, living all the time in the country at Landsberg or Wies, where he died quietly at the age of eighty-one. He was uninstructed and could hardly get his drawings correct, using wood and stucco to solve problems in stone while his more worldly brother was working with Cuvilliès on the 'rich rooms' of the Munich Residence.

Yet at Gunzbourg, Steinhausen and Wies he produced works abounding in natural genius. Steinhausen is a small pilgrimage church near Biberach in Württemberg with a ceiling fresco by J. B. The church is elliptic in shape and decorated in white, pink, beige and pale blue; even the lettering of 'Jesus' is rococo while the circular fresco of Mary as Queen of Heaven, full of green paradisal scenery, is bounded by a Versailles vision of a fountain in a glade. These upward leaping fountains (there is another in the Asam fresco of St. Maria Victoria in Ingolstadt) suggest the rococo title-page of Meissonier or the imaginary ornaments of Cuvilliès and Lajoue. Yet Steinhausen is but a preparation for Wies (near Füssen), the supreme achievement of the two brothers. The outside is plain: fields, dark woods and distant mountains (often under snow) frame the lonely scene so that the contrast within is all the more striking, a pilgrim's dream of pastel perfection. The painter to the Munich court and the rural master builder have here fused all their separate capacities. Such interiors are impossible to describe, they must be illustrated by colour and diagram and then a prolonged visit must be undertaken. Wies, Vierzehnheiligen, Zweifalten, Birnau, Ottobeuren, Weltenburg—these have to be studied, then seen, then relearnt over again for no words can evoke both light and space and colour. J. B.'s ceiling at Wies is a Day of Judgment where all is charity and forgiveness and Christ descends on a rainbow; the whole small edifice breathes delight and serenity. After the two old brothers' work at Wies was done Domenico retired to a nearby cottage where he could contemplate his handiwork and remained there until his death.

The brothers Asam (Cosmo Damian, 1686-1739, and Egid Quirin, 1692-1750) are more famous for they too were capable of building and decorating a whole church between them, yet their work is not so well known as their name for the best of it is somewhat inaccessible. Their genius is more agitated than that of the Zimmermanns; they too worked best away from cities in the remote monastic lands that bordered on the Danube. Their youthful masterpiece is Weltemburg with its magical statue of St. George slaying the dragon and its enchanting bust of Cosmo by his brother, a Cherubino arising from the stucco while at Rohr the younger brother Egid Quirin went on to create his sensational altarpiece—a theatrical tableau of the Assumption. Osterhofen and Straubing are considered their finest late work, while at Munich their carved rococo house-front can still be seen next to the dark, damaged, somewhat occluded church they built together for St. Johann Nepomuk. The brothers are the earliest of the rococo church architects of southern Germany; they studied in Rome which must have developed their sense of theatre and began to work at home in the 1720's. They combine a brilliant invention, grace and wit with the fresco-gift of Cosmo Damian and the outstanding sculptural talent of Egid Quirin.

One more church architect must be mentioned, Johann Maria Fischer (1691-1766), who sprang from a line of Upper Palatinate masons and began to work in Munich with the Asams and Cuvilliès, then became the architect for the greater monastic orders, especially the Benedictines. In richness of conception he was the equal of Neumann and, like him, finished off his work with superb decoration. He, too, was extremely prolific and was connected with thirty-two churches and twenty-three convents, but he never became a builder of palaces, and of his life we know next to nothing. Although his designs go back to Austria and Italy and he was well versed in French art, he never travelled. His finest churches are Diessen (on the Ammersee), Ottobeuren (near Memmingen in the south of Bavaria) and Zweifalten in Württemberg. This is indeed a marvellous creation where his lofty spiritual quality combines with the dazzling stucco of J. M. Feichtmayer and the moving sculpture of Christian. The church is surrounded by hills and woods, its precinct encircled by a quiet little stream.

The exterior is billowing and gracious, the inside extraordinarily rich; the pulpit drips with golden waterfalls and is ornamented with skeletons rising from the dead while greenery cascades to the serpent on its base and is faced by another full-scale model by Christian of the vision of Ezekiel in the valley of dry bones. The art of rococo here brings the whole of the great church under its genial domination. There is a throne with rococo chair and two confessionals by the entrance which must be unique; one is a stucco box carved with a swaying palm grove, the columns encrusted with vegetation while in the other the stucco is carved into a catastrophe of falling columns. Ottobeuren is on an even grander scale.

One other exquisite church remains of the mid century—Neu Birnau, a pilgrimage church at the west end of the Lake of Constance on a hillside among meadows and orchards. Peter Thumb was the architect and Joseph Anton Feuchtmayer in charge of the stucco. The entrance doors are grey with pink facing. Inside is a blaze of colour, a ceiling fresco containing a real mirror with gold busts below to catch the reflected sunshine from it and everywhere patches of green—in interstices in the scroll work or at the top of the pink altar columns where it is echoed by green plants and the green in the cracks of the honeycomb pergola above the altar and again in St. John the Baptist's outspreading tree. There are several statues of an elongated El Greco character and on a wall-memorial Death has been reduced to the dimensions of a dried sea-horse while from the pulpit near by a girl's head as fresh and secular as Mozart's Barbarina looks out while from below another head peers.

The strangest figure of the German rococo is certainly Cuvilliès (1695-1768); this Walloon from Soignies was a dwarf of under four feet high. Although of French origin, he worked entirely abroad and before 1711 had become the page of the exiled Elector Max Emmanuel of Bavaria, with whom he returned to Munich from Brussels in 1715. After an apprenticeship as a military engineer, he was sent to Paris where he studied under Blondel from 1720 to 1724. In 1725 he became court architect to the

Elector and succeeded Effner, the creator of Nymphenburg and Schliessheim. His books of ornaments are fertile and original variations on the themes of Lajoue but his opportunities for realising them on the grand scale were much greater. Apart from work (now badly damaged) at Brühl outside Cologne, he produced three triumphant interiors, the five rich rooms in the Residence (1730-37) the Amalienberg (1734-39) both decorated by J. B. Zimmermann, and the Residence theatre (1753). Both the theatre and these rooms in the Palace have now vanished utterly. Jacob Burckhardt considered these rich rooms 'the most beautiful rococo which exists on earth, excelling in inventiveness and subtle elegance anything I have seen'. There were particularly fine *chinoiseries*, a bedroom in white and gold and wine-red, a long picture gallery hung with silk and a blending of all the sea-borne themes of French *rocaille* with German hunting scenes and northern woods. Here the Elector Karl Albrecht dreamt his luckless dream of Empire which was to end so tragically. The theatre (now restored to use with most of the original panelling) ('Rococo art at its absolute culmination.' S. Sitwell) was a vision of white, gold and crimson, the key-note of which was the Royal Box and four circular tiers of boxes each with rococo ornamentation; it held only six hundred and thirty-seven people, and here Mozart conducted the first performance of his opera *Idomeneo* (1781).

A link between Church and State is formed by the monastic libraries whose frescoed oval ceilings, undulating book-cases and allegorical statuary proclaim an opulent calm where the atmosphere is deeply religious although no detail can offend the delicate susceptibilities of an unbeliever. St. Gall in Switzerland, Fürstenzell, Wiblingen near Ulm, Dillingen and Schussenried in Württemberg are among the loveliest. There are also rococo gardens like the Jardin de la Fontaine at Nîmes and above all at Veitschöcheim outside Würzburg. Expelled from the shrubs which are confined to high enormous formal hedges forming a series of '*cabinets particuliers*', Nature seems to flower in Tietz' statuary, exquisitely exuberant and robust yet like rococo china, touching, even pathetic. Trains, trams, gasworks and factory chimneys, waiting greedily for the end, cluster and hoot round the alleys and the delicate grottoes.

> Unwater'd see the drooping sea-horse mourn,
> and swallows roost in Nilus' dusty urn.

One last word to those who want to study the rococo, Hurry! A style which ignored frontiers, which convoluted all it touched from a cathedral to a chamber-pot, which included all classes, whose message was movement, spontaneity, intimacy, formal extravagance and spiritual delight, which brought love and warmth for a half lifetime into gloomy interiors, which in its day was daring and contemporary and universal as no other has been since—unless we elevate *art nouveau*, cubism and surrealism to an authority they do not merit—such a creative fire as swept through every capital from Lisbon to Leningrad, Cork to Constantinople, is nothing if not perishable and attracts to itself an undeviating hatred. Even as I write some façade is crumbling; a ceiling flakes, panelling is being stripped, plaster-work crushed, chimneypieces torn out, a Chippendale looking-glass cracks and innumerable pieces of china are thumbed and shattered—('The period of rococo may well be called the age of porcelain and without a sympathetic understanding of rococo no appreciation of the art is possible.' Honey). So hurry, before the last cartouche, the fading arabesque, the final *cul-de-lampe* goes the way of Sans-Souci and Schönbornslust, Belle-Vue and Bruchsal.

> Another age shall see the golden ear
> Im-brown the slope and nod on the parterre,
> Deep harvests bury all his pride has plann'd
> And laughing Ceres re-assume the land.

5

THE WALLACE COLLECTION

It is difficult to return to an old love. When once everything is familiar and wardrobe, speech, childhood, mannerisms have all been lived through or rejected, admired or hated, it is difficult to return. For the Wallace is a 'closed collection'; nothing new can be added to it; we change while it remains the same. And at the very end of the romance we are left regretting its own losses, the objects that should have been part of it and weren't—the Houdons, the splendid tapestries, the marvellous books. And yet there is a change—for new people come to look after the collection who understand it better. Such a one is Mr. Francis Watson, author of the Catalogue Raisonné of the Furniture which has just appeared. Under his touch the collection really seems to flower, the secret drawers spring open, the beautiful woman we have known becomes glowing and mysterious, rich with a subtle promise of pleasure. The Past lives. To love the past is a religion, collecting is a form of prayer. As the objects assemble (sometimes in a juxtaposition which was theirs two hundred years ago) the devoted craftsmanship with which they were made, the devoted connoisseurship with which they were loved, breathes from them and this exhalation is infectious and can transform a student, a pair of lovers, an artist by its radiance, enriching their sensibility for ever. For the Wallace Collection is serenely happy. Manchester Square is a good square, Hertford House a magnificent mansion, 'a clean well-lighted place'. The walls, hung in silk by Lord Duveen, are made for pictures, the pictures chosen to give immediate pleasure. Only the Watteaus can make one cry. The Sèvres china in its vitrines sings like a coral reef seen through a glass-bottomed boat, the commodes glisten like bulls at pasture, the snuff-boxes are like tropical shells. I remember a lady saying to Sir Robert Abdy that she did not know what to do with her dog in London, it was so bored and restless. He looked at her gravely. 'Couldn't you take it to the Wallace Collection?' Among the snuff-boxes are two or three in such exquisite taste—one green, one rock-crystal, one scallop-shaped in pure gold that I used to make a point of asking my girl friends to choose one to see if they would pick these out. I can't imagine applying such tests in the Musée des Arts Décoratifs or the National Gallery, it is something in the air of Hertford House where Houdon's Madame de Serilly, the bust which the Duc de Morny took on his campaigns so that it should be the first thing his eyes rested on when he woke up, still sets the tone.

The Wallace Collection is two things: the finest collection of French eighteenth-century art in the world and the happy ending to a human drama, a drama of mania and greed and hate like a Greek tragedy. We must observe two things, a collection of objects, and a family history. The Seymours who became earls then marquesses of Hertford in the second half of the eighteenth century were not of very great interest though they play a large part in the affections and correspondence of Horace Walpole. As far as the collection was concerned they are responsible only for a few family portraits and a Reynolds and a Romney, but by being enormously rich and mixing in court circles (the first Marquess was ambassador to France at the height of the rococo) they *lived* that eighteenth century which their descendants were to collect. They ate off the china dishes which would end up in showcases, commandeered the beds and chairs which museums would fight over, sprawled over the tapestries, dropped their snuff-boxes and ordered others, had themselves painted by Gainsborough and attended the fêtes and parties the minutest detail of which would one day make decorative history. They were consumers for collecting had hardly begun. Without their careless display and grace of living there would have been no humus where the nostalgia which animates all collectors could ripen.

Among the great aristocrats who were busy creating what we mean by the eighteenth century none fulfilled his historical mission more equably than the Duke of Queensberry who, as Earl of March, had become involved with an Italian opera singer and afterwards with another Italian, the Marchesa Fagnani, by whom he had a daughter. This child, the celebrated Mie-Mie, married in 1798 the third Marquess of Hertford, politician, rake, collector, and the friend and adviser in artistic matters to the Prince Regent. She inherited two fortunes and bore two children, the fourth Marquess (the collector in chief) and Lord Henry Seymour (Milord Arsouille), whose real father was Talleyrand's crony, Montrond. The third Lord Hertford began his career as a statesman, continued it as a man of affairs and pleasure and ended it as a 'stock-jobbing sybarite' interested only in money and sex. He developed the passion for low company which goes with overweening pride and allowed sensuality to invade his being to such an extent that he had to be carried to the brothel in his chair, dying, worth two millions, after a particularly squalid debauch. One must not judge a life by its ending. Four novelists have succumbed to the glamour of Lord Hertford; he is Balzac's Lord Dudley, he is Disraeli's Lord Monmouth in *Coningsby* and Thackeray's Lord Steyne in *Vanity Fair*. Bulwer Lytton introduced him into *Pelham*. There is also an authentic account of an evening with him in the memoirs of Hariette Wilson. Disraeli alone understood the political importance of Hertford and tried to see the complete man when his cold calculating intelligence, utter selfishness and immense charm were not clouded over by his continuous debauchery. It was natural that such an egotist should become estranged from his wife and persecute his two sons until both spent long periods abroad to avoid him. Something of the relationship between Tiberius and Augustus can be noted here for as a result of his treatment by his accomplished father the fourth marquess grew up a resentful timid recluse. He had his mother, however, to preserve his heart intact and prevent a complete atrophy of feeling and also an income, on his father's death in 1842, of at least one hundred thousand pounds a year. At first Lord Hertford, his brother Lord Henry and their mother, Mie-Mie, formed an inseparable trio occupying two adjoining houses, 2 Rue Laffitte and 1 Rue Taitbout as well as Bagatelle and Lord Henry's property at Sablons. It would be interesting to know if Lord Henry was merely an aggressive hysterical psychopath or a full-fledged paranoiac, but this great dandy, bully and founder of the Jockey Club does not really belong to our story except to suggest that Mie-Mie must have possessed unstable tendencies which were transmitted to both her sons. Lord Hertford (1800-70) is a character whom it is necessary to love in order to understand. He must have constantly been the butt of his father's cynical and worldly observations and witnessed his ill-treatment of his mother and he used his money to construct a hard carapace between himself and the world while his feelings towards her became sublimated into a taste for beautiful things, pictures in particular, while his aggression, the sense of frustration which was brought on by his inability to make use of his gifts through pride and shyness, expressed itself in the competition of the sale-rooms, in snatching from the high and mighty (kings and emperors if possible) the possessions on which they had set their hearts. Where people were concerned he was a miser (his doctor could not even extract a cutlet out of him), where objects mattered, a princely benefactor. He was probably the first person in France to rediscover the rococo. With his superb income he could bid for what was best in France and England. What he bought in England was mostly sent to Hertford House, some of it to remain crated till his death, for his victories were in the sale-room, not in vulgar gloating over the spoils. His letters to his agent Mawson survive and are models of charm and tact as if they were equal partners. 'I confess I do not much like the portrait of an old man,' he writes, 'however fine it may be; it is not pleasing . . . I only like pleasing pictures.' His income according to Yriarte grew to a quarter of a million pounds a year; there was simply nothing he could not get, the best clocks (there is a legend that one man spent a lifetime trying to synchronise all 200 of them and only succeeded on the day of the Marquess's death), the most superb examples of French furniture, the rarest Sèvres (including the sailing ship in apple green which symbolises the arms of Paris), tapestries, statues, books and pictures. Everything which would have been most prized in the reign of Louis XV and XVI must be his. His taste in contemporary painting was less certain. He bought only one Delacroix and admired equally Bonington and Meissonnier. We cannot enjoy the art of our own time through taste alone, we need intelligence. Not that the Marquess was stupid but the events of his time passed him by: 'il n'aurait même pas écarté le rideau de sa fenêtre pour voir une revolution passer dans la rue'. The clue to his character is in a sentence. 'Il a vécu toute sa vie dans un milieu inférieur; il y apportait même avec ses intimes une manière d'être dissimulée, peu conforme avec le "cant" anglais et il affichait une sorte de cynisme que les deux ou trois amis intimes qu'il a conservés jusqu'à sa mort regardaient comme sa masque d'emprunt.' Of course, he loved animals.

When a very young man, at Brighton, the fourth marquess had had a mistress who was to bear him an illegitimate son, brought up first as Richard Jackson and then as Richard Wallace, and employed as companion to Mie-Mie and general secretary. In 1850 he replaced Lord Henry Seymour in Lord Hertford's will though he was probably unaware of his parentage or his destiny. Wallace was also a born collector (he began with a cup of rock-crystal) whose tastes veered more to the Renaissance, he was also a born connoisseur and used to tour the antique shops with Lord Hertford and General Claremont where 'his opinion invariably used to prevail', but he was also something quite different, an unwarped human being. The close air of total selfishness which hangs over old Q (Queensberry), the third and fourth marquesses, Lord Henry and, I am afraid, round Mie-Mie, is dissipated and we can take our ease with a man of his time, generous, even extravagant (he had to sell his own collection to pay his debts), a Bohemian and a lover of his contemporaries. If the third marquess was prepared to pay Balzac's debts because of his enthusiasm for 'La fille aux Yeux d'or' and if the fourth marquess encouraged

Meissonnier and liked shopping with Louis Philippe, Richard Wallace went much further. Though a relatively poor and unknown young man he was a friend of 'La Présidente', Madame Clésinger, and he took her on a tour of the Italian lakes, thus winning the interest of Flaubert and the Goncourts. He bought a Meissonnier at her sale and when he inherited great wealth in 1870 befriended her with a handsome settlement and encouraged her to re-open her salon. Nobody came for her former lions had found other cages and she relapsed philosophically into an old age of bridge. But Wallace had escaped from the world of auction catalogues and had tasted that of Baudelaire. There is a photograph of Lord Hertford, Wallace and his mistress, the future Lady Wallace, on the terrace at Bagatelle which is redolent of the period. Lord Hertford always looked rather like a yak, but Wallace has an aura of love and good living, of true connoisseurship—the cosmopolitan grand seigneur.

In 1870 Lord Hertford died. He was fond of showing his cousin and heir, General Seymour, a writing-desk. 'I'm just a barren old bird,' he would say, 'but there's something in there which will interest you.' It proved to be his will leaving everything (except his entailed states) to Wallace who during the Franco-Prussian war moved his treasures to England for safety. He then settled down as an English gentleman and was created a baronet. His own illegitimate son carried on the family tradition of not marrying and was disinherited. 'Will bastardy never cease in our family!' Sir Richard exclaimed. Like his father he became more and more of a recluse and there is a record of him inviting guests to Bagatelle who sat down alone to an exquisite meal while conscious of a sliding panel opening and shutting behind which glowered their host's sombre poetic eye. In the end beautiful things drive out people; as each beloved object represents a triumph of a human craftsman, his contribution towards an ideal society, so they belittle the prattling spectator and make a wilderness around them. Sir Richard continued to collect—armour, Renaissance objects, the splendid rococo chandeliers, he even bought back his rock-crystal goblet but he refused to die smothered by his own possessions or to enjoy triumphing over his rivals in the sale-rooms. He began to make plans to leave the collection to the nation. These at first were frustrated. 'It seems hard,' he complained, 'that when one wishes to do good there should be so many difficulties in the way,' and all his Seymour ancestors might have guffawed 'I told you so'.

He died in 1890 and his remains were buried at his request under Lord Henry Seymour's with whom he had once found the warmth which the Marquess lacked. He left Hertford House, the collections and the Paris houses to Lady Wallace who bequeathed Hertford House and its collection to the nation and the contents of some of the floors in Bagatelle and the Rue Lafitte to Sir John Murray Scott, a mammoth of a man who had been secretary to Wallace and, possibly, the lover of his wife. Sir John, whose treasures themselves were worth a million even when the main collections had gone, left his share to Lady Sackville who won a sensational case against his family and then sold it to Messrs. Seligmann of New York. In *Pepita* her daughter Victoria Sackville-West described their visits to the genial Sir John in the Rue Lafitte, the servants skating over the parquet in their polishers, the marvellous furniture, the huge giant of a man dropping louis d'or which he was too fat to pick up while the nimble Lady Sackville (her mother had been a Spanish dancer) scrambled for them. Sir John died of a seizure in 1913 while talking about the history of the collection among the family portraits in the Founder's Room. It was the last explosion of the Seymour magic, the memories of Wallace and the Franco-Prussian War, the whole vast accumulation of wood and bronze and canvas crated and packed and piled up like a Pharaoh's treasure; the terrible invisible weight of the past had been too much for him. It is wiser to look at such things than to own them. Life must go on.

The paintings in the Wallace Collection centre round the French school, it is particularly rich in Watteau, Boucher, Pater, Lancret and Fragonard. The Watteaus alone are world-famous. There are also Guardis, many Dutch pictures and a collection of Bonington. The miniatures include several group scenes and there are many earlier paintings as well as portraits of the English school. The furniture collection is probably unique, through the inclusion of such celebrated pieces as the Bureau du Roi Stanislas which once belonged to Beckford, the Versailles staircase, the Caffieri commodes, the Vernis Martin, the Avignon clock and many, many others. The Sèvres is, I think, the best in the world and everything is displayed with the utmost felicity. Lord Hertford would have been deeply horrified. If only the tapestries and the books from Paris had been included—the Houdon of Sophie Arnould, the boiseries, the statues from the garden at Bagatelle, the silver—but we are back at the beginning! Even Madame de Serilly's little boudoir can never make the journey from the Victoria and Albert to join her bust. Frozen at last within the walls of Hertford House all the objects which were once used and lived with, broken and replaced in the careless days of Queensberry and Selwyn, expressions of the pre-revolutionary *douceur de vivre* which their descendant was so passionately to seek are now rendered innocuous and sterile. It is a closed collection.

6

CABINET OF CLAY

THE world of old china is red in tooth and claw, it 'tosses with tangle and with shell' like coloured caverns under sea. Collectors prowl, quiet men with murder in their hearts who will give the price of a farm for a lover and his lass and incarcerate them in a bank-vault; speculators pounce knowing that a broken harlequin is safer than the Bank of England and has risen to thirty times its value since 1939; scholars rage who have given all their time to searching for the vanished factory of Limehouse (its wares have never been found); scientists with acid-test and violet-ray debate with art-historians, aesthetes battle with crooks.

Humble people who desire to possess the past through some particular object, nurse their incorrigible dream. One day, driving through a remote village, they will catch the glint of apple-green and mazarine blue from a cottage window. 'Four Seasons, they do say, from old Miss Mosspot up at the Hall, proper dusty they get, let ee have'n for thirty bob.'

There is something about old china. What is it? So many fakes, so many breaks, yet always more left; so much 'expertise', yet so much to discover; so expensive, yet bargains always to be found; so brittle, so diminutive, so commercialised, yet strong enough to run a whole gamut of style and mood. A minor art, in a perishable and luxurious material, which is above all the new and private discovery of the rococo, it is most exquisite, most feminine, most touching in the years between 1740 and 1760.

In one quarter was a maypole dressed with garlands and people dancing round it to a tabor and pipe and rustic music, all masked, as were all the various bands of music that were disposed in different parts of the garden; some like huntsmen with French horns, some like peasants, and a troupe of harlequins and scaramouches in the little open temple on the mound. On the canal was a sort of gondola, adorned with flags and streamers, and filled with music, rowing about. All round the outside of the amphitheatre were shops, filled with Dresden china, Japan, etc., and all the shopkeepers in masks. . . .

This Venetian fête, held at Ranelagh to celebrate the peace in April, 1749, is one of the purest moments in English *rocaille*, and the whole scene, as Horace Walpole described it or Boitard engraved it, is like an elaborate group in porcelain. One wonders if the 'Japan, etc.' might have included the first specimens of Chelsea.

For Chelsea is the glory of our own rococo, Sprimont our greatest director and the only one to enjoy for all too brief a moment (through the patronage of the Duke of Cumberland) some of the privileges of Meissen and Sèvres. Besides manufacturing the loveliest of artificial pastes and employing first-class artists like O'Neale and Willems, and possibly Roubiliac, Sprimont was the first to celebrate the spirit of the countryside in those rabbits and cauliflowers, apples and melons, sunflower plates and giant vegetable dishes which combine perfection of craftsmanship with the rustic insouciance of England under George and Caroline.

In softness of paste and beauty of figures Chelsea alone can rival, perhaps surpass the Continent. As the rococo style gives way to neo-classicism so later factories like Derby and Worcester become more formal and more commercialised, their vision of the world less felicitous. By the nineteenth century originality, except for that of Billingsley at Nantgarw, has almost departed. 'Judge the art of a country, judge the fineness of its sensibility, by its pottery, it is a sure touchstone,' writes Mr. Herbert Read. A sombre reflection.

7

POSEIDON'S KINGDOM

THE discovery of the underwater mask (assisted by the frogman's flippers) is as momentous as the development of the ski after 1914. Two strips of wood opened up the world of snow and made us free of the winter element; now an arrangement of talc and rubber has given us possession of a summer paradise. It is an event of enormous importance. Once you have taken to swimming with a mask in warm, clear, salt water such as the Mediterranean, the drab world above is done with; it will soon seem inconceivable that people used to go in to bathe without being aware of the treasure underneath. The new continent we have discovered 'beneath the wave's intenser day' with its beauty-spots and scenes of desolation, its kaleidoscope of shifting weed, its rocks and valleys and their quivering gaudy population, serene and habit-loving, is something we must become part of once and for all to which a lifetime is too short to surrender.

The revelation, however, has hitherto been confined to athletes since diving to twenty or thirty feet with a heavy gun in pursuit of crafty rock-fish is only for the young and strong; but the athletes are apt to become bores about it: they argue, they plead, they boast, exterminate the *méru*, drive the sea-bass from its breeding ground, get involved in disputes with professionals and stain the wave with blood. Let us hope the future will belong to the fish-watcher and naturalist, to those equipped with colour film and underwater camera and with the love and patience to study the same fish year after year—the life-cycle of an octopus or jewfish, the courtship of the conger. We need new hotels for fishwatchers on virgin beaches of North Africa or Sardinia, maps of the best underwater scenery (such as already exist for the Esterel), and eventually we shall demand submarine national parks and sanctuaries with their froggy guides and game-wardens before the sportsman's dream—a double-barrelled spear-gun with powerful cartridges of compressed air—paves the way for syndicate and battue.

Those who must enter this azure world, like the Spaniards in Mexico, with a gun in their hand, will learn from Mr. Ivanovic how to use it. He gives an admirably clear account[1] of the different makes, of the necessary equipment and its purpose. The mask comes first; it should be large of vision, easy to clean and empty, and the breathing tube should be joined to it. Flippers are nearly as important: if they fit well and are not too heavy they free the hands completely, swimming ceases to be a conscious operation, we dive and glide without effort, can stray far from base, mount currents, stay in longer. Since nearly all the fish in the Mediterranean make at some time for shallow water, especially for those plateaux which reach almost to the surface an hour's row from land, fish-watching can be enjoyed by those who don't dive without the risk of a *coup de pompe* or a broken ear-drum. For those who wish to hunt, the latest information will here be found with good chapters on weather and the kinds of sea-bottom and how to choose them.

Where Mr. Ivanovic disappoints is in his refusal to tell us anything about fishes, though his photographs include some fine monsters from the Red Sea. For knowledge of them we must consult a good French text like *Dix mètres sous la mer*. Fortunately the smallest fish are among the prettiest to watch; the beginner will find more going on in a patch of rock and sand a few yards from shore than in vast deserts like the Bay of Nice or from a boat in mid-ocean. It is just as thrilling to see a pipe-fish for the first time, a sea-horse or a ray in flight as to pursue a flock of *sars* for the pot, while the staring eye and swivelling jaw of a *murena* or the groping of an octopus allow us to partake of the terror of primitive man.

[1] *Sub-Marine Spearfishing*, by I. S. Ivanovic (Kaye).

The great value of the mask and tube is that by virtue of them we participate in the fishes' universe; it is a world of astonishing colour yet eventual monotony and perhaps it is as well that we have to come out; but, while wind and weather permit, it is almost perfect. Gliding on a gusty day along some sandy trail through the rocks, following a melancholy sea-bass on its afternoon saunter around the apple-green Sèvres and Pompadour rose of the fidgeting weed where silver *oblades* nibble like angel-fish and midnight-blue castagnoles pose against the limestone or the unbelievable emerald of the peacock-labrus undulates through the shifting grass; swimming on while the wind claps and drones in our breathing tube, the lapis lazuli water goes by and a Greek bronze or Roman amphora, a present from Thetis, our mighty mother, lies, for all we know, round the corner—thus we find a new world opening before us, one which it lies still in our power to preserve—or to exterminate.

8

UNDERWATER MAN

I MAKE no apology (a phrase I have always wanted to use)—I make no apology for returning to the subject of underwater exploration, gogglefishing or whatever we are going to call it. The art—or science or sport—is now perfected to the point at which it must go forward in one of two directions: aesthetic or scientific. What it cannot continue to be is a branch of angling, for as more and more people take this up it becomes utterly destructive. There is hardly a single large fish to be seen off the coast of the Riviera and soon the minor fauna of the rock-pools will suffer the fate of the Devon coral groves after they were celebrated by the father of Edmund Gosse. A ban on the use of underwater guns from Marseilles to Menton until other measures for the conservation of wild life during the breeding season (which largely coincides with the swimming season) are undertaken would be a useful beginning. But most useful of all is knowledge, and because it is so crammed with knowledge *The Undersea Adventure*[1] is a valuable book.

We may classify underwater books under three headings, the practical, the adventurous and the scientific. There are several practical handbooks for those who wish to destroy fish in their nests during the mating season; there are adventure stories, of which the most spectacular are by Hans Haas; and there is one which is both adventurous and scientific, Commandant Cousteau's, the most inspiring which has hitherto risen out of the waters.

[1] By Philippe Diolé. Translated by Alan Ross (Sidgwick & Jackson).

M. Diolé may not be a great diver or a great scientist or a great naturalist but he is the first underwater journalist, the first writer to see that man has discovered a new paradise which is both healing to the spirit and rewarding to the senses and which offers an endless field to our curiosity. His all-round vision is his strength. He is the first to have a chapter on seaweed, on the possibilities of the ocean-bed as a source of food-production, on the kind of poetry or the kind of philosophy that the underwater man will produce or the kind of love-making he may be privileged to watch. He is the first contemplative diver and his writings may help to turn beginners in the direction of the naturalist with a notebook rather than the sportsman with a gun:

> For the first time in human history man and fish are finding themselves face to face in the same water, breasting the same weed. I can remember the time when fish were less frightened for their lives and would come up to nose my harpoon. Now their education is complete, they know we are murderers and flee at sight. . . . Let us confess; we have gone down into the sea, into this unlooted palace, with the mentality of the line-fisherman. In this world under-water we might have become, not a feared and hated spoil-sport, but an understanding witness and a tolerated guest. For that we should have had to grasp the fact that fish were receptive to communication, that they could be tamed and perhaps one day domesticated. These discoveries we owe to the self-contained diving apparatus, to this instrument for increasing knowledge which has come too late. Yet the harm done is not irreparable.

Mr. Ross's rendering makes very pleasant reading, though I believe he has translated, in the introduction, 'calanque' as 'sand-dune'. The problem of names for fish, however, requires to be settled. It looks as if he has translated 'loup' (sea-bass) as sea-dace and the exquisite little 'castagnole' as 'sea-bream'. And what is a 'drum-fish'? Since all books on underwater fishing emanate from the Mediterranean and their cradle is Provence, I suggest that once and for all Provençal names are retained, a *saupe* is a saupe, a *loup* is a loup, a *castagnole* a castagnole.

It is a tragedy for us that the new art of sea-loitering or fish-watching is impracticable in northern waters. The ideal surroundings are those where rock and sand are close together and where the coast has been neither scraped nor dynamited. Corsica is better than France and Sardinia or Djerba are more fortunate than Corsica. Only the Mediterranean is both warm and clear and free from sharks, and I think if I could set out on an underwater holiday I would make for Corfu or Ibiza and try to study the same group of fishes day after day in all their mysterious monotony. We may not learn much about fishes from watching them, but from their absolute and cheerful rightness in their blue medium we can learn to make peace with ourselves.

9

NEWS FOR ANIMAL-LOVERS

THIS is a delightful book[1] which steers between the same author's more solid *Wild Animals in Captivity* and the anecdotal method of Dr. Lorenz. Dr. Hediger is the director of the Zurich Zoo; he has also worked in the excellent collection at Basle, and has travelled over the world in search of animals. His approach is that of a biologist who happens to love and respect the living objects of his scientific research, and all animal-lovers can learn something new from this modern outlook.

Man is now exterminating the animal world by the mere speed of his own multiplication; there is simply not room for large or rare animals as well as human beings. There is probably not a jungle elephant in Africa, according to Dr. Hediger, which has not been shot at. Zoos and national parks therefore become increasingly important in so far as animals can breed in them. On the Yale chimpanzee farm in Florida there are more than fifty native-born chimpanzees extending to the third generation. We are watching the emergence, in fact, of a new kind of ape, an all-American chimpanzee. Those of the St. Louis zoo have taken very kindly to motor racing and the best driver, Pancho, can get out of a jam by moving into reverse. Only one of these chimpanzees, alas, is happiest with pencil and paper.

We must not therefore think of zoos as bad places—except, of course, when they are bad zoos where the animals are not given enough to do or where we do not understand enough about them

[1] *The Psychology of Animals in Zoos and Circuses*, by Dr. H. Hediger (Butterworth).

to provide rubbing posts, concrete termitaries, urine baths, wooden play blocks, and various other devices agreeable to their temperament. Animals in captivity are liberated from disease and from the cycle of preying or being preyed upon. This security sets free a considerable amount of energy which must be prevented from decaying into boredom. From scientists and curators like Dr. Hediger we can build up a truer picture of what animals are like in a wild state and thus look after them better.

The home is immensely important; most wild animals have homes and hate leaving them; they like to use the same tracks and to be at the same place at the same time for they are creatures of habit. And besides their obsession with routine and their eternal vigilance against man their other regular preoccupation is with their position in society. Among forty-one monkeys there will be 820 different relationships; similarly, a procession of small boys from a school by the sea reveals but little of the intense and complicated system of mutual relationships within it. Every group of animals has a leader, not always the obvious one for among the ibexes it will be a female. Lions and tigers high in their group are less obedient to the tamer than those lower down. 'Bettering oneself' occupies most of the animal's life and leads also to the greatest sexual prizes and eventual leadership of the herd. How different from the captive chimpanzees who have learnt to beg coins off each other to put in food machines!

The first animals to be kept in captivity were the giant sloths of prehistoric Patagonia, the last is the golden hamster of which the whole population derives from a female and twelve young caught at Aleppo in 1930; two pairs only began the breed in England. The escape of the chinchilla is also phenomenal.

The newest discovery in acclimatisation comes from the enormous aquarium at Marineland, Florida—a tame porpoise. This proves the truth of the old Greek legend of Arion and the dolphin. For a young adult porpoise named 'Flippy', handed over to a lion-tamer, has proved one of the most intelligent pets in the world. 'The confidence of this legendary sea-creature, its exaggerated human eyes, its strange breathing hole, the torpedo-shape and colour of its body, the completely smooth and waxy texture of its body and not least its four impressive rows of equally sharp teeth in its beak-like mouth, made the deepest impression on me. So new, strange and extremely weird was this creature, that one was tempted to consider it as some kind of bewitched being.' Underwater fishing may lead to the domestication of further unexpected pets, but few have the porpoise's unremitting activity and well-developed brain.

Dr. Hediger includes a masterly essay on lion-taming, which he regards as almost one of the visual arts; there are studies of snakes fighting, the birth of a giraffe and the 'gibbon's day'. Occasionally he drops a piece of fascinating information, as that the cells of a live sponge, when passed through a sieve, will reassemble into the original animal. He writes also of the sleep of elephants and decides conclusively that dogs dream for one has been observed to make hunting noises when some artificial pine-needle essence was placed by its sleeping nose.

10

THE OTHER HALF

BOOKS about animals generally suffer from facetiousness and sentimentality. There would seem a conspiracy to keep the lords of creation in ignorance of the strangeness of the world, permanently unaware that the lower the life-form, the nearer it approaches to a condition of perpetual ecstasy. Zoos are concentration camps in which we triumph over the ringleaders of ancient civilisations—fish, reptile, bird, mammal—whom we suspect to have led lives richer than our own. 'As unlike as two peas. . . .' All the world's fauna which subscribe to such slogans of discrimination incur our envy and must do a stretch in aviary or formicarium without benefit of aphis.

Dr. Lorenz introduces each chapter of his book[1] with a few words in the whimsical pet-side manner of the old-fashioned naturalist but only to lull his reader into accepting the extraordinary information which is to follow. A home-made aquarium—how deceptively simple. By precisely balancing the relationship between plant, insect and fish it should never be necessary to change the water. Shall we exactly reproduce the bottom of an alpine lake or experiment with some ferocious, monogamous and philoprogenitive occupant like stickleback or cichlid? A moment later we are following a learned and fascinating account of their courtship patterns.

The same technique is used in a brilliant chapter on jackdaws wherein is the revelation of a whole new language. Thus jackdaws have a pecking order. A high-up male can mate with a low-down

[1] *King Solomon's Ring*, by K. Z. Lorenz (Methuen).

female who then assumes the husband's rank in the pecking order—as in human society. But a high-up female can never mate with a male who is lower in the pecking order. This seems extraordinary at first, but a little thought will reveal that it is apt to be true in a highly socialised institution like a government office.

Dr. Lorenz keeps all his subjects in a state as near as possible to complete liberty: ravens, grey-lag geese, cockatoos descend from the air when he gives the signal; a parrot flies in and out of rooms looking for him with a cry of 'Where's the doc?' and jackdaws fill his ears with chewed-up worm. Is this love? Yes; but it is also in response to a stimulus based on an understanding of their behaviour. The jackdaw which feeds him will peck his hand to pieces if it holds a wet bathing-dress, because a black object in a hand means a jackdaw in distress and all the other jackdaws are called to liberate it. If this happens twice he will be branded for life as an enemy.

Talking birds, with the possible exception of the raven, do not know what they are saying. No parrots have yet been taught to ask for 'water' when thirsty or 'food' when hungry, even if they exclaim 'good morning' only in the morning. The language of birds is like the language of people coughing at a concert. It is unpremeditated and spontaneous and the desire to communicate is of secondary importance.

Yet the borderlines of animal intelligence are immensely hard to define. When tangled up a monkey can unwind its leash by going round in the opposite direction while a lemur can never do so. The destructiveness of higher animals seems a source of pleasure. Why do they precipitate the deluge or the crash? Is it boredom or revenge or to provoke punishment and forgiveness? Why does my coati always unhitch the telephone or smear its tail with unguents? Why are some animals, lemurs and kinkajous for instance, particularly fond of alcohol? Dr. Lorenz quickly makes one realise how ignorant we are of dogs, cats and parrots. How many people know that dogs descended from a wolf strain have entirely different temperaments from those whose ancestry is pure jackal? The former recognise one master only, choose him a month earlier than other dogs and will never accept another.

This is a minute sample of the information contained in this absorbing book. It should make all who read it wish to enlarge their vision and understanding of the world by accepting some member of an archaic civilisation as their guest. We cannot maintain flocks of geese and jackdaws in our homes but we can most of us accommodate one animal or bird in a state of true liberty.

If we take the dog and the cat as norm and mark them I for intelligence, A for affection, C for cleanliness and H for hardiness we can establish a scale by which the petworthiness of all other species can be measured. Monkeys receive a plus for I and a minus for C and H, guinea-pigs a minus for I and A and it will be found by long trial and error that the best pets (apart from dogs, cats, lemurs, woolly monkeys, sea-lions and cheetahs) all come from the Viverridae and Mustelidae. Mongoose, civet, genette, otter, beaver, badger, marten, even weasel, can all be tamed when taken young and are clean (which coatis and kinkajous are not) and hardy (as monkeys and marmosets seldom are). The raven is the most intelligent of birds but the parrot, affectionate and vegetarian, runs him fairly close, though its gift of mimicry seems biologically meaningless.

In liberty animals develop their passions and intelligence which makes them better companions as well as fitter subjects for observation. Mysterious biological processes such as 'releasing' and 'imprinting' can be watched; according to Dr. Huxley's foreword to this book they were largely discovered by Dr. Lorenz. 'Imprinting' may lead to embarrassment for it is the process which causes creatures to fall in love, like Titania, with the objects with which they are familiar at the time of their awakening. In such circumstances a peacock may refuse all hens and desire only a giant tortoise. 'It is typical of this extraordinary state of fixation of sexual desire on a particular and unnatural object that it cannot be reversed.'

22

LIVING WITH LEMURS

AFTER twenty years I have a ring-tailed lemur again; my sixth. I still think them the most delightful of all pets; it is their owner, not the breed, who has deteriorated. Yet a singular doubt has grown. Are they clockwork? How do they differ from a machine?

I used to think of them as possessing an unearthly quality—ghosts; *lemures*, like their name—uncanny, primitive, remote; man's one authentic ancestor. Their plaintive cry, their eyes of melting brown under long black lashes, the indescribably forlorn and touching quality of their expression as if dimly aware of their predicament halfway between man and beast, a terrier's head on a fur-lined Pharaoh's body, toenails as well as claws, hands that grip fruit yet cannot peel it. . . .

And now they remind me of Arab musicians. 'How unutterably sad,' I said of such monotonous singing. 'No—the sadness is in you,' my companion replied—and indeed the musicians were shaking with silent laughter. The lemur's typical plaintive cry, for instance, which certainly results from loneliness, from any separation from the herd, is also automatically reproduced in answer to any sound of the same pitch—children's voices or the mew of a cat.

A lemur, in fact, has about six noises each with its corresponding body posture, and runs through them in regular order like the gear changes on a car. They fall into three groups.

1. EMOTION	NOISE	POSTURE
Anxiety, hunger, etc.	=short mew	=skipping with imaginary rope
loneliness, recognition	=plaintive cry sometimes prolonged to a sob	=head lifted, cheeks blown out

2. EMOTION	NOISE	POSTURE
Excitement, irritation, play	=metallic, *bdib, bdib, bdib*	=leaping, bouncing
alarm	=short croak	=stares at suspicious object, jumps to safety
anger	=high squeak	=biting, clawing

3. EMOTION	NOISE	POSTURE
Pleasure	=purring	=licking and cuddling up
sex (males only)	=nasal whinny	=tail held over head and stiffly waggled

Lemurs are inclined to bite when food (or what they consider food—i.e. eyeblack, toothpaste) is taken away from them or when picked up roughly or much against their will, or when sexually rebuffed. If the ribs or armpits are tickled they are compelled to purr, to abandon any other posture and to start licking whatever lies in front of them.

They are, I believe, affectionate and devoted to only one master or mistress whom they will follow or precede closely; yet they appear quite promiscuous, like married couples at a cocktail party. They resent all ties or dependency and have a deep-rooted love of freedom; their temperament is amiable, steadfast, sunny and mischievous. The basic play-form is 'catch me if you can.'

This is how they play together; an impertinent tap or nip is followed by a delirious chase ending in a boxing and wrestling match. They express themselves by their agility and will reserve their longest leaps for the largest audience—they seem to like best children and the very old.

Lemurs regard cats as being germane to themselves and will immediately attempt to groom them; dogs are generally to be teased. They are almost fearless, but all dislike aeroplanes and large birds. They rely on their brilliant timing to get out of the way, will jump on the dog's rump or advance backwards upon it in a manner that even large hounds find completely unnerving.

Their front teeth form a currycomb; the canines grow back like fish-hooks and can give a most painful bite; in addition the males have a blunt claw inside the elbow with which they can rip and tear in moderation; all box cleverly, 'southpaws' who lead at their opponents' eyes.

When a lemur is let loose in a strange room it does not skulk in corners and investigate smells, like a dog or cat, but immediately establishes a four-wall circuit until it can leap round the room at picture level. Each new leap is tested with hilarious *bdib-bdib-bdib-bing*. In these circuits, pictures, china and even quite large pieces of furniture come rapidly to grief and—since lemurs are beautifully precise and sure-footed—it is clear that they enjoy the crash and jingle of breaking glass or cascading Chelsea. Out of doors they will choose some fragile and elastic shrub and bounce up and down on it, like children on a clump of rushes. They will always answer and come when called yet show the greatest reluctance to being caught, except when feeling tired or cold.

At night they prefer to sleep in a bed, will find their way to the bottom like a hot-water bottle and remain quiet for hours. They rise at dawn. They will not foul their bed but it is impossible to house-train them; any perch above ground is considered a privy.

On the other hand they can be controlled to some extent through the times when they are fed and, being vegetarians, are seldom noxious. They will consume between two and three bananas a day, one or two bits of bread or cake, some grapes or a few leaves of lettuce. They must be protected from alcohol or they become topers.

Lemurs are not greedy and spend very little of their time in eating. Sleep, play and fur-combing come first. Their coat is short, thick and extremely soft with a smell of young kitten. They enjoy travelling and will sit for hours looking out of a railway window.

What are the limits of their intelligence? If tied to a post they immediately become hopelessly entangled and, unlike a monkey, can never unwind themselves. They will not run carrying their leash in one hand, as I have seen a monkey do, but can tug at it if it is bothering them. They altogether lack the imitative impulse of monkeys and their hands are extremely clumsy.

Matches and match-boxes fascinate all lemurs though they have great difficulty in manipulating them; newly cut wood usually sets up the elbow-clawing reaction.[1] Their sight and hearing are excellent and they perceive everything; in fact, they may well be much more intelligent than anyone has supposed since their reproachful glance or sneer or look of love is subtle almost to the point of imperceptibility.

They never appear as if they are trying to say something—they are too self-satisfied, too much the dandy to give way to emotion. Their parting protest, however, can lacerate one with guilt.

The ring-tailed lemur (*lemur catta*) has a fairly short history. It appears in a Chinese painting of the eighteenth century and in several eighteenth-century pictures, one a charming Stubbs of the Duke of Atholl's family. With the gibbon, Humboldt's woolly monkey, the sea-lion, cheetah, beaver and otter it is in the top flight of pets; it is hardy, diurnal, clever, sensitive and devoted, reasonably clean and very easy to feed as it can be let loose for long stretches in the garden.

Before the war there was a great rush on lemurs and the French Government has now prohibited their export from Madagascar. They are preserved, like the Australian koala, in their dwindling forests. I am not sure that this is the right policy; it would be better to enclose them in various tropical and subtropical zoos where the climate suits (even an English summer day drives them into the shade) to encourage them to breed in captivity.

But breeding is difficult for human beings seem to exercise a fatal fascination; lemurs will spurn their own image to pursue the huge creatures who, like monkeys and apes, are descended from them, who once possessed a tail with sixteen rings and the lost virtue of irresponsibility.

[1] Mr. Ivan Sanderson wrote to me that the horny excrescences release a glandular secretion.

12

NO PEACE FOR ELEPHANTS

A REVIEWER should have no feelings, only judgment and his judgment should recognise no values other than literary. Until a machine is invented which can vamp out a criticism of a book, he should try to be that machine. Sometimes, however, his feelings intervene and where no literary element is present to distract him they may even boil over.

Herr Oberjohann is, or was, since no biographical details are provided after 1938, a German explorer, intrepid, resourceful, who because of his 'passion for animals', obtained employment with various dealers, notably Hagenbeck and went out to stock his zoos and circuses. 'Not content with capturing animals, Oberjohann was always intent on studying their behaviour and psychology, on understanding them and making himself understood by them.' *Wild Elephant Chase*[1] describes the cream of four years of hardship and adventure in the Lake Chad region, where, he was told, the largest elephants in Africa were to be found, tormented by insects but secure in their impregnable swamps from man.

When Herr Oberjohann arrived, like Tribulat-Bonhomet the swan-killer, in his home-made leather suit, with his guns and beaters and whip and pipe, the herd numbered about two hundred. For the next four years the animals were to know no peace while Herr Oberjohann dogged their footsteps, examined their droppings and abducted nineteen small calves, all of whom died, their grief-stricken mothers going mad or being shot, together with any adult animals who allowed him to approach them. In addition he

[1] By Heinrich Oberjohann (Dobson).

conducted some experiments to prove that baby elephants who were impregnated with his scent were trampled to death by their mothers. We can therefore estimate that he reduced the herd by about fifty during the four years in which he 'understood' them.

Occasionally he permits a crocodile tear to water his home-made buckskin:

> I looked over at the dying cow; she was bleeding profusely and a big patch of the water in front of her was coloured a deep blood-red. . . . Now the sounds from the cow grew. She was talking in her own tongue, the elephant language. I wished I could understand what she was saying. It was an uncanny sound and it got under my skin, for it was through my own brutality, my crime against nature, that this elephant mother lay dying. I longed to escape. I refused to remain any longer as witness to this tragic scene. I wondered whether the people back home, whether Carlo Hagenbeck himself, had any idea of the unspeakable tragedy which is involved in robbing a fellow creature of its freedom.

In the next chapter he has quite recovered:

> I fired; the leading elephant went down on his knees. One of the cows, refusing to be frightened off by the death of her companion, rushed wildly ahead. . . . I fired again. The cow collapsed. Now I turned my attention to the baby elephants.

Mindful of the casualties of Hiroshima, we proudly call this the Atomic Age but future historians may look back on this century as the time when man finally exterminated everything larger than himself and ceased to be a trustee for the older forms of life on his planet: whales, basking-sharks, dugongs and manatees, sea-lions, sea-leopards and sea-elephants, walruses and polar-bears, giraffes —and elephants. Capable of living to a hundred, of kissing, of combining together, of thinking ahead and endowed with extra-sensory perception or telepathy, their continued existence is clearly intolerable.

Perhaps the French authorities of the Chad region could take them under their control, perhaps the four Powers who control tropical Africa could pool the remaining herds in a safety zone as in the Belgian Congo. Meanwhile we can do little but hamper Herr Oberjohann's further exercises in 'understanding' by omitting to read a book in which so much fascinating elephant lore is purchased at such fearful cost by a man who, knowing he is doing wrong, is yet unwilling to stop.

13

A PLEA FOR WILD LIFE

ALAN MOOREHEAD'S *No Room in the Ark*[1] is the best-written book about big game since Hemingway's *Green Hills of Africa*, though it might be considered somewhat superficial; for Mr. Moorehead is neither a naturalist nor an ethnologist but a brilliant journalist with a love of the wilderness and a keen eye for animal personality. It is essentially a work of propaganda, an impassioned plea for the protection of wild life in Africa written with great charm and persuasion, a fitting complement to *No Room for Wild Animals*, the moving film on the same subject.

Mr. Moorehead visited several parks and reservations and also some of the most unspoilt game country in Kenya, Uganda and Tanganyika as well as the Kruger and other South African parks and a portion of the Belgian Congo.

The position is roughly that everywhere in Africa the game is dying out: it can be preserved only by the Governments concerned and in the end this can be financed only by big-game hunters and tourists. The national parks, therefore, are, at one end of the scale, genuine reservations maintained in the interests of the animals and a few scientists who are allowed in to study their ecology (the Albert Park and Garamba Park in the Belgian Congo); at the other end mere Whipsnades (as the Kruger Park is in danger of becoming) or else simply State-controlled game areas.

It is a human instinct to kill the goose which lays the golden

[1] Hamish Hamilton.

eggs and the enemies of national parks far outnumber the friends —they are the poachers and the traders who live by the poachers, the natives who compete with the animals and the friends of those natives, the sportsmen who like to take a potshot at anything that moves and the politicians who wish to develop all the land for agriculture or industry.

The animal-lovers have two arguments—the humanist line that we are the trustees of life on the globe and should take steps to preserve it in all its strangeness and diversity and protect all rare forms from extinction and the sentimental argument that it is wrong to inflict pain and death on weaker creatures. There is also the one powerful economic argument that the tourists will come to see the game and that their currency is more important than the loss to agriculture.

The human problem is the most difficult. Thus in the Belgian Congo the pygmies, themselves a rare animal, do a lot of harm to other rare animals by their hunting and use of poisoned arrows; and in Tanganyika the Serengeti Plains, scene of the fabulous migration of huge herds of ungulates, are also being infested by more and more Masai with their herds of cattle or by new settlements of Kikuyu. The Masai cattle are prestige animals and use up all the water, formerly available for the thirsty antelopes.

The Belgians, whose government of the Congo is an enlightened autocracy, recognise that a national park is an entity whose whole ecology must be preserved and studied. They want both to keep the fauna and flora and to watch their interaction in their primitive state. The tourist is something of a nuisance. They rightly make fun of the Whipsnades at the other end of the scale where all the animals are affected by the cars and the cameras and kept in bounds by an electric fence.

In between is a school which believes in reasonable control of the parks to prevent predators multiplying too fast or food-crops dying out. The worst evil is poaching which can be defeated only by financial grants on a large scale (this brings the tourist in) and by higher penalties sanctioned by public opinion. The greatest danger is that when the countries are handed over to native

African Governments the African indifference to wild life—and passion for meat and hunting—will destroy what the enlightened bureaucrats and devoted game wardens have built up. There is no national park in Ghana.

Yet this is far from being a depressing book; for the sombre argument is more than compensated for by the deep happiness, even spiritual serenity which Mr. Moorehead derived from his expeditions. He has fallen in love with Africa and especially with East Africa and particularly with its noblest inhabitants—the primitive warrior tribes and the sacred trio elephant, giraffe, and gorilla. Though he writes charmingly about all animals, even the crocodile, even the wart-hog, he is most interesting about elephants, and the best moment in the book is when he is face to face, after arduous stalking, in, I am thankful to say, a British national park near Kabale, with an adult male gorilla.

> I had not been prepared for the blackness of him; he was a great craggy pillar of gleaming blackness, black crew-cut hair on his head, black deep-sunken eyes glaring towards us, huge rubbery black nostrils and a black beard. . . . He was the most distinguished and splendid animal I ever saw and I had only one desire at that moment: to go forward towards him, to meet him and to know him: to communicate.

In 1948 the International Union for the Conservation of Nature and Natural Resources was founded at Fontainebleau and here, perhaps, is the germ of the world organisation which can protect the vanishing wild life of the world before it is too late.

14

BIRD'S-EYE VIEW

I SHOULD like to communicate the continuous enjoyment I have derived from this book[1]. It is not particularly well-written; it is a little untidy and it credits us with an interest in birds, bird-watching and bird-name-dropping which we do not all possess. But even if I do not love birds, I happen to like the American wilderness and never have its various aspects been so refreshingly combined by two such experts.

Mr. Peterson and Mr. Fisher are both dedicated naturalists, kings of the bird world in the fullness of their passion and their powers. Mr. Peterson was able to show Mr. Fisher 600 different American species—a record—in a 100-day journey, covering 25,000 miles. He met Mr. Fisher at Gander, took him down the east coast to Key West, along the Mexican border, into the nearest Mexican jungle, over the Arizona deserts, up through California, and finally to Alaska. Every hour of the journey was planned in advance, a chance tea-stop at a tiny copse was calculated to produce its long-sought rarity. It was like being shown round England by Mr. Betjeman.

America, zoologically speaking, is a reformed spendthrift living happily on a meagre annuity which fifty years ago would have been squandered in a day. It was then that the lumbermen, plume-hunters, sportsmen, fur traders, had done their worst, exterminating large animals like the buffalo or birds that, like the American pigeon, seemed innumerable, felling the giant sequoias, clubbing to death the harmless herds of fur-seal and sea-otter, eliminating the egret, forging the dust-bowl.

[1] *Wild America*, by Roger Peterson and James Fisher (Collins).

But now no country takes more care of its vanishing fauna and the United States leads the world in preservation of the countryside and the system of national parks. 'Never have I seen such wonders', writes Mr. Fisher, 'or met landlords so worthy of their land.'

The national attitude to wild life has changed profoundly; there are innumerable bird-watchers and the sea-otter is perhaps on the increase. It is the revelation of this new attitude which partly contributes to the exhilaration which one feels on every page of this entrancing book. Though the great herds and vast extent of primeval deciduous forest have gone, small pockets are preserved and the minutest breeding ground of a threatened species immediately receives attention. There would seem only two recent failures: the ivory-billed Florida woodpecker, 'the rarest bird in the world', may now be extinct; and the Californian condor seems doomed on account of its inefficient breeding habits and the shortage of sheep carcasses.

The marvellous variety of North America is brought out by vivid glimpses of different life-zones and extremes of vegetation. I was particularly entranced by the Ramsay Prong in the Great Smokies:

> Leaving the great forest was like coming out of a dream: not a sinister dream, for there is nothing terrifying in the grandeur of Great Smoky's deciduous woodland. It is just big beyond belief and benign in its bigness. I thought it the most beautiful forest I had ever seen.

Next came the woods of Georgia, where the wild *magnolia grandiflora* drops its great petals into beaver-made pools, then the Florida Everglades. In the Mexican excursion we glimpse the tropical forest where the six-inch butterflies dazzle the dark glades. 'The first sight of the great blue Morphos flapping slowly along the forest roads', wrote Wallace, 'can never be forgotten.' Louisiana's Avery Island reveals the courting herons entwining their necks; the hordes of egrets and herons, once almost extinct and saved by the resolution of one man, bloom like huge beds of white and russet flowers. In the Arizona deserts we study the

Saguaro tree; we visit the Grand Canyon and the Hopi Indians, the sea-lions of the Californian coast, the huge redwoods and the mysteriously lovely rain forest of the Olympic peninsula.

The best thing in the book, I think is Mr. Fisher's account of the seal grounds immortalised by Kipling, the Pribilof Islands off the coast of Alaska. Here butchery has become scientific and we witness a system no more, or no less, cruel than a Chicago stock-yard. A 'great natural resource' is now intelligently harvested and yields a profit of a million dollars a year for the American people. The seals are herded, stunned, stabbed and skinned before you can recite 'the beaches of Lukannan', and none are processed unless of the correct size and weight.

Wild America is a travel diary written alternately by Mr. Peterson who provided the introductions, the statistics, and the Americana, and Mr. Fisher who supplied the emotional impact, the fresh eye. It is really Mr. Fisher's book and Mr. Peterson should be proud of his guest. Besides a succession of lovely places, of rare birds and animals, we meet with very pleasant people and escape to a community free from sterility or cattiness. There are no cocktail parties, no smears, no politics, no anxiety, no resentment; only the changing aspects of the wilderness, the beauty of birds and their names, the thrill of the chase under the tall shadow of Audubon who first saw, loved and illustrated this Eden.

15

WILDERNESS AND CITY

ANDALUSIA is my favourite island: it has all one needs, except a restaurant and a bookshop, for permanent exile. It is bounded on two sides by the sea, on the west by the broad Guadiana, on the north by the Sierra Morena, its eight capitals are rich and rewarding, it includes the whole of the highest mountain range in Spain and the length and breadth of its most famous river; from Jaén to Huelva and Almáden to Algeciras there is every climate and all types of scenery—and only one real eyesore, the main square of Torremolinos. It is only in Andalusia that Spain has made up its mind what it really wants to be.

Of all its cities Cordoba is the most typical, the least spoilt, the most mysterious; Seville is a modern capital, Malaga and Granada tourist traps; the British are in Huelva and the Americans in Cadiz, but Cordoba is genuine, too hot in summer and too cold in winter to attract a foreign colony, centre of a vast agricultural region which rolls up to the river that laps against the mazy oriental town.

At the mouth of the Guadalquivir which first achieves greatness at Cordoba, are the *marismas*, one of the largest areas of marsh in Europe and along the Atlantic or western side, behind the dunes, lies Doña Ana's game reserve, an area of some 70,000 acres, protected since the seventeenth century. It is a lucky month when two books appear, both good ones, on these two special areas and I dedicate my review of them, like a bull, to their only common denominator, the Marques del Mérito, one of the four protectors of the wilderness and also of the Cordoba *Campiña*.

Portrait of a Wilderness[1] is the record of three ornithological expeditions in which such grandees as Sir Julian Huxley, Lord Alanbrooke, Doctors Roger Peterson and James Fisher (authors of *Wild America*) took part. The superb photographs were taken by Mr. Eric Hosking. The 'portrait' develops from two earlier books which should be in the library of all lovers of nature and of Spain: *Wild Spain* and *Unexplored Spain* by Abel Chapman and Walter Buck, published in 1893 and 1910. Bloodthirsty exterminators of so many creatures wiser and kinder than themselves, they yet had a genuine appreciation of wild nature and magnificent opportunities to gratify it; and to them belong the first discoveries of the Coto of the Lady Anna and the best map of it together with the credit for stimulating Mr. Mountfort's interest.

The Coto (public not admitted: this means us) contains one shooting-box or 'palace' and several kinds of country over which one flies on the Seville-Las Palmas route. Besides flamingo, egrets, night herons and many rare waders, there are several different kinds of eagle and vulture, together with hoopoes, bee-eaters, orioles, storks, bustards, kites, stilts, down to the 'little brown jobs', as Dr. Peterson called the warblers while the animals include lynx, boars, genettes, mongoose, red deer, and an occasional wolf (the last five wild camels were stolen in 1950); there are also some interesting lizards and snakes of which only one, Lataste's viper, is truly dangerous. Leeches, ticks and horse-flies patrol the whole area.

Mr. Mountfort is not a writer but he is a happy chronicler of three spring festivals of bird and man in congenial surroundings, including an account of the wonderful pilgrimage to the 'Rocio'. Do not think we cannot learn lessons in our own psychology from bird-watching:

> The arrival of the parent with food created an immediate change in the entire appearance and behaviour of the young eagle. In place of the self-confident, aggressive little creature I had been watching, it became a whining grovelling incessantly crying baby.

[1] By Guy Mountfort (Hutchinson).

Except that any bird takes preference over the rare and beautiful lynx, the genette, the deer or the porcupine, *Portrait of a Wilderness* is a very satisfactory book which soothes and calms the reader; the expeditions achieve all they set out to do; the peace and beauty of the wilderness are in safe hands. Chapman can shoot no more bustard or flamingo. The Spaniards are beginning to learn.

Mr. Haycraft deserves a success with his first book.[1] He is a natural writer. Here is an economy of language, a rapidity of effect, a rightness of epithet, an underlying wit and sympathy which would endear him even if he had nothing to say. And (as Mr. Gerald Brenan points out) he has plenty to say for he has really lived in a Spanish city and come to know it through giving English lessons. These lessons develop into a full-fledged Institute so that we witness the building up of a successful career as well as the vicissitudes of the intellectual's typical love-affair with a new city.

The impact of Cordoba is extraordinary. Everyone wants to leave; a whole *bourgeoisie* is trapped there, unable to earn a full living, yet the question endlessly proposed, 'How do you like Cordoba?' must always be answered by superlatives. Mr. Haycraft likes everything and tries to understand everybody; he sees the frustration and unhappiness which afflict the Spanish professional classes, suspected of republicanism and wedged between the rich landowners and the orthodox *petite bourgeoisie*; he hears their cry for help yet he is aware that there is no easy political solution and continues to give his English lessons.

Meanwhile there is Andalusia, the fairs and the dancing, Roman pavements, Moorish remains, wine and flamenco:

> Suddenly she started singing like an animal howling at the moon . . . emitting long cracked howls, her mouth moving like a prehensile sucker. But the men continued talking.
>
> 'Animals!' shouted Paco again. 'This old woman's a thousand times better than you. She's known the days when dancing and singing weren't artificialised—when we didn't have to pay such big taxes!

[1] *Babel in Spain*, by John Haycroft (Hamish Hamilton).

When Spaniards were at peace with one another! Animals! Be quiet! She's a million times better than you!'

The men smiled but stopped talking.

'If only she knew that a grandee of Spain had been listening to her!' said Paco when she had finished.

Is Cordoba different from anywhere else? I think Mr. Haycraft proves that it is. It is not Reading on the Guadalquivir. The Spanish cycle of gaiety and gloom is more spectacular, the relations between the sexes, between the classes more extreme, the wit fiercer, the religion deeper, the humanity more evident. 'In Andalusia friendship to the foreigner is so generous and openhearted that it is difficult to sustain it on the same level for long. Here indeed making a friend is often like drinking a glass of beer which has a deep layer of froth on top.' In Reading it is like going on all fours and blowing at a fire till one suddenly discovers that one has got warm without it.

16

DISCOVERIES OF A PLANT-HUNTER

In a world of changing values it is the duty of a critic to attempt, where possible, a stabilisation. Let us admit that English architecture reached a peak in the eighteenth century and declined after 1840, and let us also admit that English gardening reached a peak a century later and has declined only since 1940. We can still enjoy, in fact, gardens which are a tangible expression of a great aesthetic vision and which, owing to taxation and labour shortage, are now past their prime, but only just.

These gardens are the result, like the pictures in the Wallace Collection, of a perfect combination between capitalist and agent. Intelligent patronage has produced the best possible results, because the expert botanical knowledge and adventurous individualism of the garden-owners have reacted on the sterling qualities of the seed-collectors whom they have employed: the Williams family in Cornwall, Lord Aberconway, Mr. Lionel de Rothschild, Mr. G. H. Johnstone, Colonel Stern and the Loders are to modern gardening what Lord Burlington and his friends were to modern architecture. They have given our country, with its dismal climate and limited resources, world leadership in the acclimatisation of rare and exotic species and in the production of new hybrids.

Wilson, Forrest, Farrer, Rock and Kingdon Ward are the great plant-collectors who have fed the judgment and curiosity of the great garden-owners and thus helped to transfigure our landscape by the introduction of new species from the mountain paradise of Yunnan. Farrer was his own master, Wilson collected mostly for institutions but the relationship of Forrest to his patron, Mr. J. C. Williams, of Caerhays, was closer than any partnership; they seem to have formed together a perfect human animal both scientific and creative. *Journeys and Plant Introductions*[1] is a tribute to the work of George Forrest (1873-1932) who, an almost ideal collector by physique and training, spent his life in journeys to the Tibetan-Burmese-Chinese watershed and died suddenly while out shooting just when his last and greatest collection had been packed. Among his seeds were those of the truly marvellous black magnolia whose blossom he never lived to see and which can be observed in lonely splendour among the dank Douanier Rousseau thickets of Lanarth. This must have been a difficult book to put together for collectors in the field are seldom literary artists and there is nothing to do but record various introductions, except in one or two large groups like rhododendrons, primulas and magnolias where the collector's personality is vigorously manifested.

'Though rhododendrons are indigenous to most parts of China, the real home of the genus is, unquestionably, those high Alpine regions on the Chino-Tibetan frontier, which form the basins and watersheds of the Salween, Mekong and Yangtze; there, somewhere about 98-101 degs. E. long., and 25-31 degs. N. lat., the genus reaches its optimum.' This still centre of the rhododendron world Forrest never succeeded in finding, but we must be thankful that he carried out such thorough exploration in the days before the Bamboo Curtain had descended and that the specimens he brought back, unlike the miserable giant panda, have increased and multiplied.

Rhododendron Griersonianum and *sinogrande* are among the most spectacular of the 300 new varieties he introduced: 'One morning, in early May, 1934, the late Mr. John A. Holmes arrived at the Royal Botanic Garden bearing an immense truss of *R. sinogrande* which he had picked the day before in his garden at Arisaig. He had walked the length of Princes Street carrying shoulder high the huge truss, supported with gigantic leaves, like

[1] *Journeys and Plant Introductions of George Forrest*, ed. Dr. J. Macqueen Cowan (Oxford, for the Royal Horticultural Society.)

a magnificent umbrella. On the way he was stopped, questioned, almost mobbed, but at last in triumph reached the garden.'

Primula malacoides, *Pieris forrestii*, *Camellia saluensis*, *Abies forrestii* 'King of Silver Firs', *Daphne retusa*, *Gentiana sino-ornata*, *Magnolia nitida*, *Osmanthus Delavayi* are among the choicest plants introduced or reintroduced by Forrest as well as those very rare shrubs like Gordonia, Hartia, Manglietia, Rhodoleia and Saurauja which are found only in one or two privileged collections. One day our countrymen will appreciate that men like the late J. C. Williams and George Forrest, the living Mr. Kingdon Ward and Lord Aberconway also represent an optimum; the fusion of scientific knowledge with aesthetic judgment, resulting in that most perishable and elusive work of art, a botanical garden.

PART TWO

THE GRAND POSSESSORS

2

ON RE-READING PETRONIUS

I FIRST read Petronius when I was at school and though I had no idea what most of it was about, I had two editions by the time I left, two more a year later and two more since then—yet it was only the other day I read him for the first time since that elm-heavy summer thirty years ago. I was perfectly right. It is a very great book.

Not great—magical perhaps is a better word and, what is even rarer, it is a humane book. Imagine that nothing at all survived of our literature but one or two poems and histories and a long novel like Proust's of which but a few disjointed fragments reached posterity and formed the only record of how we talked or loved or ate or felt about poetry or painting or friendship or money. Imagine a few remarks of the Duc de Guermantes or some head waiter as all that was known about our pronunciation, together with a dinner party at Mme Verdurin's coming down intact and a crepuscular glimpse of Swann and Odette, Marcel and Albertine. How our posterity would pore over every sentence! Yet, though in Petronius we possess a fragmentary Roman Proust, how few have studied him; how little known to generations of boring novelists is the secret of his rapidity of style, of his visual clarity, biting dialogue, intellectual fastidiousness or of the haunting fugacity of the picaresque—that art which keeps characters on the move from waterfront to waterfront, brothel to palace, adventure to adventure. 'I dimly saw Giton standing on the curve of the road in the dark and hurried towards him.' Thus we are introduced to one of the principal characters. The analysis of such a book could help many young writers to give movement and montage to their characters, the lilt of transience which is the breath of readability.

There are at least four Petroniuses whom for convenience we have rolled into one: (1) the historical Petronius of Tacitus, (2) the author of the *Satyricon*, (3) the author of the prose fragments and (4) the writer of some separate poems. The fragments (preserved by grammarians) indicate that he came from Marseilles, a place, as Tacitus said, 'where Greek refinement and provincial puritanism meet in a happy blend' but the fragments are all dated very much later and one of the puzzles about this extraordinary book is that it would seem, even in antiquity, to have been very little known. The *Satyricon* itself tells us nothing about the author except that he is looking at low life from a standpoint which is above it and that he is very interested in a poet who must be Lucan. Trimalchio tries to sing a song by Menecrates whom Nero greatly admired. The Petronius of Tacitus is a historical figure, the artist in extravagance, the dandy who idled into fame and who after being an efficient proconsul in Bithynia became the arbiter of Nero's pleasures until he aroused the jealousy of Tigellinus. When he found the plot against him had succeeded, he committed suicide at Cumae, 'the finest death' according to Saint-Evremont 'in all antiquity'. 'The reflection arises at once,' writes his editor, Mr. Michael Heseltine, 'that, given the *Satyricon*, this kind of book postulates this kind of author.'

We have then a picture of a great nobleman such as haunted Versailles or perhaps like Charles II's Lord Rochester, of a poet and lover of low life who finds time between governing Asia and amusing his Imperial master to write an enormously long work of which we possess fragments only of Books 15 and 16. There may have been twenty-two like the *Odyssey*. He belongs to a strange world: to the little group of writers who effected the transition between the Augustan age and silver Latin. The next generation, Tacitus, Suetonius, Juvenal, Martial, the younger Pliny and Quintilian came through the tunnel of the terror into the prolonged sunlight of the Antonines but our group all come to violent ends. Seneca, Petronius and Lucan were forced by Nero to kill themselves, Persius died very young and the elder Pliny perished in the eruption of Vesuvius. As far as the arts are concerned, the Rome of the Julio-Claudian emperors was only at the very beginning of decadence. There is nothing *fin-de-siècle* about Petronius, rather an enormous gusto. What was the *Satyricon's* real subject? Is Trimalchio's banquet a parody of Nero's entertainments or is it written especially to amuse him together with the hostile criticism of Lucan? Is it a *roman à clef*? I think myself that, like James Joyce's *Ulysses*, it had something to do with Greek literature; the fragments we possess all deal with Greek-speaking cities, especially those which are on or near the sea. There are lecturers called Agamemnon and Menelaus, a charmer named Circe with a maid called Chryseis. The four main characters and a great many minor ones have Greek names and a theme runs through it like a parody of epic doom: The Wrath of Priapus. Encolpius (whose name means 'cuddlesome') is the narrator, a young man with literary ambitions and all the physical graces; high-tempered but quick to forgive and with a deep and constant affection for his young companion Giton and some kind of tie with a rival, Ascyltos, who might be described as a neurotic hearty. There are also men of learning who gravitate around the three adolescents and several insatiable ladies of fashion. Though the tone is homosexual, the *Satyricon*, as Saint-Evremont remarked, is the only classical work where *galanterie* appears in the relation of the two sexes as in the delicious exchange of letters between Circe and Polyaenus. Encolpius has been in trouble at some time: 'I fled from justice, I cheated the arena, I killed my host,' he moans, and Ascyltos calls him 'a filthy gladiator who was kicked out of the ring, one who strikes people in the dark'. He has robbed a shrine of its sacred images and he is constantly profaning the mysteries of Priapus who punishes him by a psychological impotence which he remedies with difficulty only to infringe the sacred rites once more. When the story opens we find him near Naples at Cumae; later on, the three learned scallywags sail round to Croton on the instep of Italy. Fragments allude to Marseilles and Egypt and there is a reference to a quarrel in the

Porch of Hercules which indicates Rome. Encolpius, I think, was an Epicurean: Epicurus is mentioned as 'divine' and as the 'very father of truth'. And when Encolpius has to take another name he chooses Polyaenus, a disciple of Epicurus while only an Epicurean could proclaim 'at all times and in all places I have so lived that I have spent each day as if it were my last'. I think we were meant to appreciate a conflict between the sunny reasonable sceptical attitude of Encolpius and the Dark God whom he provokes and the God's priestesses with their superstitious rages and horrible medicines.

The novel is written in alternate passages of prose and verse which produce a peculiar effect rather like a staccato recitatif which leads up to an aria but the verse arias are not as memorable as the prose recitatif; they are less tense and vivid; good minor poetry and nothing more. I would like to give an example of the prose which holds, I think, something of the magic of this novel. Encolpius is speaking:

I came into a gallery hung with a wonderful collection of various pictures. I saw the works of Zeuxis not yet overcome by the defacement of time, and I studied with a certain terrified wonder the rough drawings of Protogenes which rivalled the truth of Nature herself. But when I came to the work of Apelles the Greek which is called the One-legged, I positively worshipped it. For the outlines of his figures were defined with such subtle accuracy that you would have declared that he had painted their souls as well.

I cried out as if I were in a desert, among these faces of mere painted lovers, 'so even the Gods feel love. Jupiter in his heavenly home could find no object for his passion, and came down on earth to sin, yet did no one any harm. The Nymph who ravished Hylas would have restrained her passion had she believed that Hercules would come to dispute her claim. Apollo recalled the ghost of a boy into a flower, and all the stories tell of love's embraces without a rival. But I have taken for my comrade a friend more cruel than Lycurgus himself.'

Suddenly, as I strove thus with the empty air, a white-haired old man came into the gallery. His face was troubled but there seemed to be the promise of some great thing about him; though he was shabby in appearance, so that it was quite plain by this characteristic that he was a man of letters, of the kind that rich men hate. He came and stood by my side. . . .

'I am a poet,' he said, 'and one, I hope, of no mean imagination. . . .'

'Trimalchio's supper' is rather top heavy for the book as we possess it. I think the important character is Encolpius and he has to be kept in constant motion. What a prose writer he is—of a fine lady's tears 'when this designing rain had ceased'. '*Tam ambitiosus detumuit imber*' and his Existentialish reflection on the drowned merchant, who happens to be the only virtuous character. 'Make a fair reckoning and you find shipwreck everywhere' (*si calculum bene ponas*, *ubique naufragium*).

Petronius died in A.D. 66 and Herculaneum was engulfed in A.D. 79. There was just time for the *Satyricon* to find its way into one of those libraries in the 'Sirenland' which its author loved. If the world cared anything for literature, we might live to see a sustained effort of the United Nations to excavate all that the lava has buried—buried yet not always burned—and perhaps then the missing volumes will turn up. I know that I would sacrifice any cargo the space-ships bring back from Venus or all the minerals on the moon for a sight of those rolls in their charred cases, and for a few more episodes of these aesthetes in adventure. In the picture gallery Eumolpus said that in an age that worshipped drink, sex and money there could be no more great art; people would no longer take the trouble to write well and would rather earn a gold ingot than own an Old Master. Like many whose gaze is fixed with longing on the past, he was apt to find himself looking into the future.

2

FRANÇOIS VILLON

An obstinate sadness hangs about the death of the Middle ages as about the end of winter; something harsh and rude lingers on, a bank of blackening snow while primrose and violet bloom elsewhere. So it is with the France of Louis XI: Chaucer has long since flourished, and Petrarch and Boccaccio; across the Alps the high Renaissance is in full bloom, but no whisper of it has reached murky Paris, a frost-pocket of feudal strife and academic obscurantism where, in 1438, fourteen people were devoured by wolves in one night, where secret police and inquisition burrowed and perjurers were boiled in oil.

A hundred years of war had impoverished it and another hundred were to elapse before the laughter and grace of Rabelais and Ronsard; yet from this indigence of flesh and spirit rose one of the great lyric poets of all time:

> First of us all and sweetest singer born
> Whose far shrill note the world of new men hears
> Cleave the cold shuddering shade as twilight clears. . . .

Several qualities distinguish François Villon from all other poets; he is not, like some aesthetes, 'l'ami du criminel', but in his own right a robber and a murderer, a member of the dreaded rogue's fraternity of 'La Coquille'. Hence the note of genuine ferocity in his scenes of low life, the sincerity of his visions of goodness and of his moments of remorse. When a poet has three times been condemned to death and has bitten on the 'poire d'angoisse' (the gag which is thrust on those who wait for torture) he will speak of grief and passion with authority. Villon is an absolutely personal poet, his best work is all autobiographical and when we open him he is with us in the room:

> Finally as I sat here writing,
> at nine o'clock this night, alone
> and merry, these bequests inditing,
> I heard the bell of the Sorbonne,
> as always at this hour, intone
> the angel's message of salvation;
> whereat I laid my labours down
> to pray at my own heart's dictation.

Yet this most Catholic poet reflects the decline of the Age of Faith, the Dance of Death is in all he writes; the corruption of the Church, the fires of justice and man's mortality seem to blot out the fair Christian vision. No poet has so loved the underworld, the underdog, the old, the outcast and the poor. In spite of his personal and romantic attitude this inspired gangster has a dominating sense of form. His poetry is ornate, classical to perfection, riddled with elaborate rhyme and acrostic; his feelings bubble forth with divine simplicity but his wit is intricate with double meaning and his compression is the translator's despair. Notice the exquisite line, three from the end of this verse, which telescopes the brief glory of old courtesans into the cheap fires they sit by. 'C'est d'humaine beaulté l'issue. . . .'

> Ainsi le bon temps regretons
> Entre nous, povres vieilles sottes
> Assises bas, à crouppetons
> Tout en un tas comme pelotes
> A petit feu de chenevottes
> Tôt allumées, tôt éteintes;
> et jadis fûmes si mignottes
> Ainsi on prend à mains et maintes.

> So we make moan for the old sweet days
> Poor old light women, two or three
> Squatting above the straw-fires' blaze,
> The bosom crushed against the knee.

Like fagots on a heap we be,
Round fires soon lit, soon quenched and done;
And we were once so sweet, even we!
Thus fareth many and many an one.

Thus Swinburne; now for Mr. Cameron:

Tis thus we mourn for good old days,
Perch'd on our buttocks, wretched crones,
Huddled together by the blaze
Of some poor fire of forest cones,
That dies as quickly as our moans,
A briefly-lit, brief-living flame—
We who have sat on lover's thrones! . . .
With many a man 'tis just the same.

Notice how well Swinburne recovers from a sentimental start, how each fails at 'mains et maintes' and deviates from literal meaning over 'pelote' and 'chenevotte' to suit their rhyme.

In translating these ballads Swinburne has the better of it, but the value of Mr. Cameron's book[1] (value which would be double were the French included) lies in his translation of the whole of Villon's work from the difficult archaic original into a living seventeenth-century diction. In England we know the ballads well but remain much too ignorant of the exquisite chain of stanzas in which these jewels are set. Villon's eight-line narrative verse with its rich rhymes, its changing moods and sighing caesuras, is like the monotonous music of raindrops in the lulls and gusts of the south-west gale, and in the long lament for his youth it reaches the heights of great poetry:

I mourn the season of my youth
(in which I revell'd more than most
Before old age had brought me ruth).
Youth drank with me no final toast;

[1] *Poems of François Villon.* Translated in the original verse-forms by Norman Cameron (Cape).

François Villon

It did not march on foot, nor post
Away on horse; how did it go?
Suddenly in the sky 'twas lost,
And left no parting gift below. . . .

Mr. Cameron's translation is generally admirable; his achievement is a most timely benefit and should lead many back to an artist by whom our favourite poets have been inspired and whose secret of fire, melody, wit and pathos is so disastrously lost.

3

SHAKESPEARE: I

SHAKESPEARE is the only supreme writer about whose identity doubts are continually raised.

The fact that this recurring doubt persists deserves analysis. There are three reasons for it. The first is that everything we know about William Shakespeare, the actor-manager of Stratford, contributes little or nothing to the image we should like to form of Europe's greatest writer. Some of it is downright injurious. This disappointment is particularly felt by other writers, especially Americans, including Emerson, Hawthorne, Whittier, Mark Twain and Henry James. George Moore was an English example. All felt that the discrepancy between the personality of the man of Stratford and the genius that brooded over the great plays was so complete as to suggest some deliberate hoax or gigantic blunder.

The second reason derives from the curious fact that the information we possess about Shakespeare of Stratford and the contemporary tributes to Shakespeare the dramatist do not mesh in together. There are no accounts of pleasant after-theatre suppers, no gossip-columns, no letters from him, no visual descriptions, nothing to link the author of the plays whose name was even then something of a household word with the litigious social-climbing bourgeois of Stratford, busy with his enclosures and foreclosures. This lacuna, together with the 'missing years' of Shakespeare's youth (1582-94), permit a wide range of speculation.

Thirdly the unsupported and unscholarly claims which eighteenth- and nineteenth-century 'bardolators' made for their hero laid them open to very damaging refutals or to equally preposterous counter-claims. All those who believe that S. S. (Shakespeare of Stratford) was not the author of the plays are convinced that they were written by someone of superior social position and/or education to the man of Stratford, someone familiar with Courts, who travelled abroad, particularly in Northern Italy, who had read deeply (even Marlowe was a brilliant university man); and who in addition had a particular knowledge of law, duels, heraldry, falconry and so on.

The supporters of rival claimants all agree that a hoax was perpetrated because their claimant, being a nobleman, could not publish under his own name, and/or because there were treasonable elements in the plays which would have got him into trouble. In any case a great many books were published in Elizabethan times without the author's name. 'Shake-speare' (they argue) was either a pseudonym like 'Martin Marprelate' or signified that the genial actor-manager had allowed himself to be bought by one or several of the stage-struck peers acting in unison (the 'grand possessors'). During the nineteenth century Bacon was the chosen substitute and because the Baconians were dealing with the bardolaters, they were the most virulently anti-Stratfordian. In the first half of the twentieth century the Earl of Derby was put forward (popular in France); and today the favoured candidates are the Earl of Oxford and Marlowe.

All heretical theories of Shakespeare's identity are brought up sooner or later against Ben Jonson and the First Folio. Seven years after Shakespeare's death the introductory poems at last link the man of Stratford with the authorship of the plays and with the first of Jonson's tributes—and the monument is in place.

At this point all apologists for the rival claimants bid farewell to probability and set out to prove that Jonson was bribed and that the monument was a fake. Jonson alone knew Shakespeare personally as an actor and as the author of the plays (even if he didn't think much of them) and said so. He must be rubbed out.

Now there are very few facts which will stand up to the onslaught of determined critics over a hundred years, and one might say that several dents have been nicked in the Stratford monument and in the First Folio—in particular, in Jonson's poem on the

Droeshout portrait. It is possible to claim that Jonson was the kind of man who might be bribed or intimidated into keeping up a deception (which he sticks to in the passage on 'Our Shakespeare' in *Underwoods* (1630); but it is impossible to prove it. It is easier to suggest that Shakespeare carried out the deception so perfectly that he never allowed Jonson to suspect he was not the author. Some champions maintain that he double-crossed their claimant.

Who were these claimants? Dr. Gibson, in what is a very fair-minded analysis of the literature that has grown up around them,[1] investigates four: Bacon, Oxford, Derby, and Marlowe. He also discusses many of the confusions and obscurities which provide an opening for these unorthodox theories. Beginning as an agnostic, he tells us, he ends up dissatisfied with the evidence and above all with the unscholarly methods, the *suppressio veri* of many of these exponents, their wild improbabilities; until he finally concludes that more problems are solved if the actor-manager *were* the author than by any other explanation.

The Bacon case (apart from cryptograms and the lunatic fringe) rests on the fact that Bacon alone had gifts commensurate with the authorship of Shakespeare's plays. There are also many verbal correspondences between them and his own works. The best refutation of the Baconians is a psychological one. He is not a poet but an anti-poet; his whole cast of mind is alien to Shakespeare's even if he could have taken the time off to write the plays from his own large body of work.

The Earl of Derby (1560-1641) provides a better *Spiel-raum* for theorists; he was four years older than Shakespeare which puts the early works on less tight a schedule; he also outlived him by many years but in complete retirement; he was known to have written comedies; his brother Lord Strange had a troupe of actors in which Shakespeare may have performed; his initials were W. S., he was a true Renaissance prince of many accomplishments who may have visited Nérac and the Court of Henry IV which is

[1] *The Shakespeare Claimants*, by H. N. Gibson (Methuen).

described in 'Love's Labour's Lost'. He was near enough in succession to the Crown to have some political significance—hence the need for anonymity. The Derby case has been put forward with great ability by Professor Le Franc and afterwards by Dr. Tytherley (*Shakespeare's Identity*, 1953).

The case for Oxford (1550-1604), who certainly wrote poetry and comedies, is popular in America. Here we have a nobleman with the necessary background, who was also a poet. In his case, however, the work schedule has to be thrust backwards and the plays written long before they are generally supposed to have been while the flattering dedications of 'Venus and Adonis' and 'Lucrece' to Southampton become nonsense. Oxford's temperament also lacked the large charity and benevolence of the dramatist's; he was a melancholy, self-centred man.

With Marlowe we break new ground. His champion, Mr. Calvin Hoffmann, an American journalist, claims that Marlowe's assassination was a blind, that he was spirited out of the country by his protector, Thomas Walsingham, on the eve of his arrest and torture, and that he sent the plays back to his old patron (with whom there was also a homosexual tie) from Italy. They were then handed on by him to Shakespeare. Dr. Gibson dismisses this theory with skill and force.

I am very surprised that he did not include a brief chapter on Rutland, a claimant who has always appealed to me, perhaps because Mr. Claud Sykes's book *Alias William Shakespeare*, seems one of the most readable, excitingly and skilfully argued. One might call this theory the Mozartian syndrome, for Rutland's dates (1576-1612) involve making him into a teen-age prodigy who wrote the two long poems and the early plays when he was sixteen. He was a man of culture with a fine library, who visited Italy and also went on an embassy to Elsinore.

There is, of course, no reason why the plays must have been written by a great nobleman; any travelled courtier would do. At the bottom of the scale is the other William Shakespeare of Essex and London, and higher up is, for instance, Sir Edward Dyer, of Alden Brook's *Will Shakespeare and the Dyer's Hand.*

Of course there are many arguments Dr. Gibson has had to leave out. He does not mention such fearful problems as Willoby's 'Avisa', or Spenser's praise of 'Aetion'; moreover, he seems not to have heard of Mr. R. C. Churchill's *Shakespeare and his Betters* (Max Reinhardt, 1958), which deals with exactly the same subject and uses some of the same arguments and includes an excellent bibliography: or of Professor Georges Conne's *The Shakespeare Mystery*, which pokes gentle fun at all the theories (except Marlowe) by accepting all the claims one after the other.

Meanwhile I am convinced that there is no getting round Jonson or even the new evidence about Shakespeare's minor activities which is slowly accumulating. But one is always grateful to the heterodox for introducing one to such delightful people as Oxford, Derby, Rutland and Dyer, 'wiser and kinder than public faces. . . .' May Time guard their secrets!

4

SHAKESPEARE: 2

EVERY generation deserves a good new book about Shakespeare's Sonnets—despite the awful warning of Professor Sir Walter Raleigh:

> There are many footprints around the cave of this mystery, none of them pointing in the outward direction. No one has ever attempted a solution of the problem without leaving a book behind him; and the shrine of Shakespeare is thickly hung with these votive offerings, all withered and dusty.

Of course, if there had been no dedication, there would have been no problem, for every impartial critic would be forced to admit that, whether by accident or design, the Sonnets are very nearly clueless. Theories could proliferate, but all on a basis of 'not proven' and we would all agree with another forgotten critic, Churton Collins:

> If certainty about them can ever be arrived at, it can only be attained by evidence of which, as yet, we have not even an inkling. The probability is, that it was Shakespeare's intention, or rather Thorpe's intention, to baffle curiosity, and, except in the judgment of fanatics, he has certainly succeeded in doing so.

Collins, however, immediately proceeded to stick his neck out:

> For our part, we are very much inclined to suspect that they owed their origin to the fashion of composing sonnet-cycles, that those cycles suggested their themes and gave them the ply; that the beautiful youth, the rival poet, and the dark lady are pure fictions of the imagination

—a theory to which Raleigh might seem to be replying when he wrote:

> That they were made from the material of experience is certain: Shakespeare was not a puny imitative rhymster. But the processes of art have changed the tear to a pearl, which remains to decorate new sorrows. The Sonnets speak to all who have known the chances and changes of human life. Their occasion is a thing of the past; their theme is eternal.

He agrees with Wordsworth:

> With this key,
> Shakespeare unlocked his heart.

Mr. Leishman[1] is of the same opinion, but he has tried to show that a great many subjects and images are indeed '*exercices de style*' and borrowed from the great tradition of Renaissance sonnet-writing and from the classical authors. No one who is the least bit of a poet himself can fail to recognise the note of sincerity, of deep suffering which emanates from many of the Sonnets and which can be contrasted with the artificial quality of some of the others.

In spite of such exercises, the general note of the Sonnets is one of muffled anguish, of sadness, weariness, even of self-pity which is perhaps a characteristic of the paganism of the late Renaissance, but which also suggests an element of personal defeat, some shattering experience of betrayal and unrequited love.

But when we look for facts we come up against a wall. The poet is given a blank notebook which he gives away, and he himself presents a blank notebook. Are there one or more 'lovely boys'? Or more than one lady? Who was Mr. W. H.? Who was the rival poet? One would like a Royal Commission of a poet, a scholar and a judge to examine every sonnet—starting with completely open minds—in order to decide what the emotional and factual

[1] *Themes and Variations in Shakespeare's Sonnets*, by J. B. Leishman (Hutchinson).

content of each amounts to, and, finally, to deduce from this what kind of a person wrote them; to distinguish, as it were, between Mr. Eliot and J. Alfred Prufock.

There has already been a book, Mr. Gittings's *Shakespeare's Rival*,[1] which attempted to solve one problem and which identifies the rival poet with an intriguing versifier of the Essex circle called Markham, author of a panegyric on Essex's brother.

This involves two suppositions: one that Shakespeare and the rival poet were fellow competitors for patronage; the other that the line about the 'Full proud sail of his great verse' is completely ironical, and that the sonnet portrays an extreme contempt. But the author of the sonnets seems indifferent to worldly success, except as a passport to the 'lovely boy', and appears genuinely alarmed about the rival poet's powers of seduction; he is defeatist rather than competitive. The idea of a Maltby-Braxton duel with Markham does not seem to me to accord with the tragic preoccupation with time and mutability and fading beauty set against the immortality of verse which dominates the Sonnets. But Mr. Gittings's book is full of Elizabethan literary detail and I can recommend it.

Mr. Leishman is not concerned with these problems so much as with the poetic content of the Sonnets, and of seventeenth-century sonnets in general (he is the translator of Rilke and the author of a book on Donne). It is therefore the more unfortunate that he launches out with two sweeping statements.

The first is that 'Mr. W. H.' was William Herbert, Earl of Pembroke, despite the fact that he was always known as Lord Herbert, and was Earl of Pembroke when Thomas Thorpe brought out the Sonnets in 1609, and that as such Thorpe inscribed other volumes to him. There are other difficulties which Mr. Leishman does not go into, and since the dedication to Mr. W. H. comes from the publisher and not the author of the Sonnets it may refer not to the man who inspired them but to the man who procured them, or indeed the wrong inspirer might have been

[1] *Shakespeare's Rival*, by Robert Gittings (Heinemann).

chosen. Mr. Leishman also sails happily into a whirlpool of controversy over what is called sometimes 'the dating sonnet'.

> The mortal moon hath her eclipse endur'd
> And the sad augurs mock their own presage;
> Incertainties now crown themselves assur'd
> And peace proclaims olives of endless age.

'I have found no reason to change my conviction that Shakespeare is here alluding to the death of Queen Elizabeth I in 1603 and to the unexpectedly peaceful transition to her successor. . . . The one certain allusion to a definite and datable public event.'

But surely the allusion is far from certain: Professor Hotson has written at length to prove that the 'mortal moon' is the Armada, a death-dealing crescent of ships, and he has given other instances of both words in these senses, while several authorities maintain that the allusion is to Elizabeth's grand climacteric in 1595, an ominous event about which prophecies were made and sermons preached. Let us equate the Virgin Queen with the moon-goddess Cynthia; even so does 'eclipse' mean death, or a possible illness? I think Mr. Leishman should have dealt with these problems.

What he has done, however, is to illustrate the Sonnets by means of a wealth of allusion. He does not suggest that Shakespeare borrowed from Petrarch, Tasso, Ronsard, Du Bellay, Michelangelo, and all the others, but he shows at great length what themes and conceits were common property. Some of them are abstract or far-fetched, some of them extremely convincing. Thus when he quotes certain passages from Ovid, particularly the Metamorphoses, one feels something click. It was a somewhat arrogant quotation from Ovid which was the motto for 'Venus and Adonis' and it is a good idea to clear one's mind of Jonson's sneer about 'little Latin' when approaching the author of the poems.

I have read the Sonnets many times since I was at school, and have only one conjecture which I should like to inflict on the world. In Sonnet 64, line two:

Shakespeare: 2

When I have seen by Time's fell hand defaced,
The rich proud cost of outworn buried age . . .

is not 'coat' (the armorials which grow blurred on costly tomb-stones) a possible emendation for both sound and sense?

5

MONTAIGNE

THIS is an expensive book[1]; however, it contains 1,100 pages and a brand new translation of Montaigne into a contemporary English which preserves both the spirit and the letter of the original. I thought I had caught Mr. Frame out once, when he seemed infelicitously to use 'bellyache' as a verb; but no, the French was 'crier au ventre'. So I finally proclaim that it is a small sum to pay for the pleasure of having one of the great writers of the world restored to us like a cleaned picture, at a time when we most need him. I should like to see the book carved up immediately into Penguins, with English, not American, spelling.

Montaigne is the supreme humanist: one can object to humanism even as Pascal objected to Montaigne but to consider his achievement in the second half of the sixteenth century in a French province torn by civil war and religious persecution as anything but wholly admirable, and indeed almost miraculous, is to fail as a man, a critic, and a reader.

He did, of course, write too much. His aim was to produce the first and greatest of modern spiritual autobiographies, a series of self-portraits like Rembrandt's which also reveal us to ourselves and it was not until he reached the third book that he achieved this for the nature and demands of his masterpiece grew but slowly apparent to him. Too much of his early work is the mere ingestion of his reading, the classics poured into Renaissance

[1] *The Complete Works of Montaigne.* Newly translated by Donald M. Frame (Hamish Hamilton).

dress. He was a Catholic who loved Socrates more than Christ, a Frenchman who was more at home in the world of Plutarch, a Jew after the order of Ecclesiastes or the author of the Wisdom of Solomon.

Jewish mother and feudal father, Lopez and Mountain, the combination is ideal: the gentleness and scepticism and intellectual energy of the one, the large responsibilities and appetites of the other. It is not a whimsical or sentimental mind—Florio erred here—but a tenacious, inquiring and corkscrew spirit adorned with a Shakespearian glut of images. He thought deeply all his life about death and love and virtue, the meaning of morality and the nature of happiness. The titles of his essays are misleading for they often open with a digression and then settle down to the steady contemplation and analysis of one of these ideas. His Judaeo-Gascon mind moves in an oblique pattern—statement, example, reservation, counter-statement, example, counter-reservation and back to the statement again, now doubly enriched.

What better interpretation could we find for Messalina's behaviour? In the beginning she made her husband a cuckold in secret, as people do; but carrying on her affairs too easily through his stupidity, she soon disdained that practice. Now behold her making love openly, acknowledging her lovers, entertaining them and favouring them in the sight of one and all. She wanted him to feel it. When that animal could not be awakened for all that, and made her pleasures flat and insipid by the over-lax facility with which he seemed to authorise and legitimise them, what did she do? Wife of a healthy, live emperor, and in Rome, the theatre of the world, at high noon, in a public festival and ceremony, and with Silius, whom she had been enjoying a long time beforehand, she got married one day when her husband was out of town.

Does it not seem as if she was on her way to becoming chaste through her husband's nonchalance, or seeking another husband who would whet her appetite by his jealousy, and who by opposing her would arouse her? But the first difficulty she encountered was also the last. The animal awoke with a start. One is often worse off with these deaf and unconscious people. I have found by experience that this extreme tolerance, when it comes apart, produces some of the harshest acts of vengeance.

I apologise for this long quotation but I think it reveals the complexity of Montaigne's mind, no whit inferior to that of Freud or Proust. The recital of Messalina's infidelities is brought to a stop by a sudden revelation—'she wanted him to feel it'. When Claudius takes no notice (the analysis proceeds) her pleasures pall and so she devises the ultimate insult to his pride, the bigamous marriage to her lover. Then comes the reservation—was she not really looking for a husband who would be jealous? But if so—counter-statement—it was too late. The Emperor has them all put to death. Then comes the quite unexpected final statement, verified by personal experience: the extremes of tolerance and jealousy meet. She obtains for herself and her lovers the punishment she has unconsciously desired.

I suppose the best-known essay is the last ('Of Experience') but I confess that my favourite is the celebrated 'On Some Verses of Virgil'. This, which Montaigne claimed would remove his book from the drawing-room to the boudoir, is really a treatise on sex, on what a middle-aged man ought to know. (Montaigne thought men were too old for love at fifty, women at thirty.) But it is also, like the last chapter of 'Ulysses', a passionate plea for a deeper understanding of women. 'I say that males and females are cast in the same mould, except for education and custom the difference is not great. . . . We are almost always unjust judges of their actions as they of ours. . . . Women are not wrong at all when they reject the rules of life that have been introduced into the world, inasmuch as it is the men who have made these without them.'

The essay ends with one of his most beautiful S-shaped inversions. Old men grow harder to please as they grow more unpleasing. They should eschew love and leave it to the young. On the other hand it is the only thing that will keep them young.

Another of my favourite essays is 'On Coaches', for it contains the superb attack on the behaviour—then fairly recent—of the Spaniards in Mexico and Peru: 'I am much afraid that we shall have greatly hastened the decline and ruin of this new world by our contagion, and that we will have sold it our opinions and our arts very dear. . . . So many cities razed, so many nations exterminated, so many millions of people put to the sword, and the richest and most beautiful part of the world turned upside down for the traffic in pearls and pepper.'

And this leads me to the essay on cruelty, with which I absolutely agree: 'Among other vices I cruelly hate cruelty, both by nature and by judgment, as the extreme of all vices. But this is to such a point of softness that I do not see a chicken's neck wrung without distress.' And cruelty springs from intolerance ('I have been vexed to see husbands hate their wives for the mere fact that they themselves are doing them wrong') and reminds one of the motto which he had painted on the roof of his circular library (which we can still see), the 'bold saying of Pliny': 'There is nothing certain but uncertainty, and nothing more miserable and arrogant than man.'

Scepticism, irony, doubt were not in Montaigne conducive to despair and inaction so much as correctives to arrogance, intolerance, cruelty, over-certainty and error. His last and greatest essay is full of magnificent assertion. 'There is nothing so beautiful and legitimate as to play the man well and properly, no knowledge so hard to acquire as the knowledge of how to live this life well and naturally; and the most barbarous of our maladies is to despise our being. . . . It is an absolute perfection and virtually divine to know how to enjoy our being rightfully. . . . [Jouir loyalement de son être. . . .']

There are times when one longs for the French to be set down beside Mr. Frame's magnificent translation, particularly in certain passages of exquisite precision or unexpected poetry as when he compares the cries of Untouchables warning the higher castes of their presence to those of gondoliers navigating blind corners or when he absolves us all of guilt for seeking vain pleasures:

> I, who boast of embracing the pleasures of life so assiduously and so particularly, find in them, when I look at them thus minutely, virtually nothing but wind. But what of it, we are all wind. . . . Mais quoi? Nous sommes par tout vent.

6

SAINT-SIMON

THE reading of Saint-Simon's memoirs is a major literary experience and demands three weeks preventive detention in a nursing home or country house; meanwhile here is an admirable selection[1] in an excellent translation from all the passages in the forty-three volumes which deal with Saint-Simon at Versailles, the very nub of the story. I have read it with the greatest enjoyment and I shall read it again, including Miss Nancy Mitford's Introduction, so pertly pertinent, and her useful, breezy footnotes. What a writer he is—and what a subject! The long decline of the Sun-King who was also France, who was also Europe, pitilessly observed by a young courtier whose allegiance lay elsewhere, a Gibbon of the antechamber, a Tacitus of the *chaise percée*, a Proust in periwig.

Those who had the entrée entered the private apartments by the mirror-door that gave on to the gallery and was kept shut. It was only opened when one scratched at it and was closed again immediately.

It is thus, discreetly and through the looking-glass, that we should enter Saint-Simon to witness the struggle for power in fancy dress, the extraordinary figures grouped around the king.

At what point shall we begin our study of the supreme egotist, *le Rayonnant*, in his magnificent poise and composure? Through his royal appetite?

[1] *Saint-Simon at Versailles.* Selected and translated by Lucy Norton with an Introduction by Nancy Mitford (Hamish Hamilton).

I have often seen the King consume four full plates of different kinds of soup, a whole pheasant, a partridge, a large dish of salad, two great slices of ham, mutton served with gravy and garlic, a plate of sweet-cakes, and on top of that, fruit and hardboiled eggs.

Or his Hatmanship?

For ladies he took his hat quite off, but more or less far, as occasion demanded. For noblemen he would half remove it, holding it in the air or against his ear, for a few moments, or longer. For landed gentlemen he only touched his hat. Princes of the Blood he greeted in the same way as the ladies.

Or shall we study him calling indefatigably on Madame de Maintenon, his huge pockets stuffed with snippets from the mail supplied by snooping postmasters from all over the kingdom? Or see him in a rage, a paroxysm of selfishness?

'Why should I mind who succeeds me? Are they not all grandchildren of mine?' Then with a sudden rush of impatience, 'Thank God that she has miscarried, since it was bound to happen! Now, perhaps, I shall not be thwarted in my excursions and everything else that I want to do by doctor's orders and midwives' argufying. At last I can come and go as I please and they will leave me in peace.'

A silence during which you might have heard an ant walking succeeded this outburst. All eyes were lowered, people scarcely dared to breathe. Stupefaction reigned. Even the gardeners and the craftsmen working on the buildings stood still.

Round him cluster other extraordinary and overprivileged people. Madame de Maintenon, Monseigneur (the eldest son), a bored and torpid glutton—'immersed in his fat and gloom, albeit with no desire for wrong doing, he would have made a most abominable king'—and Monsieur, the King's brother,

a little pot-bellied man, whose heels were so high that he seemed to walk on stilts. He decked himself out with rings, bracelets and other jewellery like any woman, wore a long black and powdered wig, spread out in front, and ribbons everywhere. He covered himself with all manner of perfumes and was the very pattern of elegance. They said that he used a touch of rouge.

His son, afterwards the Regent Orleans, was what history books call a profligate and married to the King's daughter by Madame de Montespan who thereby possessed the 'witty languishing manner' of the Mortemarts. The precise nature of this wit and private language eludes us and so is all the more tantalising.

Round this terrifying group frisks the little Duchess of Burgundy whose husband is Monseigneur's heir and who enlivens everyone by her familiarities, even picking the intercepted letters out of the King's pocket and reading them aloud. With her untimely death the King's own sun sets:

> With her death, all joy vanished, all pleasures, entertainments, and delights were overcast and darkness covered the face of the Court. She was its light and life. . . . Indeed mourning for her has never ceased, a secret involuntary sadness has remained, a terrible emptiness that never can be filled.

I hope I am managing to convey by these quotations the power of Saint-Simon and the unusual excellence of the rendering, especially since the ducal style was atrocious and often made matter which was dull in itself additionally obscure. Saint-Simon was what used to be called a 'Die-hard'; his loyalties were to his father, who had loved Louis XIII, to the old nobility and their leaders, the Dukes of France, whom he saw rendered impotent and ridiculous by the calculated policy of the King and the encroachments of lawyers, parliament, and bourgeoisie.

He was at Versailles as a young man but was not a witness of the glorious morning, of the days of Condé and Turenne, Colbert and Vauban, Racine, Molière, La Rochefoucauld, Madame de Sévigné and La Fontaine. He himself was as intelligent as anyone who came under his observation, he was a friend of the future Regent and assisted him in getting rid of his most dangerous rival, the royal bastard the Duc de Maine.

Saint-Simon hated these royal bastards as usurpers, 'fruit of a double adultery', even as he hated the policies which had corrupted the nobility and impoverished the whole kingdom. When he saw the bastards and the lawyers humbled simultaneously by the 'King's speech' from the new throne he exploded in a paean of justified revenge like a great gong.

Now, at last, my eyes could see the fulfilment of my prophecy. I could rightly congratulate myself that all this had been brought about by me, and that I enjoyed the shining splendour of that hour in the presence of the King and all that august assembly. I triumphed, I was avenged, I rejoiced in my vengeance, I delighted in the satisfaction of my strongest, most eager and most steadfast desires. I was even tempted to feel that now nothing else mattered.

After reading Saint-Simon (a pleasure in itself) one can never be quite the same; the innocent will learn more than they wish to about human depravity, the wicked that they will be found out, the ambitious that even seventy years of kingship of most meticulous order must come to an end.

7

LORD HERVEY

IMAGINE that we are looking through a small hole into a lighted room in which many candles are burning; there are heavy curtains, clumsy rococo furniture, two tables set for chocolate and cards. A group of six in their embroidered coats and wigs move about like clockwork figures going through a series of motions which are always identical.

The florid King struts and scolds, enlarges on war and genealogies, the amiable Queen yawns over her knitting, the two Princesses remain silent, the fat Prime Minister grows wise, then coarse and over-familiar while the courtier, exquisite and affected, agrees with everyone, his doll-like beauty masking a cold ambition. The younger Princess never takes her eyes off him. When the figures pass the long windows they gaze outside and throw up their hands in horror. 'Booby, puppy,' mutters the King, 'Monster,' cries the Queen, 'Nero,' hisses the courtier as the Prince of Wales disappears in a burst of vulgar applause. King, Queen and Chamberlain resume the tirade—'Monster, booby, changeling'—to Sir Robert Walpole, their Prime Minister.

The scene, with innumerable slight variations, is played for nearly ten years, a comedy of hate for perfectly selfish people. Then tragedy enters with a ray of genuine feeling for the Queen dies. 'She then took a ruby ring off her finger, which the King had given her at her coronation, and, putting it upon his, said, "This is the last thing I have to give you—naked I came to you, and naked I go from you. I had everything I ever possessed from you, and to you whatever I have, I return".' 'Poor woman, how she always found something obliging, agreeable and pleasing to say to everybody,' mused the King, 'and always sent people away from her better satisfied than they came. *Comme elle soutenait sa dignité avec grace, avec politesse, avec douceur.*' Her death, in 1737, puts an end to the memoirs; five years later the Minister falls and the courtier dies, aged forty-six. 'The last stages of an infirm life are filthy roads,' he writes, for already he had become a laughing-stock.

The present edition[1] of his memoirs is an abridgment by Mr. Romney Sedgwick of his admirable edition of 1931. All the tedious politics have been omitted, and we are left with the concentrated essence of the original, a sustained conversation-piece of the Court and its struggle with the Prince of Wales of which Lord Hervey was a privileged and indeed unique observer.

We know very little about the first half of the eighteenth century, of the detailed lives of Pope, Gay and Congreve before Boswell and Horace Walpole, Gibbon, Selwyn and Sterne come to let the daylight in. The Court in particular is in semi-darkness and the small hole through which we have been looking is Lord Hervey's eye. It was observant, accurate, unprejudiced, steeped in Tacitus and Suetonius and its owner was conscious of his extraordinary position as half-lover of the Queen, half-favourite of the King, half-colleague of the Minister, a secret man-of-letters grounded in the Hanoverian desert. 'The King used often to brag of the contempt he had for books and letters; to say how much he hated all that stuff from his infancy.'

Lord Hervey himself remains something of a mystery and will always do so. How callously he relates the death of his mistress, Miss Vane, how feelingly he describes the death of the Queen, his patron! And how abrupt is the transition from the 'handsome beau' of 1720 to the 'coffin face' of a few years later. One day I believe this little rococo group will come to be studied as a case-history of power-mania. It is a disease which rusts both head and heart and makes people callous and stupid. The King dreams of absolutism and military glory with indestructible egotism, the Queen aims at power through him, the Minister at influencing the

1 *Lord Hervey's Memoirs.* Edited by Romney Sedgwick (William Kimber).

King through her. All dread the young Prince: he represents the future.

Only the courtier, his political ambitions frustrated, understood real power as Tacitus understood it, and obtains it through these memoirs.

8

BOSWELL FOR THE DEFENCE

It is ten years since the dazzling arrival of Boswell on our scene with his English publisher's modest claim: 'The Boswell papers are the largest and most important find of English literary manuscripts ever made.' After the marvellous gaiety and freshness of his *London Journal* ('the most carefully and elaborately written of all Boswell's journals', wrote Professor Pottle) had established him as the major diarist 'between the poles of Pepys and Rousseau', he seemed to go somewhat off the boil; his years abroad were given over to drudgery and melancholy and the protracted social climbing that sometimes leaves a bad taste. In short, there has been a tendency to patronise him or find him a bit of a bore. 'Boswell suffered from a radical sense of insecurity and a basic lack of confidence,' Professor Pottle has added, and the familiar methods of righting this imbalance, through drink, duchesses, and father-spotting, have grown rather tedious. So when he turned up unabashed on the threshold of 1960 with another three hundred and fifty pages of self-revelation, one hesitated to let him in.

We need have had no qualms. *Boswell for the Defence*, edited by William K. Wimsatt, Jr., and the aforesaid Frederick A. Pottle[1] is easily the best volume since Boswell's *London Journal*, and for two reasons—the massive interventions of Dr. Johnson and the emergence of Boswell as a man we can truly admire. It is also a beautifully constructed book which appears to possess a musical form; the dialogue between Johnson's cello and Boswell's violin

[1] McGraw-Hill, New York.

dominates the first section while in the last we hear a new and sombre theme, the struggle for a man's life.

If one could sum up the English eighteenth century in a phrase, I would choose this:

JOHNSON: I remember once being with Goldsmith in Westminster Abbey. While we surveyed the Poets' Corner, I said to him, '*Forsitan et nostrum nomen miscebitur istis*' ('Perhaps even our names may be joined to theirs'). When we got to Temple Bar he stopped me, pointed to the heads upon it, and slily whispered me, '*Forsitan et nostrum nomen miscebitur istis.*'

We no longer exhibit traitors' and criminals' heads until they drop to pieces but we have no Poets' Corner, either. In those days hope and fear were closer companions and one could legitimately quote Ovid and expect immortality, yet for indigent Jacobites the scaffold and the debtors' prison were also realities. When we analyse the appeal of the eighteenth century, it is based not on such luxury or fantasy or ceremony as the age possessed but on simplicity. It was a small world with fewer people and they with a nicer sense of their human importance and with more clean-cut emotions. We seek it out for its life-giving properties and these are to be found not in externals but in conversation, in love, in affection, in adventure. The reciprocal friendship between Boswell and Johnson and the interplay of their compensatory talents constitute one of the great life-giving forces in literature. In his *Life of Johnson*, Boswell subordinates himself to his hero who epitomised the age he lived in; in the *Journal*, he allows his own forward-looking sensibility full scope.

In this new volume, many pages (now reinserted) were taken out by Boswell for the *Life* so that it becomes a matter of concern to us whether we are simply reading the *Life* over again. Fortunately we are not and though the *Life* contains many expansions and additions to the present material, there is also much suppression of invaluable personal feeling. Here is an example. In Boswell's *Life*:

On Friday, April 10th, I dined with him at General Oglethorpe's, where we found Dr. Goldsmith. Armorial bearings having been mentioned. . . .

And here is the new journal for 1772:

I dined at General Oglethorpe's, at his house in Lower Grosvenor Street. . . . Mr. Johnson and Dr. Goldsmith and nobody else were the company. I felt a completion of happiness. I just sat and hugged myself in my own mind. Here I am in London, at the house of General Oglethorpe, who introduced himself to me just because I had distinguished myself; and here is Mr. Johnson, whose character is so vast; here is Dr. Goldsmith, so distinguished in literature. Words cannot describe our feelings. The finer parts are lost, as the down upon a plum; the radiance of light cannot be painted. . . . It was somehow like being in London in the last age.

Sometimes this journal gives names that are suppressed in the *Life*, sometimes additional brush strokes are present. Thus, when Johnson addressed Sir Adam Fergusson at their first meeting, 'Sir, I perceive you are a vile Whig,' Croker added a footnote to his edition of the *Life*: 'These words must have been accompanied and softened by some jocular expression of countenance or intonation of voice.' Yet the new journal tells us that 'He was very loud and violent. . . . He was disgusted by Sir Adam and called him to me a narrow Whig with just the commonplace arguments.' Again, in the journal, Johnson says, 'No, Sir, riches do not gain respect. They procure court being paid,' which is watered down in the *Life* to 'They only procure external attention.' There is a visual capacity in Boswell that is almost suppressed in the *Life*. Some of his descriptions of meals and interiors are three-dimensional. Boswell on his visits to London (1772-73) is a married man whose 'valuable wife' has to be left behind in Scotland while he seeks his fortune at the bar. To his credit, he manages to be faithful to her despite the dangers of walking home at night 'through a variety of fine girls. . . . I confess I was a good deal uneasy'. He is, in fact, now *rangé* and we see his career as a barrister occupying more and more of his time so that when he returns to Scotland in 1773, he seems just another fortunate young man of good family with a sensible, understanding wife, a difficult though eminent father, the beginnings of a successful practice and a footing among the men of letters and the highest legal clique. All seems set for the Country Club. For at that time only London was not provincial and even London was besieged by leering Irish charmers and thrusting young Scotsmen with fine-sounding names. 'Sir,' says Johnson, 'I will do you the justice to say that you are the most *unscottified* of your countrymen. You are almost the only instance of a Scotchman that I have known who did not at every other word bring in some other Scotchman.'

But before the self-satisfaction of Edinburgh becomes oppressive, another note is struck. 'This was a day of complete sobriety and diligence. . . . I went in the afternoon to the prison and conferred with my old client John Reid.' Reid had been Boswell's first criminal client, a butcher whom in 1766 he had successfully defended against a charge of sheepstealing. Now (July, 1774) Reid had been arrested on another charge of the same kind, for receiving sheep he knew to be stolen and butchering them. He was an elderly, crafty and somewhat gloomily religious man and his personality tolls like a bell through the rest of this journal. This time Boswell could not obtain his acquittal and he was sentenced to death. Then begins the struggle to save him. It is here that the incipient greatness of Boswell appears—it is easy for a young man to accept the defence of petty criminals which more successful lawyers will not undertake and to score an occasional victory; it is not difficult to take a fashionable interest in a client under sentence of death and thereby satisfy the macabre romantic yearnings of the time. But Boswell goes far beyond this and works indefatigably to get the sentence changed to transportation. He pledges his influence with his grand English friends. The condemned cell invades his home. Yet he continues to act from a qualified belief in Reid's innocence (that he received the sheep not knowing them to be stolen); rather than from an indignation with the state of the law. He wants, above all, to get his man off. It is left to a contemporary Glasgow lawyer, John Wilson, Jr., to point the modern moral: 'Can any sober thinking person believe it that in a country which boasts so much of its knowledge and refinement, there should exist a law assigning death as the punishment of the crime of stealing eighteen sheep?'

Perhaps because his own father was among the judges who rejected his defence, there was an incentive to win this case but the Boswell who refused to give up, who spent so much of his spare time in the 'iron room' (the condemned cell), returning covered with vermin to his unsympathetic lady, is a champion whom any of us would welcome in such a situation. 'I thus pressed him; and while he stood in his dead clothes, on the very brink of the grave, with his knees knocking together . . . he most solemnly averred that what he had told concerning the present alleged crime was the truth.'

In spite of such events Boswell belongs. to the company of divine comedians; it was his friend Johnson whose sanity struggled so hard with the tragic sense of life. Boswell could always get drunk. 'It gave me much concern to be informed by my dear wife that I had been quite outrageous in my drunkenness the night before; that I had cursed her in a shocking manner and even thrown a candlestick with a lighted candle at her. . . . I therefore most firmly resolved to be sober.' You smile? But remember—'We are so formed that almost every man is superior, or thinks himself superior, to any other man in something; and, fixing his view upon that, he is in good temper with himself.'

A man capable of such bland but deadly observation is not to be disparaged.

9

LETTERS OF HORACE WALPOLE

WALPOLE'S letters are like music for the harpsichord: there are times when they seem unimaginably lovely and moments when they sound intolerably monotonous. But there is no room for the tinsel cliché in a selection of seventy from several thousand. His correspondence was addressed to carefully chosen recipients each of whom represented a facet of himself and Mr. W. S. Lewis is here[1] perhaps a little too concerned to present Walpole as a commentator on international and American affairs and so has had to exclude some of the warmest and most intimate juvenilia in the interest of the more mature set-pieces. As an introduction, however, this selection could hardly be bettered: all the themes and all the correspondents are here (with notes, not always accurate) and the reader can move on from them to study that aspect of Walpole—as author, antiquarian, politician, man of pleasure—which appeals to him most.

The letters range from 1736 to 1797 during which time Walpole became two different people: a man of his period who reflected quite unconsciously the rococo charm and clumsiness, the violent contrasts of the first half of the century as well as the pomp and urbanity of the second, he grew also to be more and more his real self.

It is this dual essence which gives to his letters their extraordinary charm and mystery. 'I fear 'tis growing old;' (he was twenty-five) 'but I literally seem to have murdered a man whose

[1] *Letters of Horace Walpole*. Selected by W. S. Lewis; introduction by R. W. Ketton Cremer (Folio Society).

name was Ennui, for his ghost is ever before me.' But it was a second apparition, called 'Zeitgeist', who had adopted him as a life-tenant. 'Mr. Bateman has a cloister at Old Windsor furnished with ancient wooden chairs, most of them triangular, but all of various patterns, and carved or turned in the most uncouth and whimsical forms. . . . I have long envied and coveted them. There may be such in poor cottages in so neighbouring a county as Cheshire. I should not grudge any expense for purchase or carriage.' The request is so casual that we forget what an unusual state of feeling such a commission represented in the year of grace —and Chippendale—1764. These flashes have a timeless quality and reveal our own sensibility co-existing with sedan-chairs and highwaymen.

The limitations of Horace Walpole have frequently been pointed out. The sage of Strawberry Hill was a snob and so imprisoned in his caste that he seemed to require a poultice of rank and fashion, endlessly renewed, to alleviate an early fever of lovelessness and insecurity. His snobbery was but one expression of a kind of terror, 'a rainbow on a dark cloud', which caused him to flee from the deepest expression of emotion and from all that was revolutionary in the mind of his age; he deliberately chose an artificial world and an artificial medium to describe it. He moves away from genius—even as he quarrelled with Gray or Rousseau —from an instinct of self-preservation.

He pays the penalty and one looks in vain through all his voluminous writings for the revelation, the breaking of the mountain torrent that was just outside his hearing—in Coleridge and Wordsworth, or even in 'Don Giovanni', Chateaubriand or Goya. Possessing the wit and imagination to emerge from his microcosm, he preferred to remain there, spellbound by the rococo; and for that refusal to endanger his industry and talent he was both punished and rewarded. If he could never achieve a sublime phrase neither could he perpetrate a bad sentence: the harpsichord music will produce the most enchanting effects; the lighter and gayer the words, the more elusive the sadness while the virtues of his century, good taste, sincerity, measure, breeding will never desert him; his enjoyment of life, his curiosity about the past, his devotion to his friends will remain constant; the rhythm of his prose will achieve the music which his vocabulary is denied.

For not only was Horace Walpole with his exceptional observation and precision of feeling the perfect journalist; he seems, as when he visits Stowe or Versailles or the Paris salons, to wish to tell us exactly what we want to know. His eye appears glued to the moving spectacle—and suddenly his hand is stretched out to offer us the glass. When, if ever, we come to unravel the nature of consciousness, the secrets of Time and personality, it may well be that this lifetime of double vision, this obsession with the present and with posterity, may provide a significant clue to the aristocratic prisoner who seems so strangely to beckon to us. 'This little concert lasted till past ten;' (notice his individual cadence), 'then there were minuets, and as we had seven couple left, it concluded with a country dance. . . . . A quarter after twelve they sat down to supper, and I came home by a charming moonlight.'

20

COLLECTOR'S PROGRESS

THE arrangement of consciousness which we know of as Horace Walpole nursed a grand design: to present a complete picture of his time through a planned exchange of letters with an ambassador, an antiquary, a don, a field-marshal, a man of the world and a series of intelligent and fashionable women between the ages of twenty and seventy. As an eighteenth-century Whig he was prevented by scruples from ensuring the publication of such intimacies during his lifetime; the calculation, therefore, depended on an element of risk. Would the recipients preserve his letters? Would they ever be reunited to form the whole which he intended? Would the allusions be understood?

The dissolution of his earthly envelope proved a temporary setback; a more serious obstacle was the revolution in taste engineered by the earnest Victorian bourgeoisie which tried to discredit the frivolous occupations of a more favoured age. Macaulay's hostility delayed the plan. But Lord Orford (as Walpole became) was possessed of both patience and cunning. In his youth he had coined a word, 'serendipity', the gift of finding one thing while looking for another, which he had bestowed on the Princes of Serendip in a fairy tale and by which scientists now explain the discovery of penicillin. He instigated an aeolian agitation of his missing letters: trunks sprang open, caskets slid across attic floors, the correspondence with Lady Ossory appeared in 1848, and, ten years later, he had chosen his general editor.

Peter Cunningham kept Walpole before the public for half a century until he could find a successor. Mrs. Paget Toynbee's annotated edition would have contented most authors but the egotism of the living seems but a faint anticipation of that hunger for perfect and perpetual presentation which attends the personality, once rid of its imperfect shell. Around 1920 Lord Orford had a brainwave. His next editor should be an American; he should be trained from youth to the task, he should be free from all financial cares and, unlike his predecessors, take nothing for granted. He should collect, collate and comment not merely on letters but on all the objects, pictures, furniture with which Walpole had ever come into contact, beginning with his own library. Secure from invasion, Strawberry Hill should rise again beyond the sea.

For this role the noble shade selected an inconspicuous and moderately well-to-do young man who, without much aptitude or knowledge, was drifting into book-collecting, one for whom 'the eighteenth century was a fancy-dress affair with everyone giggling in wigs and tights, all except Dr. Johnson, who rolled about on his bottom and said, "Too-too-too".'

By the summer of 1923 the callow Mr. Lewis had got to York and the shade of Walpole brought serendipity into play. For thirty-five shillings Mr. Lewis bought the edition of Jesse's *George Selwyn and his Contemporaries* which had come from Lord Home's library and which included thirty-four pages of manuscript notes by the amazing Lady Louisa Stuart, notes which Mr. Lewis was fortunately to make available in a limited edition. After reading them with delight he opened Austin Dobson's *Eighteenth Century Vignettes* at random and found 'Lady Louisa could give points even to that inimitable gossip Horace Walpole himself.' The seed had fallen and Walpole now acted with the lightning rapidity of the disembodied. He introduced Mr. Lewis to the future Mrs. Lewis who would not only put another fortune at his disposal but encourage his collections and not hinder them; and, on the same day, he sent Mr. Lewis wandering into Scribner's to chance upon a set of rarities from the Strawberry Hill press for sale. "There is no point in my buying those things," I said to my brother, "and stopping there. If I buy them I shan't stop until I have the finest collection of Walpole in the world."

'Serendipity,' Mr. Lewis remarks, 'leads collectors into the mysterious extra-sensory world where telepathy, clairvoyance and premonition are commonplace. . . . All ardent collectors believe that they have a sixth sense when it comes to their man.' Walpole of course would put it differently. What has once been joined, he might say, is always seeking to come together, it is the sheer stupidity and destructiveness of life itself that the supervital are up against. As a child is prompted at his lesson, so the living have to be nudged and prodded through their famous sixth sense if they are to look beyond their noses. Envious of Walpole's assured immortality across the Atlantic, in 1925 a rival lightweight began to agitate. 'Evans (of Elkin Mathews) told me that a great cache of Boswell manuscript was reported by John Drinkwater to be at Malahide Castle, outside Dublin. I repeated the news to Professor Tinker . . . he told Edward Newton about them, and Newton told Colonel Ralph Isham.' The poet has the hunch, the collector has the money, the aristocracy the possessions.

The most agreeable interludes in this wholly agreeable book[1] describe Mr. Lewis's raids on certain eccentric descendants of Walpole's correspondents. There is something right about his fecund depredations. In fact there is something right about Mr. Lewis altogether. He does not mind whether he is sensible or nice—he is a collector! He writes vividly and pawkily (Walpole has seen to that), he has got together a great collection, a fine library and a splendid edition and made arrangements that this master-key to the eighteenth century will be preserved intact for the future; he has made himself a scholar, one of the rich who have put more into the world than they have taken out, who can sleep sound and say with the sensible, inquisitive and loyal arch-aesthete who has taken care of him, 'when by the aid of some historic vision and local circumstance I can romance myself into pleasure, I know nothing transports me so much'.

[1] *Collector's Progress*, by Wilmarth Lewis (Constable).

22

HORACE WALPOLE AND POSTERITY

BOSWELL, Walpole and Beckford are the three windows of the English eighteenth century which open outwards. These men betray an awareness of posterity which was alien to their contemporaries, a desire to communicate with the unborn. Walpole and Beckford also possessed a consuming interest in the past; and it may well have been speculation about the past which led them to consider how they themselves would appear to the eyes of the future.

This idea was rudimentary in Beckford but dominating in Walpole who, like Boswell, was gnawed by the desire for fame. Boswell wished to be associated, above all, with his intellectual superiors; Walpole to become the first object of pilgrimage to the visiting foreigner. All three wrote picturesquely and vivaciously in styles which had little in common with the elaborate Ciceronian of the period. Today Boswell appeals to the common man, Beckford to the aesthete, Walpole to the scholar and social historian.

I should like to add to the intellectual, but he must turn to Hume, Voltaire, Rousseau or Diderot: Walpole, typically, had no use for these and preferred Fontenelle. Whereas recent additions to the Beckford canon tend to diminish his stature by the pettiness which they reveal, Boswell goes from strength to strength and may still have some surprises while our knowledge, of Walpole, under Mr. Lewis's guidance, is nearing completion. The last two volumes of his correspondence contain his letters to a varied group of young men and women confidantes. But there is still a gap of half a dozen volumes in the middle, presumably to be filled by the major correspondences with Chute and Lady Ossory.

Horace Walpole[1] consists of the Mellon lectures delivered by Mr. Lewis last year, and wisely he has not rewritten them. I have never heard Mr. Lewis lecture but it must be a delightful experience, judging by his captivating *Three Walks in Eighteenth-Century London*; and his *Horace Walpole* is a near-masterpiece which I commend to everyone, the high cost of the book being compensated by the many excellent illustrations. Into these lectures Mr. Lewis has poured all his scholarship and all his devotion; they are the fruits of a lifetime distilled into an elixir of two hundred pages, beautifully condensed and simplified, a labour of love not wanting proper references and one of his inimitable indices.

Was Horace Walpole really as intelligent, as forward-looking, as kindly as he makes out? I have always had my reservations about him; perhaps I was unwittingly influenced by Victorian disapproval, perhaps I am too provincial, perhaps I was shocked by his gloating over the trial and execution of the Jacobite peers which is hard to reconcile with Mr. Lewis's belief in his progressive humanitarianism.

I think perhaps it is his snobbery which puts me off. Mr. Lewis maintains that he was not a snob, that he merely upheld the caste system in which he grew up and his place in it while corresponding on equal terms with men of merit like Gray and scholars like Cole. But the fact remains that this sensitive artist who was equipped to deal with the profounder issues of life, to recognise the best in the art and literature of his time or, like Laclos or Chamfort, to dissect its corruption, wasted a vast amount of his time and talent in mere chronicling of aristocratic meetings and matings, often of people he hardly knew. For this the social historian can be grateful but the literary critic who perceives the bruised sensibility—demanding endless reassurance—of this artist in words, is often led by his triviality to the brink of despair.

[1] *Horace Walpole*, by Wilmarth Sheldon Lewis (Hart-Davis).

Mr. Lewis is aware of such charges but his reply to them, I think, is to overvalue Walpole's literary output, to rate his *Anecdotes of Painting*, his *Catalogue of Royal and Noble Authors*, his *Castle of Otranto*, his Strawberry Hill productions on too high a plane and to attach an exaggerated importance to his political memoirs. The lecture on Walpole's politics is most revealing for in his politics Walpole allowed his aggression to emerge (and very aggressive he was, full of injured party venom).

One must remember that he was the son of our first and most powerful Prime Minister who grew up at the centre of a power-intoxicated ruling clique before one condemns him for not having met Blake or admired Rousseau or helped Chatterton. It is a near-miracle that he became what he was: the discoverer of the Gothic and the chronicler of the Rococo, a *pierrot lunaire* of English prose and a soul-mate of the soul-searching Madame du Deffand. Mr. Lewis, while avoiding Freudian speculation, hints at the consequences of his upbringing:

> Both (parents) contributed to his inner uncertainties; his mother by her possessiveness and hatred of his father; Sir Robert by his initial aloofness, by the rejections of Horace's mother, and by his power. From childhood Horace was pulled back and forth between love and hatred, fear and confidence, desire for money and contempt for it, pride and humility, idealism and disillusionment, his flair for friendship and his dislike of people at too close quarters. He had to find the middle way between these conflicts if he was going to have fame in his own right apart from his father's, very early he saw that he could get it by writing the history of his time in his own informal manner.

Mr. Lewis also attributes to this love-hate for a much calumniated father Walpole's weakness for lost causes and underdogs (e.g. his defence of Richard III), while his confused feelings about both parents were so powerful as to condition his whole life to complete and apparently effortless chastity. Like many a subsequent charmer he suffered from claustrophobia of the heart.

All his friendships came to grief sooner or later and left him embittered. 'In our cold climate friendship seldom ripens much,' he told Pinkerton. 'A friend is a name for a more constant acquaintance.' In Mr. Lewis he has found the friend of his dreams, and, judging from this last bewitching volume, the friendship has not been one-sided. Under his influence Mr. Lewis seems to have mellowed in grace and gained in stature.

12

BECKFORD'S FANDANGO

HERE is a most welcome book[1] full of new material about a fascinating personality, agreeably presented and quite admirably edited.

There are several good reasons for liking Beckford: he wrote well; his sensibility is a precursor of our own; then again he visited the places of which one is never tired of hearing: Portugal, Spain, Italy, Switzerland in all their charming eighteenth-century heyday and finally he was an aesthete with the money to indulge his dreams as well as his tastes, to build legendary Fonthill, own the Bellini of The Doge now in the National Gallery and the 'bureau du roi Stanislas' now in the Wallace Collection. Whoever wonders what they would do if they were fantastically rich will find the life of Beckford a delightful day-dream and be grateful to the vindictive puritanical scandalmongers who refused him his peerage, drove him out of the country and kept him abroad to secrete letters and journals like resin from a wounded pine tree.

Those who are branded with E for Escapist will already know Rutter's *Fonthill* and Beckford's *Vathek*, his *Monasteries of Alcobaça and Batalha*, his *Sketches of Italy, Spain and Portugal*. The importance of this journal is that it provides the original text from which—many years later—these Iberian sketches were drawn, all personal details being then omitted.

The journal is both a literary and a human document. Beckford was one of the first great magnates to be driven abroad by the

[1] *The Journal of William Beckford, 1787-88*. Edited by Boyd Alexander (Hart-Davis).

breath of scandal and the death of his young wife had caused further accusations to be made against him by malevolent philistines.

When shall I cease acting the part of the Wandering Jew and being stared and wondered at as if I bore the mark of God's malediction on my countenance? I am almost ready to give up the contest and build my nest in the first country who will promise to keep the English at a distance.

I have been haunted all night with rural ideas of England. The fresh smell of my pines at Fonthill seemed wafted to me in my dreams. The bleating of my sheep and lowing of herds in the deep valley of Lawn Farm faintly sounded in my ear. And shall I banish myself forever from these happy scenes of my childhood? My heart beats. I am bathed in tears.

The young Beckford had many weapons against homesickness and persecution. He was an irresistible charmer (for charm allied to wealth *is* irresistible) and wherever he went both in Portugal and Spain, created a fever of general amorous consternation; he had many intellectual interests, the deepest being a love of music and he had powerful friends, headed by the Queen of Portugal's favourite, Marialva, who doted on him. The theme of the journal is Beckford's attempt to get presented at Court while Robert Walpole, the British Ambassador, is determined to stop him. Beckford affected an interest in the Catholic religion worthy of Madame de Pompadour in similar circumstances and it was hinted that a presentation might lead to his settling permanently in the country and bringing his wealth there. On the other hand the presentation could be made only through his Ambassador and since Beckford's powerful relatives made no move to suggest it, the obstinate red-faced Walpole won the battle and the creator of *Vathek* was laid low by the cousin of a rival dilettante, the author of *The Castle of Otranto*.

What was Beckford like? Oh, for a first-hand description of his musical gifts for he was constantly dancing, playing and singing. How good was he? He claimed that, as a child, he had taught the child Mozart 'Non più andrai', he mentions his fandango, his singing of Brazilian 'modinhas' and Spanish 'seguidillas', his minuets, 'all my talents lay this night in my heels and I kept cutting *entrechats à huit* and leaping over chairs and tables without intermission', 'my singing, playing and capering subdues every Portuguese that approaches me', 'notwithstanding my evil temper, I never sung so well in my life—three octaves clear, falling as plump as a hawk on its prey'.

If he were, like Nero, perhaps, an exquisite performer in the most evanescent of the arts, it might account for the scrappiness and monotony, the general lack of progress in his literary output. For he was twenty-seven when he kept this journal. *Vathek* had already appeared and for the next sixty years he wrote nothing more but the description of the two monasteries.

His reputation is now inflated, I fear, for the dazzle of his promise has blinded us to the meagreness of his performance even as his early misfortunes help us to overlook the iron complacency and aggressive frivolity, the snobbery and dull antiquarianism which are to eat away his long and useless life. But don't let's join the preachers. 'The night was serene and delightful, the folding doors which communicate with the veranda thrown wide open, and the harmonious notes of French horns and oboes issuing from thickets of citron and orange; not a breath of wind disturbed the clear flame of the lights in the lustres, and they cast a soft gleam on the shrubs shooting up above the terraces. . . . I danced several minuets.'

13

SAMUEL ROGERS

LONGEVITY is a virtue, life is to be lived out; it is right that monarchs congratulate centenarians. Longevity is particularly desirable in an age of great ideas and great achievement, and if it be near to the vortex of these events, more praiseworthy still.

Few existences are more to be envied than those which savoured the *douceur de vivre* of the high eighteenth century, the climate of the French Revolution, the phenomenon of Napoleon and the Romantic Revival. For a complete life I would add a whiff of Victorianism at the close. Talleyrand, Chateaubriand, Wordsworth, Landor come to mind, Luttrell, who in his eighties was fascinated by 1848, and of course Goethe—but there is much to be said for Rogers, the banker bard of St. James's Place: 'Few men have been more extensively known or more universally courted; his conversation is remarkably brilliant and his wit pure and original.'

His dates, 1762-1855, are impeccable (though I wish he could have hung on till Bovary, 1857) and all his life he sought out interesting people. His *Table Talk*,[1] though lamentably insufficient, is an authentic glimpse of a golden age. With an income of five thousand a year he often helped genius in distress, made up his friends' quarrels, produced pretty books and gave famous breakfasts. As a poet he was a master of melodious commonplace which at times could quicken into something better; 'Human Life'

1 *The Table Talk of Samuel Rogers*. Edited by Morchard Bishop (Richards Press).

is strangely rapid and comprehensive and he wrote one lovely pre-romantic couplet;

> And terraced walls their black reflection throw
> On the green-mantled moat that sleeps below.

Now we come to the mystery. Why was he so hated? For he was not merely envied or disliked but most particularly loathed by very sensitive people. Tennyson and Carlyle did not think much of him, Byron wrote a most penetrating and ferocious poem about him—and as for Coleridge, 'If I believed it possible that the man liked me,' he wrote to Beaumont, 'upon my soul I should feel exactly as if I were tarred and feathered.' A more telling image crops up in the unexpected pages of Captain Gronow. 'The mild venom of every word was a remarkable trait in his conversation. One might have compared the old poet to one of those velvety caterpillars that crawl gently and quietly over the skin, but leave an irritating blister behind.'

The clue, of course, is envy. Rogers had, in common with Edmond de Goncourt and so many others, a longing for popular success and when he found his kind of poetry superseded, he tried to identify himself with his successors and used his money to purchase fame. A cold eye, a keen memory and a bad liver accounted for the rest aided by the cynicism which great wealth induces. No rich man wrote so well about cottages. 'Madame de Staël one day said to me, "How sorry I am for Campbell! His poverty so unsettles his mind that he cannot write." I replied, "Why does he not take the situation of a clerk? . . . When literature is the sole business of life, it becomes a drudgery: when we are able to resort to it only at certain hours, it is a charming relaxation".'

Rogers, in fact, was the prototype of the modern patron, of the small, neat, frugal millionaires who compete with their protégés, who try to paint instead of getting someone to paint them, who privately print their own works, who pick brains for ballets, lend cottages to poets and then sue them for the telephone bill and who encourage talent in order to devour it. The new poets saw through this connoisseur of ingratitude in whom they recognised the worst aspect of themselves.

For his faults—he has but one—
'Tis but envy, when all's done
He but pays the pain he suffers.

This does not prevent his *Table Talk* from being an indispensable book. In some ant-colonies there is a beetle which has learnt to resemble an ant; when two worker-ants meet and one regurgitates a drop of delicious nectar to invigorate his comrade, this beetle nips in and bolts off with it. 'That's the Bard, the Beau, the Banker.'

14

ON BEING WON OVER TO COLERIDGE

SOMEBODY should write an essay on the cult of Coleridge, one of the strangest phenomena of modern times. Here is a man who was accounted a failure and who accounted himself a failure, sick, neurotic, frustrated, author of some lovely but fragmentary poems, mouthpiece of German metaphysicians, eclipsed by Wordsworth during his lifetime, by Keats after his death, a whale stranded on the nineteenth-century sea-front: and now, owing to the devotion of editors and critics, emerging as the greatest of them all, almost the subject of a new religion.

Sir Herbert Read hails him as the founder of modern scientific criticism—the true inventor of existentialism, 'gestalt' and Jung's Collective Unconscious, as well as the greatest of transcendentalists and precursor of Freud: large volumes are written about the genesis of his poems, the implications of his prose; every scrap is treasured, every erasure annotated.

'One of the great seminal minds of the nineteenth century,' Mr. House calls him and he is coming into his own as our great English sage, a worthy protagonist for Goethe and Voltaire. His failure clothes him in refreshing mists like a fog-ridden mountain of problematical altitude whereas every stone on their bald summits is numbered and worn threadbare. 'There is something inherently mean in action,' he wrote. 'The Almighty more or less made a mistake in creating the universe.' There is consequently nothing mean about Coleridge. He is the least vulgar of writers; every hint of accomplishment disappears in that great lachrymose, self-pitying eye. His failures are on a giant scale as if he failed for our sakes that we might raid his huge quarries and carry off the half-finished blocks without guilt of plagiarism:

> Hitherto, I have laid my eggs with ostrich carelessness and ostrich oblivion—the greater part indeed have been crushed underfoot; but some have crawled into light to furnish feathers for other men's caps and not a few to plume the shafts of the quivers of my calumniators.

When I try to analyse my own strong prejudice against Coleridge I find that it springs from an inability to understand metaphysics and consequent dislike of them, an impatience with his dilapidated existence which betrays a fear of it and above all from my horror of 'The Ancient Mariner'. I cannot believe that this is a good poem. I cannot believe that the sensitive ears which are ravished by the prose melodies of Coleridge or the delicacy of some of his blank verse can support this barbarous jingle. Yet they do.

'This is made fully apparent,' writes Mr. House, 'in that wonderful pair of stanzas in which the thought and verse are in shape identical, but with opposite content':

> And I had done a hellish thing
> And it would work 'em woe:
> For all averred I had killed the bird
> That made the breeze to blow.
> Ah wretch! said they, the bird to slay
> That made the breeze to blow!
>
> Nor dim nor red, like God's own head,
> The glorious Sun uprist:
> Then all averred, I had killed the bird
> That brought the sun and mist.
> 'Twas right, said they, such birds to slay,
> That bring the fog and mist.

The first four lines seem to me like the patter of a comedian, the beginning of the second stanza contorted and ambiguous and the opposing sentiments of the sailors equally lifeless. Surely such a stanza (which was to lead Oscar Wilde astray in 'Reading Gaol') belongs to the jingling small change of poetry and enforces too many rhymes and repetitions to sustain a long poem? How can it be compared with a contemporary expression of the same sentiments like Wordsworth's 'Hart-Leap Well'?

Mr. House's lectures,[1] however, have been converting me to Coleridge and are completing the good work begun by Sir Herbert Read's eulogies. It is through the notebooks and the letters that one begins to love him and Mr. House is an authority on these notebooks, most of which have never been published:

> I write melancholy, always melancholy: you will suspect that it is the fault of my natural Temper. Alas! no—this is the great Cross in that my Nature is made for Joy—impelling me to Joyance—and I never—never can yield to it—I am a genuine Tantalus.

Coleridge in fact stands head and shoulders above all other guilty men, patron saint of those artists (and they include the most exquisite) who are prevented not so much by vanity and sloth from committing themselves to masterpieces as from a deep horror of the enjoyment and relief. Perfection is the Albatross they fear to slay:

> I was followed up and down by a frightful pale woman who, I thought, wanted to kiss me, and had the property of giving a shameful Disease by breathing on the face.

This is a guilt dream; it is Coleridge who half-heartedly pursues his Muse, fearful of contaminating her with the sickness of being himself.

In one fragment I might hazard a conjecture. 'O Sara wherefore am I not happy,' he writes in his notebook one stormy night, 'why for years have I not enjoyed one pure and sincere pleasure! one full joy!—one genuine Delight, that rings sharp to the Beat of the Finger!—all cracked, and dull with base Alloy—Di boni! mihi vim et virtutem vel tu . . . eheu! perdite. . . . But still have said to the poetic Feeling when it has awakened in the Heart. "Go! Come tomorrow".' The dots represent erased Latin words—did he

[1] *Coleridge*, by Humphry House (Hart-Davis).

perhaps write 'Perdidi musam tacendo,' 'I have lost the Muse by my silence,' quoted from the 'Pervergilium Veneris'?

But not all these fascinating notes are depressing:

> Fowls at table—the last dinner at Gallow Hill, when you drest the two fowls in that delicious white sauce which when very ill is the only idea of food that does not make me sicker.

Mr. House is the most understanding of critics and his interpretation of 'Frost at Midnight' and of the first version of the Ode to Dejection increases the stature of the poem and the poet. What can one say of this magnificent romantic youth who carried intuition and lucidity with him into the long years when his inspirations had deserted him and who so perfectly dissected his own condition?

> Instead of a covey of poetic partridges with whirring wings of music or wild ducks shaping their rapid flight in forms always regular (a still better image of verse) up came a metaphysical bustard, urging its slow, heavy, laborious, earth-skimming flight over dreary and level wastes....

'Do not call him poor Coleridge!' Lamb was right. 'Call him Coleridge.'

15

HAZLITT'S *LIBER AMORIS*

THE *Liber Amoris* is a record of the most unfortunate love story in literature from Propertius' meeting with Cynthia to Baudelaire's with Jeanne Duval. It is something between a work of art and a case history containing some of the loveliest pages in English and some of the silliest, aiming at the perfection of art but held back by too close a proximity to the raw and painful experiences of life. There is nothing else like it in the language. It remains a *pièce unique*, a romantic catastrophe.

Let us first observe the episode as the world saw it: Benjamin Robert Haydon is writing to Miss Mitford (1822):

> Hazlitt at present gives me great pain by the folly with which he is conducting himself. He has fallen in love with a lodging-house hussy, who will be his death, he has been to Scotland to divorce his wife although he has a fine little boy by her; and after doing this to marry this girl, he comes back to find she has been making a fool of him in order to get presents and in reality has been admitting a lover more favoured. Hazlitt's torture is beyond expression; you may imagine it. The girl really incited in him a devoted and intense love . . . he talks of nothing else day and night. He has written down all the conversations without colour, literally as they happen; he has preserved all the love letters, many of which are equal to anything of the sort, and really affecting; and I believe, in order to ease his soul of this burden, means, with certain arrangements, to publish it as a tale of character. He will sink into idiocy if he does not get rid of it.

In 1822, Hazlitt was 44 years old. He had been married in 1808 and had lived apart from his wife since 1819. For two years he had been living in lodgings off Chancery Lane kept by a tailor named

Walker who had three daughters. Though his marriage had been a sensible one for his wife had intellectual tastes and a little property, it was not founded on mutual attraction and their temperaments were utterly dissimilar. Sarah Hazlitt was prosaic, secretive, conventional and thrifty, her husband brilliant, reckless, moody and improvident. He had never been loved nor ever had a happy love affair; young girls, he said, drove him mad; he developed a taste for low life and he suffered from a sentiment of physical inferiority which was kept alive by the personal attacks on him in right-wing papers. 'Pimpled Hazlitt' was a favourite epithet and *Blackwood's Magazine* described him as a 'small fetid blear-eyed pug'. In fact, like many political journalists, he was attractive when animated and insignificant when silent and brooding. 'His figure was indeed indifferent,' wrote Barry Cornwall, 'and his movements shy and awkward, but there was something in his earnest irritable face, his restless eyes, his black hair, combed backwards and curling (not too resolutely) about a well-shaped head, that was very striking.'

For the last year at his lodgings he had been titivated by the morning visits of his landlady's daughter, Sally Walker, who brought him his breakfast, sat on his lap and kissed him. 'Her face was round and small' (I quote Barry Cornwall again) 'and her eyes emotionless, glassy and without any speculation (apparently) in them. Her movements in walking were very remarkable. For I never observed her to make a step. She went onwards in a sort of wavy sinuous manner, like the movements of a snake. She was silent, or uttered monosyllables only, and was very demure. Her steady unmoving gaze upon the person whom she was addressing was exceedingly unpleasant. To this girl he gave all his valuable time, all his wealth of thought, and all the loving frenzy of his heart. For a time I think that on this point he was substantially insane—certainly beyond self control.' There must have been a manic depressive streak in him and I believe that the transition from depression to mania (cf. Goethe) is generally accompanied by falling in love which is, perhaps, provoked by glandular disturbance. Sally Walker was like a cancer of the soul to Hazlitt, an obsessional growth on the spirit set in motion through sexual repression and the last middle-aged clutching at innocence and youth. She attacked him in his weak spot as an insect paralyses a grub and from that moment genius was of no avail; 'glued to a bitch', he was in the grip of a disease that had seized on a centre of retarded adolescence. 'By Heaven, I doat on her. The truth is, I never had any pleasure, like love, with anyone but her.' He developed the true manic loquacity and on the same day told five people (two of them strangers) of his passion, down to the minutest detail. Some of his original letters are hysterical, obscene and illegible and he develops the typical exhibitionism, reading aloud his most abject letters, boasting of imaginary success, behaving to his wife and friends with meanness, aggression and blatant want of tact. He is clearly possessed and, at moments, consciously so, though perhaps not aware that his rising tide of mania will also protect him, will enable him to write a whole volume of essays in less than a month and at the last float his hopeless passion into the wide ocean of rage rather than incur the lee shore of self-destruction.

Sally Walker is attractive in the way of so many artful modest maidens of the early nineteenth century, Juliets of the back parlour, paintable by Etty or Fuseli. A servant girl's conventionality appeared modesty, her sententiousness high principles, her ignorance simplicity, her lumpish heaviness deep understanding. A quiet flirtatiousness, the prevarication of indifference and the gleam of cupidity wove round her victims a mysterious texture of unfathomable charm. She would make the perfect whore, he thought, 'she has an itch for being slobbered and felt'—or the perfect wife. Seizing with the suicidal chivalry of middle age on the latter suggestion, he persuaded Mrs. Hazlitt, in return for a settlement, to go to Scotland to divorce him and they set out in the spring of 1822 for the indifferent Reno of the North.

Mrs. Hazlitt kept a diary of her trip to Scotland. It is an extraordinary document. She and Hazlitt frequently met to arrange the details of the divorce and she was always asking him for small sums of money which he owed her. As he was famous and seldom paid, she soon acquired a reputation for thinking of nothing else. Those who have examined this journal have pronounced her phlegmatic and callous. I think she was a proud and undemonstrative woman who loved her husband and tried to deaden her mortification by compulsive walking. Although each painful scene laid her low with stomach trouble, she covered one hundred and seventy miles in a week. 'Mrs. Bell said that he seemed quite enamoured of a letter he had been writing to Patmore; that in their walk the day before, he pulled it out of his pocket twenty times, and wanted to read it to her; that he talked so loud and acted so extravagantly that the people stood and stared at them as they passed, they seemed to take him for a madman . . . walked to the Glasgow canal; seemed so restless; as if I could go mad; and could not swallow, I was so choked.'

Like many abandoned wives of men of genius Sarah Hazlitt continued to observe paintings and landscape with the eyes her husband had opened for her and one day as she was leaving the picture gallery at Dalkeith Palace, she met Hazlitt and a friend coming in. In a letter to Patmore about Sally he writes afterwards, 'Do you know I saw a picture, the pattern of her, the other day at Dalkeith Palace (Hope finding Fortune in the Sea) and the resemblance almost drove me out of my senses.' [Originally 'I saw a picture of her naked figure . . . and it drove me mad'.] When they met a week later, Mrs. Hazlitt asked him if he thought it a good collection. 'No,' he said, 'very poor; there were but two tolerable, one a female figure floating in the water in an historical picture, which he thought a copy of some good picture. I told him I had remarked it and thought that figure exceedingly good. The other was a Claude but in a very dirty condition.' Three days later they had a long and final discussion when he tried to explain the nature of his infatuation, how Sally had made a dead set at him from the first . . . ' "she was not at all pretty; her eyes were the worst and had a poor slimy watery look, yet she was well made and had handsome arms". I said it did not appear to me at all the beauty he used to admire, which was plump, and she was as thin and bony as the scrag end of a neck of mutton; that I thought the female figure in the picture at Dalkeith House much more to his taste; he fancied it was like her. I said it was much nearer my form in the thighs, the fall of the back, and the contour of the whole figure; he said, I was very well made. He said he had two opposite opinions of Sarah Walker at different times. . . . He asked me where I should be in town and I told him at Christies; he inquired what sort of people they were. I told him a very respectable quiet young couple lately married; he desired me to take care of myself, and keep up a respectable appearance, as I had money enough to do so. He wished he could marry some woman with a good fortune, that he might not be under the necessity of writing another line.'

The *Liber Amoris* is in three parts—the Overture, a series of dialogues which present the characters in their period of felicity, then the letters to Patmore from Scotland, and finally the denouement, a long letter to Sheridan Knowles from London. There are also some fragments of diary. We see Hazlitt in three keys; the gallant lover as with Sally, the doggy or despairing one with Patmore, and the self-contemplating artist in the Journal. Hazlitt made a considerable effort to produce a work of art and rewrote many of the letters, toning down his ravings and accusations until he very nearly succeeded. It is instructive to compare the rough and finished states, and I give the first and second 'romanticised' version of the passage recounting his visit to Rosslyn.

I

'I was at Roslin Castle yesterday, and the exquisite beauty of the scene, with the thought of what I should feel, should I ever be restored to her, and have to lead her through such places as my adored, my angel-wife, almost drove me beside myself. For this picture, this ecstatic vision, what have I instead as the image of the reality? Demoniacal possessions. I see the young witch seated in another's lap, twining her serpent arms round him, her eyes glancing, and her cheeks on fire. Damn the unnatural hag: Oh! Oh! Why does not the hideous thought choke me? It is so, and she can make no more confidences. The gentleman who lodges in the old room is a red-faced, pot-bellied, powdered gentleman of sixty—a pleasant successor! For what am I reserved? The bitch likes the nasty, the wilful, and antipathetic. That was why she pitched upon me, because I was out of the ordinary calculation of love. . . . Where, how shall I be released from these horrors? . . . Get some-one to try her or I am destroyed for ever. It would be sweet and full revenge. You may try her if you like—a pot-belly and a slender waist match by contrast. Do they not? I shall soon be in town and see. Pity me, Pity [a word indistinct].

'Looking in the glass to see why I am so hated, I think I see FREEDOM written on my brow.'

2

'I was at Roslin Castle yesterday. It lies low in a rude but sheltered valley, hid from the vulgar gaze, and powerfully reminds one of the old song. The straggling fragments of the russet ruins, suspended smiling and graceful in the air as if they would linger out another century to please the curious beholder, the green larch trees trembling in between, with the blue sky and white silver clouds, the wild mountain plants starting out here and there, the date of the year on an old low doorway, but still more, the beds of flowers in orderly decay, that seem to have no hand to tend them, but keep up a sort of traditional remembrance of civilisation in former ages, present altogether an amiable subject for contemplation. The exquisite beauty of the scene, with the thought of what I should feel, should I ever be restored to her, and have to lead her through such places as my adored, my angel-wife, almost drove me beside myself. For this picture, this ecstatic vision, what have I of late instead as the image of the reality? Demoniacal possessions. I see the young witch seated in another's lap, twining her serpent arms round him, her eye glancing and her cheeks on fire—why does not the hideous thought choke me? or why do I not go and find out the truth at once? The moonlight streams over the silver waters: the bark is in the bay that might waft me to her, almost with a wish. The mountain breeze sighs out her name: old ocean with a world of Fears murmurs back my woes! Does not my heart yearn to be with her; and shall I not follow its bidding?'

Perhaps because Hazlitt was hard up (a general consequence of infatuation) and had even been arrested for debt—or perhaps through neurotic insensitiveness, the *Liber Amoris* appeared too soon and after inadequate gestation. The effect was disastrous and the book was attacked on all sides. Few, beside De Quincey, could appreciate the exquisite prose-poetry or the disturbing transitions from subjective to objective in this forerunner of modern psychology. Crabb Robinson wrote in his diary: 'Finished early Hazlitt's disgusting "New Pygmalion", such a story as this is nauseous and revolting. It ought to exclude the author from all decent society.' Half a century later the little book deterred Stevenson from writing the life of our most imaginative essayist since Bacon.

Hazlitt had hoped to be cured by the knowledge of Sally's infidelity but four months after the publication of his book he was still passing most of the night watching her door. 'If we have drunk poison, finding it out does not prevent its being in our veins.' What repels so many people about the *Liber Amoris* is indeed the helplessness of a brilliant mind in the grip of adolescent lust. Hazlitt is unmanned by it, he is no longer master of himself and this morbidity is something that, like jealousy, we cannot forgive in other people because we so dread it for ourselves. Fortunately a trip abroad and the rewarding company of Landor (who relished his account of the divorce) and of Stendhal (who gave him *De l'Amour*) worked wonders. He married (again unhappily) a widow with a little money, and died in 1830. His last words were, 'Well, I have had a happy life.'

Mrs. Hazlitt did not re-marry and on her son announcing his engagement she wrote advising him, 'to pay ready money for everything, to lay by a little every year in case of a family or illness, and to let neither of you have any secret or separate schemes unconfided to the other'. Of the 'slimy marble varnished fiend', 'the little damned incubus', 'the poor hapless weed', the 'sweet apparition' whose lingering glance, as she turned in the doorway that August morning, had set in motion such a coil, we can only conjecture.

16

DIDEROT

DIDEROT is a figure whose stature is steadily growing, although there has been no *Life* of him in English since Lord Morley's. If Montesquieu, Voltaire, Rousseau and Diderot are the four great minds of the French Enlightenment, then of those four Diderot's is the one which is still expanding, whose thought is least understood, richest in implication; the others have already exerted their fullest influence.

Since Freud singled out *Le Neveu de Rameau* for a special tribute, and French critics began to praise *The Nun*, *Jacques le Fataliste* and the *Dialogue on the Blind*, or to study his art criticism (the first of its kind), we have been aware of the peculiarity of his genius, lit by flashes of romanticism dear to humanist and Marxist alike, to both poet and philosopher and far more imaginative than the usual name of 'Encyclopaedist' would suggest.

Mr. Crocker's *Life*[1] is readable and intelligent, but just lacks the literary quality which would enable him to dominate his subject, and so I can pronounce it only a good biography of the second order.

Some of the blame for this must be attributed to Diderot himself for his life has a ramshackle quality, an air of drift, since it pursued two aims, philosophy and literature on the one hand and bourgeois solidity on the other.

I wish I could admire him more than I do. Frothy, sentimental, emotional, incorrigibly optimistic, benevolent, discursive,

[1] *The Embattled Philosopher: A Life of Denis Diderot*, by Lester C. Crocker (Spearman).

amorous, greedy, the brilliant son of the cutler of Langres lacks the superb mastery of life which distinguishes Montesquieu—and, above all, Voltaire—or the neurotic intransigence of Rousseau. Despite his great gifts there was about him something vapid and foolish, the inevitable 'Talker's Alibi'.

> I seemed extraordinary to them, inspired, divine. Grimm didn't seem to have eyes enough to see me, nor ears enough to hear me. Everybody was astonished. I myself felt a contentment within me that I can't express. It was like a fire burning in my depths that seared my breast, spread over them and set fire to them. It was an evening of enthusiasm of which I was the hearth.

The quotation is from one of his letters to his mistress, Sophie Volland. These letters, though sadly mangled by his conventional descendants, give us an absolutely living picture of the French eighteenth century—a living but not a very pleasant one. We hear the actual tones of Diderot, Holbach, Madame Aîné and other *habitués* of the *philosophes* but with a note of vulgarity and exhibitionism which makes one heartily glad not to have been there; such selfishness, such conceit, such crudity, such mountains out of molehills, all conveyed with an indulgent smirk to the mistress who was too dowdy to be invited. And at home the nagging wife ('quite unsuitable, poor thing') with her spite and jealousy, and ignorance and poverty; his meals served separately to punish her. . . .

We do not read the *Encyclopaedia* today, though we collect it for its plates; yet it was a stupendous achievement to which he gave up twenty-five years.

> 'This work,' he wrote to Sophie, 'will surely produce in time a revolution in the minds of men, and I hope that tyrants, oppressors, fanatics and the intolerant will not gain thereby. We shall have served humanity; but we shall be reduced to a cold and insensible dust for many years before we have any gratitude for it.'

The philosophical dialogues contain his most prophetic and brilliant work, while the *Neveu de Rameau*, in which he seems to be confronted by his subconscious self, has also the charm of re-creating a morning among the chess players of the Palais Royal in the heyday of Louis Quinze's reign. It is a fantastic piece which I have never been able to get through to the end, despite its quite dazzling beginning, and this I attribute partly to Diderot's flightiness and word-intoxication and partly to my own inability to grasp abstract ideas. I give a passage, written in one of his rare moods of despondency, which we can all understand:

To be born in imbecility, in the midst of pain and cries; to be the plaything of ignorance, error, need, sickness, wickedness and passions; to return step by step to imbecility, from the time of lisping to that of doting; to live among knaves and charlatans of all kinds; to die between one man who takes your pulse and another who troubles your head; never to know where you come from, why you came and where you are going! That is what is called the most important gift of our parents and of nature. Life.

To his credit he gave his life to contemplation of this predicament and to the attempt to solve it benevolently by work, intelligence and imagination, for other people. A great mind, a great humorist, a philosopher—and yet.

17

STENDHAL'S LETTERS

There should be a pale blue wrapper round certain books meaning 'You can read your way out of anything with this. It is another world and a better.' A red wrapper would mean, 'Another world, but a sadder.' Thus the letters of Flaubert are magnificent but harrowing, the correspondence of Baudelaire slow torture—only in the world of Stendhal do we sail away to forty years of good-humour. 'Apart from this everything goes well: we have not seen a woman since the postmistresses of Poland, but by way of compensation we are great connoisseurs of fires,' so he begins the Retreat from Moscow. 'I, too, have had a grapple with the void. It is only the immediate experience which is disagreeable, and the horror of it comes from all the silly nonsense that is put into our heads at the age of three'—so he announces his last illness, with the strange prophecy of his end: 'There is nothing ridiculous about dying in the street, provided one does not do it on purpose.'

Though he considered himself an unhappy man and knew boredom as only artists know it, he had a sunny and optimistic disposition and he had imbibed from his grandfather (like George Sand) something of the rational art of happiness of the eighteenth century. Of the three writers in the age of transition who grew up under Napoleon and led the way to modern literature, Stendhal is the most solid and indestructible. Constant could not fertilise a whole generation by 'Adolphe' alone; Chateaubriand formed a sombre leaf-mould round Flaubert and Baudelaire. The writers influenced by Beyle's 'On me lira vers 1880' are still emerging.

'My habitual state of being is that of one unhappily in love who adores music and painting. I have set an exquisite sensibility to seek out beautiful landscapes. That has been the only object of my travels. I have valued contemplation above everything else, even a reputation for wit.' Such is the romantic Stendhal's definition of himself. But there are two others: the realist and the man of action. The realist could observe the unhappy love affairs of the romantic while conducting his consulship at Civita Vecchia, enjoying Roman balls, analysing political trends and satirising social follies. The man of action had the makings of a hero and fell with Napoleon in 1815.

In every work by Stendhal we can perceive the fusion of these personalities which exist in rather different proportions in Balzac and Delacroix. On the whole the realist predominates and gives a somewhat flinty aroma, a whiff of the garrulous and lonely old bachelor to the correspondence; but the inclusion of many love letters in this book redeems the *côté boulevard* by a *côté salon*; Stendhal was fortunate to live at a time when love still had its dangers and drawing-rooms their magic so that his abandonment of the pursuit of glory was not embittering. He wrote very few letters about his books and the three drafts of his acknowledgment of Balzac's great tribute to the *Chartreuse de Parme* form almost an autobiography. His correspondents were chiefly worldly and beautiful women or worldly and cynical men. It is regrettable that the superb exchange with Mérimée published by 'Fontaine' is not included but in the letters to Di Fiore we find a charming relationship with a cultivated younger man which went on until his death.

Mr. Norman Cameron has made an excellent translation which crowns Mr. Lehmann's admirable and necessary continental series. The selection,[1] by M. Boudot-Lamotte, does not however seem a great improvement on the original correspondence as published in 1851 with a golden introduction by Mérimée. We lose many admirable letters of his later life (including the one on England) in return for the priggish early letters to his sister and a few love letters which one would be sorry to miss.

[1] *To the Happy Few. Selected Letters of Stendhal* (John Lehmann).

I am not a Beylolater, I need a *fond noir à contenter* in my heroes, but of all those who lack it, the seed of Epicurus, Stendhal is the least stupid. We can never dismiss him as insensitive or shallow. He has the quality which Norman Douglas in his travel books inherited from him of a serene acceptance of himself and of the universe, coupled with a prickly wit, critical curiosity and an unchanging admiration for love and youth and courage. It was right he should know Byron or dig up Etruscan tombs and find a bust of Tiberius. Could Horace have said good-bye better? 'I have great hopes of recovery. Nevertheless I want to say farewell to you, in case this letter may be the *ultima*. I truly love you, and you are not one of a crowd. Farewell, take events cheerfully as they come.'

18

BALZAC

THERE has been no translation of the *Comédie Humaine* into English in this century. Every generation requires its own rendering of the great books of the past. These three volumes in one[1] make an excellent beginning. Kathleen Raine's translation is smooth, readable, vivid and accurate.

The book has one serious defect which makes one hesitate to recommend the considerable outlay. The last volume of the trilogy is a dull anti-climax. 'I recommend the reader to take this section as fast as he can,' writes Mr. Raymond Mortimer in his introduction. But why include it? The third volume should have been *Splendeurs et Misères* which deals with the hero's return to Paris, not with the undeserved misfortunes of a provincial printer. Pace and interest need not have been sacrificed.

Having made this complaint, let us abandon ourselves to the marvellous genius of Balzac. At first we set out slowly and quietly on our magic voyage. Gradually the enchanted universe of the *Comédie Humaine* grows nearer and clearer; ultimately we are engulfed by it. Once more we live through the great theme of the French romantic novel (whether by Balzac, Flaubert or Proust), the conquest of Parisian society, glittering and poisonous as a moonlit *datura*, by the handsome young poet and lover who one day will turn and trample on it.

What separates Balzac completely from other novelists of the period, such as Thackeray, Scott, Dickens, Dumas, is that he is a

1 *Lost Illusions*, by Honoré de Balzac. Translated by Kathleen Raine (Lehmann).

great and conscious artist who cares intensely about the writer's situation. Lucien de Rubempré, coming to Paris in 1821 when a little younger than the century, with a bourgeois father and an aristocratic mother, penniless and consumed with literary and social ambition, is faced at once with the same predicament which many a young writer who wishes to live by his pen and go out in the evenings is tackling today. Shall he invest in a dinner jacket? Or the big Oxford Dictionary? How can he write if he does not learn about society? How can he go out in society without more money than writing can bring in?

The greatness of Balzac lies in his having, like all romantics who survive, both experienced and surmounted every temptation. His account of journalism is of something more evil and corrupting than we have to face, even as his picture of the great world describes rewards which are now beyond our reach. *A Provincial Celebrity in Paris*, the second of these volumes, seems even now a work of pure genius, a marvellous morality for all who have inhaled, as age creeps on, the miasma from their wasted time. The indictment deepens through the book: 'I know Lucien! He wants the harvests without the toil—that is his nature. Social duties will eat up his time and time is the capital of those whose intelligence is their only fortune'. . . . 'Every writer goes about with a parasite in his heart, a sort of tapeworm which eats up his feelings as they hatch. Which will survive, the parasite or the man? As talent increases the heart dries up. Any man who is not a colossus is left at the end, either without heart or without talent. You are fragile and delicate; it will break you.'

> Lucien walked home, turning over in his mind that terrible verdict, whose profound truth seemed to him to throw light on the literary profession.
>
> 'Money!' a voice kept crying. . . .

The passage illustrates Balzac's intuitive knowledge of damnation. The insoluble dilemma, the death of the heart is sketched out in two or three sentences; and then the abrupt transition—not to repentance, but to a new kind of crime—as what Balzac called 'the beat of that great pendulum money struck like a hammer, blow after blow, on his mind and heart'.

The retribution which overtakes Lucien is perhaps over-indulged in. The misery he causes those nearest him is over-coloured even as the insincerity of his own remorse is most subtly portrayed. Alas for great novelists—one and all they are dominated by evil: Lucien, Charlus, Emma Bovary, Becky Sharp, infallibly the active and wicked steal the limelight from the virtuous. Balzac's good characters may love virtue; their creator is obsessed by vice. Greed, lust, revenge, treason: a gong seems to sound in his prose when they are touched upon. The illusions which are lost are those of first love and poetic glory, the ones which remain are of vanity and worldly success. For great novelists have need of society and so must re-create it, nor dare they allow it to perish utterly in the flame of their satire.

The supreme greatness of Balzac resides in his grand romantic conception of life which is never weakened but rather illuminated by his own intellectual disillusion. Lucien seems entirely destroyed by his trip to Paris; but, after all, he is only twenty; the illusions reform in clearer focus; for him life is only just beginning. The romantic's last word is never said.

19

SAINTE-BEUVE

ENGLISH biographers of French authors have a special problem. What use are they to make of the crop of superb biographies, the life-work in some cases of dedicated scholars, which have come out in France in the last few years? Stendhal, Mallarmé, Baudelaire, Flaubert, have each their passionate editor to mount guard over them; M. André Billy and M. André Maurois have both done some of their best work recently on the Romantic period. Rather than be put off by M. Billy's definitive life of Sainte-Beuve Sir Harold Nicolson has ruthlessly pillaged the two volumes and on at least three occasions paid a handsome tribute.[1] Short of translating the whole work, it is difficult to see what else a biographer, confronted with the fruits of modern French research, can be expected to do.

No two biographies are alike, for in every one enters an element of autobiography which must always be different. Sir Harold is concise, astringent, and occasionally severe. He tells us he is repaying a youthful debt of gratitude to a favourite author, yet since there is not one cell of his organism but has been replaced many times over, the links with his early self are few indeed and there are moments when his present dignity is outraged: 'In later years the Goncourts heard him bleating to the Princess Mathilde on this same eternal subject.' It is for the Goncourts to use such a word, not Sainte-Beuve's biographer.

Of recent years the scales in which art and life are balanced have been heavily weighted in favour of living. 'Encore un moment,

[1] *Sainte-Beuve*, by Harold Nicolson (Constable).

M. le Bourreau,' cries the artist to his conscience, and hopes for the best. But the choice has to be made and it is easier when there is illness or a physical disability, a limp, a stammer, asthma or T.B. to turn the scale. Ugliness and bladder trouble gradually withdrew Sainte-Beuve from circulation and helped him towards the decision, taken in childhood by his unconscious self and melancholy cast of mind, to renounce the world, not for the Church as he had once hoped but for that distillation from two thousand years of frustration which is literature.

There are two Sainte-Beuves: the critic who took his final vows in his early forties and whose life, except for a few friendships and a late incursion into politics as a senator, is withdrawn and sedentary, revolving round his 'Lundis' in a glorious treadmill; and the poet and lover whose failure in both rôles was the fertilising tragedy.

Sainte-Beuve's love-affair with Madame Victor Hugo is a classic of adultery. It should be printed as a case-history and handed to every young couple as they leave the Registrar. 'But he was my best friend,' Hugo might have exclaimed. 'Of course, no point in it otherwise, was there?' 'And he admired my work so much.' 'And you his?' 'We both felt so sorry for him, he was practically one of the family.' 'That's what they said about you.' It was the revenge of the Iago of talent upon the Othello of genius, a deeply horrifying story for all who build their happiness on the shifting sands of the heart.

Hugo, great poet, great lover, and great egotist, had won his Adèle after years of devotion; he had not yet been unfaithful to her though his theatrical activities took up much of his time. But stupidity (and Madame Hugo 'had,' according to Sainte-Beuve, 'the brain of a peahen') is not static, it grows in rancour and develops its own sullen envy; the inferiority complex, once established, manufactures its own revenge. Violated by night and neglected by day Adèle Hugo fell a by no means easy (for she was virtuous) but inevitable victim to the assiduous probing malice and hypocrisy, the unfrocked personality of Sainte-Beuve whose decaying creative gift, in attendance on Hugo's effortless, inexhaustible prodigality, was rotting into hate. To such a nature a rival's happy marriage is a challenge; an endearment, a casual connubial aside, the merest flicker of two-ness a mortal insult.

Loneliness had quickened Adèle's powers of compassion; unhappiness drove Sainte-Beuve desperate; and Hugo, overconfident like all the over-sexed, had one other weakness. He could not set aside the Romantic's respect for passion, the belief that a great love was outside the law. He did not therefore feel morally justified in sending Sainte-Beuve packing when he first confessed to his feelings. The elephant let the pigmy, with his poisoned arrow, come too close.

One can read the story from Hugo's point of view in André Maurois's wonderful biography. Here we see it only from Sainte-Beuve's, but even so his hate and cruelty peep out from underneath the loneliness and devotion; he betrays his friend to the utmost of his ability, boasts of the misery he has caused and finally comes to loathe his mistress. For him there was to be no more real love. His mind could command friendship; anything more he would have to buy. Hugo, after great bitterness, was liberated for his long career of infidelity and, without Sainte-Beuve, the ravishing Juliette Drouet would never have fallen into his arms.

Madame Hugo's punishment was that for the rest of their lives she remained always there. 'If any blame attaches to the beginnings of such a passion. . . .

> La faute disparait dans sa constance même
> Quand la fidélité, triomphant jusqu'au bout
> Luit sur des cheveux blancs et des rides qu'on aime,
> Le Temps, vieillard divin, honore et blanchit tout.'

Victor Hugo to Juliette Drouet? No—Sainte-Beuve to his Adèle.

Let us not confuse the issue: a writer can ask to be judged by his work, and here the five-year period of Sainte-Beuve's unhappy love is soon forgotten. As a critic Sainte-Beuve had two faults; he was indifferent to some of his gifted contemporaries, a coward about Baudelaire, a dolt about Flaubert; and he neglected (according to Proust) to write with that passionate intensity which we find in those books which are the 'children of solitude and silence'.

He strove to entertain. But in *Volupté* and in his poems he had tried magic and failed.

He was a classicist and in his studies of the seventeenth and eighteenth century he is unsurpassed. He was the inventor of modern criticism and one of the most agreeable essayists of all time. His notebook, *Mes Poisons*, reveals a remarkable aphorist and what he called his 'âme élégiaque'. 'I am a classic,' he wrote in *Mes Poisons*, 'in the sense that there is a degree of irrationality, absurdity or bad taste which can spoil a work of art for me for ever afterwards.' Besides having scholarship, taste, and enthusiasm he was, according to Sir Harold and M. Billy, despite his faults a 'man of good will'.

Sir Harold has taken down his ill-favoured bust, cleaned it, talked to it, judged and forgiven and put it back on a brighter shelf, in a more prominent but no less lonely position.

20

DELACROIX

It was Baudelaire who compared Delacroix in society to the crater of a volcano artificially concealed by a clump of flowers, even as it was he who seized the fundamental nature of Delacroix's genius: 'Une passion immense doublée d'une volonté formidable, tel était l'homme.' This was, of course, the passion of the Romantics, but the will-power sprang from the cold and intellectual desire for perfection which led him to reject almost every quality of the French Romantics except their sense of pageantry and drama. He was the first to suspect their idea of progress and belief in inspiration, as Flaubert and Baudelaire were afterwards to do and thus to affirm the particular note of the nineteenth century with which we find ourselves in harmony.

Judging Voltaire shallow and Hugo pompous he had to create an ideal companion—himself—even as, disliking at the beginning of his life the classicism of Ingres and at the end the realism of Courbet, he became the one painter to bridge the gulf between them.

His heredity is revealing: his mother belonged to a family of royal furniture-makers, the Oebens and Rieseners, his putative father was a lawyer who signed the death-warrant of Louis XVI, his real father is supposed to have been Talleyrand. The great minister certainly used some of his influence to help the family, and made things easy for the unsuspecting young painter by that secret assistance whose provision, according to Balzac, is one of the few pleasures which we can share with the gods. Besides a strong physical resemblance, some other attributes of the diplomat are certainly present but no two worlds remain mutually more exclusive than the power-haunted political society of the father and the vision of the lonely artist who could write, of his studio, 'All my ambition is bounded by these walls.'

The *Journal* of Delacroix consists of one very early section which might have been kept by any art student of high fancy and a long interior monologue from which the key year 1848 is unfortunately missing. The present edition,[1] admirably introduced and translated, reduces the three French volumes to 400 pages of India paper which fit in the pocket. The notes could be fuller but after this charming edition it is unlikely that it will be necessary to translate or abridge these journals again.

And what of the journal itself? It is a painter's, not a writer's diary; two-thirds of it is technical and so lacks the tragic brilliance of Baudelaire's journals or the wrought-iron gossip-column quality of the Goncourts. It is a painter's record of his impressions and difficulties, the self-portrait of a proud and aloof artist who opposes the times in which he lives, who regards mechanical inventions as disasters and the desire for change as a disease of the human spirit. The message of the journal is stoical: 'The practice of an art demands a man's whole self.' Work, work, work, he proclaims, and meditate on the great ones. All else is vanity and boredom. 'Evening party at the Tuileries. I came home feeling even sadder than after poor Visconti's funeral. The faces of these rogues and worthless women make me sick; their flunkeys' souls hidden under their embroidered uniforms.'

Like many great and isolated figures, Delacroix builds a private Pantheon for himself: for Mozart's music he will go out, for his worship of Rubens there is an occasional pilgrimage to Belgium, for the sea ('Water, water, of which I never grow tired') there is Dieppe, but the true life is within. 'I have been saying to myself and I cannot say it too often for my happiness and tranquillity (they are one and the same) that I must and can live only through the mind; the food it needs is more necessary than bodily food.'

[1] *The Journal of Eugène Delacroix*. Translated by Lucy Norton, with an introduction by Hubert Wellington (Phaidon Press).

In pursuit of music Delacroix sometimes had to emerge at night. Unfortunately for us he describes his friends too briefly. A combat between fly and spider or some ants and a beetle is minutely rendered but what can we make from such an entry as 'went to call on Madame Sand. That good-natured fellow Chopin played for us,' or 'M. Baudelaire called just as I was starting work. . . . His views seem exceedingly modern and progressive.'

Yet it was Baudelaire, had Delacroix but known, who was to draw a far more life-like portrait of him than the diaries furnish, depersonalised as they are by the artist's classical reserve and by that deep reverence for the masterpieces of the past which inhibited the parade of his own accomplishments. Beneath the endless bouquets for Mozart and Michelangelo, Rubens and Racine, the volcano rumbles. Sometimes there is an explosion. 'He's always scheming to make money out of small pictures. He's finished! He's beginning to say: "It's too late now" like all lazy people who have been in the habit of saying confidently "I've got plenty of time".'

21

FLAUBERT

It was time a really good life of Flaubert appeared in English, if only to incorporate new facts which have come to light in the last few years. Important discoveries have been made by M. Gerald Gailly who has filled in the background of Flaubert's crucial love-affair at Trouville which forms the basis of *L'Education Sentimentale*: he has laid bare facts which even Flaubert did not know. It was because Elisa Schlésinger was not actually married to Maurice Schlésinger (who had rescued her from an unfortunate early marriage) that she put up with his infidelities and could not feel justified in allowing herself to love the youthful Flaubert, thus risking the illegitimacy of her daughter being made public. This tragedy in her early life was unknown to Flaubert who constructed his vision of romantic love round her inscrutable virtue. The double tension to which she was subjected may have prepared the way for her eventual insanity.

Mr. Spencer, besides assimilating all this new information (he even suggests there is evidence that Flaubert hanged himself in his bath), has managed to write a very good book[1]; he presents a mass of facts skilfully and easily and his own judgments are both scholarly and searching. There is, however, a certain tendency to be dry and priggish, as in his suggestions that Flaubert would have benefited from a psychiatrist or that he was blasphemous in his aesthetic mysticism. It is easy to adopt a superior tone about the dead if we do not have to write their books; and by applying modern psychology to them we are apt to render their greatness as artists all the more inexplicable.

[1] *Flaubert: A Biography*, by Philip Spencer (Faber).

Perhaps only those to whom art is a religion can love Flaubert and therefore understand him. Mr. Spencer comes very near to this but seems to be deliberately holding himself back. His attitude to Flaubert's books suggests that all, except *Un Coeur Simple*, were interesting failures and yet he recognises his immense stature as a novelist: 'He stands, firm and downright, in the main path of literature, offering a permanent challenge.'

The difficulty is that to write a life of Flaubert which is not also a critical study of his work is like presenting a film on the life of a seal with the words 'Of course we shan't see what it does in the water.' He himself proclaimed that happiness was to be found only in the turning of a phrase. Like Baudelaire's his life, apart from his books, is a desolation. Both men spend their time looking back over their shoulders at their vanished youth. All the themes of the one are in *Novembre*, of the other in *La Fanfarlo*, both written while their authors were in the early twenties. It is only their perception of these early experiences which deepens and changes. Now Thibaudet's *Flaubert* is one of the most perfect works of criticism in any language, one which makes it almost impossible to write at length of Flaubert's art and this is perhaps why intelligent people like Mr. Spencer and Mr. Francis Steegmuller in his *Flaubert and Madame Bovary*, have been thrown back on his life. And his life, however brilliantly analysed, is unsatisfactory.

At first we have an ideal picture: 'L'homme c'est rien, l'oeuvre c'est tout'; the high priest renounces the world and retires into his ivory tower to perfect his art. But closer analysis would seem to show that the ivory tower was thrust upon him. His father and beloved sister die simultaneously a few months after the splendid young giant who is reading in Paris for the Bar is himself disabled by a mysterious illness, perhaps epilepsy. Duty and ill-health require him to give up his career, retire to Croisset and look after his mother and motherless niece. But, going with Mr. Spencer even further into the affair, we receive the impression that Flaubert subconsciously caused the ivory tower to be inevitable. The illness may have been a form of hysteria; once back at base it mysteriously disappears while he gathers obligations round him like the shell of a caddis-worm.

Prometheus has formed his chains and found his vulture, and now for the rest of his life he will rail against the *bourgeoisie* of Rouen and the venality of his friends in Paris, use his mother as a shield against other women and expiate his *bourgeois* guilt by the enormous labours which he undertakes and by his denunciations of the society to which he will always belong. Does his comfortable income, however well spent, give him the right to condemn those who adopt journalism for a living? Such doubts affect French circles today and partly account for the reaction against Flaubert. Mr. Spencer tries hard to dispel them.

The best way to do so is to turn to what he wrote, to allow ourselves to be engulfed by that fantastic and yet solid agglomeration, the brilliantly coloured and even lethal cloud which goes circling round for ever, in its twelve word-perfect volumes, haunting us with its passionate disillusion and causing us to hope and despair at an opening sentence: 'Pendant un demi-siécle les bourgeoises de Pont l'Evèque envièrent à Madame Aubain sa servante Félicité. . . .'

22

BAUDELAIRE

THIS year (1961) marks the centenary of the *Fleurs du Mal* and I wish there was a small exhibition to commemorate it. Meanwhile, as a preliminary, here is a self-portrait in the form of a translation of most of Baudelaire's important letters with a biographical commentary[1].

The two editors are redolent of the campus: simple, sensitive souls who give adequate but not exciting translations, a great many facts and rather too many observations. I prefer Arthur Symons's translation of Baudelaire's letters to his mother or Pascal Pia's 'Baudelaire par lui-même' as a simple presentation. But it is a point in favour of the Hyslops that while loving and sympathising with Baudelaire up to the end, they do not feel they must explain him or that it is necessary for them to proclaim some new theory, Freudian, existentialist or otherwise, to justify all their trouble.

For those who cannot read French and want to learn about Baudelaire this self-portrait is a moving and solid introduction. But whereas Flaubert's letters are a feast in themselves, Baudelaire's are insufferable the moment one loses sight of his poetry. If the devil reads aloud to those who take their meals in hell, as is the rule in a monastery, I think these letters would be an ideal curriculum; one is conscious of the air, the life, the hope, slowly being sucked out of a human being, of an increasing weariness and dissimulation, of small sums of money, debts, loans, publishers'

1 *Baudelaire: A Self-Portrait*. Selected Letters translated and edited by Lois and Francis Hyslop (Oxford).

royalties and rates of interest gradually acquiring a life of their own like giant cockroaches in a delirium tremens.

'One doesn't marry again when one has a son like me. . . .' It was the withdrawal of his mother's affection from him to his stepfather which poisoned his youth and which instigated the blend of financial-cum-emotional blackmail of his mother which was to last his lifetime and acquire a more and more controlling hold on her after General Aupick's death in 1857:

As for me, I loved you passionately in my childhood, later on, suffering from the weight of your injustice, I was guilty of a lack of respect. . . . The harm is done through your imprudence and my mistakes. We are evidently meant to love each other, to live for each other, to end our lives as honourably and as peacefully as possible. And yet in the terrible circumstances in which I am placed, I am convinced that one of us will cause the death of the other and that finally we will succeed in killing each other. After my death it is obvious that you will not go on living. I am the only thing that keeps you alive. After your death, especially if you were to die from a shock caused by me, I would kill myself. That is beyond all doubt. Your death . . . would not improve anything in my situation, the legal guardianship would be maintained, nothing would be paid and, worst of all, I would have the *horrible sensation of utter loneliness*.

This superb and harrowing letter ends with a confession that he has appropriated 400 francs of someone else's money to pay his worst debts. His mother sent him 500.

As M. Sartre has pointed out, the whole scenery of Baudelaire's tragedy was set by him in youth—the 12,000 francs of debts which he was never to get rid of, and which increased with interest faster than they could be paid off. The angry stepfather, the legal guardianship established to protect the rest of his tiny capital, the coloured mistress, rapacious and uncomprehending who contracted syphilis and left him under a permanent obligation to provide for her, the bad reputation, the bohemian habits, sloth and general unemployability were all part of a supreme design for failure, an unbeatable combination.

Baudelaire, whose intelligence and imagination were as twin Rolls-Royce engines, had managed permanently to foul his superb installation yet never quite prevent the motors from turning. What was the true significance of his helplessness? What maintained his equilibrium between genius and impotence? It could not be some secret knowledge of how to get the best out of himself since, after his twenties, when some of the best poems were written, the machine was slowly running down and in the last six years of his life produced hardly anything. The equation between his passion for life and his horror of life did not remain constant, the resolutions which he made increase in rigour until they become unenforceable.

The 'flaw' and the 'jinx' from which he suffered, the fatalistic belief in the positive force of evil, are like some small error of workmanship which will gradually incapacitate a huge vessel: around 1857-61 the will was in a position to execute the commands of genius; both were in their prime, though there was already a dearth of new material. The second edition of *Les Fleurs* (1861) was the masterpiece of which he had dreamed: 'in this *atrocious* book I have put all *my heart*, all *my love*, all *my religion* (travestied), all *my hate*'. And in his last letter but one he writes to Catulle Mendès after his stroke: 'The last line of the poem entitled "Bien loin d'ici" ' (a masterpiece of evocation) 'should be preceded by a dash in order to give it a kind of isolation and separation from the rest.' 'Peace of mind, give me peace of mind,' he implored his mother, who could not release this solitary from his self-confinement because she could never restore the lap from which he had fallen; but in his art, his perfect, hated, dreaded and maltreated art he found peace and bestowed it, so that even Mr. Beckett's Hamm can quote him: ' "Tu reclamais le soir, il descend, le voici!" Jolie ça!'

23

A BAUDELAIRE CONUNDRUM

THE cult of French literature during the war was a feverish gesture of solidarity, a protest against isolation. Since then a reaction has set in and I doubt if more interest is shown in contemporary French writing here than our neighbours take in ours. The war names—Sartre, Malraux, Camus, Gênet, Michaux, Paulhan—are always sure of a hearing but we no longer keep up with the new magazines or grapple with the young poets, any more than we read and re-read the once consoling and endangered classics or travel with Racine or Rabelais in our pocket. At the same time we must go on reading French; the habit is unbreakable for we need a literature whose authors do not live on Green Line bus routes or lunch at their clubs, whose civilization is observed through a sheet of glass. We have never experienced anything like the vivarium of Versailles, the salons or the Terror, the battle of *Hernani* or Mallarmé's Tuesdays; we have no café life. When we read too much English literature we grow depressed by the unalterable bourgeois scene which has survived so many literary groups, even as it will outlast our own. Oxford common-rooms, London squares, Sussex cottages, sausages, landladies, publishers' cocktail parties, Sunday afternoons—one can fit almost every English writer into the familiar mould; tea is being served behind the house with the blue plaque as expertly as when the great man lived there, be he Addison or Gosse, Colley Cibber or George Moore. Thackeray or Gray or Pater are not so far removed from us in manners and habits as Valéry or Gide or Proust. My favourite writers are those whose sensibility is more modern than their surroundings, who, like Baudelaire or Flaubert, died just before it became necessary to wear a collar and tie and whose floppy cravats are almost the last we see before the universal dinginess of modern neckwear enforces equality.

*

Both are authors whom one can read and indeed write about for ever. Among the strangest phenomena of French literature today are the lives dedicated to nineteenth-century authors by their twentieth-century disciples. Crépet on Baudelaire, Dumesnil on Flaubert, Martineau on Stendhal, Mondor on Mallarmé—they are not so much latter-day Boswells as projections into the present of the personalities of these old masters, the genius of the dead artist appearing to re-create itself into a devastating arrangement of consciousness which seizes hold of the living mind and invests it like a fortress. When we study how a dead writer was occupied every day we get to know him better than he knew himself, and such knowledge can be dangerous. We know now why Mme. Schlésinger could not permit herself to love Flaubert. We know now that when Baudelaire resolves to visit Flaubert at Croisset, his will will not prove equal to the voyage; we know, with each move into some cheap hotel, exactly how many other cheap hotels lie ahead of him.

A scholar's life is often a long one, and when it is entirely devoted to the study of one man the few outstanding mysteries attain an exaggerated importance. A lacuna in Baudelaire's adolescence, his attempted suicide, the true nature of his relationship with Jeanne or of her lost letters to him obsess and harry the patient investigators to whom all the rest is daylight. That three-letter dedication of *Les Paradis Artificiels*, how it torments them! 'À "J. G. F." ' 'It's quite impossible to suppose for a moment that it could ever have been intended for such a vulgar creature as Jeanne Duval, one so completely indifferent to poetry,' writes M. le Dantec (editor of the 'Pléiade' Baudelaire) when referring to the appearance of these strange initials over the poem *Héautontimoroumenos* in the second edition of the *Fleurs du Mal.* Others have pointed out that the preface to *Les Paradis Artificiels* would be entirely above Jeanne's head from the very first sentence. '*Ma chère amie—Le Bon Sens nous dit que les choses de la terre n'existent que bien peu, et que la vraie réalité n'est que dans les rêves.*' What is needed in fact is a refined and cultivated muse with a philosophical turn of mind who has shared some of the poet's extra-sensory expeditions into the world of hashish and opium. The existence of such a paragon was established by a letter to M. Porché (another Baudelairian) from a M. Robert Jacquet, who said he was both the grandson of a painter and the nephew of a lady who had been entrusted with the confidences of a Mme. Juliette Gex-Fagon, to whom Baudelaire had been introduced in the Louvre by the sculptor, Pradier. Pradier (who had also presented Flaubert to Louise Colet) died in 1852. Mme. Gex-Fagon lived on the Ile St. Louis, on the quai d'Anjou, while Baudelaire was near at hand in the Hôtel Pimodan; she had copper-coloured hair, a rose carnation skin, a mind avid of sensations and a naive affection for the poet. It was not, however, a love affair but a romantic friendship. She hoped to save his soul and, in gratitude for her care in the opium dens, he reminded this Electra in the dedication of De Quincey's friendship for Anne: '*tu devineras la gratitude d'un autre Oreste dont tu as souvent surveillé les cauchemars et de qui tu dissipais d'une main légère et maternelle le sommeil épouvantable*'. When *Les Paradis* appeared in 1860 and the new *Fleurs* in 1861 bearing the mysterious dedications, Mme. Gex-Fagon may have been dying. We learn that the dedicatee was ill, one 'qui tourne maintenant tous ses regards vers le ciel, ce lieu de toutes les transfigurations'.

*

It would seem that the mystery is now solved were it not for the odd fact that M. Jacquet gave no address and that M. Porché was unable (by 1943) to verify his assertions or even his identity. Let us now examine the evidence for Jeanne. In the *Héautontimorouménos* (which was originally intended as an epilogue to the *Fleurs du Mal*, and whose title is taken from Terence by De Quincey) Baudelaire tries to explain his sadomasochist temperament to his victim and to justify the suffering he has inflicted. '*Je suis la plaie et le couteau*,' and the dedication to *Les Paradis* also concerns a woman whose love has been of the deepest significance to him, '*C'est à une qui, quoique malade, est toujours active et vivante en moi.*' Now Jeanne had indeed been very ill and taken to the hospital with a stroke in 1859, and M. Crépet is convinced that the two dedications were acts of reparation on Baudelaire's part, protestations of a resumed friendship, remorseful courtesies for the ruined, ailing quadroon whose disintegration he records at the same time in the marvellous sonnet sequence, *Un Fantôme*. As is often the case the dedication is a kind of epitaph, though Baudelaire was to continue to live with her '*en papa et tuteur*'. In that case to write above her head, to pay her classical compliments, to assume that she was of the élite who 'find happiness an emetic', is to honour her, to treat her on a level with Gautier and the other dedicatees and thus to rebuke the friends who considered her an evil and stultifying influence:

> Les stupides mortels qui l'ont jugée amère.

And he writes to his mother at this moment (October 1860) that for eighteen months he had been kept from suicide only because he could not bear to leave Jeanne penniless, '*cette vieille beauté transformée en infirme*'. If the J. G. F. of *Les Paradis* is indeed Jeanne (and the publisher Poulet-Malassis thought so), it remains but to solve the meaning of the initials. Here again there are two schools. M. Crépet suggested that they referred to the initials of her real name or else '*À Jeanne, généreuse, grande, ou glorieuse femme*', while M. Mouquet and M. Pommier have opted for '*À Jeanne, gentille femme*', a romantic archaicism employed in an early dedication used either by Baudelaire or his friend Privat d'Anglemont. To this solution M. Crépet eventually rallied.

*

But '*À Jeanne, gentille femme*' seems hardly worth so much mystification and appears to lack the aroma of secrecy which initials usually possess. I should like to make one more suggestion.

Letter to Poulet Malassis, May 3rd, 1860

Maintenant, je ne blague pas. Une terreur me prend, relativement à la note pharmaceutique de la fin. Réfléchissez-y-bien. Il suffit de la malveillance d'un méchant bougre, dans quelque sale journal, pour nous créer un embarras. (Reference to a chemist's advertisement on the preparation of opium or hashish which was to terminate *Les Paradis Artificiels* and for which he might be prosecuted.)

Je pense à la tireuse des cartes, qui m'avait prédit que j'allais rencontrer une fille très grande, très mince, très brune, âgée de. . . . Or, je l'ai rencontrée.

Vous connaissez son autre prédiction. Il est encore temps. La dédicace, c'est J. G. F. Préparez donc C à ma visite.

To the Same. No date

Mon cher,

Voici le billet D. j'espère que vous avez écrit aujourd'hui un mot à C que j'irai voir demain. Ne vous moquez pas de moi, à cause de mes histoires de tireuse de cartes. Qu'y aurait-il d'étonnant dans ce fait qu'un agent trop zélé trouvât immoral qu'à la suite d'un livre sur l'opium et le haschisch on indiquât les différentes préparations des substances et les différents avantages ou incommodités attachés à chacune d'elles?

It would seem that a fortune-teller had once made two predictions: that he would go to prison (?), as might happen were he to be prosecuted again for an immoral book, and that he would meet '*une fille très grande, très mince, très brune*'. An exact description of Jeanne Duval. 'J. G. F.', then, refers to his private destiny: '*À Jeanne, ma grande fille*' (in a letter of December, 1859, he addresses her as '*ma chère fille*'), and the initials can also be traced in the last line of the dedicatory sonnet which brought her cycle to an end ('*Je te donne ces vers*'):

> Statue aux yeux de jais, grand ange au front d'airain.

The fortune-teller may even be the '*vieille hydropique*' whose evil scented pack contained the 'handsome knave of hearts and the queen of spades' whose sombre talk of their dead love in his most splenetic sonnet symbolized their decaying passion.

But there is still a possibility that the visit was quite a recent one, that the prediction referred to yet another dark, tall, thin beauty whom he had met since Jeanne's illness in 1859, a name in the *carnet*, an Aglae or Agathe, a Negress like the Laure whom he brought to sit for Manet and that his irony, the '*poison noir*' of the '*victimebourreau*' in J. G. F.'s poem has triumphed over the commentators: '*Il importe d'ailleurs fort peu que la raison de cette dedicace soit comprise*,' he writes in *Les Paradis*, and in a rough draft he is even more explicit: '*Je désire que cette dedicace soit inintelligible.*'

24

GÉRARD DE NERVAL

There is no disease more mysterious than schizophrenia; it is a kind of madness which some sensitive people, at odds with reality, seem able to wish upon themselves: 'the mind is invaded by morbid mental growths', as one doctor has put it, and these growths bring with them a richer mental texture than the normal, a flood of images, a religious conviction of the significance of trifles, of the mystical communication between spirit and matter.

Gérard Labrunie was born in 1808, a contemporary of Tennyson and Poe; his mother died of hardship while with his father, an Army doctor, on Napoleon's campaigns; the boy heard the news at the age of seven, and was at the same age removed from the care of his mother's relations at Mortefontaine. He grew up idealising the peasant girls of the Ile de France, and being faithful to the image of his mother through a succession of platonic love affairs which culminated in his devotion to the actress Jenny Colon; she married a flute player and died young, thus precipitating the second crisis in the deep and sensitive nature of the poet who was now writing under a romanticised version of his mother's name.

His father strongly disapproved of the literary career which had begun so brilliantly with a translation of Goethe's 'Faust', and there is something pathetic about the letters, full of lies and boasts and guilt, which Gérard all his life addressed to this most unsympathetic man. Like his bosom friend Gautier, the youthful Gérard was a journalist of genius, able to turn out plays, stories, articles and dramatic criticism which all possessed the endearing, imaginative quality of Lamb and De Quincey. He was also a great traveller who did much to bring Germany before French eyes, who interpreted Wagner and Heine and who wrote one of the most fascinating books about the East.

It was not until the wing of insanity had brushed him that the peculiar element in his work, the conversion of reality into dream and thus into an artistic whole, took him right out of the vapid contemporary scene. His stories of his early loves, 'Angélique' and the magical 'Sylvie', culminated in his mystical novel, 'Aurélia', in which he is revealed as a prose Van Gogh, even as the banal verses of his early years were suddenly transformed into the magical sonnets which made him the equal of Hölderlin and Rimbaud. He comes at the end of the French romantics, a dreamer and an agreeable entertainer whose gifts were paralysed, like Baudelaire's, by a weight of neurosis and financial embarrassment but who lacked the terrible lucidity of Baudelaire and who drifted into greatness in the asylum of Dr. Blanche.

'It is kind of you to have come. Our poor Dr. Blanche is mad; he thinks he is at the head of an insane asylum, and we inmates pretend to be demented in order to be agreeable to him.' Nerval's last years were passed in a clouded state in which the female figure of Isis shed a moonglow over his imagination; he was possessed by the living dead and by mystical heroes from the mythical past; the doctors shut him up, he said, because he could heal the sick.

He forced his release from the good doctor's asylum and took to the Paris streets. One winter dawn he found himself down to his last coppers in the lowest street of Paris, the rue de la Vieille Lanterne. He knocked at a doss-house where one could sleep on straw. Nobody opened, and this he took to be the final rejection. With a piece of string he hanged himself from the lamp-post. In his pockets were two sous, the visiting card of Baudelaire's friend Asselineau, and a page of the corrected proof of 'Aurélia', which is now before me in a Paris bookseller's catalogue, priced at £100.

Gérard de Nerval

Books on Nerval are rare. Mr. Rhodes's[1] is very full and well-documented, though lamentably expressed from start to finish. It coincides with the appearance of a complete one-volume Nerval in the French Pléiade.

[1] *Gérard de Nerval*, by S. A. Rhodes (Peter Owen).

25

THE GONCOURTS

THE original Goncourt Journal was published in nine volumes and there has already been an English abridgement, published in this country by Secker & Warburg, with a useful glossary. Since 1956, however, there has been access to the original uncut version from which Edmond de Goncourt made his selection. Now comes a new translation and abridgement[1] which makes use of the censored material and which therefore supersedes all others. One can rely on Dr. Baldick and know that the best use has been made of this.

The modern movement in literature arose in the middle years of the French nineteenth century, the creation of writers born around 1820 (Flaubert, Baudelaire, 1821, E. de Goncourt 1822, Renan 1823, Dostoevsky 1821, Turgenev 1818). To these we must add the next crop: Verlaine, Rimbaud, Villiers, Mallarmé and Maupassant, Zola, Huysmans; with Lautréamont and Laforgue to complete the founding fathers. Rimbaud and Lautréamont are not mentioned by Goncourt, despite his exaltation of prose at the expense of poetry while Laforgue and Villiers meant next to nothing to him. His loyalties, or rather his disloyalties, were pledged to his own group and his own generation. Like Henry James he 'saw all round Flaubert' and could never stop worrying away at his reputation, though it caused him less pain than Zola's (the disciple who outsold the master). In every literary movement there is always someone with more taste than genius, a cold fish who looks on and bides his time.

[1] *Pages from the Goncourts' Journal.* Edited and translated by Robert Baldick (Oxford).

Envy dictated about 60 per cent. of all comment on books and writers in this journal and so we must be grateful, for a little more success on the stage or the best-seller list would have robbed us of a masterpiece. 'I shall die not knowing what is to become of the two great projects of my life intended to ensure my survival' (the other was the Academy Goncourt). 'My constant preoccupation is to save the name of Goncourt from oblivion in the future by every sort of survival. Survival through works of literature, survival through foundations, survival through the application of my monogram to all the *objets d'art* which have belonged to my brother and myself.'

This partakes of the tycoon. No true writer would wish to be remembered by anything but his books. Edmond de Goncourt had written about forty; they included the first lively but serious rehabilitations of the eighteenth century, some excellent realistic novels about prostitutes and servant-girls and circus performers and bohemian painters—as if George Moore, shall we say, had been welded into Edmund Gosse. The younger brother Jules was somewhat spoilt, an impertinent and juicier element in the aesthetic combination but he died in 1870; the diaries run from 1851 to 1896.

Edmond de Goncourt was preoccupied with literary reputation and with the sex-life and diseases of authors, particularly when there was a connection between them. He seems to have a special affinity with bladder trouble—so many entries are devoted to Sainte-Beuve's and Daudet's complications in this field. He watched his beloved brother die of syphilis of the brain, he observed the same fatal illness in Flaubert, Maupassant, Murger and so many others, including Baudelaire. It was the heyday of syphilis when every amorous man of letters might in a rash instant condemn himself to an atrocious death; it was also the heyday of modern medical jargon when doctors and surgeons frequented literary society, discussing their patients' ailments and operations. Searching for an epithet the man of letters watched his friend's scalpel cutting into his stomach 'like a knife into a banana' (Turgenev) and looked forward to producing the right word for it at the next Magny dinner. What extraordinary dinners they were!

> Dinner at the Café Riche with Flaubert, Zola, Turgenev and Alphonse Daudet. A dinner of men of talent who have a high opinion of each other's work, and one which we hope to make a monthly occasion in the winters to come.
>
> We began with a long discussion on the special aptitudes of writers suffering from constipation and diarrhoea; and we went on to talk about the mechanics of the French language. . . .
>
> Our old dinner of five was revived today with Flaubert missing. . . . The moral difficulties of some of us and the physical sufferings of the others brought the conversations round to death—and we went on talking about death till eleven o'clock. . . .

A discussion of the author's sexual experiences or an attack on some established reputation like Homer's or Hugo's generally provided the brighter side of the picture. What took place at these dinners was really a liberation of spirit among these hard-working writers deprived of normal outlets (Goncourt called himself and his brother the John the Baptist of Neurosis) who were also living under strict censorship. Flaubert and Goncourt believed in celibacy as essential to a serious artist and Sainte-Beuve would have agreed. The bawdy dinners brought their repressions into the open as well as their doubts about their work and their fear of age, infirmity, death and oblivion. Such conversations had never been recorded before and are enough to constitute the importance of the Journal. We see the modern sensibility grow in boldness before our eyes.

Like all great diary-keepers Goncourt had to wait for his fame and suffer from the slights of his contemporaries, taking his revenge in the perpetual belittling of them (a habit which, in Sainte-Beuve, he detested and attributed, perhaps rightly, to an inadequate sex-life). The Princess Mathilde, the royal protectress of Sainte-Beuve, Flaubert and the Goncourts, moves like Athena through the pages of their spiritual Odyssey.

The Goncourts were *rentiers* and were opposed to socialism, bohemianism and the Commune, but without Flaubert's peculiar detestation of the *bourgeoisie*. Edmond was too Parisian, too interested in the arts and decoration, too much the aristocratic aesthete to be tortured by it. He was unable to understand intellectual prejudice and sufferings and picks constantly on the coarseness of Flaubert without seeing that this was a mask. Now that we know how deeply Flaubert was in love with the original of his Mme Arnoux we are not taken in by his crude brothel-boasting.

> Neither Flaubert, for all his bragging about such matters, nor Zola, nor I have ever been seriously in love and we are all incapable of describing love, only Turgenev could do it; but he lacks precisely that critical judgment that we could bring to the task if we had been in love as he has.

And this seven years after the 'Education Sentimentale'!

The new additions to the Journal are invaluable and give point to much that has seemed insipid before. It is now necessary to have two copies of this only successor to Boswell, one of the whole nine volumes (in French) and Dr. Baldick's for the sake of the admirably crisp translation plus the new material. His selection and compression are excellent for he sticks to the main themes—sex and literature—and doesn't bother with the politics and aestheticisms of minor personalities. Everyone should enjoy this extraordinary picture of the relaxations of genius and the splendours and miseries of a great creative epoch.

26

HUYSMANS

HUYSMANS is a prose drug whose aroma is so subtle, so fetching, that there is in existence a flourishing society of its addicts. I have been hearing about this book for two years and here it is.[1] I wish I had written it myself. Very occasionally we can still find a good writer about whom far too little is known and a small voice tells us: 'There's room for a book there.'

But how seldom is such a book written in a way which combines all the available information with the ability to sort it out and put it together, carefully, perspicaciously, humbly, wisely. Dr. Baldick's *Life* bulges with a mass of new information, nearly all of it interesting, about one of the most fascinating of writers and most enigmatic of men. All who enjoy the French nineteenth century should lay hold of this volume and salt it away for the next wet evening.

If we consider Flaubert, Baudelaire, Edmond de Goncourt (born within a year) as members of a key generation who fused romanticism with realism to produce two great books and one important minor one, we can find a resemblance in their followers. Influenced chiefly by Baudelaire: Verlaine. Influenced entirely by Flaubert: Maupassant. Influenced by Baudelaire and Flaubert: Mallarmé, Villiers. Influenced by Flaubert and Baudelaire: Huysmans. Villiers (like Barbey) fails in the long run through dissipation and loss of vitality. Mallarmé and Huysmans, both sober

[1] *The Life of J. K. Huysmans*, by Robert Baldick (Oxford).

stayers, exercise an ever-potent influence on those who read them. What they have done well is so significant that there is awfully little left.

The persistent quality of Huysmans's work is a disillusioned *aigre-douceur*, a taste of generous vinegar. He is a master of prose; no penetrator of illusions has possessed so keen a visual sense, so rich a palette. He towers over all the other novelists of the end of the century. He was also a man of great integrity whose life was a spiritual pilgrimage in search of the absolute, of a rewarding satisfaction. He found it, after years of aesthetic experiment and controlled sensuality, in the Roman Catholic Church; particularly in the doctrine of suffering of which the Crucifixion is a symbol as the true condition of humanity. This discovery came just in time to help him to bear a terrible illness.

Otherwise his life was completely uneventful; he was a bachelor and a Civil Servant, a novelist and art critic, he travelled a little and nibbled at monasteries. He grew up at the moment when excitement was beginning to go out of the literary life, when writers were becoming government officials and adopting safe professions, when the young Claudel could observe the unfortunate Verlaine and Villiers 'wearing in their eyes the remains of their genius like prostitutes' fur tippets'. By a fearful paradox the increasing humdrum of the writer's existence was equalled only by the enormous documentation which he left behind him. A famous man was beginning to sit on a pile of paper as high as the Great Pyramid. This will become the ultimate despair of all biographers, but in Huysmans's case the material could just be assimilated. Yet when a biographer can write of his subject (and more than once) 'it was the beginning of a busy week' (not month, or year) 'for Huysmans,' and quote several descriptions of the same incident, he begins to seem like a Channel swimmer before whom the cliffs constantly recede.

Huysmans himself had a way of collecting bores, nearbrows, amorous young women, half-unfrocked priests, seedy satanists, penniless charlatans; and it often takes Dr. Baldick ten or twenty pages to get rid of one of them. It is interesting to observe how even an author's conversion to Catholicism can partake of the spirit of the time.

He had written, he said, a satanic book full of Black Masses. He now wanted to write another which would be white, but he knew first that it would be necessary to whiten himself. And so he had come to the Abbé Mugnier for the help which only a priest of the church could give him.

'Have you,' he asked, 'any chlorine for the soul?'

All Huysmans's books are autobiographical and each occupies a higher jumping-off point in his spiritual odyssey. They are not really novels but an attempt, by simulating fiction, to force the reader to accept a combination of erudite essays and personal comment which he would otherwise reject. One novel only, *Là-Bas*, has a real construction and it is one of the greatest novels I know. The evil which curiosity about the past uncovers marches in accelerating pursuit of the horrors lurking in the present and the two sinister themes are brought together in the dénouement; the book is a marvellous achievement. *À Rebours*, though so much better known, is really a bundle of essays of uneven excellence; the later novels are smothered in documentation.

One can say of Huysmans, therefore, that the man, though not more interesting than his work, is not often surpassed by it and that to read a good biography of him is to learn almost as much as we would from his books. His character is strange and baffling and I would not presume to lay it bare. There are times when one longs for this sensual faun to rush out of his government office and set the Seine on fire, when the endless routine of small scandals, petty gratifications, poverty and sickness associated with the literary life nearly drives one crazy. But then we must remember that we see it, even with Dr. Baldick, through the wrong end of a telescope, for the experience of the artist, in actually writing, cannot be communicated.

27

PROUST

As a rule I dread this kind of book[1]: the intrusion of the brash, cocksure and semi-illiterate anaylst into the Broceliande where genius and neurosis wander hand in hand is seldom rewarding.

The artist is proved to be a criminal-homosexual-alcoholic-voyeur-and-exhibitionist, but no explanation is forthcoming for his art which sets him for ever above his alco-chums. Flaubert said that he felt a special kinship with madmen and criminals, yet he was neither; Proust, for all his neurosis, became as penetrating a psychologist as Freud himself.

Therefore I was delighted to find that Dr. Miller never departs from a perceptive reverence for the greatness of his subject, going out of his way to claim for Proust discoveries concurrently made by Freud and treating him as a neurotic whose understanding of his own case was profoundly original and expressed in a stupendous work of art—a work which Dr. Miller continuously helps to explain and illuminate.

Proust's need for integration was great. His anxiety and the actual danger of fragmentation of his impulses was imminent. Luckily he was sufficiently gifted to follow the only lines along which both his parents gave their approval: literary creation. He was unable to lead an active life. He had the genius and, one might say, the neurosis, for just this one kind of aesthetic sublimation, oriented toward the past rather than the present or future. The content of his emotional

[1] *Nostalgia: A Psychoanalytic Study of Marcel Proust*, by Milton L. Miller, M.D. (Gollancz).

life was largely centred around the need to deal with unconscious aggression against those whom he loved very dependently. . . . The successful writing of his books probably prevented psychosis. The creative aspect of his whole existence provided restoration, reunion with all he loved most and felt he must have lost, particularly his 'eternal union' with his mother.

As Dr. Miller sees it, the birth of Proust's younger brother, when he was two years old, caused torments of jealousy and insecurity and led to a 'separation-complex'. 'Something happened, in Proust's development, to impede his masculine procreative function.' 'Fear of separation from the beloved runs through Proust's writing as the essence of love itself.' 'The infinite repetition of the themes of love, jealousy and separation-fear gives one the impression that the author was aware of how he was driven by a repetition-compulsion.' This separation-anxiety about the mother is found in many sufferers from asthma.

Proust's weaning, in the novel, from the overwhelming mother-influence, the Combray-Venice of his nostalgia, is accomplished by the substitution of first his grandmother (whose love for him is wholly unselfish, being uncomplicated by his father's presence), then by a brother-figure, Robert de Saint-Loup (Robert was Proust's brother's name, Loup, a nickname for himself), until from his new playmates he goes on to their mothers, so that in the novel the little Marcel has, besides his own family, a brother, Saint-Loup, a spare grandmother, Mme de Villeparisis, three mother-substitutes, the Duchesse de Guermantes, Odette, and Madame Verdurin, a couple of fathers, Swann and Charlus, and three sister girl-friends with boys' names, Albert(ine), Gilbert(e) and André(e).

Elstir and Bergotte are fathers-in-art and Bloch a comic brother, while royal goddesses, the Princesse de Guermantes, the Princesse de Parme, the Queen of Naples, circle above him, even above snobbery, beckoning him on, in his state of 'perpetual anxiety and frustration, constantly needing love and reassurance from every direction'.

It is to Proust's credit as a novelist that he refuses to be bogged down in what is in reality a fantasy-world of social climbing, one where Prince Charming to the chagrin of his middle-class father Dr. Proust—or Norpois—or Legrandin—soars ever upward on the royal beanstalk; he perceives that love is as much more important than friendship as friendship than social position, more important, in fact, than anything, for the humble, elusive, androgynous Albertine destroys the reality of both duchess and mother, even as love itself can be subdued only by art. Or rather not until we are utterly defeated in love can we be driven to accept the idea of expiation through art, when anguish, like a guided missile, hurtles on us out of the blue.

For Proust could not support normal love. Children, and the reliving of childhood through them, the casual brutish intimacy, the synchronised selfishness or unthinking self-sacrifices of domesticity, were all beyond him—'Certainly, personal charm is a less frequent cause of love,' he wrote, 'than a speech such as: "No, this evening I shall not be free".' To fall in love then, for Proust, was to fall in fear of separation and therefore to fall in jealousy since all the pent-up anxiety based on his mother's 'betrayal' was diverted to a new phantom. His only solution was to sequestrate the loved one under lock and key since he lacked the aggression by which rivals are fended off and driven away. To declare one's love verbally is to incur contempt and the deception against which there is no redress.

The great love-stories in Proust are therefore all unhappy and the beloved is always unworthy of the lover: Odette betrays Swann, Albertine the narrator, Charlus comes to hopeless grief over the unspeakable Morel, while Saint-Loup loves an ex-prostitute; Proust seems to exercise the neurotic artist's right to veto every normal situation. The men are infinitely more sensitive than the women and Proust's theory that love is the most painful of human illusions reveals by its defeatism where he departs furthest from normal belief and thereby most wounds or infuriates those who have charitably taken on trust all his other flagrant aberrations.

But it may be from their knowledge of the stupidity, falsehood and greed, of the very worthlessness of the people they love that certain artists are quickened before it is too late, driven at last to express themselves in competition with the pregnant mother by their urgent awareness of the pathetic perishable phantom—the Albertine or Jeanne Duval, real only in their lies—whom they have made the unwilling repository of their hopes and sorrows:

And it is because they thus contain all the hours of days gone by that human bodies can do such injury to those who love them, because they contain so many past memories, joys and desires, already effaced for them, but so cruel for one who contemplates and carries back in the domain of Time the cherished body of which he is jealous, jealous even to the point of desiring its destruction.

28

LÉAUTAUD

This is a book[1] for a worldly guardian to slip into the hand of a young man who proposes to earn his living by his pen. It is guaranteed to make an underwriter of him. There can have been few literary careers more outwardly unrewarding. Poor, solitary, shy, proud, egocentric, a caustic debunker and deflater, Paul Léautaud had to wait till his eighties for his moment of glory, when his voluminous and misanthropic outpourings made him the star turn of French broadcasting.

Like a good Stendhalian he kept a journal all his life (an activity which is usually nourished by a private income). This journal for the years 1898-1907 Mr. Sainsbury has reduced to one volume: when I say that the journal for 1908 alone consists in French of more than 300 large pages it will be seen that this is no mean feat. Mr. Sainsbury's method is excellent as a comparison with the French will show. He concentrates on the main themes in the journal: the friendships, love-life and literary occupations of the author, yet he has eliminated a mass of irrelevant detail.

The translation is good, though I do not think 'you have unusual troubles' is quite right for '*vous avez des maux bizarres*' when the doctor is trying to reassure the dying Huysmans and there are some slips, as in the titles of Jarry's books.

Here is Léautaud's credo:

I have lived for no other purpose but to write. I have felt, seen, and

[1] *Journal of a Man of Letters*, by Paul Léautaud. Translated by Geoffrey Sainsbury (Chatto & Windus).

heard things. I have studied people and their sentiments in order to write. I have preferred that to material welfare or facile reputation. I have often even sacrificed the pleasure of the moment, my most secret felicities and affections—and even those of others, before whose pain I haven't flinched—in order to write what gave me pleasure to write. And from all that I derive a deep satisfaction (*un profond bonheur*).

With such a vocation one wonders why recognition came so late. The answer lies in his upbringing for as readers of *Child of Montmartre* will remember his childhood was similar to that of the stray cats he was afterwards in such quantities to adopt. The sensation of being completely unwanted by both parents, by-product of a liaison between a minor actress and the prompter to the Comédie Française, caused him to become the confidant of the cocottes with whom he was thrown in contact and who reminded him of his mother and to nourish in protest a fierce pride and independence, a love of solitude which was really a defence mechanism and which led to a series of rebuffs unconsciously calculated to perpetuate the feeling of being unwanted.

This masochism is seen clearly in operation in everything to do with the Prix Goncourt which occupies an enormous role in the Journal. It is quite clear that this unworldly recluse is obsessed not only with winning the Prix Goncourt but with everything to do with the Foundation. His ambition would seem to be to get the prize and also join the celebrated 'Ten' who then received a small income. His novel *Le Petit Ami* was seriously considered. But now his masochism intervenes. He withdraws his next book on the eve of publication and thus ends his career as a creative writer (for the next forty years he is dramatic critic or on the editorial side of the *Mercure*) and he refuses to meet the influential Huysmans.

On Huysmans's death the vacant seat was given to Jules Renard whose journal would probably yield some cross references to Léautaud. The fear of entering his new book and still not getting the prize must have been the dominating factor. The love of solitude (and Léautaud dedicated a book to solitude) is clearly thrust upon him.

His dogs and cats enabled him to wield power and compassion unadulterated by competitiveness and envy. His relations with women are typical: while secretly longing to be a pasha or a pimp he is unable to marry or live alone and is usually found living with some girl who is busy getting up steam to leave by reading about the other women he hankers after in his famous diary.

His vocation was greater than his talent (usually it is the other way round) and I think his failure as a writer is due to his mistrust of humanity, to puritanism of style (he abhorred all images) and to the rodent ulcer of his egocentricity. For this colossal egotism was unredeemed by the powers of imagination which would raise it to the universal. A comparison of his account of the death of Charles-Louis Philippe with Gide's will illustrate this. Unlike Gide's journal, his diary has no open windows. One can imagine Léautaud as an English writer, someone between Gissing and Orwell, performing hatchet jobs for Dr. Leavis, droning and wasping for many years in the bitterer weeklies while acting as a no-man for some successful publisher. On the other hand he won and kept the friendship of some very interesting people—Marcel Schwob whom he did not respect and Rémy de Gourmont whom he did.

His last words, according to Mr. Pryce-Jones, who contributes a lively introduction, were to his nurse 'Maintenant foutez-moi la paix' and his journal carries a warning, in red, 'No letters—By request.' Of his love of animals he writes 'Since I came home I haven't stopped thinking of him [a dog] and of all the poor abandoned creatures, lost, dying of hunger, terrified of everybody. That's the sort of thing I find infinitely more touching than all these stories of accidents to miners.'

The greatest compliment I can pay Mr. Sainsbury is that his version is more readable than the unabridged original; one is grateful for his omissions. What survives and gives pleasure is the frankness and toughness of Léautaud in literary matters, his weakness and irresolution in affairs of the heart and the honesty which kept him at the hub of the other writers of integrity who were centred round the *Mercure de France*. One need not be sorry for him. 'There's just one thing I wouldn't want changed, and that's my family. It has brought too much grist to my mill. . . .' 'I was asked the other day: "What are you doing nowadays?" "I'm busy growing older," I answered, "it's a wholetime job".'

29

ALAIN-FOURNIER

HENRI ALAIN-FOURNIER was born in 1886 and, like his friend Péguy, was killed soon after war broke out in 1914. His greatest friend, Jacques Rivière, who married his sister, was taken prisoner at the same time and survived until 1925. Five years younger than Apollinaire and as many older than Cocteau, Alain-Fournier belongs to the French 'lost generation', the flower of youth and talent who went happily and instantly to battle, dying for a cause they knew to be right before disillusion and war-weariness had set in.

Alain-Fournier's short life of twenty-eight years contained only three movements. Childhood, a lonely intense ecstatic childhood in the breckland of Sologne where his father was a village school-teacher; youth, haunted by the vision of a beautiful girl with whom he had five minutes' conversation and who was to be the love of his life; and early manhood, devoted to the integration of this ideal love and the lost paradise of his childhood into a work of art which appeared in 1913 (a year before *Du côté de chez Swann*) as a novel, *Le Grand Meaulnes*. Into this novel he put almost everything that had happened to him and the whole of his inner life. A year later he was dead.

> Heureux ceux qui sont morts dans une juste guerre
> Heureux les épis mûrs et les blés moissonnés.

A few days ago I heard a familiar voice on the wireless exhorting the young: 'Above all, skip the romantics!' 'Skip poetry, skip literature,' he might almost have said, 'away with rebellion, loss, inspiration and wonder.' For it is what an artist does with his romanticism that constitutes modern literature.

Henri Alain-Fournier not only accounted the world well lost for love (his youth is a chronicle of failed examinations) but considered love well lost for art. He stumbled on the same vision of the lost paradise as Proust but while Proust devoted his imagination and intelligence over many years to digesting the honey-dew through Bergsonian philosophy, Alain-Fournier was more robust and at the same time more mystical. He was determined to create a magical world that was only just around the corner, plausible in space and time. His world derives from *Dominique* and *Sylvie*, *Axel* and Kipling and Hardy, above all from the overwhelming satisfactoriness of Debussy's *Pelléas et Mélisande*; it is a world of symbolism suddenly immersed under a cold douche of reality and emerging strengthened, as in the work of his two contemporaries, Eliot and Kafka, a closed ingrowing vision.

When he was twenty he wrote:

> My credo in art and literature is childhood. To succeed in expressing it without any childishness (cf. Rimbaud) with its depths which border on mystery. Perhaps my future book will be a continuous and unconscious coming and going between dream and reality. . . .

And later:

> I only like the marvellous when it is firmly bound up with reality, not when it overwhelms it or surpasses it.
>
> Je cherche la clef de ces évasions vers les pays désirés, et c'est peutêtre la mort après tout.

The objection usually made to *Le Grand Meaulnes* as a novel is that the first part, the evocation of childhood, is so much the best. To a romantic, childhood is the only time; the rest of life a sequel. But Alain-Fournier was quite aware of this; he was determined to go forward from the difficult point although he knew that solutions are the bane of mysteries, that they assuage curiosity but never satisfy the secret hopes which mysteries engender. 'Well, listen, it's all ended, the fête is ended,' cries the bridegroom,

Frantz de Galais, and for two-thirds of the novel we must continue with its repercussions. The sequel is adult and exciting.

Mr. Gibson's biography[1] should be read by all who love Fournier and all who wish to learn how to construct a work of art. It is admirably done and the threads and patterns of this brief, uneventful but enormously rich and poetic existence are brought out with sympathetic scholarship. Writers who desire to learn how magic is made should not skip this.

[1] *The Quest of Alain-Fournier*, by Robert Gibson (Hamish Hamilton).

PART THREE

THE MODERN MOVEMENT

2

HENRY JAMES

'I TAKE possession of the old world—I inhale it—I appropriate it,' wrote James to his parents from London in 1875. He was to spend a year in Paris and several more in Bolton Street, in what was to prove his adopted country.

When one looks at the current flight of the intelligentsia to America where everyone stays until their permits are up it seems hardly credible that the most gifted American of his generation should have elected to live in England out of admiration for our way of life and the conditions it afforded his work. Why did he not choose France? 'The longer I live in France' (a letter to his brother supplies the answer) 'the better I like the French personality, but the more convinced I am of their bottomless superficiality.'

The important factor for the novelist, granted the initial dissatisfaction with his own country, was that he could never be really accepted by the French, only by the Franco-Americans ('I saw that I should be an eternal outsider'), while in England he could burrow deep into the social ramifications of society. 'I think a position in society is a legitimate object of ambition.'

As a disciple of Balzac, James considered people in high position as the natural subjects for his art. In England a ruling-class which still governed the greater part of the world would throw open all doors to the intoxicating charm and deferential intelligence of this handsome, bearded, impeccably punctilious stranger. The miracle was to happen once again when the most brilliant American of a succeeding generation fell into our arms, like James to be rewarded with the Order of Merit. Can we do it a third time?

Sir Robert Lowell, Dame Mary McCarthy, the Viscount Lolita...?

Professor Edel quotes James's familiar indictment of America from his *Hawthorne*:

No sovereign, no court, no personal loyalty, no aristocracy, no church, no clergy, no army, no diplomatic service, no country gentlemen, no palaces, no castles, nor manors, nor old country houses, nor parsonages, no cathedrals, no little Norman churches, no great university nor public schools, no literature, no lords, no museums, no pictures, no political society, no sporting class—no Epsom nor Ascot. . . .

And best of all—no nannies. What is much less known, in fact quite unfamiliar to me, is James's extraordinary prediction in a letter to his brother of January, 1878.

I have a sort of feeling that if we are to see the *déchéance* of England it is inevitable, and will come to pass somewhat in this way. She will push further and further her non-fighting and keeping-out-of-scrapes policy—until contemptuous Europe, growing audacious with impunity, shall put upon her some supreme and unendurable affront. Then—too late—she will rise ferociously and plunge clumsily and unpreparedly into war. She will be worsted and laid on her back—and when she is laid on her back will exhibit—in her colossal wealth and pluck—an unprecedented power of resistance. But she will never really recover as a European power.

Victorian England then seemed to him the strongest and richest power in the world. 'My dream is to arrive at the ability to be, in some degree, its moral portrait painter.'

Professor Edel is a meticulous, sympathetic if rather flat biographer and this second volume[1] carries his hero (born 1843) up to the age of forty. The book leaves nothing to be desired for fullness and accuracy or for the understanding of the great Irishman[2] and his circle. It records the day-by-day struggles of a young novelist with an unerring sense of vocation and a private income to provide himself with 'a position in society'.

[1] *Henry James: The Conquest of London*, 1870-83, by Leon Edel (Hart-Davis).

[2] His grandfather emigrated from County Cork.

He tried Rome, Paris and finally London; he was determined not to marry. He liked to work most of the day, and see people in the evening; he dined out one London season 140 times and met all the other professional diners out; otherwise he ate at his club. It is a life without adventure, without passion, without ambition, except to write well, a Balzac without debts, a Proust without pederasty. 'I know what I want—it stares one in the face as big and round and bright as the full moon; I *can't* be diverted or deflected.'

The prudent social advancement of the 'bachelor of Bolton Street', the cultivation of the right hostesses, the most worthwhile old ladies, the passing muster with the harpy husbands, the friendships with a few sympathetic but correct young men on the same moving stairway would prove an intolerable chronicle were it not for the development of his genius. Small wonder that, in later life, he grew so fond of Hugh Walpole.

This genius was greatly furthered by his friendships in Paris with Turgenev and Flaubert. Professor Edel tries to remove the bad impression that James's strictures on Flaubert have produced and stresses the great sympathy between them. I am not altogether convinced and I think a few more years in literary Paris, perhaps a few sessions with Verlaine, Rimbaud, Mallarmé, Villiers would have done him a world of good. 'How many more strange flowers might have been gathered up and preserved.' For James's best work lies outside this volume of the biography and during all this time he was rather aiming to be a fashionable best-seller—which, with *Daisy Miller*—he nearly became. *The Portrait of a Lady* is the transitional masterpiece which closes this first period. Professor Edel's book is a 'must' for all James-lovers; a 'may-be' for the rest.

2

GISSING

In the snow-bound country small-hours the intensity of the silence becomes a form of life-giving medium like the blood which the ghosts sip in Homer. The last spirit to materialise has been that of Gissing, whose *Private Papers of Henry Ryecroft*[1] I have just read for the first time. What a marvellous book!

The *Private Papers* were published in 1903, a few months before Gissing's death at the age of forty-five. They were written in seven weeks (exquisite hoax!) at St. Honoré les Bains, and purport to be the journal of a year spent in country retirement by a battered literary hack who has been left an annuity of three hundred a year by a friend.

About a hundred little essays take the reader through the four seasons, from spring to the first appearance of the lesser celandine beside the author's beloved Exe. Ryecroft is ten years older than Gissing, older at times even than the estuary by which he potters, a disciple of Lao Tse and Epicurus, an elegiac and a quietist, drunk with books and liberty and the beauty of England. 'Here was a man who, having his desire and that a very modest one, not only felt satisfied but enjoyed great happiness.'

Why is this such a good book? It is a daydream, a puritan's self-forgiveness on the edge of the grave, releasing the vision of an ideal life as seen by a tired, ill, impoverished and unhappily married Londoner whose imaginative intensity gives an almost eerie quality to the daily round which he so realistically depicts. Then, too, he happens to be a very intelligent man, in bitter

[1] By George Gissing. Introduction by Cecil Chisholm (Phoenix House).

opposition to the modern age; there is plenty of aggression in his philosophy; for he understands that the man who seeks his own peace will always have the world for his enemy:

> More than half a century of existence has taught me that most of the wrong and folly which darken earth is due to those who cannot possess their souls in quiet; that most of the good which saves mankind from destruction comes of life that is led in thoughtful stillness. Every day the world grows noisier; I, for one, will have no part in that increasing clamour and, were it only by my silence, I confer a boon on all.

A third virtue is the style, which might be described as 'semi-precious', for it lingers near the edge of preciosity (so common in the 'nineties) but never trips over. A keen, exact eye for the details of the countryside, an astringent critical gift, a vein of satire, a touch of epigram keep the mixture light, crisp and sparkling yet set like a jelly in the mellifluous prose.

A much greater artist, like Horace, might have varied the pace and changed the mood more often while a writer who was actually living such a round would have recorded some of the horrors, the boredom and inertia which descend in high summer and deep winter; but then he would have lacked the strange earthy hunger of the imagination peculiar to the ailing Gissing. And of course in a way he cheated. A misanthrope seldom receives an annuity of three hundred a year out of the blue, a misogynist seldom finds a housekeeper who is more of a treasure than any wife, nor a Londoner a climate as ideal as that of Ryecroft's Topsham.

In his excellent introduction Mr. Chisholm speculates how this book will be received today. Ryecroft was an extreme petty-bourgeois reactionary, a pacifist, a hater of democracy and a lover of Shakespeare and Johnson, Sterne and Lamb, order and the roast beef of old England. He was determined, for one year, to put the clock back. He was right, however, not so much in his politics as in his spiritual outlook. Everything he says about freedom, independence and literature holds good today. We cannot write well unless our minds are happy and stimulated; the spirit thrives only in close contact with nature, and when away from herd emotions, financial anxieties and great possessions. All else is vanity, and as Chamfort said when he left the Court 'qui quitte le parti, le gagne'.

'I should like to add to the Litany a new petition: "For all the inhabitants of great towns, and especially for all such as dwell in lodgings, boarding-houses, flats, or any other sordid substitute for Home which need or foolishness may have contrived".'

For all of these a mind—and a legacy—like Henry Ryecroft's.

3

NORMAN DOUGLAS

THIS would seem to be the first edition of *Old Calabria*[1] for twenty-five years. It belongs to the great tradition of English travel books: it is more solid than all the author's other work, and may well be that for which he is longest remembered.

It is introduced by Mr. John Davenport, who has some robust and original comments to make on the author. I knew him quite well myself, though I do not suppose I penetrated far beneath the surface. He was a happy man and though, I expect, very selfish, he managed to make others feel happy. This serene, ironic gaiety was not a pose nor did it proceed from an abdication of life: 'One can make just as big a fool of oneself at seventy as at thirty,' he once assured me at a time when infatuation for some young person caused him to spend painful evenings on the Big Wheels and switchbacks of a Paris circus.

Happiness is so rare among intellectuals that one wanted to know more about it. What philosophy had engendered it? What teachers, what lovers, what books? It was here that 'Uncle Norman's' reserve became impenetrable. The philosophers he admired most were those who had lived longest: Democritus, Xenophanes, Xenophilos of whom nothing is known but some hundred and fifty-odd summers.

I am inclined to think the source of his inner content was his Scots temperament and his good breeding which made him not expect too much from himself but assume the rôle of privileged

[1] By Norman Douglas (Secker and Warburg).

onlooker without self-questioning. And he was very Scottish, with a pawky and dreadful humour, as when he re-entered a Capri café to ask 'Has anyone found a toothpick tasting of ham?' I remember seeing him set off with some younger men on an expedition to the Chartreuse de la Verne. They had not taken provisions because there was supposed to be a restaurant nearby, but Douglas lingered behind a moment, gave out his extraordinary dry crackle of a laugh and with a clownish leer revealed the end of an enormous salami under his jacket.

No author was less literary; he never rolled words or gargled quotations yet his silvery tones could infuse a fine nuance of melancholy. His scientific training was the source of his thoroughness as an observer and even of his originality. For, on the whole, he did not always write very well. Time and again in enjoying his sensibility one is brought up short by a cliché or some tritely poetic expression. For this reason he is more memorable in attack than eulogy, though here too a hint of journalism would creep in.

On the eucalyptus:

> I never lose an opportunity of saying exactly what I think about this particularly odious representative of the brood, this eyesore, this grey-haired scarecrow, this reptile of a growth with which a pack of misguided enthusiasts have disfigured the entire Mediterranean basin.... A single eucalyptus will ruin the fairest landscape. No plant on earth rustles in such a horribly metallic fashion when the wind blows through those everlastingly withered branches; the noise chills one to the marrow; it is like the sibilant chattering of ghosts; its oil is called 'medicinal' only because it happens to smell rather nasty....

And so for another hundred lines, an uneven *tour de force* which never comes to a head. Here is a more poetic, but, even so, strangely tawdry piece on Croton:

> The temple has vanished, together with the sacred grove that once embowered it; the island of Calypso, where Swinburne took his ease (if such it was), has sunk into the purple realms of Glaucus; the corals and sea-beasts that writhed among its crevices are engulfed under mounds of submarine sand. There was life, once, at this promontory. Argosies

touched here, leaving priceless gifts; fountains flowed, and cornfields waved in the genial sunshine. Doubtless there will be life again; earth and sea are only waiting for the enchanter's wand.

No, it is not as a writer of prose but as a human observer, historian, master of dialects, wine-bibber, walker and botanist that Douglas shines in *Old Calabria*. Even as a controversialist he is beginning to date: 'The quaint Alexandrian *tutti-frutti* known as Christianity.' Well, let it pass.

His travel books have a quality we lack today; he knew not only the languages but the dialects, he met people the hard way by walking and by being alone, he frequented the vanishing world of priest, mayor, chemist and village schoolmaster—then cabined and confined by poverty and malaria, now self-consciously Hollywood.

Who now in those once remote parts could find such wine (symbol of humanist tradition and sociability) so cleverly:

> To this end, I generally apply to the priests; not because they are the greatest drunkards (far from it; they are mildly Epicurean or even abstemious) but by reason of their unrivalled knowledge of personalities. They know exactly who has been able to keep his liquor of such and such a year, and who has been obliged to adulterate it. . . . And failing the priests I go to an elderly individual of that tribe of red-nosed connoisseurs, the coachmen, ever thirsty and mercenary souls. . . .

4

OSCAR WILDE: I

'OSCAR WILDE has been dead long enough for an opinion of him and his work to be formed without prejudice,' opens Mr. St. John Ervine. His impartiality is maintained for two pages, after which, with a rapid gear-change, he reaches the cruising speed of bumbling vituperation which is kept up for the rest of the book[1].

An Ulsterman who has written lives of Carson and Craigavon, Mr. Ervine seems to have a temperamental and racial bias against Wilde; he combines the aggressiveness of Carson with the malice of Brookfield and yet there is something almost mechanical about his virulence, as if he feels real to himself only in moral indignation. 'Hate is a form of atrophy and kills everything but itself,' wrote Wilde in prison: and in this book it leads, despite some interesting dramatic criticism, to distortion and misrepresentation.

Thus, though by all accounts the disposition of Robert Ross was angelic, Mr. Ervine portrays him as a kind of monster. And of Wilde he writes: 'He bragged and boasted of his success, and demanded that his sycophants should boast and brag of it too. He sneered at rivals and belittled those who produced and performed his plays. They were unworthy of him. There was always a derogatory word on his lips for someone. . . . Other writers must be mentioned, if mentioned at all, only in derision.'

Now if there is one fact uniformly vouched for about Wilde it

[1] *Oscar Wilde: A present-time appraisal*, by St. John Ervine (Allen & Unwin).

is his total absence of malice: in this respect he was almost unique among wits. 'I knew Wilde,' said the late Bishop of London, Dr. Winnington Ingram, 'and in spite of his one great vice—which was surely pathological—I never met a man who united in himself so many lovable and Christian virtues.' As to this vice, Mr. St. John Ervine lays down the law like a Bottomley come to judgment: 'Ross, Wilde and Douglas were habitual and incorrigible liars, as all pederasts are. . . .' Bold words! But do they account for the extraordinarily long shadow which Wilde still casts from his tomb in Père Lachaise, or help us to understand the mystery of his tragedy?

Gratefully we turn back to the wisdom and charity of the present Lord Queensberry's account of the men who destroyed his inheritance, to Mr. Montgomery Hyde's admirably documented *Trials of Oscar Wilde*, and to the good humour and good sense of Mr. Hesketh Pearson. Best of all are the brief accounts of the two poets who saw beneath the mask—Yeats and Gide[1]. Indeed, it was in answer to Gide's disparagement of his writings that Wilde exclaimed: 'J'ai mis tout mon génie dans ma vie; je n'ai mis que mon talent dans mes œuvres'—what a cry of despair from the admirer of Ruskin and Arnold, the devoted disciple of Flaubert and Pater, the poet with a first in 'Greats' who knew that his art, however successful, had taken a wrong turning and who obscurely divined that some catastrophe was required to bring him back to the world of thought and poetry.

He wanted, of course, a catastrophe that was symbolic, not real; as he said to Gide, 'I must go on as far as possible. Something is bound to happen . . . something else.'

It was because, underneath his mask of flippancy, he was in despair that he allowed himself to fall completely under the spell of Lord Alfred Douglas. A man of forty is not destroyed by an undergraduate except by unconscious consent. Wilde's old life, his plays, his marriage, his social success were turning to dust and ashes. The 'great white caterpillar', as a lady described him,

[1] *Oscar Wilde*, by André Gide (William Kimber).

awaited the exhilarating puncture of the sandwasp, hopefully abdicating to an egotism fiercer than his own.

Douglas was a gifted and desperate young man in search of a substitute father; how could Wilde know that he would be treated exactly as Douglas had used his own poor Caliban of a parent, and eventually come to reproach Douglas in almost the same terms as Queensberry had used? 'You are the atmosphere of beauty through which I see life,' he writes at first; and even at the end, when he is becoming what Mr. Ervine calls 'a drunken sponger in the back-streets of Paris', he explains his fatal return to Douglas in a letter to Ross: 'I cannot live without the atmosphere of Love; I must love and be loved, whatever price I pay for it. . . .'

Wilde's truest remark was also made to Gide: 'My great mistake, the fault for which I can't forgive myself, is that one day I ceased my obstinate pursuit of my own individuality, stopped believing in it because I listened to someone else, stopped believing I was right to live like that and began to doubt myself.'

I take this 'someone' to be Douglas, an Alcibiades at war with society, who lured the happy aesthete of the 'eighties off his pedestal of wit into the gloom of the underworld and the glare of the law courts. 'And I? May I say nothing, my Lord?'

'His lordship made no reply beyond a wave of the hand to the warders, who hurried the prisoner out of sight. . . .'

5

OSCAR WILDE: 2

FIRST let us honour that rare combination, the scholar-publisher. Mr. Hart-Davis has got together enough Wilde letters to fill 800 pages, weeded out the inessential and the forgeries and contributed a mass of footnotes both necessary and readable, including thumb-nail biographies of all the recipients which are models of compression. The index is a pleasure, and I regret to say that this costly and splendid book,[1] fruit of so much exacting labour, is a 'must' for everyone who is seriously interested in the history of English literature—or European morals.

I use the word 'regret' purposely. For after reading through the whole volume carefully (including my third reading of *De Profundis*, for Mr. Hart-Davis includes the final—British Museum—text) I did regret having to give up three days to Wilde. 'I have put my genius into my life and only my talent into my work,' he said to André Gide; and it is in his letters that a man's life and work run closest.

But my three days with Wilde's letters are no proof of his genius. On the whole they are viscous, even oppressive, they adhere rather than delight and one is left with the impression of having escaped at last the clutches of some great greedy beetle. It is the same feeling as we get with Sade's letters. Perhaps prison, among other damage, gears people too closely to trivialities, to petty grievances about possessions. Certainly *De Profundis* is an obsessive piece of writing, a quicksand of self-pity and recrimination in which the reader is soon up to the neck.

[1] *The Letters of Oscar Wilde.* Edited by Rupert Hart-Davis (Hart-Davis).

Of the thousand letters here printed I should say that two-thirds were about money. It is an element in the condition of authorship that a great many letters must be about money; a writer is a fisherman with many lines out who must go around giving them all a tug. But Wilde's 'business sense', of which he was evidently proud (and which was really an obsession with money), caused him to expatiate at great length on royalties and percentages, while after his release from prison nearly every letter includes a request or demand and he suffered agonies from being quite penniless until some friend or publisher, often themselves impecunious, could send him ten or twenty pounds: one night Wilde said that by bankrupting him Queensberry had ruined him even more effectively than by putting him in gaol.

Early success had made him extravagant. Luxuries became necessities, prison was only a temporary alleviation of a psychological urge to play the king. Free again, he was like a great stranded whale, beached and blowing for his native element, the 'red and yellow gold' which had once come so easily. The only way to ease such sufferings is for friends to unite and provide an allowance which is paid in cash monthly, or better still weekly or even daily, taking in return any products of the pen. This is more or less what was being done for Wilde at the end by marvellous friends like Ross, Turner and More Adey.

It seems to me that with the years we all feel more and more guilty about Wilde and the paternal system of punishment which upheld the father (Lord Queensberry) and sent the prodigal off to stitch mail-bags with public howls of righteous sadism. Homosexuality, flogging, prison, capital punishment—they form one deep chord in our puritan natures.

When I last wrote about Wilde I suggested that he had himself desired his notoriety and punishment, partly out of a need for self-destruction, an instinct to free his talent from the unreality of success, partly from a desire to challenge the hypocrisies of social convention; and there are lines in the letters that support this claim:

> Why is it that one runs to one's ruin? Why has destruction such a fascination? Why, when one stands on a pinnacle, must one throw oneself down? No one knows, but things are so.

But a reading of the letters as a whole does not support this view. Wilde was clearly bowled over by Douglas. He never expected Queensberry's retaliation and walked straight into his trap. The truth only dawned on him in prison.

> Time after time, I tried, during those two wasted weary years, to escape, but he always brought me back, by threats of harm to himself chiefly. Then when his father saw in me a method of annoying his son, and the son saw in me the chance of ruining his father, and I was placed between two people greedy for unsavoury notoriety, reckless of everything but their own horrible hatred of each other, each urging me on, the one by public cards or threats, the other by private, or indeed half-public scenes, threats in letters, taunts, sneers. . . . I admit I lost my head. I let him do what he wanted. I was bewildered, incapable of judgment. I made the one fatal step. And now—I sit here on a bench in a prison cell. (To Ross, Nov. 1896.)

I think this is a true explanation. Wilde failed to understand the nature of the mutual hatred of Queensberry and his son, or how the son, by replacing his real father with the doting extravagant Wilde, was also casting him for the hated role. Was there much difference between his telegram to his father—'What a funny little man you are'—and his later message to the sick Wilde: 'When you are not on your pedestal you are not interesting. The next time you are ill I will go away at once.' Money incidentally also runs all through *De Profundis*. Wilde seems to think no one has ever kept anyone before.

Wilde's tragedy resulted from his need for love. It so happened that just after creating Dorian Gray he met his *garçon fatal*, then an undergraduate at Oxford who was being blackmailed. Wilde came to the rescue of beauty in distress and fell, perhaps for the first time in his life, hopelessly in love. He was on the hook, and even when he protested against Douglas's failings, his scenes, his extravagance, his petulance, the near-madness of his rages, he could not see that this invulnerable rival egotism was part of what kept him on the hook. Two kinds of desperation ran together. Wilde wrote his only real love-letters to Douglas, he was the 'graceful boy with a Christ-like heart', 'my immortal, my eternal love', 'my sweet rose, my delicate flower, my lily of lilies, it is perhaps in prison that I am going to test the power of love . . . I have had moments when I thought it would be wiser to separate. Ah! moments of weakness and madness.' 'You have been the supreme, the perfect love of my life. There can be no other.'

Perhaps the real tragedy of Wilde's life—assuming that prison or some equivalent suffering was necessary to the rehabilitation of his talent, as he sometimes believed—lay in the bad planning of his release. By going only as far as Dieppe and settling at Berneval he seemed on the threshold of a new and simpler existence, happy in freedom, natural beauties and little pleasures. But once these wore off, it was the *fin de saison* and the weather became British. Wilde easily succumbed to Douglas's appeals and went to join him in Naples.

'My only hope of again doing beautiful work in art is being with you.' When the friends protested at this ominous renewal he wrote defiantly to Ross, 'I cannot live without the atmosphere of Love. I must love and be loved whatever price I pay for it. . . . When people speak against me for going back to Bosie, tell them that he offered me love, and that in my loneliness and disgrace I, after three months' struggle against a hideous Philistine world, turned naturally to him. Of course I shall often be unhappy, but I still love him: the mere fact that he wrecked my life makes me love him.'

The Douglas family cut off Bosie's allowance, Mrs. Wilde cut off his and the poverty which neither could tolerate soon forced them to separate. Wilde's last reference runs, 'Bosie I have not seen for a week. I feel sure he will do nothing [for Wilde]. Boys, brandy and betting monopolise his soul. He is really a miser: but his method of hoarding is spending: a new type.'

Other lines of speculation suggested by the letters: whether Wilde's career would have been saved if he had joined the

Catholic Church at Oxford, as he so nearly did; or if he had, with his double first, become a school inspector, as he tried to do. Perhaps what emerges from his letters is his fatal indifference to the real demands of a talent. No one talked more about art and artists or worked less. He mistook greed and lust and vainglory for life and allowed insincerity and affectation to seep through everything he wrote, with such fatal facility, so that he survives only through his one comedy and a couple of melodramas.

He had all the gifts of a great writer except the conscience and was behind, rather than ahead of, his time. His two letters on penal reform to a daily newspaper are models of vigorous polemical writing, without humbug, and as modern as his early letters to his parents from Italy. They show what he might have done without his exhibitionism. But then we should not have had his conversation.

Mr. Vyvyan Holland deserves a word of special thanks for allowing the letters to be printed in their entirety.

6

THE BREAKTHROUGH IN MODERN VERSE

When did modern poetry begin? And how? And what is it? These questions sound impossible to answer and so instead of replying to them, I should like to record some events which can be accurately dated and leave it to the reader to decide how far they are relevant.

One thing is certain, modern poetry exists; it has claimed new areas for its own, it has developed a new sensibility and enlarged our consciousness; there is something intelligent and energetic about it, an integrity, a depth of imagination which we recognise immediately and whose absence we are quick to detect.

*

The winter of 1907 was a cold one. One night the lecturer in French and Spanish at Wabash College, Crawfordsville, Indiana (he had taken a master's degree in Romance languages at the State University of Pennsylvania), went out late into a blizzard to post a letter. On the street he ran across a girl from a stranded burlesque show, penniless and hungry. He fed her and took her to his rooms, where she spent the night in his bed and he on the floor of his study. (We can believe this in 1907.)

When he left in the morning for his eight o'clock class, the two maiden landladies, the Misses Hall, went up to do the cleaning. They discovered his visitor and at once telephoned the President of the College and several trustees. The dismissed lecturer (he was then twenty-two) took a cattle-ship to Gibraltar and then walked through Spain and Southern France to Venice, where he published his first book of poems, *A Lume Spento*. Later in the same year he came to England, where he was to remain until 1921.

Ezra Pound had two very remarkable qualities: he was a poet and, despite his passion for the past, a deeply original one. He was also something rarer than a poet—a catalyst, an impresario, a person who both instinctively understood what the age was about to bring forth and who helped it to be born. We recognise this quality in Apollinaire, in Cocteau, in Diaghilev, in André Breton. Apollinaire also combined a backward-looking vein in his own poetry with a flair for discovering what was forward-looking in others; he was five years older than Pound and grew up at the centre of the modern movement instead of having to find his way there from the periphery.

Arrived in London in 1908, Pound produced two more books the next year, one of which was reviewed by Edward Thomas in *The English Review*, and he began to throw his weight about.[1] He formed a coterie of promising writers who lunched once a week to discuss poetry and very soon met Yeats, who was regarded as the outstanding poet of the 'nineties, a devotee of all that was aesthetic and occult: 'a great dim figure with its associations set in the past', Pound called him.

In these early books of Pound's the influences are from the 'nineties and the early Yeats, and Browning, especially the latter's method of introducing fully-drawn character studies by casual conversation ('That's my last Duchess')—and, of course, the formal rhyme-structures from the Provençal. Yeats was twenty years older than Pound and, for all his success, was becoming deeply dissatisfied with his work and his life, long sacrificed to an unhappy love-affair. There is no doubt that Pound's peculiar serum immediately began to take: 'This queer creature Ezra Pound, who has become really a great authority on the troubadours,' wrote Yeats to Sir William Rothenstein in December

[1] *Personae* (dedicated to 'Mary Moore of Trenton if she wants it') and *Exultations*. The *Review* was edited by Ford Madox Ford with assistance from Norman Douglas, Conrad and others.

1909. 'A headlong, rugged nature, and he is always hurting people's feelings, but he has, I think, some genius and goodwill.'

*

1912 was an important year for Pound. He brought out his fifth book of poems, *Ripostes* (dedicated, incidentally, to William Carlos Williams), in which his authentic voice began to be heard. It is a tone of cool, relaxed dandyism, playing with the forms of the Greek and Latin epigram, yet capable of a deeper magic—as in 'Portrait d'une femme' ('Your mind and you are our Sargasso sea' or 'The Tomb at Akr Çaar', or his bleakly alliterative adaptation of the Anglo-Saxon 'The Seafarer'). At the end of the book Pound included the 'poetical works' of a new friend, the youthful T. E. Hulme.

> They are reprinted here for good fellowship; for good custom, a custom out of Tuscany and Provence; and thirdly, for convenience, seeing their smallness of bulk; and for good memory, seeing that they recall certain evenings and meetings of two years gone, dull enough at the time, but rather pleasant to look back upon.

This dates the poems between 1910 and 1912. Here is one of them [1908]:

> A touch of cold in the autumn night
> I walked abroad,
> And saw the ruddy moon lean over a hedge
> Like a red-faced farmer.
> I did not stop to speak, but nodded,
> And round about were the wistful stars
> with white faces like town children.

If that is not a modern poem—but we must hurry on. During the winter of 1912-13 Yeats was ill with a digestive disorder and sometimes unable to read. Pound came to read to him in the evenings, and even taught him to fence. (He also knew ju-jitsu and once threw Robert Frost over his back in a restaurant.) Wordsworth and Bridges were among the poets they read and discussed —at a later sojourn they read through the whole of Landor. Pound soon became indispensable and was taken on as Yeats's secretary. In the autumn of 1913 the pair settled down for the next three winters at Stone Cottage in Ashdown Forest. 'Ezra never shrinks from work, a learned companion and a pleasant one. . . . He is full of the Middle Ages and helps me to get back to the definite and concrete, away from modern abstractions; to talk over a poem with him is like getting you to put a sentence into dialect. All comes clear and "natural",' Yeats wrote to Lady Gregory.

It was then that they planned the selection of letters to Yeats from his father which Pound eventually edited (1917). Yeats passed on to Pound a prize for £50 which he received from *Poetry, Chicago* (editor, Harriet Monroe). I do not think it is far-fetched to see Pound's bias towards the 'definite and concrete' as influencing Yeats in the stupendous transformation, which bore fruit in his next book, *Responsibilities* (Cuala Press, 1914). It begins with the great prelude:

> . . . Pardon that for a barren passion's sake,
> Although I have come close on forty-nine
> I have no child. I have nothing but a book,
> Nothing but that to prove your blood and mine.

and ends with 'A coat' (first draft 1912):

> I made my song a coat
> Covered with embroideries
> Out of old mythologies
> From heel to throat;
> But the fools caught it,
> Wore it in the world's eyes
> As though they'd wrought it.
> So let them take it
> For there's more enterprise
> In walking naked.

'Yeats,' said Pound, 'is much finer *intime* than seen spasmodically in the midst of the whirl. We are both, I think, very contented in Sussex.' The main event was a visit to Wilfrid Blunt on his seventieth birthday, when Yeats made a speech and a group of poets, headed by Pound, presented the old poet-squire with a book each in a stone casket made by Gaudier-Brzeska. He regaled them with roast peacock 'in the pride of his eye'.[1] Pound's talent as an impresario led him naturally to editing and he was soon occupied with *Poetry*, *Chicago* (and Harriet Monroe), *The Egoist*, London (and Harriet Weaver), and Ford Madox Ford's *English Review*. He begins to mention the names of Lawrence, Lewis and Joyce, and by 1915 he is deeply involved in the successful transaction by which Yeats obtained for Joyce, then teaching in Trieste, a civil list grant of £75.

In 1914 he edited his first anthology, *Des Imagistes*, with poems by several well-to-be-known writers, Joyce, Aldington, H.D. He had also come to know Wyndham Lewis soon after his arrival and to be associated with him in *Blast* and also with Cubism and Gaudier-Brzeska about whom, in 1916, he wrote a book. *Blast* was a large, thick, luscious magazine, the first number of which (1914) is rather disappointing. It held a dinner on the fifteenth of July. 'We were the first organised youth racket,' wrote Lewis afterwards.

In his *Gaudier*, Pound explains how his poems are written. He once saw several beautiful faces in the Paris Métro and, walking down the Rue Raynouard, 'found the equation, a pattern, little splotches of colour, like a non-representative painting'. He wrote a thirty-line poem and destroyed it as 'work of secondary in-

[1] January 18th, 1914. 'All the poets behaved well except poor X—.' The peacock was Yeats's suggestion and was followed by roast beef. A paper read by Yeats proclaimed, according to Pound, his new manner. The poets were Richard Aldington, F. S. Flint, F. Manning, John Masefield (absent), Sturge Moore, Victor Plarr and Yeats. Bridges, because of Blunt's political opinions, could not be invited, Belloc came down after lunch.

> 'We who are little given to respect,' declaimed Pound,
> 'Respect you, and having no better way to show it
> Bring you this stone to be some record of it.'

tensity'. Six months later he made a poem half the length. A year later 'I made the following haiku-like sentence:

> The apparition of these faces in the crowd:
> Petals on a wet black bough.

I dare say it is meaningless.'

*

But his greatest discovery comes in a letter to Harriet Monroe of September 30th, 1914: 'I was jolly well right about Eliot. He has sent in the best poem I have yet had or seen from an American. PRAY GOD IT BE NOT A SINGLE AND UNIQUE SUCCESS. He is the only American I know of who has made what I call adequate preparation for writing. He has actually trained himself *and* modernized himself on his own.' The poem was 'The Love Song of J. Alfred Prufrock', which Harriet Monroe sat on warily till June 1915.

Pound's own programme was limited to three points which he had first published in 1913. He had dwelt on the necessity of distinct presentation of something concrete: on accuracy and economy of language—'to use absolutely no word that does not contribute to the presentation' and, regarding rhythm, on the necessity of composing 'in the sequence of the musical phrase, not in the sequence of the metronome'. Eliot must have wholeheartedly accepted all three.

*

Thomas Stearns Eliot was born in Saint Louis in September 1888, and is three years younger than Pound. He comes of a distinguished New England family of Wessex origin and went up to Harvard in 1906. He spent a post-graduate year in Paris, 1910-11, and was in Germany with a travelling fellowship in the summer before the war. When the war broke out in 1914 he had moved to England, and was reading Greek philosophy at Merton College, Oxford, at the time he sent Pound his poems, for which Conrad Aiken had tried unsuccessfully to find a publisher.

As he dates them from 1909, these early poems of Eliot are really contemporaneous with the early Pound and with T. E. Hulme—but the year of his flowering is without question 1915, when 'The Love Song of J. Alfred Prufrock' at last appeared in *Poetry* (June). In July the second or war number of *Blast* contained the two 'Preludes' and 'Rhapsody on a Windy Night', while 'Portrait of a Lady' was published in *Others* (U.S.A.) in September, and three more short poems in *Poetry* for October.

In November, Pound brought out his *Catholic Anthology* (catholic in taste, he meant), being 'determined to get Eliot between hard covers'. This is an astonishing book and certainly the first in the canon of modern poetry, containing, besides five poems by Eliot, a new poem by Yeats and poems by Carl Sandburg, William Carlos Williams, Maxwell Bodenheim and others. In 1914 Pound had married the daughter of Yeats's friend, Mrs. Shakespear. In 1915, Eliot too got married. This was also the year of Lawrence's *Rainbow* and Virginia Woolf's first novel, *The Voyage Out*.

In 1916 Eliot published four more poems in *Poetry* (including 'La Figlia che piange'), but his great year was 1917, when his first book, *Prufrock and Other Observations*, was published at a shilling by the Egoist Press, London, while his second, the anonymous *Ezra Pound, his Metric and Poetry*, came out in New York (November). 1915 had been the year of Pound's adaptations of Chinese poems, *Cathay*, and 1916 of his first volume of truly modern work—chiefly songs and epigrams—*Lustra*, a light-hearted narcissistic essay in linguistic deflation.

Dawn enters with little feet
Like a gilded Pavlova
And I am near my desire,
Nor has life in it aught better
Than this hour of clear coldness,
The hour of waking together.
[in a garret]

*

It will be seen that there is now an increasing acceleration, that the Pound-Eliot streams have become a river and that the whole movement, first of 'Imagists', then of 'Vorticists' (names chosen by Pound), like Cubism in France, was well under way by 1914, only to come up against the blind holocaust of the war. Hulme was killed, so was Gaudier-Brzeska; Lewis became a bombardier; Ford joined up; Joyce remained in Trieste and Zürich, although the 'Portrait of the Artist as a Young Man' continued to appear in *The Egoist*; Lawrence suffered persecution; neither Pound nor Yeats took any part in what the latter called the 'bloody frivolity' of the war. Eliot was trying to earn a living by journalism but eventually registered.

So this movement, in all its energy and subtlety, was maimed and permanently slowed down by the 'march of events'. These young men were denied the insouciant gaiety and freedom of experiment to which every new generation is entitled and also the opportunity of slow self-development through scholarly research. Yeats, however, found his voice in the Easter rebellion of 1916 and wrote his magnificent 'I have met them at close of day' in September of that year. His new-found realism dominated the next slim volumes, *The Wild Swans at Coole* and *Michael Robartes and the Dancer* (Cuala Press, 1917 and 1920). But Pound and Eliot by now were without a country, and it was to be ten years before these patriarchs of the Lost Generation finally adopted erastian England and fascist Italy as their spiritual homes. Pound in England, with his shock of hair, red beard, ten-gallon hat and velvet jacket, striding about the streets with head thrown back and shouting out lines of his poetry, 'Damn it all! All this our South stinks peace' in Bellotti's, was, according to Lewis, always a fish out of water.

'Ezra started out in a time of peace and prosperity,' wrote Aldington, 'with everything in his favour, and muffed his chances of becoming literary dictator—to which he undoubtedly aspired —by his own conceit, folly and bad manners. Eliot started in the enormous confusion of war and post-war England, handicapped in every way. Yet by merit, tact, prudence and pertinacity, he succeeded in doing what no American has ever done—imposing his personality, taste and even many of his opinions on post-war England.'

*

These first books of our brief literary renaissance have a particular beauty. They come before the more self-conscious era of limited editions from costly private presses or the uniform assembly line of modern poets which we associate with Faber's. The *Catholic Anthology* (Elkin Mathews, 1915), with its Cubist cover, opens with Yeats's 'Scholars' ('Bald heads forgetful of their sins') and then goes straight into Prufrock:

> Let us go then, you and I
> When the evening is spread out against the sky
> Like a patient etherized upon a table;
> Let us go through certain half-deserted streets . . .

I can never read the opening of this marvellous poem without feeling that it is a piece of modern music, that I am sitting back in my seat at the first hearing of the Debussy Quartet—of which I am reminded by that sudden shatteringly discordant metaphor, 'like a patient etherized upon a table', in the third line. And as for the end—

> I have heard the mermaids singing, each to each,
> I do not think that they will sing to me.
> I have seen them riding seaward on the waves,
> Combing the white hair of the waves blown back
> When the wind blows the water white and black
> We have lingered in the chambers of the sea
> By seagirls wreathed with seaweed red and brown
> Till human voices wake us, and we drown.

—though we know it so well, the changes of mood—the flat beginning, the gathering crescendo with the harsh, astonishing vowel-sounds and rhymes, and the bold repetition of 'white', leading to the lovely dying cadence where 'red and brown' replaces the 'white and black' of the storm—never cease to intoxicate; like the three 'Preludes' and the 'Rhapsody', on the enormous thick blotting paper of *Blast*. How many realized that here was an urban lyricism, an absolutely original sensibility, something serenely new?

The winter evening settles down
with smell of steaks in passage ways
Six o'clock
The burnt out ends of smoky days . . .
The conscience of a blackened street
Impatient to assume the world.
I am moved by fancies that are curled
Around these images and cling:
The notion of some infinitely gentle,
Infinitely suffering thing . . .

*

To heighten the effect of these poems, or of a purely cubist experiment like Pound's 'Dogmatic Statement on the Game and Play of Chess' (which is really a 'vorticist' painting), or of the general Picasso-awareness of *Blast* under Lewis's dominating personality, one should contrast them with the ordinary poetry which was currently produced. 'The situation of poetry in 1909 or 1910 was stagnant to a degree difficult for any young poet of today to imagine' (T. S. Eliot). There was Bridges, to whom (in 1915) Yeats sent Pound's *Cathay*, and academics like Binyon and Sturge Moore, and there were the first two series of *Georgian Poetry* (1911-12 and 1913-15) edited by Edward Marsh. These were particularly disliked by Pound. The contributors to both series were Lascelles Abercrombie, Gordon Bottomley, Rupert Brooke, W. H. Davies, Walter de la Mare, John Drinkwater, James Elroy Flecker, Wilfrid Wilson Gibson, D. H. Lawrence, John Masefield, Harold Monro and James Stephens. Ralph Hodgson appeared in the second, G. K. Chesterton in the first.

I have read through both volumes but, *grisé par l'art moderne*, found them all lush or arid, whimsical or insipid. Pound thought Brooke the best of the bunch and his 'Fish' is, I think, an interesting poem, but to enjoy these warblers it is essential to forget

Pound's three points and to like obsolete words with false sentiments and to listen to the metronome. There is no melodic line. There is one border-line case: Harold Monro, owner of the Poetry Bookshop and publisher of the *Chapbook* (not to be confused with Harriet Monroe, editress of *Poetry*, *Chicago*), who greatly encouraged the modern school and was gradually influenced by them. He alone appears in both *Georgian Poetry* and *Catholic Anthology*, and Pound and Eliot eventually wrote articles on him, treating him as a sincerely repentant late-comer. His poem 'Suburb' is already (1914) both pure Betjeman and a trailer for part of 'The Waste Land', or a story by Huxley.

. . . In all the better gardens you may pass
(Product of many careful Saturdays),
Large geraniums and tall pampas grass
Adorn the plots and mark the gravelled ways

Sometimes in the background may be seen
A private summer-house in white or green.

Here on warm nights the daughter brings
Her vacillating clerk
To talk of small exciting things
And touch his fingers through the dark.

He, in the uncomfortable breach
Between her trilling laughters,
Promises, in halting speech,
Hopeless immense Hereafters.

She trembles like the pampas plumes,
Her strained lips haggle. He assumes
The serious quest . . .

Now as the train is whistling past
He takes her in his arms at last.
It's done. She blushes at his side
Across the lawn—a bride, a bride.

*

The stout contractor will design
The lazy labourers will prepare
Another villa on the line;
In the little garden-square
Pampas grass will rustle there.

*

It will be seen that I have not attempted to explain why or how Ezra Pound, born in Idaho (though really an Easterner), or T. S. Eliot (a New Englander from Saint Louis), were or became poets. It is our good fortune that some divine restlessness sent them forth on their travels and brought them to our shores, where Yeats and Ford Madox Ford and Harold Monro and Wyndham Lewis were waiting to receive them. Both Pound and Eliot had a very unusual combination of gifts—revolutionary élan, first-class minds, and a most fastidious and critical ear. One is always surprised by Pound's taste, he is indeed the Catullus (a *gamin* Catullus, wrote a reviewer) of Yeats's 'Scholar' poem which, I fully believe, was intended for him. De la Mare, too, had such an ear, but belonged, like Graves, to the traditional Georgian song-canon.

Perhaps the war, although it interfered with their natural pattern of growth, gave them both an additional stiffening. But whatever the cause, the two expatriates came of age. The Pound of 'Lustra' is still a minor poet. With *Quia Pauper Amavi* he attains a stature which is worthy of the admiration since bestowed on him. The book was published by John Rodker at the Egoist Press in 1918—since it was also the publisher of Lewis's *Tarr*, Eliot's *Prufrock*, Marianne Moore's *Poems* and Joyce's *Portrait of the Artist*, the Egoist Press has a claim to fame similar to Elkin Mathews before it, and The Hogarth Press immediately after. The book consists almost entirely of long poems and includes the first three Cantos and 'Homage to Sextus Propertius'. The Cantos have not yet begun to belch forth huge lumps of prose like a faulty incinerator and include the lovely Elpenor passage paraphrased from Homer, while 'Homage to Sextus Propertius', complete with howlers, grows better at each re-reading, a complete identification of one fame-struck, slightly wearying dandy with his dazzling archetype. The passage of time encrusts the howlers with a hoary rightness.

In 1917 Yeats got married and Ezra Pound was the best man, while in Chicago Margaret Anderson founded one of the brightest of all magazines, *The Little Review*, to which Pound was appointed foreign editor. He started her off with a splendid poem by Yeats, 'In memory of Major Robert Gregory', and Yeats announced his opinion in a generous letter: 'When I returned to London from Ireland, I had a young man go over all my work with me to eliminate the abstract. This was an American poet, Ezra Pound.' Pound also brought them stories by Lewis and the serialisation of Joyce's *Ulysses*, which began in 1918: both these ended in disaster, for several numbers of the magazine were banned on account of them although Miss Anderson was defended by the Maecenas of the whole group, the Irish-American collector John Quinn.

The Irish rebellion, closely involving two of the women he loved (Maud Gonne's husband, John MacBride, was shot), was an extraordinary inspiration to Yeats and events in Ireland continued to arouse him till his visit to Oxford—

> When long ago I saw her ride
> Under Ben Bulben to the meet
> The beauty of her country side
> With all youth's lonely wildness stirred,
> She seemed to have grown clean and sweet
> Like any rock-bred, sea-borne bird;
>
> Sea-borne or balanced on the air
> When first it sprang out of the nest
> Upon some lofty rock to stare
> Upon the cloudy canopy
> While under its storm-beaten breast
> Cried out the hollows of the sea.

1922 was the year of triumph for Yeats. His *Later Poems* came out, illustrating his whole development from *The Wind among the Reeds* to *The Second Coming*, from 1899 to 1921. He also brought out his autobiography, *The Trembling of the Veil*, and a volume of his plays and eight more poems, including 'All Souls' Night' (the beginning of his intellectual manner), at the Cuala Press. Although Middleton Murry thought the *Wild Swans at Coole* (1919) 'eloquent of final defeat' and Pound pronounced him 'faded' in 1920, the greatest triumphs of his poetic life were all before him.

Eliot however seemed to be making heavy weather by 1917 and after failing to earn his living from journalism, took up working in a bank. His poetic output fell off slightly. There were four poems (three in French) for *The Little Review* in July 1917, four more in September 1918, three in 1919, the superb *Gerontion* in 1920, and then nothing till 1922. These were the years when Eliot was making a reputation as a critic, the years of his first collection of essays in *The Sacred Wood* (1920), and during which the Prufrock volume, enlarged by the new poems which appeared as The Hogarth Press *Poems* (1919), became *Ara Vos Prec* in 1920 (with *Gerontion*) and *Poems* 1920 in America.

In 1918 Sweeney comes on the scene, sensual among the nightingales, and a major difference between Eliot and Pound grows more apparent: Eliot understands suffering, 'the last twist of the knife' and becomes a deeper, ultimately Christian writer. Pound remains lightheartedly pagan, open to wonder and moments of lyrical sadness, but never portraying a stronger emotion than indignation, and that very rarely. His Hell, as Eliot was to point out, is for Englishmen he didn't like, not for himself. In *Lustra* Pound claimed that this cool, formal, elegiac dandyism was the best way to puncture the Georgians, the lush Swinburnian and Tennysonian cadences, the romantic inflation. He called it a 'work of purgation of minds'. Lacking the tragic sense of life which leads to the understanding of other people, his portraits as a result grow increasingly artificial, 'an art in profile'. Propertius is there without his anguish; and Pound's other major poem describes Hugh Selwyn Mauberley, an anglicised Prufrock who has walked out of Henry James to be intaglio'd by Gautier and who is too much a cardboard man even to be hollow. But *Mauberley* (Ovid Press, 1920) in which Pound bids his lethargic English audience a disdainful farewell, is a chain of lyrics flung out like a pattern of islands—'scattered Moluccas' which are a perpetual delight.

As whole books have been written about these exquisite poems and a Warden of All Souls has devoted much space to annihilating their defunctive music, I will only say that every other one seems perfect. [They include the most bitter anti-war poem ever written.] 'His true Penelope was Flaubert': that is what distinguishes Pound from all other revolutionaries; he flies his jolly roger from the ivory tower. Both *Quia Pauper Amavi* and *Mauberley* went unsold and uncelebrated and his increasing dislike of post-war England—where the Sitwells had replaced his own shock-troops, and where the gay demobilised second wave with Huxley, Graves, Robert Nichols and Sassoon gathered at the Café Royal and Tour Eiffel instead of Bellotti's and the Vienna Café—as well as his native restlessness drove him in 1921 on to Paris where he could continue to be foreign editor of *The Little Review* and discover the novelist Hemingway, the poet Cummings and the composer Antheil all within a year of his arrival. Here Joyce, financed by Miss Weaver at Pound's suggestion, had preceded him. He there ceases to be the clear-sighted troubadour and becomes the full-blown international exhibitionist, Gertrude Stein's 'Village Explainer', Lewis's 'Revolutionary Simpleton'. He had, however, one more midwifery duty to perform.

December 24th, 1921: Letter to T. S. Eliot

. . . The thing now runs from 'April' to 'Shantihk' without a break. That is nineteen pages and let us say the longest poem in the English langwidge. Don't try to bust all records by prolonging it three pages further. . . . Compliments, you bitch. I am wracked by the seven jealousies. . . .

March 18th, 1922: Letter to William Carlos Williams

Eliot, in bank, makes £500. Too tired to write, broke down; during convalescence in Switzerland did 'Waste Land', a masterpiece, one of most important nineteen pages in English. Returned to bank and is again gone to pieces physically. . . .

Of course I'm no more Mauberley than Eliot is Prufrock. Mais passons. Mauberley is a mere surface. Again a study in form, an attempt to condense the James novel. Meliora speramus. . . .

Eliot's 'Waste Land' is I think the justification of the movement, of our modern experiment, since 1900. It should be published this year.

It was. One should read it every April. In America it won the Dial prize and came out both in the magazine and as a book; in England it appeared in the first number of the *Criterion*, which Eliot was to edit and which also contained a review of *Ulysses*. The *annus mirabilis* of the modern movement was drawing to a close. Yeats's *Later Poems* and *The Waste Land*, *Ulysses* and *Women in Love*, *Jacob's Room* and Valéry's *Charmes*, with *Le Serpent* and the *Cimetière Marin*—the breakthrough is complete. I have left out two important minor poets, Marianne Moore (also from Saint Louis), who was first published in 1921, and the war-poet Wilfrid Owen (1920), and one major one—Edith Sitwell, because she deserves a study in herself and grew up in total isolation from any of these influences—a Christina Rosetti crossed with Pope—maturing considerably later. Her early works, especially *Façade* and *Bucolic Comedies*, and the poems in *Wheels*, do belong to this period, but it would not be easy to relate them, because they still tend to be formal exercises in technique until the *Sleeping Beauty* (1923).

In fact the Sitwells' part in the breakthrough, with their magazines *Wheels* and *Art and Letters*, is a separate, almost a self-contained subject. When Wyndham Lewis started to attack her, Yeats wrote to him (1930):

Somebody tells me that you have satirized Edith Sitwell. If that is so, visionary excitement has in part benumbed your senses. When I read her 'Gold Coast Customs' a year ago, I felt, as on first reading 'The Apes of God', that something absent from all literature for a generation was back again, and in a form rare in the literature of all generations, passion ennobled by intensity, by endurance, by wisdom. We had it in one man once. He lies in St. Patrick's now, under the greatest epitaph in history. Yours very sincerely, W. B. YEATS.

In the *Pisan Cantos* (1949) Pound, who has at last become acquainted with grief in his solitary cage at an American prison camp, recalls these formative years and 'lordly men to earth o'er-given'—Hulme and Ford and Blunt opening the door 'from a fine old eye the unconquered flame' and his three winters with Yeats

'At Stone Cottage in Sussex by the waste moor'.

7

YEATS'S CRUCIAL YEAR

YEATS was born in 1865, one of that generation of massive late Victorians who were to dominate our literature as their contemporaries Proust, Gide, Valéry, Claudel have done in France. He was our last great poet, perhaps because he was the last poet to speak for his nation. Mr. Eliot is something different, he is the laureate of our fragmentated age; the poet, critic, scholar, man of letters who tries to hold together a collapsing culture. He is not a monolith like Yeats, serene in his seventy-five years of fecund egotism, years devoted entirely to the writing of poetry or poetic drama and, except for a brief senatorial interlude, to reconciling the claims of philosophy and spiritualism.

This volume of his collected letters[1] contains nearly a thousand pages and, even so, many correspondents (Ezra Pound for instance) have had to be left out. Yeats was a tireless letter-writer and some of these series, as with Lady Gregory or Mrs. Shakespear, run for thirty or forty years. As one of those who are almost suffocated by the obligation of replying to even the most enchanting missive, I view these triumphs of order over chaos (for that is what these life-long mutual exchanges become) with growing respect and some dismay.

Yeats was a sound rather than a great letter-writer; he has no sparkle and very little fire; he is of the kind who seem to be issuing a daily bulletin rather than having in mind a particular recipient (this may be because all his letters to Maud Gonne are missing). Nevertheless this indispensable volume reveals his whole life.

It is a life lived entirely in and for the mind and therefore un-

[1] *The Letters of W. B. Yeats.* Edited by Allan Wade (Hart-Davis).

eventful except in so far as the mind embraced a cause, the literary renaissance of Ireland, which brought it into conflict with realities. It is not a visual mind; art, music, architecture, places, even books, play little part in his rich speculative inner life, bound up with Celtic fairy stories, myths, Indian mysticism and his intimations, some very startling, from the spirit world. The poetry comes as a surprise: a quite dull letter may lead up to a breath-catching set of verses.

So conventional is the formula of reserved intimacy (every letter is signed W. B. Yeats irrespective of destination) that one can hardly believe one has read correctly when the veil is lifted and he proposes, at fifty-one, to two young women within a month. But then he only began to live at fifty, and the difference is quite extraordinary between his letters before and after that crucial date.

Sept. 12, 1914.—England is paying the price for having despised intellect. The war will end I suppose in a draw and everybody too poor to fight for another hundred years, though not too poor to spend what is left of their substance preparing for it. Gregory, who is in London, writes describing the Zeppelin raid.

May 11, 1916.—The Dublin tragedy has been a great sorrow and anxiety. . . . I have little doubt there have been many miscarriages of justice. . . . I am trying to write a poem on the men executed—'terrible beauty has been born again'. I had no idea that any public event could so deeply move me—and I am very despondent about the future. At the moment I feel that all the work of years has been overturned, all the bringing together of classes, all the freeing of Irish literature and criticism from politics.

In the last twenty-five years of his life Yeats wrote the greater part of his finest poetry, developed his philosophy into 'A Vision', wrote his memoirs, married, and brought up two children. This is also the period of his best letters, of a ripening and hardening of his personality, a shedding of his vaguer, more easy-going, faintly priggish and precious eighteen-ninetyish self. His unrequited love for Maud Gonne, who had married MacBride in 1903, was perhaps laid to rest when (after MacBride had been shot) her daughter Iseult also rejected him.

There followed a highly successful return to reality and sexual matters, hitherto ignored altogether, begin to crop up with increasing frequency, almost dominating the very latest letters. These are by far the best; they show his unique judgment, his unerring encouragement of talent (Joyce, Wyndham Lewis, Edith Sitwell), his delightful appreciation of high-spirited young women writers like Lady Gerald Wellesley or Miss Ethel Mannin, his intimacy with the supernatural (to Mrs. Shakespear). Towards the end of every letter he has the habit of dropping some profound remark or some delicate self-revealing picture.

> When men are very bitter, death and ruin draw them on as a rabbit is supposed to be drawn on by the dancing of the fox.
>
> As my sense of reality deepens, and I think it does with age, my horror at the cruelty of government grows greater. . . . Communist, fascist, nationalist, clerical, anti-clerical are all responsible according to the number of their victims. I have not been silent. I have used the only vehicle I possess, verse.
>
> We poets would die of loneliness but for women, and we choose our men friends that we may have somebody to talk about women with.
>
> Passion to me is the essential. I was educated upon Balzac and Shakespeare and cannot go beyond them.
>
> I am an old man now, and month by month my capacity and energy must slip away, so what is the use of saying that both in England and Ireland I want to stiffen the backbone of the high-hearted and the high-minded and the sweet-hearted and sweet-minded so that they may no longer shrink and hedge when they face rag-merchants like ——.

The last of these quotations from the musings of this exemplary and dedicated life reveals the one weakness in the careful editing—too many names left out. Is not a gibe from a great poet preferable to oblivion?

8

EZRA POUND AS CRITIC

WITH exemplary piety, Mr. Eliot, like a scarab with its ball, continues to propel the collected works of 'Il miglior fabbro' over the watershed of the twentieth century. 'I hope that this volume[1] will demonstrate,' he writes, 'that Pound's literary criticism is the most important contemporary criticism of its kind.' This is a high claim which, coming from the other most important critic of his time, must be carefully considered.

Mr. Eliot divides the work into three sections: discussions of general ideas and critical standards (including 'How to Read'), essays on favourite authors of the past ('The Tradition') and reflections on young writers and contemporaries. He tells us what to look for:

> Pound has said much about the art of writing, and of writing poetry in particular, that is permanently valid and useful. Very few critics have done that.
>
> 2. He said much that was peculiarly pertinent to the needs of the time at which it was written.
>
> 3. He forced upon our attention not only individual authors, but whole areas of poetry, which no future criticism can afford to ignore. Mr. Pound is more responsible for the XXth century revolution in poetry than is any other individual.

Let me say at once that I find this volume more interesting than either Pound's letters or his translations; it contains both long

[1] *Literary Essays of Ezra Pound.* Edited and introduced by T. S. Eliot (Faber).

passages of close reasoning and brief notes and manifestoes which reveal the dry chirrup of this armchair cricket, the many-sided riches of his casual, muddled mind. He nominates his team: Wyndham Lewis and Gaudier-Brzeska (as artists), Joyce, Eliot, Jules Romains, William Carlos Williams, Aldington, H.D.; his pet precursors—Laforgue, Corbière, Rémy de Gourmont; his school —'Imagism'; his short list for the guillotine (Vergil, Milton, Tennyson); his ancestral gods (Confucius, Cavalcanti, Arnaut Daniel, the Elizabethan translators Golding and Douglas, Ovid, Catullus, Villon and Landor). It seems at first an immensely varied list, but, as one reads on, the same quotations from Provençal or Anglo-Saxon recur, the same phrases, the same jokes. The field is much more limited than it seems when we first look down on it, and certain vanities of universal erudition are more perceptible. 'De la Sade' for 'Sade', Parrhasius mistaken for a poet, not a painter—or two mysterious lines of Daniel hopelessly mistranslated.

The erudition in fact forms part of the pedagogic Zen shock-tactics of Mr. Pound with his class of young expatriates, even as the jocular disrespect for their predecessors is also part of their treatment, a literary osteopathy for a stiff-necked generation.

The most interesting essay seems to me to be that on Henry James, because reverence and disrespect here meet in a tidal race, the winds of modernity blow against the currents of Mr. Pound's American piety and the conflict is alive and foaming. In all his comments on French writers there is something to be found, but, though he may have rediscovered great tracts of medieval or renaissance or oriental literature, he blazes a very tiny trail. 'I leave these notes, rough as they are, to indicate a stock of matter needing explanation.' The formula might be repeated.

I enjoy his digs at Milton, Wordsworth, Tennyson, Gosse, Swinburne, and Dryden's 'outstanding aridity' without agreeing with them, and I deeply appreciate his attempts to clean up the lumber-room of poetry, to cut away vagueness and rhetoric and leave only what is vivid, clean, inspired, genuine and precise; but I cannot help wondering if the whole conception of *avant-garde* is not rather absurd when applied to his group of patient, gem-polishing Alexandrian archaists. Compared to Rimbaud, Mallarmé, Laforgue, or even Yeats and Hopkins, there is very little that is *avant-garde* about Aldington and H.D., and it seems to me that *Prufrock* and *The Waste Land* owe far more to Laforgue and the Elizabethans than to Mr. Pound, to whom the latter poem was dedicated. And I doubt whether Auden or Dylan Thomas owed him anything.

Perhaps there is no such thing as an *avant-garde*, only a few uncorrupted sensibilities who cling together in times of rampant militarism or commercialism to challenge their elders.

9

WASTE LAND AND T. S. ELIOT

I

For the next ten years this at first involuntary expatriate [Mr. T. S. Eliot] was condemned to labour at no profession in particular under constant financial strain . . . finally entering the foreign exchange department of Lloyds Bank (£120 per annum to start, no meals). When the United States Navy tendered him a medical rejection in 1918 he had for some years been working fifteen hours a day.

II

A grant from the American Philosophical Society made possible the collection of material, a Fellowship from the Guggenheim Foundation gave me [Mr. Kenner] leisure to write most of the book, and aid from the Committee on Research of the University of California at Santa Barbara financed the typing of the manuscript.

At this point, I should like to close my case and call no further witnesses, leaving the public to meditate on the fate of genius forty years ago and the rewards of talent today. For Mr. Kenner[1] is very talented; he performs tireless arabesques and figures of eight about Mr. Eliot like an expert young skater (I do hope he is young) round an old snowman. He 'explicates' and 'intuits', to use two of his words, until we are dizzy. Mr. Toynbee *jeune* considers this book to establish the pre-eminence of American criticism over our own. Mr. Davenport ambiguously crowns it as 'far and away the best book on T. S. Eliot'. I found it a brilliant but maddening display of auto-intoxication.

The reason is not far to seek. I am envious. It is no secret that I

[1] *The Invisible Poet: T. S. Eliot*, by Hugh Kenner (W. H. Allen).

was in receipt of a most generous grant from the Krutch foundation for a commentary on the greatest and most mysterious of English poems (pens, ink and paper supplied by the General Post Office, for I write only on telegraph forms) and that my subsidies ran out before I had got beyond the first line of what would have been a seminal work of English criticism.

Three Blind Mice

'I know of no more lambescent onset, no more miraculous *donnée*, no more shattering epiphany outside the Japanese Hai-Kai of what is in its bland defiance of the natural order where even one nystagmic rodent is the infelicitous (no feline intended) exception, so chamfered a challenge to our ambient seriousness. This basic ideogram stems entelechically from the remote sub- or preconscious of our anthropoid order. At first we are stunned (and it was intended that we should be stunned) by those three long vowels, like the toc toc toc of Molière's curtain rising, and by the range of consonant from dental to labial.

'A brief methodological examination reveals, however, the absence of the incantatory "oom" sound as in "om mani padme hum" which gives the spinning-top vibration of the universe. Applying this tuning fork to the melodic structure (and if ever there incantation were, this is it) we perceive the basic hum only if the words are pronounced with a Scotch accent.

' "See hoo they roon," supplies us at once with the true provenance of the poem—for it could not be articulated in any other way. We are still faced with the original difficulty—when even one blind mouse (Blind = castrated) is a *rara avis* how came that there were three—and all in running order? What is a mouse? in campus parlance—a young woman ("Dig that mouse with the bedroom hair") and what are three—and blind as well? The three Fates whose Greek name "Moirai" suggests the French and Roman dormouse—*loir*—so.

Three blind moirs
See who they rune . . .

'The last tumbler falls into place. "Fare forward!" '

A thin, firm minor music, of ceremonious intricacy, dissolving the world of Tiresias, Hamlet and Mrs. Equitone, creating in the zone vacated by that world 'a place of solitude where three dreams cross', a visionary process in which a symbolic stair has (incidentally) a banister, and three symbolic leopards sit quietly because their stomachs are full; a wholly transparent network of allusions, tautly nourished, like a nervous system, from secret sources among which research will discover nothing irrelevant; a religious poem which contains no slovenly phrase, no borrowed zeal, no formulated piety; this improbable achievement subsumes for good the secular Eliot whose traces of original Richard Savage precipitated in his poems an arresting residue of gritty substantiality.

This prolegomena to his exegesis of 'Ash Wednesday' is Mr. Kenner's way of saying that Mr. Eliot's conversion bore fruit in a change of attitude and in a group of poems which are perfect of their kind, and it is a brilliant way of saying it, but a typical paragraph in a whole book of clotted, overwritten commentary. After all, why drag in Richard Savage, a near-criminal who bears no relation to the secular Eliot, a young Harvard man trying to earn a literary living? How can a line like 'Pray for us now and at the hour of our death' be said not to include borrowed zeal or formulated piety?

I admire Mr. Kenner's devotion to Mr. Eliot; to have known and loved Mr. Eliot's poetry from Prufrock to Sweeney was a major experience of my youth. I can still read it and about it for ever. I can even accept Mr. Kenner's thesis that Mr. Eliot, a foreigner in our midst, set about adapting himself perfectly to his environment by acquiring the protective colouring of the literary establishment and thus rendering himself invisible and anonymous. No lyric poet presents fewer personal clues.

What I dislike about Mr. Kenner is the fatal atmosphere of the lecture-room, the subsidised incandescence which plays about his subject and which ends by wearying us. Perhaps the easy life of Santa Barbara prevents him from grasping the key factor in Eliot's greatness as a poet which comes not from imitating Laforgue or digesting Bradley or from restoring neo-classicism to the moribund Georgians but from the deep awareness of personal unhappiness which, like Baudelaire's, breaks through the formal conventions of his verse.

Three poems which Mr. Kenner does not discuss and a clue in *Ara Vos Prec*, which he seems not to have read, reveal the nature (*experto crede*!) of that ever-present sense of loss somehow connected with hyacinth and lilac that makes this loveliest of months so cruel.

20

D. H. LAWRENCE AND A DISCIPLE

THE impact of genius on talent is frequently intolerable like boiling water in a valuable teapot. Once or twice the precious object survives, then with a sharp explosion, usually inaudible, a ghastly fissure spreads from base to handle and the association is terminated. Mr. Witter Bynner, with a name which once seen is never forgotten, like Lascelles Abercrombie or Fredegond Shove, with a considerable private income, a handsome young secretary and a mud-house in New Mexico, had all the requirements of a minor poet and could indulge both in verse plays and gracious living, a typical hero of our time.

In flight from bitter winters a phoenix settled in Santa Fé and his peace was shattered. The stranger took possession of his soul, found work for the secretary, instigated a move to old Mexico, ironed out any originality Mr. Bynner might have possessed and drove him into a position of impotent envy. Writing catty letters about the Master, siding with his wife in their appalling quarrels and producing an occasional imitative poem in which admiration vied with petulance, were his only resources: he had become a disciple.

It would be natural at some future date for him to avenge a mortification of the ego which was all the more painful because Mr. Bynner had never sought out Lawrence nor chosen, as do most disciples, a particular vehicle for his spiritual humiliations. He was no teapot but a New England cranberry jar. What is remarkable is that after waiting thirty years, instead of releasing his feelings by satire or parody, he should have enlarged his narration of the eventful months in Mexico into a full-length critical work which deals with every aspect of Lawrence as a writer as well as with his private life.

Such thoroughness reveals both the author's innate sense of justice, his devotion to Mrs. Lawrence and his life-long preoccupation with his unexpected visitor. *Journey with Genius*[1] is, therefore, something not to be missed on any account by a lover of Lawrence; it is not malicious and, coming from the 'Owen' of Lawrence's *The Plumed Serpent*, it is even disinterested. Mr. Bynner was overwhelmed by Lawrence as an author but disapproved of him as a man with all the New Englander's inherited right to be considered an expert in the heart's good manners.

And if one is not a lover of Lawrence? If one has read so many books about the Phoenix by the various Turtles that the very name 'Lorenzo' casts a chill? If one regards the genius, for all its authenticity, as dissipated, the artist as lost in the seer, the seer vanquished by the tub-thumper, the triumphant neurotic rooster, always cross, always right, always the exception, always the only one to know best and always saying so three times to make it true? Natural genius everywhere exudes; marvellous images, memorable insight, ravishing phrases: 'Then quickly they hoisted the wide white sail. The sail thrust up her horn and curved in a whorl to the wind.' But the genius is an outcrop: it never dictates the shape of a book or even the form of a poem. 'Art for my sake,' he joked, and was taken at his word.

There is too much about Mr. Bynner in the book. He takes himself almost as seriously as he does 'Lorenzo', and quotes interminably from diaries, poems and letters which all possess the same metallic tea-table rattle. He is a bore out-bored, a sorcerer's apprentice who cannot turn the tap off and some secretary should have taken his job in both hands and bid Mr. Bynner reduce his stock by at least a third.

I have always felt that there should be an anthology of Lawrence for that is the fate in store for prolific writers who dissipate their genius; it would include the whole of *Sons and Lovers* and

[1] By Witter Bynner (Peter Nevill).

much of *Women in Love* and *The White Peacock*, a few chapters from other novels, much from the travel books, some of the animal poems, many stories, a few letters, all the accounts of the famous last supper at the Café Royal, Norman Douglas's Florence luncheon, bits of Huxley, Garnett, and the various 'turtles' and Mr. Bynner's wonderful travelogue of the Mexican journey (particularly his account of the Lawrences bathing).

Genius is always the same thing, whether in Mozart or Shakespeare or Lawrence or Proust or Blake or Baudelaire; it is an immediate perception of the universal harmonies of life, of the shape and essence of all living things, and with that the gift of tongues, the imagery to express this perception. What people do with their genius afterwards is another matter, and what other people write about those who have not done with their genius the best they could is another matter still. 'Blow, blow, thou winter wind. . . .' Yet even so the flamelike quality of the Phoenix, at two removes, is still scorching.

22

THE LETTERS OF D. H. LAWRENCE

THE first volume of Lawrence's collected letters, edited by Aldous Huxley, is now thirty years old. These two new volumes[1] do not pretend to be complete. They, too, are a selection and include most, but not all, of the 1932 edition, in full, with as many blanks cleared up as death permits, and a great many additional letters, including a whole early correspondence with Blanche Jennings (discovered in 1959 in Liverpool) and many unpublished letters to his wife, to Richard Aldington, David Garnett, Aldous Huxley and the Murrys, and, above all, the crucial correspondence (the longest in the book) with the patient Koteliansky.

Aldington and Garnett are two of the three to whom this book is dedicated and Huxley's Introduction to the original volume is included as an appendix. David Garnett celebrated his seventieth birthday last week, and here he enters on the scene in 1912. 'You should see him swim in the Isar, that is effervescent and pale green, where the current is fearfully strong. He simply smashes his way through the water while F(rieda) sits on the bank bursting with admiration, and I am green with envy. By Jove, I reckon his parents have done joyously well for that young man.' An idyllic introduction. Yet a month before he was writing to the same recipient (David Garnett's father):

Curse the blasted, jelly-bound swine, the slimy, belly-wriggling invertebrates, the miserable sodding rotters, the flaming sods, the

[1] *The Collected Letters of D. H. Lawrence.* Two Volumes. Edited by Harry Moore (Heinemann).

snivelling, dribbling, dithering palsied pulseless lot that make up England today. They've got white of egg in their veins, and their spunk is that watery it's a marvel they can breed. They *can* nothing but frog-spawn—the gibberers! God, how I hate them! God curse them, funkers, God blast them wish-wash. Exterminate them, slime. . . .

Why, Why and Why was I born an Englishman! My cursed, rotten-boned, pappy-hearted countrymen, *why*, why was I sent to *them* . . . God, how I hate them—I nauseate—they stink in sourness. They deserve it that every great man should drown himself.

Many of these pappy-hearted countrymen were to die shortly, Lawrence was to survive—such is the irony latent in all class or racial strictures—but it provides a glimpse of the fire which was consuming him.

I assume we all agree that Lawrence was a genius even if we are not unanimous as to what was his greatest book or even that he was a great novelist. His tragedy was that he was a sick genius, passionately in love with life yet compelled to view it through an increasingly distorted lens. No one had a more unerring instinct for the truth about places and people, yet illness caused him to round on friend and friendly environment alike; one day it's the North ('The North has gone all *evil*'), another time it is Italy, or France or Majorca or Europe. 'Europe *is* a bit depressing. What the devil's the matter with the world?' 'The place gets on my nerves all the time, the people are dead and staring. I can't bear their Spanishy faces, dead unpleasant masks, a bit like city English. . . .'

These two volumes divide Lawrence's life in half, before and after 1920 (his literary output was from 1909-31, for several volumes were published posthumously). He was a natural letter-writer, he wrote letters as a bird sings and everyone who cares for literature should possess these volumes or get them from the library and push off as soon as possible into the brief-coursed river of his life with its many rapids and broad unexpected sunny reaches. Although the best letters are to be found in the first, I am afraid either the death-wish or the love of gossip caused me to concentrate on the second volume. There is a period in every writer's life when writing letters is a phase of his creative expansion, when they supplant other means of expression. Later on they become a relaxation or a chore.

Lawrence, however, keeps it up to the end. One can compare his famous third letter to Lady Ottoline (February 1st, 1915), 'I want you to form the nucleus of a new community which shall start a new life amongst us—a life in which the only riches is integrity of character' with the last but one (April, 1929), 'Yes, I remember your coming to Sussex—stepping out of an old four-wheeler in all your pearls, and a purple velvet frock—and going across the meadows. . . . It is a pity something came across it all and prevented us keeping a nice harmony. But life does queer things to us, and it takes us a long time to come to our real steady self.'

I once asked Lady Ottoline if she thought it had been more difficult for her to reach her position in the world of letters, starting from Welbeck, than for Lawrence from his miner's cottage, a few miles away; she was convinced his path was smoother. A considerable part of the later correspondence deals with the battle with the British public or rather with its magistrates, Home Office officials and policemen whom Lawrence had to fight during the last years of his life, between hæmorrhages.

I hope some of those who confiscated his paintings, burnt his books, impounded his manuscripts, pilfered his mail, badgered him out of the country and campaigned against *The Rainbow*, *Pansies* and *Lady Chatterley's Lover* are alive to read these letters and are in sufficient possession of their faculties to understand something of the damage they caused to this proud and exquisitely sensitive man by their vindictive smallness of spirit.

One wonders what Lawrence would have thought of the Chatterley Trial. 'It's the most improper novel ever written and as Jehovah you would probably find it sheer pornography. But it isn't. It's a declaration of the phallic reality. I doubt if it will ever be published,' he wrote to Koteliansky in 1928; and he explained to Lady Ottoline 'About Lady C—you mustn't think I advocate perpetual sex. Far from it. Nothing nauseates me more than promiscuous sex in and out of season. But I want with Lady C to make an *adjustment in consciousness* to the basic physical realities.'

And he concludes: 'There is a brief time for sex, and a long time when sex is out of place.' One is apt to forget that Lady Chatterley was twenty-three, the same age as Don Giovanni.

Such a magnificent book yields many hundred quotations but I think it is better to regard it as a kind of non-stop performance which one can enter at any moment, like the life and letters of Byron, and at whatever moment one chooses there is genius fizzing away, soaring with early greatness or desperately disputing every inch of its retreat—there are the faithful friends, like the Huxleys and the Brewsters, indispensable villains like Murry ('He's licked all the gum off me. I'm no longer adhesive' . . . 'It's no good our meeting—even when we are immortal spirits, we shall dwell in different Hades') and younger ones with no quarrels behind them, like Rhys Davies and the Crosbies. And there are all the women—Frieda and Jessie Chambers, Brett, Mabel Dodge, Catharine Carswell; and the best and the worst of all the places, Eastwood and Zennor, Mexico and New Mexico, Taormina, Capri, Florence, Bandol, and the places where he wanted to settle like Southern Spain and the West of Ireland—think of Lawrence writing *Lady Chatterley* in Ireland! 'It's time there was an *enormous* revolution.'

12

JAMES JOYCE: I

THIS is no time to attempt a critical estimate of Joyce. Wilson's forty pages in *Axel's Castle* (Scribners) have done that best. He has died this week, but it will be a year or two before anything can be said about him which is worth saying. In the next period of expansive leisure, when we can read again and reassess the past, he may well take the place which Henry James has lately occupied, that of the Forerunner in vogue, the fine product of a vanished and alien civilisation which by its completeness and remoteness stirs the imagination and so enters into communication with its successor. Joyce was the last of the Mammoths, not perhaps quite the last, for there is still Gide, Claudel, Vuillard, Bonnard, in France, but I know of none in America and England, and by Mammoths I mean those giant inhabitants of the middle class who believed in life for art's sake, and were prepared to devote sixty or seventy years of unremitting energy and patience, all their time, all their money, all their mind to it. We see them browsing in small herds through the 'sixties and 'seventies and 'eighties, Impressionists, Post-Impressionists, Ivory Tower dwellers, Realists, Parnassians, their food the experience of a lifetime obtained through a giant curiosity, a private income and a deep sense of security, for their protective bourgeois colouring, their rich dark suits and stiff collars, their comfortable homes and devoted women disguise them completely and merge perfectly into the contemporary bourgeois landscape. With the turn of the century the herds thinned out, the feeding grounds deteriorated, the last war had somewhat the effect of an ice age yet the pastures which had supported Cézanne and Flaubert, Degas and Henry

James continued to nourish Moore and Yeats and Proust, Joyce, Gide, and Valéry. Now most of them are gone and the ice cap is returning with velocity.

Joyce was not a revolutionary. His life contained only one revolutionary gesture, his departure from Ireland after the final suppression of *Dubliners* (1912) which was to have been brought out in 1904. He produced a fierce poem, *Gas from a Burner* (1912), which contains some excellent hate of Ireland and left his country never to return. He then taught English in the Berlitz schools, where he was working at Trieste when the last war broke out, after which he moved to Zurich. It is odd to think that there must exist many Italians who learnt their English from this lord of language, who was quietly acquiring every known tongue in his spare time. *Dubliners*, an admirable collection of short stories, was finally published in 1914. It shows Joyce torn between the realism of the 'modern movement' and a decadent Celtic romanticism. In 1916/7 he published *A Portrait of the Artist* through the Egoist Press. It is a quite remarkable book, adult, sensitive, unreassuring, in which the two veins of Dublin realism and Celtic romanticism are woven into an elaborate fugue. After the publication of *Ulysses*, which was due to the courage and devotion of Sylvia Beach, he became, through a private benefaction, financially secure, and was able to live the kind of life he wanted which was that of a well-to-do high priest of art, remote from equals and competitors and not too accessible to admirers, in a luxurious apartment in the Rue de Grenelle. It was there that I used to go to see him, or else in his room at the American hospital in Neuilly, when I was writing an article on *Ulysses* and *Work in Progress*. I had read *Ulysses* with passion; it is very much a young man's book, packed with the defeatism and the guilt of youth, its loneliness, cynicism, pedantry and outbursts of bawdy anarchist activity. Guilt about a dying mother, boredom with an actual father, search for a spiritual father, reliance on robuster friends, watery and lecherous cravings for girls, horror and delight in failure, horror and fascination for the gross calm, bitchy, invincible feminine principle as exemplified in Molly Bloom, 'Queen of Calpe's rocky mount, the raven-haired daughter of Tweedie'; it was like, and always will be, nothing one has read before.

At that time there was a complete cult of *Ulysses*. Books were written about it. Stuart Gilbert provided a fascinating crib; there was a map of Dublin with the journeyings of Bloom and Stephen in different coloured inks, and on 'Bloom's Day' (June 16th) there was a celebration, Joyce going to the country with a few friends and admirers for a picnic, one of which was ruined by a clap of thunder for which Joyce had a genuine terror. I could not write about *Work in Progress* without having it explained to me and so my talks with Joyce ended up in my being put on to construe. 'Now, Mr. Connolly, just read this passage aloud and tell me what you think it means.' 'It's about the Danish walls of the original Danish encampment—er—I mean Dub-b-lin—the black ford? Ford of the oxen? Hill on a fort?' 'No, no, no—I refer to the three cathedrals of Dublin, Mr. Connolly, the only city, you know, to have three cathedrals.' It was not quite like being at school, it was like going to breakfast, after one had left school, with one's schoolmaster. In theory you were grown up, in practice you weren't. After one difficult passage about Roman Dublin intoned by Joyce in his magnificent voice, he paused. 'You know, of course, to what I refer, Mr. Connolly?' 'No, not exactly.' 'I refer' —there was a moment of acute embarrassment—'I refer to a Lupanar.' After the tutorials he would go to the piano and sing Dublin street ballads with a charming, drawling, nasal parody of the old itinerant singers. He talked endlessly about Ireland. 'I am afraid I am more interested, Mr. Connolly, in the Dublin street names than in the riddle of the Universe.' He was even interested in Irish cricket, and always, when I knew him, wore the white blazer of an obscure Dublin club. He was very proud of his family, and like all the Anglo-Irish, a snob. In Paris he liked good food, especially a Montparnasse restaurant called Les Trianons and going to the opera and order and wealth. Sometimes, however, he went out with Hemingway or Lewis and got drunk. He always seemed to be two men, the legendary Joyce, blind but patient, pompous, cold, easily offended, unapproachable, waiting to be spoken to, with a strange priestly blend of offended dignity, weakness and intellectual power and underneath the warm, sympathetic bawdy Dublin character. In the years to come something really important could be written about him. Revolutionary in technique, yet conservative in everything else, so deadly respectable in his life, so fearlessly sensual in his writings, so tortured with the lapsed Catholic's guilt—the '*Agenbite of Inwit*', so obsessed with his own youth that his clock seemed literally to have stopped on June 16th, 1904, and yet so determined to create a mythical universe of his own. We will never have the time, the security or the patience in our lifetime to write like him, his weapons 'silence, exile and cunning' are not ours. I hope but only for the time to read through him and one day make a study of this literary anti-Pope, this last great mammoth out of whose tusks so many smaller egoists have carved their self-important ivory towers.

[1941]

13

JAMES JOYCE: 2

'THESE letters should be read in conjunction with an authoritative biography of James Joyce'—the first words of Mr. Gilbert's excellent introduction define this book.[1] These are not letters which portray a man or tell his story so much as chips and shavings which fly from the machine while *Ulysses* and *Finnegans Wake* are getting themselves written. Few great writers, I feel, can claim such dedication to a self-appointed task, for, if family matters be excluded, there is hardly a line here which does not deal with Joyce's work and the mechanics of having it printed, published, reviewed and understood.

James Joyce does not reveal or wish to reveal his character, his 'sluggish, slimy, slithy, sliddery, stick-in-the-mud disposition'. He flirts with no woman and unbends with no man, not a Jim is heard, not a humorous quote: only Mr. Budgen inspires a certain playfulness. This does not make his letters dull; they present an absolutely closed world into which the reader must crawl like a speleologist and watch the subterranean grottoes unfold before him until, in 1940, all grows dark again.

Mr. Gilbert stresses this formal reserve, which made Joyce even ask to be referred to as 'Mr. Joyce' throughout 'James Joyce and the making of Ulysses', and I still possess a telegram summoning me to the Euston Hotel in 1929 and signed 'Joyce' which I took to be the Christian name of a girl I knew; a misunderstanding which was never cleared up satisfactorily with either of them.

The whole *schema* by which Joyce lived is growing more and

[1] *Letters of James Joyce*. Edited by Stuart Gilbert (Faber).

more unfamiliar. We live in an age when highbrows prefer music to literature, middlebrows painting and lowbrows television, and when the prestige of the written word, the whole cultural heritage of literary 'happy families' is a fading dream. Joyce, who made and kept a vow never to write prefaces or give a lecture or grant an interview, saw himself as among the great revolutionaries, a lord of language like Dante, or a king in exile:

> You must know that the Opera in Paris is considered, not without some reason, by the Paris intellectuals as beneath contempt and the spectacle of the immensely illustrious author of Ulysses endeavouring to hustle crowds of journalists and protesting admirers into that old-fashioned playhouse to hear antiquated music sung by old-timer Sullivan was too much.

His attitude to psychoanalysis, as far back as 1921, can only be described as irreverent:

> A batch of people in Zurich persuaded themselves that I was gradually going mad and actually endeavoured to induce me to enter a sanatorium where a certain Doctor Jung (the Swiss Tweedledum who is not to be confused with the Viennese Tweedledee, Dr. Freud) amuses himself at the expense (in every sense of the word) of ladies and gentlemen who are troubled with bees in their bonnets.

'At the expense' . . . through all his life Joyce manifested a very exact regard for money. As with all who refuse many undertakings for money, he was most tenacious in the remainder. Royalties, translation rights, serialisation, small privately printed editions bulk largely in his correspondence. 'Already in 1917,' Mr. Gilbert tells us, 'Miss Weaver had made her first benefaction . . . this was followed, in 1924, by the transfer of a large sum of money' which supported Joyce and his family for the rest of his life: the Mallarmé of English prose could give up his teaching. In the same year the first fragment from *Finnegans Wake* was published in a little magazine and the artist was well away on his journey to Byzantium; never was a subsidy so graciously given, so well-deserved, so richly spent.

The most interesting letters over the long years are to his benefactress, especially when he explains the meaning of episodes in *Ulysses* or of key passages in *Finnegans Wake*. Let us look at one: the famous first sentence whose beginning completes the last phrase of the book, 'river runs'

brings us back to Howth Castle and Environs. Sir Tristram, violer d'amores, had passencore rearrived on the scraggy isthmus from North Armorica to wielder fight his penisolate war; nor had stream rocks by the Oconee exaggerated themselves to Laurens County, Ga, doublin all the time. . . .

Dear Madam: Above please find prosepiece ordered in sample form. Also key to same. Hoping said sample meets with your approval, yrs trly Jeems Joker.

Howth = Dan Hoved (head) (an island for old geographers).

Sir Amory Tristram 1st Earl of Howth changed his name to Saint Lawrence, b. in Brittany (North Armorica).

Tristan et Iseult. Passim.

Viola in all moods and senses.

Dublin, Laurens County, Georgia, founded by a Dubliner, Peter Sawyer, on r. Oconee. Its motto: Doubling all the time.

Passencore = pas encore and *ricorsi storici* of Vico. 'Rearrived' idem.

And so on for another page. How Joyce must have appreciated the reviewer of this fragment in Laurens County, who exclaimed: 'We and the Oconee river of all places in the world are in it, too.' It has sometimes been said that Miss Weaver's subsidy turned Joyce away from the realities of life and caused his genius to run to seed or rather flower itself to death in the wastes of *Finnegans Wake*; but a study of his work shows that it was always moving in this direction, that his gift for languages was leading to an obsession with language, that he sought inspiration from the form and was always drawn by his personality to the arcane and esoteric.

A letter from Wells (much finer than his strictures on Henry James) expresses the public incomprehension once and for all. Yet neither subsidy nor vocation nor the dedicated life in the quiet

Paris street can stave off the tragedies of life or the attrition of time:

> Twilight of Blindness. Madness, descends on Swift . . . unslow, malswift, pro mean, proh noblesse. Atrahora. Melancolores, nears; whose glauque eyes glitt bedimmed to imm!

His own eye-troubles, his daughter's mental breakdown, the vicissitudes of war, return him at the end to the Zurich where, in the first world war, so much of *Ulysses* was written. The wanderer, Vico-like, comes full circle.

At the end we emerge from these letters, haunted rather than dominated, pitying and wondering rather than loving this strange, arrogant, shy, kindly and meticulous scholar whose stoical reticence cannot obliterate a fundamental bitterness, even a touch of the 'injustice-collector':

> I have refused scores of requests to sit to painters and sculptors, having a very profound objection to my own image, needlessly repeated in a picture or bust. In fact years ago casual glimpses of it in shop mirrors, etc., used to send me speeding away from it. I think I was right for, underfed, overworked, ill-dressed, with septic poisoning gradually undermining my health and unable to attend to it for sheer want of time and money, I must have been a dreadful spectacle.

14

JAMES JOYCE: 3

It is strange how many figures of the 'twenties, like mammoths in a block of ice, are now reappearing in their perishable completeness—in Mr. George Painter's *Proust* and Miss Sylvia Beach's autobiography (not yet available in this country), and now in Mr. Richard Ellmann's monumental life of Joyce[1], which takes us in 800 pages through the fifty-eight-year span of the most sedentary of exiles. Allowing for extensive references this still leaves about fifteen large and solid pages for every year of the man's life.

I do not know whether to be more impressed by the scholarship, patience, industry and devotion of such a biographer or to be appalled by the standard he sets. A computing machine could not have done better. I think I must be about the only person who knew Joyce not to be mentioned in it.

There is a weakness inherent in this all-embracing method of biography which depends on the filing of innumerable interviews. Too many stray visitors appear whose reminiscences are of doubtful accuracy and seriousness. These have then to be incorporated in the larger annals as if the Person from Porlock's account of his reception formed part of *Kubla Khan*.

But Mr. Ellmann is not a computing machine and he manages to evaluate most of the evidence; in fact, when he steps in with a judgment or a brief estimate of one of Joyce's works he is both penetrating and sympathetic. It is this gift of criticism held in reserve which makes his book a truly masterly biography, wise in

[1] *James Joyce*, by Richard Ellmann (Oxford).

its completeness. If Joyce be a great writer, then this is a great book.

I say 'if' because I do not think it is altogether established that Joyce is a great writer in the sense in which Yeats or Proust is. There have been many times when I have thought so—when I first read *Ulysses*, when I met him, when I wrote a long article on 'Work in Progress' in 1929, when I hear the recording of his wonderful voice reading *Anna Livia*, when I read the last page of *Finnegans Wake*: let us say, then, he is a marvellous writer.

But I cannot feel absolutely sure of his greatness, as once I did, because I am now less tolerant of his faults. I feel that so much of *Finnegans Wake* and of *Ulysses*, even when the obscurity has been penetrated, is fundamentally uninteresting that there must be some failure of conception or execution or both, and I think it perhaps springs from Joyce's absolute refusal to let himself mature through the spiritual struggles and intellectual discoveries of his time.

His life is one of the saddest and one of the emptiest except in so far as it was filled by the joys of artistic creation. For he rejected everything—he ignored the war of 1914 and displaced himself from Trieste to Zurich, he ignored the last war and again displaced himself from Paris to Zurich, he ignored the Irish Republic which he had called for in his youth, he ignored Fascism, anti-Fascism and Communism, he despised psychoanalysis, he hated painting, took no interest in architecture or travel or objects, liked no music of his time except for a brief craze for Antheil and seems equally immune to modern poetry and literature. His clock had stopped on Bloomsday (June 16th, 1904). 'His true Penelope was Flaubert' one might say with Pound—but Flaubert did manage to live in the present, if only through his hate—as one can see from *Bouvard et Pécuchet*.

I am not criticising Joyce from a journalistic or Marxist point of view but I am trying to suggest that he fed his queen bee of a mind with inferior jelly and that from such subject-matter it could not produce the sublime or even the comic effects which were intended. He asks too much of his ideal reader. This is perhaps an English heresy and may account for the way we lag behind America in our appreciation of Joyce (or is it our lack of subsidised theses?); and perhaps I am the only person to find the plans and keys and clues and commentaries on Joyce's books more exhilarating than the originals. Is there an immaturity in his mind and humour or a blind spot in mine? Mr. Ellmann has the answer ready:

> If we ask Joyce to bestride literature like a colossus, he will disappoint us. No generals paid him visits of homage, no one called him the Sage of Dublin. As he makes clear enough himself, in the world's eyes he began as a bad boy and ended as an old codger. There is much to rebuke him for, his disregard for money, his regard for alcohol and other conduct lacking in majesty or decorum. Yet we have to ask with Parsifal the question that Joyce also asked: 'Who is good?' . . . Yet as the nobility of his heroes gradually overcomes their ingloriousness, so the tenacious craftsman, holding to his idea, gradually surmounts that roving debt-ridden scene through which Joyce kept his elegant way. . . . To be narrow, peculiar, and irresponsible, and at the same time all-encompassing, relentless and grand, is Joyce's style of greatness, a style as difficult but ultimately as rewarding as that of Finnegans Wake.

I have said that his was a sad life. His two profound interests, according to Mr. Ellmann, were his family and his writings. 'These passions never dwindled. The intensity of the first gave his work its sympathy and humanity; the intensity of the second raised his life to dignity and high dedication'—but what tragedy can lurk in two most natural obsessions?

Poverty crippled the first half of Joyce's life, illness the second, and he died almost as poor as he had begun. Many artists, the majority even, have been poor, but there is something Baudelairean about Joyce's poverty—his feckless drunken father, his own miserable shifts and flittings, the duns, the bailiffs, the pawnbrokers, the borrowings of florins and shillings, the patched trousers, the missing dress suit, these become a nightmare of shabby-genteel bohemia—until one feels it is infectious, that one will rise from this book a poorer man than one sat down. I don't know which is sadder—the Dublin poverty and moon-flittings of

Joyce's parents or his days at the Berlitz school in Pola and Trieste with his children born in such unfavourable circumstances and his books also being held up and vilified by publishers with all the prejudices of the time.

It was not till he reached Zurich, in his middle-thirties, that good fortune came his way in the shape of the subsidies which were to prove his undoing. Not but what Miss Weaver acted like a goddess of tact and goodness, more devoted than Athena to Ulysses; but the sums which Joyce required to expunge and blot out the years of want and injured pride were so rightly enormous that they required the use of all capital as income. Nor was he ever able to clear the fortune from *Ulysses* which a world-wide distribution of a classic ought to have provided.

He died suddenly of a duodenal ulcer, a poor man, and Miss Weaver paid for his funeral. She was his 'true Penelope' as her name implies. All his fortune in later life was of small account compared to the troubles of his eyesight, his long, excruciatingly painful and losing fight against blindness, his many operations and the tragedy of his daughter's madness which he tried so hard to mitigate and perhaps had helped to bring on. His son's marriage also ended in disaster.

Anyone who met the Joyce family at the height of their prosperity in their apartment in the Faubourg St. Germain, must have felt there was something incongruous about the position of this highly decorative family of Italian-speaking Irish expatriates. They seemed to rotate in a social vacuum like the brilliant shadow-cabinet of a long dispossessed government.

Mr. Ellmann describes the famous meeting between Joyce and Proust in which both outshone each other in mutual ignorance of their work and Proust asked Joyce if he liked truffles. But Proust was, after all, on his home ground. If they had both known how outrageously the other overtipped, a friendship might have been formed, the Esprit de Berlitz been recognised by the Esprit de Guermantes. But though Proust and Joyce shared an aversion from happiness and made instinctively towards the tragic sense of life, the rainclouds where their genius flowered, Joyce was immune to the snobbery of our time and maintained that not one of his characters was worth a thousand pounds.

He liked nice clothes and he liked his family to have them. 'Never mind my soul, just be sure you have my tie right,' he said to an over-intense painter to whom he was sitting. Otherwise meals in good restaurants, white wine, champagne, and cures for Lucia took up his money. He did not want possessions. 'We're going downhill fast,' he told Beckett at Christmas, 1939; and Jung diagnosed father and daughter, five years earlier, as 'two people going to the bottom of a river, one falling and the other diving'.

15

GERTRUDE STEIN

'A Rose is a Rose is a Rose' is the device on the cover of Gertrude Stein's classic *The Autobiography of Alice B. Toklas*, and Mr. Brinnin quotes a friend of his: 'Well, I can go along with those first two roses of hers all right—but when she gets to that third rose she loses me.' He is not the only one, for Miss Sylvia Beach used to have in her possession a copy of the *Autobiography* in which Hemingway had inscribed three times in a similar magic circle 'Is a bitch'. And he had something there. Let us small fry give her and Mr. Brinnin the last word.

Can't you see that when the language was new—as it was with Chaucer and Homer—the poet could use the name of one thing and the thing was really there? And can't you see that after hundreds of years had gone by, and thousands of poems had been written, he could call upon those words and find they were just worn out literary words? The excitingness of pure being had withdrawn from them; they were just rather stale literary words. Now the poet has to work in the excitingness of pure being; he has to get back that intensity into the language.... Now listen! I'm no fool and I know that in daily life we don't go around saying 'is a . . . is . . . is'. Yes, I'm no fool; but I think that in that line the rose is red for the first time in English poetry for a hundred years.

No revolution in our time has failed more signally, alas, than the 'revolution of the word'. Everyone who has tried to do for language what Cézanne, Picasso or Mondrian has done for painting or Schoenberg for music, has failed. Poets have not been able to go farther than Hopkins or Dylan Thomas and retain a public; all the experimental prose-writers of the *Transition* period have fallen by the wayside; only in the theatre of Beckett and Ionesco are there signs of a breakthrough.

James Joyce and Gertrude Stein are more read about than read. It is their personalities which dominate whereas the more intelligible artists—Eliot, Hemingway or Scott Fitzgerald—are studied for their work. And who now cares about M. Pichette and his Lettrisme? Yet the attempt was worthwhile. In *Finnegans Wake* Joyce tried to create a new language in which each word carried the maximum number of potential meanings, while Gertrude Stein tried to divorce words from any meaning whatsoever, to apply to language the principles of abstract or cubist art. 'The writer expresses. He does not communicate,' as *Transition's* manifesto put it. 'The revolution in the English language is an accomplished fact.'

Why did it founder? Is the language perhaps too utterly fouled with communication ever to be cleaned? Is the economic factor too important? For while people will buy painting or listen to music which expresses without communicating, they will not support the right of the literary creator 'to disintegrate the primal matter of words'.

One should, perhaps, at this point, canvass a few readers about Gertrude Stein. How many have read the *Autobiography*? Or the easy books? (*Picasso*, *Paris*, *France* or *Wars I have Known* or *Everybody's Autobiography*)—how many the tougher *Three Lives*, *Tender Buttons*, or the mammoth *Making of Americans*?

Personally I came hopelessly to grief at a performance of *Four Saints in Three Acts* which seemed to me an intolerable imposition. But the *Autobiography* is an inspired gossip column which stands up to any amount of re-reading. It may be inaccurate, it certainly is unfair, but it is a model of its kind.

Besides being the best-seller which it deserved to become, the *Autobiography* (written in six weeks) triumphantly demonstrated the disciplines to which Miss Stein in her arcaner studies had for so long submitted. Every parody of her has failed because one cannot parody the monotonous boredom of her writing unless one has an equal amount of learning and intelligence to suppress; a smaller mind will lack the courage to be so dull.

I am unable to accept, alas, Mr. Brinnin's estimate of her literary achievement[1]; I think the success of her *Autobiography* results from her being one of the major egotists of her time (only surpassed by her brother) and therefore being able to kindle into animation every circumstance connected with herself, even as she fails as a novelist by being completely impervious to the real nature of other people. Her brother's egotism was not saddled with creative inhibitions; he could only boast and impotently deride her rise to stardom.

Where Mr. Brinnin is so successful is in seeing that there is a life of Gertrude Stein to be written which is neither the life she wrote herself, nor a self-conscious exposition of her books. While admiring his subject as a biographer should, he is scrupulously fair and cites many contrary opinions. His *Dylan Thomas in America* I felt was ferocity masked as objectivity. Here I feel he is on sure ground. The claims he makes for Miss Stein are consistently upheld; he relates her life to her work and does not stray off into hypnotised name-dropping or tedious literary quarrels.

If Miss Stein was a supreme example of selfishness, accustomed to being fussed over all her life, greedy for praise and monolithically uncharitable, her benefactions being limited to the purchase, under her brother's tuition, of Cézannes and Matisses for less than they were worth and, when independent of his tutelage, of Picasso and Sir Francis Rose, Mr. Brinnin does no more than adumbrate the possibility. His final verdict is startling:

> Gertrude Stein belongs in the last phase of the governance of reason; she is one of the last daughters of the Enlightenment. While she spent a lifetime trying to escape the Nineteenth century, her career belongs to its sunset phase, she believed exclusively in the power of efficacy of the rational mind . . . she believes in consciousness as a positive glory . . . it is difficult to be passionate about her work . . . but it is easy and perhaps

[1] *The Third Rose*, by John Malcolm Brinnin (Weidenfeld & Nicolson).

necessary to be passionate about her devoted practice of the art of language without reference to utility.

As Mr. Brinnin points out, somebody would have had to do it and she had many qualifications for attempting the breakthrough.

16

A RENDEZVOUS FOR WRITERS

'He turned off by the Rue des Quatre Vents to the venerable little street where the modern bookshop was hidden, like a cache of dynamite in a solemn crypt. This was his spiritual home: here he prepared for his private revolution, by which he was to put an end to the divided reign of art and experience, of literature and life. Somewhere on those walls was the sword he would pull out to make an end of such tyrants and proclaim the reign of a happily integrated modern soul. And inside it Miss Greville sat at her table in her brown coat looking up with her quick dark eye like a thrush on its nest.

'O if you could have known that woman, her gay fierce generous character, her American courage, her extreme wit! She made it seem possible, after all, to Kenneth that he could become a real person and so write like one, her library held the essence of that new wisdom, the technique of which Americans seemed to possess the secret and which he hoped to apply; writing at last non-intellectually about intellectual things.

'It was disheartening though to meet his fellow apprentices. Dark young men with small moustaches would meander on about their egos, looking softly at him while they spoke, like spaniels, and quietly disregarding what he said in return. There was something curiously wan about them, and at the same time rather knowing, as if they felt the arts had to make up for a great deal.

'The women were generally older, setting out on venturesome pilgrimages with Lady Chatterley as their Baedeker, and their appearance as their only protection. With them Miss Greville was kind but distant, and their sing-song exclamations faded as the mew of gulls. A few months later, however, the English men of letters found themselves rallying to avenge a new stab in the back, some unpleasant and well-founded insinuations on the sex life of their heroes. They sweated to defend Thackeray, Meredith and Jane Austen from serious charges, and it grew increasingly difficult, as these quiet ladies returned to their university presses, to prove that Byron had ever known woman.

'Besides these, there flowed a thin stream of transient maniacs and such few people of real talent as existed at the time on our small globe. These would disappear into a back room and give to the shop that atmosphere of a place where things happened which excited and stimulated all who went there. The polished silhouette of Joyce, the swarthy face and broad shoulders of Hemingway, the beard of Fargue, Gide in his cape, Sherwood Anderson—it was a place where people who normally existed, lived, and people who lived, enjoyed themselves.

'The shop was just closing and Miss Greville was bringing in the books from the shelf outside. "What have you been doing," she asked him, and he explained how he had begun a story about a young man who couldn't sleep because he always imagined the symptoms of a fatal disease were appearing, and how he picks up an English girl for company, who turns out to have been an hospital nurse and who keeps him awake retelling her experiences. It ends with her description of septicaemia.

' "It sounds very neat," she said. He resolved immediately to tear it up.'

I hope you begin to feel the atmosphere, for although these pages from an unfinished novel were written later (they are dated 1934), they give the sensation of 1928, and should serve as an introduction to Miss Beach's memoirs,[1] for she cannot herself put down how she appeared to other writers. The shop accepted letters for its customers, cashed cheques, and put people in touch with each other; I used to be shut in there while I was doing an article on Joyce, and it was through Miss Beach that I met him and Gide and Hemingway.

[1] *Shakespeare and Company*, by Sylvia Beach (Faber).

She was born in Baltimore and came from Princeton, offspring of a long line of clergymen and missionaries, but she always seemed to me like a New Englander, a Bostonian in revolt. I suppose nothing was more extraordinary than that there should be a bookshop like hers and another like Adrienne Monnier's both in the same small street, or that they should be partners in life and rivals in business—but at that time one took it for granted, and it seemed that these two had always been there and that Joyce had always ruled invisibly, like Godot, under the head of Shakespeare, with Paul Valéry and Valéry Larbaud at the 'Maison des Amis du Livre' across the way.

Miss Beach now tells us about the haphazard way it all began, on a shoe-string, in 1919. In the summer of 1920 she met James Joyce who had only recently arrived in Paris. The next day he came round to her bookshop and asked her to help him find pupils for English lessons. This led to her publication of *Ulysses* and to fifteen years of collaboration.

Her book is therefore of the greatest interest to Joyce-lovers and full of invaluable information, but even apart from Joyce, it is a charming, gay, astringent scrapbook of the 'twenties and 'thirties and full of fun about Hemingway and many others. I did not know before how Hemingway organised the smuggling of *Ulysses* into America from Canada, or of the efforts he and, among others, Gide and Spender, made to help her through the slump. This led to her having a sale in 1935 when some Joyce items had to be sold, including the manuscript of *Stephen Hero*, which went for a thousand dollars.

I think this sale may have been responsible for his changed attitude to her. Oddly enough, I turned up yesterday a letter about it. 'It was awfully kind of you to have my sale written up in the *Evening Standard* . . . a dealer wrote for a catalogue and asked if I had any curious Hemingway items. I have suggested "is a bitch is a bitch is a bitch" that you laughed at so much'—and so we are back at Gertrude Stein and Mr. Brinnin. Incidentally Miss Beach implies that Hemingway and Miss Stein remained on good terms after his attack on Sherwood Anderson, but Malcolm Brinnin, in his recent biography of Gertrude Stein, quotes a brutal rebuff from her. Who is right?

Hemingway turned up in 1921, with a letter from Sherwood Anderson and it was he again who liberated the Rue de l'Odéon from the last Germans, a fine destiny. Miss Beach, I have said, is astringent, but she is never unkind. I have seen her angry, or rather I would say righteously indignant, and she commands a pleasing irony and a gift for deflation, but with this goes an unquestioning love of literature and a great devotion to her friends.

I don't think she has ever bothered about anyone who was not an artist: money and success have never mattered to her, she has never gone in for fans and bores, there really is something birdlike about her—vivacity, energy, simplicity, unsentimentality—a bird from the Greek Anthology. I think part of her charm for artists was that having once accepted them she liked them for the oddest reasons or for their most unlikely gifts—and it was writers she liked, not painters, publicists, art critics, the whole cultural hotchpotch in which we mill around today.

Antheil was an exception—but Antheil, although a musician not a writer, was a phenomenon, a charmer like René Crevel who died so young, while nothing died young about George Antheil, except his genius. An exhibition about Miss Beach's literary associates and associations 'Paris in the Twenties' was held at the Cultural Affairs office of the American Embassy. One could read *Shakespeare and Company* up to the moment the doors opened and then dive in to this pool of the past, the not very distant past whose blue waters—Ulysses blue, the blue of the Greek flag—were so clear and invigorating.

17

ERNEST HEMINGWAY: I

It is not uncommon for a famous writer to produce one thoroughly bad book. When this happens a critic must estimate the extent of the damage, try to explain the causes, and suggest a remedy, for the world would be the poorer without the works of Hemingway whose adventurous life has been an inspiration to writers who don't want to be publishers or Government officials.

The idea for his new novel,[1] a Far-Western treatment of *Death in Venice*, is perfectly sound. Colonel Richard Cantwell (U.S. Army), who was wounded in the battle for Venice in world-war-one, revisits the city on short leave after world-war-two. He is now a very sick man and knows it, an old boar at bay, and he chooses to devote what may prove the last days of his life to his favourite city, to his last and deepest love-affair, his *sola et sera voluptas*, with a Venetian girl of noble family and to shooting duck on the Brenta marshes. His two friends are the head-waiter of the Gritti, also a war-veteran and the barman at Harry's. In an atmosphere which might have been as lovely and pathetic as the 'Halt during the Chase' of the dying Watteau, he moves through the winter city and recounts to his girl some episodes 'at command level' of the *reconquista*, the liberation of Paris and the crossing of the Rhine. At the right moment he waves good-bye to his many-islanded hostess and slips away. Meanwhile the reader should have learnt from this old Othello all he can teach and been presented with a magical love story and a work of art. To

[1] *Across the River and Into the Trees*, by Ernest Hemingway (Cape).

my sorrow, *Across the River* can be summed up in one word, lamentable.

Despite an excellent beginning, the Colonel soon emerges as one of the most unlikeable, drink-sodden and maundering old bores ever to have inflicted an interior monologue on those who can't answer back. His ladylove is a whimsical waxwork whose love scenes punctuate the book like a pneumatic drill on a hot afternoon, while the Colonel's fuddled war-reminiscences reveal a blind grudge against Generals, brass-hats, war correspondents and the British, but very little of the campaign. Bitter, sentimental and facetious, he mulls along from bar to bar like a mixture of Bloom and Soames Forsyte: 'I guess the cards we draw are those we get. You wouldn't like to re-deal would you dealer? No. They only deal to you once and then you pick them up and play them. I can play them, if I draw any damn thing at all . . . we are hung as we are hung, for better or for worse, or something, or something awful. You are one half a hundred years old, you bastard you. Now go in and take a shower and scrub good and afterwards put on your soldier suit. Today is another day.'

The novel fails because it is constructed from a false sense of values. The attitude of Hemingway is romantic and adolescent, a gesture of defiance made on behalf of all those who are brave and patient, dumb-animals in their suffering, against 'whatever brute or blackguard made the world'. This creed is not equipped for the deserts of middle-age and becomes theatrical and sentimental when too much strain is imposed on it. Drink and sex, the only comforters of real men (those with combat wounds), are a weariness of the spirit.

If Mr. Hemingway is to turn the corner he will have to cease to be a repressed intellectual as ashamed of the mind as he is outspoken about the body; he will have to study chess instead of baseball, Buddha or Saint John of the Cross rather than Belmonte and Omar Khayyám and forswear all fermented liquor. For the fault of *Across the River* (the unsympathetic unreality of the two principals) is present in a lesser degree in his earlier books, like the doggy facetiousness with which real men greet and sniff each other or the mechanical 'I love you's' which get them nowhere. The hardest task before any writer awaits Mr. Hemingway, and because he is capable of it, we set it confidently before him. At the age of fifty (which is much younger than he thinks) to take himself to pieces for a few months and then begin again on some objective task—a bestiary or a truthful autobiography would do—equipped at last with a comprehensive and adult philosophy in which the mind is recognised as what is most peculiar and wonderful in man.

[1950]

18

ERNEST HEMINGWAY: 2

By the death of Ernest Hemingway we have lost a Titan: whatever judgment we make upon his books the man was of the stature of a great novelist. He had the energy, the endurance, the personal grandeur of the Balzac, Stendhal, Flaubert, Tolstoy category. I do not think he was a great novelist but he was of the material of which great novelists are made, a Titan who still had it in him to become a god.

That we cannot put him on the highest level is not to his discredit. It is because he chose so completely to represent his era that he could never escape from its limitations; he was at heart a romantic poet who used fiction, even journalism, as his medium. It was writers as artists whom he admired—not novelists whose craft he studied. One cannot imagine him writing a book on the novel.

His first book was called *Three Stories and Ten Poems*, his first two novels were long short stories. His real novels are only three: *A Farewell to Arms*, *For Whom the Bell Tolls*, and *Across the River and Into the Trees*. He is not a novelist in the sense in which Henry James was, or Joyce or Arnold Bennett or Dreiser—or even Virginia Woolf, another poet. What concerned him was getting down the poetic nature of his own experience, not the construction of a novel as a work of art which would enforce on him its own laws.

The experience he wished to communicate could go into several moulds: the prose poem (like the first version of *In Our Time*), the didactic essay (*Death in the Afternoon*), the travel book (*Green Hills of Africa*), journalism (the articles on deep-sea fishing in *Esquire*, on the *Dangerous Summer* in *Life*), or a film like *Spanish Earth* which is pure Hemingway and a great film which should be shown again. But above all his medium was the short story: *The Sun Also Rises* and *A Farewell to Arms* were begun as short stories and *To Have and to Have Not* included one, while some of his short stories have the depth and completeness of novels. Of these the greatest in my opinion is *The Snows of Kilimanjaro* which has all the elements of an autobiographical novel and, in the present circumstances, a prophetic, almost unbearable sadness.

Wonderful as so many of these stories are, and diverse in content, they never take one away from the central point of Hemingway's genius; his stance of a romantic poet in the twentieth century. All are based, almost without exception, on the relationship between man and death, on the confrontation of man's nobility and courage with his ineluctable adversary.

When you were young you gave death much importance. Now you give it none, you only hate it for the people that it takes away.

So he wrote in 1938, but it was not true: the world was already taking on a new lease of death and very soon Hemingway was giving it his full attention from the death of Robert Jordan in *For Whom the Bell Tolls* to that of Colonel Cantwell in *Across the River and Into the Trees*. In fact everything he has written springs from the romantic protest.

'Tis a fine thing to dance and sing
While the bells of death do ring—

They dance and sing in *The Sun Also Rises*; in other books they talk and drink—but always against the same background. War provides the obvious arena for brave men to face death but Hemingway, in time of peace, also made his study of bullfighting because it is a sport in which the competitors risk their lives against death personified: boxing was a pale echo of this and gang-warfare provided another peacetime field of study. Big-game hunting and fishing also had their place, even skiing. But tennis, for example, of which Hemingway was fond, had no mention in his stories because it held no danger.

I suppose no writer has ever written so consistently of the 'moments of truth' when death stalks the adventurer (and less about lingering diseases, financial suicides, or bed-side quittances where the drama is lacking) and I cannot accept Hemingway's own explanation:

> The only place where you could see life and death, i.e. violent death now that the wars were over, was in the bull-ring and I wanted very much to go to Spain where I could study it. I was trying to learn to write, commencing with the simplest things, and one of the simplest things of all, and the most fundamental, is violent death.
>
> (*Death in the Afternoon.*)

Hemingway was already writing about dying bull-fighters in 1923, and he had been reporting the atrocities of the Turko-Greek war before that, besides being badly wounded in 1918.

One of his *Ten Poems* described a suicide in Montparnasse and his father committed suicide in 1928; and although Hemingway made Colonel Cantwell in *Across the River and Into the Trees* say 'no horse called Morbid ever won a race' I would assert that he must have had from boyhood a preoccupation with death and violence, an imagination drawn irresistibly towards the macabre—a common attribute of genius. His earliest stories, written when he was seventeen, already dealt with crimes of violence and crooked boxers.

Ernest Hemingway was born July 21st, 1899, in Oak Park, a suburb of Chicago. His father was a doctor, his mother was artistic and went in for music and painting. Their summers were spent in the wild lake district of Northern Michigan with its woods and Indians. Here his father taught him to shoot and fish:

> They were seated in the boat, Nick in the stern, his father rowing. The sun was coming up over the hills. A bass jumped, making a circle in the water. Nick trailed his hand in the water. It felt warm in the sharp chill in the morning.
>
> In the early morning on the lake sitting in the stern of the boat with his father rowing, he felt quite sure that he would never die.

At school he became both an athlete and an omnivorous reader and very soon a writer who went to work on the *Kansas City Star* rather than go to a university, before joining the American Red Cross. (His sight was too bad for the Army.) His Italian war-time experiences are described in *A Farewell to Arms*, his childhood and adolescence in *In Our Time*, that subtle counterpoint of stories and anecdotes which contrasts the war-time chaos and violence of Europe with the happiness of growing-up in Michigan.

Then came the formative years in Paris (so handy for Spain) which gave us the Hemingway we know. Only a year separates the publication of the complete *In Our Time* (1925) from the nineteen-twentyish best-seller *The Sun Also Rises* (1926), from which moment Hemingway was famous and evermore remained so, in the big lights and the big money, unable ever to hide from them.

He was an extremely handsome young man of superb physique, dazzling teeth, a British officer moustache, great courage; no one so physical and athletic had ever found his way before to sit at the feet of Flaubert, Joyce, Pound or Gertrude Stein. To his study of violent death he brought his exuberant gaiety, immense vitality, a wicked satirical gift and a lyrical sense of words, of their placing and timing.

Gertrude Stein made a writer of him out of a reporter; but his dialogue, which is flowing, natural and inevitable, was his own contribution. He had one grave fault which sprang I think from something warped in his character, a sadistic facetiousness which went with a tendency to sentimentality.

It took several forms; sneering at intellectuals, making smarty wisecracks in what should have been naturalistic dialogue, needling homosexuals, exulting in unpleasant details in the hope of giving offence, revelling in phony characters like the bloodthirsty little old lady in *Death in the Afternoon* or the suffering of hyenas in *Green Hills of Africa* or the thought-train of that Soames Forsyte in battledress, Colonel Cantwell in *Across the River and Into the Trees*.

The excessively male audience for which most of his journalism and some of his stories were written tended to bring this out and it accounts for the considerable critical coldness on the part of those who shrank from this uneasy vulgarity.

Hemingway, as a writer, was very conscious of his own failings. After the enormous success of *A Farewell to Arms* (1929) he encountered unpopularity with his two guide books to bull-fighting and kudu-slaying, and his socially-conscious novel *To Have and Have Not* was not a success although it is quite one of his best books, beautifully constructed and marvellously written.

He was saved from the bloated lethargy of success by the Spanish war which brought the romantic love of his life, the Iberian peninsula and its people, into historical greatness. He gave most of his fortune, forty thousand dollars, to the Spanish Medical Aid and this gesture alone set him absolutely apart from all other writers: it was worthy of a Titan, like his film, his despatches from Madrid and the encouragement afforded by his great prestige and loyal personality. 'Writers are forged in injustice as a sword is forged. . . .'

In Spain, as for so many others, his youth ended and after the war he went back to Cuba, where the shaggy grey-bearded be-spectacled 'Poppa' was born. His moment of glory as a man, if not as a writer, was in Normandy and Paris at the Liberation. Although a war correspondent he had somehow become a tank commander and led his regiment to the relief of the Ritz, the Travellers Club, and Sylvia Beach's bookshop, where, twenty years before, he had begun.

The proof of this last ten years will be his great war novel with its vast size and many deletions. Will it justify the artist who continued to work away inside the over-garlanded, over-celebrated, touchy, arrogant and run-to-seed 'great man' as he appears in the famous *New Yorker* interview? His last two years were built round his visits to Spain and his identification of all his youthful '*aficion*' with the career of the young bull-fighter Antonio Ordoñez whose father he had known and whose father he was becoming.

I would like to give a brief anthology but there is no room. I would include the last page of *A Farewell to Arms* because he rewrote it so many times; the whole of the twentieth chapter of *Death in the Afternoon*, the inventory of his beloved Spain; the whole of *In Our Time* because it is such a good first book; the two suppressed opening chapters of *The Sun Also Rises* (so that we can read them); the last chapters of *To Have and Have Not* and the first sentence; many, many stories, even extracts from his *Death in Venice* (*Across the River and Into the Trees*); the wonderful digressions on Paris and the Gulf Stream in *Green Hills of Africa* and the whole of his remarkable interview in *Paris Review*. No one has written more knowledgeably about sudden death or with more poetry about physical pleasures and the joy of living, no one has worked harder to give his prose a new dimension, a prose which he thought could never be written, 'without tricks and without cheating. With nothing that will go bad afterwards'.

19

SCOTT FITZGERALD: I

'LIFE is really too short for art—one hasn't time to make one's shell ideally hard. Firm and bright—firm and bright!—the devilish thing has a way, sometimes, of being bright without being firm. When I rap it with my knuckles it doesn't give the right sound. There are horrible little flabby spots where I have taken the second-best word, because I couldn't for the life of me think of the best. If you knew how stupid I am sometimes!'

*

Tell you the truth, Stearns, I had a big talent and I used it pretty well, in my good years anyway. I put down the things I saw, and nobody who looked at the things I was seeing saw more than I did. I didn't worry about proving any points, group neuroses or abortive revolutions. Maybe that's why I was more convincing.

*

Here are two imaginary writers addressing their young disciples. The first, 'the author of Beltraffio', is an invention of Henry James, the second 'Manley Halliday', a creation of Mr. Budd Schulberg.[1] Deduction. No mind can transcend its own limitations, a novelist in fiction cannot exceed the stature of the novelist who portrays him. If Halliday was indeed the first American writer of the 'twenties—'the only writer who could win the approval of Mencken and Stein and make 50,000 a year doing it'—no wonder the others fled to Paris.

[1] *The Disenchanted*, by Budd Schulberg (Bodley Head).

But Manley Halliday is not just a figment of the imagination, he is also a painstaking likeness of Scott Fitzgerald, a most delightful and talented novelist, exceptionally handsome, who, after a spectacular success and a decade of wild parties, descended the precipitous slope of American failure and died in Hollywood in tragic circumstances, grimly conscious of his unfulfilled career. With insight, sincerity and a haunting beauty of language he described in a novel the onset of his troubles, and in *The Crack-Up*, the circumstances of his breakdown. A second-hand account seems almost superfluous.

But Mr. Schulberg appears riveted by the theme. He sets up his idol with veneration, only to dismember him by the thousand cuts. He appears actually to have collaborated with Fitzgerald on a film-script which involved them in a disastrous trip east to the scenes of the novelist's former triumphs, a ten-day drinking bout which Mr. Schulberg rounds off with his hero's disgrace and death. Diabetes—via D.T.s—gangrene and a pulmonary embolism perform for the body what the laughter of undergraduates and the bullying of film-producers do for the soul. Halliday's love for his ex-wife, who is now a hopeless neurotic, adds to his betterness, and his 'disenchantment' gradually infects the earnest young Left-wing admirer who has been appointed his collaborator. Here is material for an admirable long short story, a *Death of the Lion*, heightened by some of the horror of *The Lost Week-End*. But Mr. Schulberg is determined to submerge himself altogether in Manley Halliday and for several hundred pages inhabits his consciousness and re-tells his whole story. 'Ernest speaks with the authority of his success,' wrote Fitzgerald in his notebook. 'I speak with the authority of my failure.' But Manley Halliday joins forces with Hemingway's Colonel Cantwell; they roar with the monotony of their alcoholic content.

Mr. Schulberg is a sensitive reporter, he observes everything and he includes everything, after the manner of the *New Yorker* profiles; his first ten chapters are admirable, before his gift for macabre clowning runs away with him. It is his attempt to live himself into another man's soul which fails: 'the thing has a way of being bright without being firm'. Fitzgerald is now on the road to becoming an American myth. 'The authority of his failure' is daily increasing. It is an alibi for our own. But what a sorry little myth it is! He was destroyed because like many an artist with more talent than vocation, he had worn himself out on illusions. He preferred too many other pleasures to writing. Nothing is here for tears except the one, so exquisitely unshed, which gathers throughout his later work.

20

SCOTT FITZGERALD: 2

A FEW weeks ago we considered Mr. Budd Schulberg's novel about Scott Fitzgerald, *The Disenchanted*, and summed up, perhaps a little arrogantly, against him. Now comes a full-length biography of this Valentino of American fiction. *The Far Side of Paradise*[1] is a very good book, an admirable piece of research which refuses every opportunity for fireworks and concentrates on a scholarly and sympathetic understanding of its subject and the unfolding of his sad story. Apart from his increasing stature as a writer, Fitzergald is now firmly established as a myth, an American version of the Dying God, an Adonis of letters born with the century, flowering in the 'twenties, the Jazz Age which he perfectly expressed and almost created and then quietly wilting away through the 'thirties to expire—as a deity of spring and summer should—on December 21st, 1940, at the winter solstice and the end of an epoch.

The myth encloses three ingredients: first Fitzgerald the American success, the author whose first novel, *This Side of Paradise* with its title taken from Rupert Brooke and its content from *Sinister Street*, yet became an extremely American thing, selling forty thousand copies and giving to the penniless young man just down from Princeton the wherewithal to capture his eighteen-year-old Southern belle; this myth was sustained by his stories of romantic young men and bobbed-haired young women which earned him up to forty thousand dollars a year.

Then we have the Dying God, the reverse of the medal, the

[1] *The Far Side of Paradise*, by Arthur Mizener (Eyre & Spottiswoode).

failing champion taking to drink, having his stories rejected, sinking into debt, dying penniless at forty-three in the 'Garden of Allah' as an obscure Hollywood scriptwriter. And suddenly the resurrection: the publication by his friend Edmund Wilson of his last unfinished novel and the memorial volume of his essays and letters.

The third ingredient is his marriage, the immensely happy marriage which made the Fitzgeralds seem one of the most charming, impulsive, devoted and glamorous couples in all the gay places of the world, the very spirit of the 'twenties made flesh. Incredibly handsome, successful, fêted, rich, he rose from his first popular success to *The Great Gatsby*, one of the landmarks of the American novel, his beautiful wife Zelda (to whom it was dedicated) standing beside him, and New York and New-York-in-Europe at his feet. About 1928 the decline began: 'they arrived in Paris in a haze of alcohol,' writes their biographer. 'They had a bitter quarrel during which unbelievable charges were made by both of them.'

After the relative failure of his grandly conceived but too patchily carried-out novel of Americans in Europe, *Tender is the Night*, the last years are a tale of mounting tragedy. Schizophrenia develops in Zelda, with an interdependence on the alcoholism of Scott. Even in the early days of the marriage a fatal spirit of competition existed and the myth which poor Scott best illustrates is perhaps that of betrayal in the sex-war. 'Zelda constantly making him drink because she was jealous of his working well,' wrote Hemingway, looking back. 'Money went through her fingers like water,' said his publisher, 'she wanted everything: she kept him writing for the magazines.'

A careful reading of Mr. Mizener, however, reveals a very early strain of exhibitionist, neurotic and anti-social behaviour in both of them and a more than normal addiction to drinking. They were always 'undressing in public or diving into fountains.' 'Fitzgerald got into fights with waiters and Zelda danced on people's dinner tables.' With a basic sense of social insecurity, an aggression liberated by drink or cruel practical jokes, they must often have been disastrous company even at the outset.

The combined tragedy is appalling, since Fitzgerald, though drinking himself to death, retained a brilliant insight into the process, its effect on himself and on his friends and fought back stoically; while Zelda, in her asylum, was capable of heart-rending lucidities. Fitzgerald watched the disintegration of someone he had loved as part of himself in the knowledge that he had contributed to her destruction and that her death-in-life would involve him too in emotional bankruptcy. He died in 1940; and in 1947 Zelda perished in a fire in the asylum where she was confined at Montgomery, the little Alabama town of which she had once been the beauty.

Yes, the human tragedy is almost unbearable but in the world of art, the kingdom of the page, we must acknowledge other standards. Here there is no tragedy except in the failure of great spirits to communicate their vision of the world before death or illness destroys them. The strains of Gatsby's 'neat sad waltz' will long be heard on Parnassus, the self-accusing torments of its composer never reach there. 'To get back to serious things,' as Balzac said to console a bereaved friend, 'who's going to marry Eugenie Grandet?'

21

SCOTT FITZGERALD: 3

I THOUGHT I had reached saturation point about Scott Fitzgerald. He is becoming an American imposition and I am beginning to want to deny him his pinch of incense, to refuse to sacrifice at his altar. I never want to read about another alcoholic; alcoholism is the enemy of art and the curse of Western civilisation. It is neither poetic nor amusing. I am not referring to people getting drunk but to the gradual blotting of the sensibilities and the destruction of personal relationships involved in the long-drawn-out social suicide. The greater the artist, the deadlier the process. 'There was a terrible deliberateness about the way Fitzgerald dosed himself with gin.'

However, Mr. Turnbull knew Fitzgerald when he was a small boy and the Fitzgeralds were his father's tenants on their estate near Baltimore. (Fitzgerald was one of nature's Baltimoreans.) He developed a cult for him and since he is also a professional writer the result is a most sympathetic and entertaining volume[1] worthy of all that the Bodley Head are doing for Fitzgerald. Mr. Turnbull concentrates on the man and does not provide a critical exegesis of all the novels and stories.

Besides reading all the documents, he seems to have interviewed all the surviving friends. This gives added freshness for not only does he revere Fitzgerald but he admires and tries to understand Zelda. He does not accept the Hemingway view that she was bent on ruining Scott out of envy and ran up bills to force him to write worse stories. The whole harrowing tale is re-told from the begin-

[1] *Scott Fitzgerald: A Biography*, by Andrew Turnbull (Bodley Head).

ning to Fitzgerald's pathetic funeral (aged forty-four) and Zelda's horrible death by fire in her asylum three years later.

I am an admirer of Professor Mizener's biography of Fitzgerald (*The Far Side of Paradise* published ten years ago) and I wondered how Mr. Turnbull would manage with so much of the spade work already done for him. I would have expected a stream of references to Mizener's work but there is only one, tucked away in small print among the notes at the end. 'Among previous books on Fitzgerald the most useful for my purposes were Sheilah Graham's memoir *Beloved Infidel* and Arthur Mizener's pioneering biography, *The Far Side of Paradise*.'

Both draw extensively on Fitzgerald's daughter, Mrs. Lanahan, Harold Ober (Fitzgerald's agent), the Murphys and Mr. Turnbull's mother, and of course on Fitzgerald's own copious archive, but Professor Mizener is more sympathetic to Hemingway and Budd Schulberg and Edmund Wilson. Mr. Henry Piper and Judge Biggs are also common to both. I found in many anecdotes they run neck-and-neck. Sometimes there are differences. Here are two examples. Mizener's account of the first Fitzgerald-Hemingway quarrel over Fitzgerald's timekeeping in the fight with Morley Callaghan is more full and accurate than Turnbull's, and he gives three different sources. Turnbull, on the other hand, is better on the earth-shaking teaparty with Edith Wharton. Here is Professor Mizener:

'Mrs. Wharton,' Fitzgerald demanded, 'do you know what is the matter with you?'

'No, Mr. Fitzgerald, I've often wondered about that. What is it?'

'You don't know anything about life,' Fitzgerald roared and then, determined to shock and impress them—'Why, when my wife and I first came to Paris, we took a room in a bordello. And we lived there for two weeks.'

... After a moment's pause, Mrs. Wharton, seeming to realise from his expression how baffled Fitzgerald was, tried to help him.

'But Mr. Fitzgerald,' she said, 'You haven't told us what they did in the bordello. ...'

At first when Zelda asked him how it had gone he answered her that it had been a great success, they had liked him, he had bowled them over. But gradually the truth came out, until—after several drinks—Fitzgerald put his head on his arms and began to pound the table with his fists.

'They beat me,' he said, 'They beat me! They *beat* me.' ('I owe this anecdote to a very careful note of it by Mr. Robert Chapman immediately after hearing it from Richard Knight', notes the Professor.)

And Mr. Turnbull:

Arrived at the Pavillon Colombe, Fitzgerald and Chanler were ushered into a salon where Mrs. Wharton, the confidante of Henry James, sat behind her teaset in shy majesty. There was one other guest, an American-born Cambridge don named Gaillard Lapsley. . . . Since Chanler and Lapsley were unable to break the ice, Fitzgerald descended to such platitudes as 'Mrs. Wharton, you have no idea what it means to me to come out here?' Finally in desperation, he suggested telling 'a couple of—er—rather rough stories'.

Permission having been granted by a queenly nod, a fixed smile, he began one and switched to another about an American couple who had spent three days in a Paris bordello, which they mistook for a hotel. As he faltered to a conclusion, Mrs Wharton said 'But Mr. Fitzgerald, your story lacks data'—whereupon he tried to patch it up without success.... Mrs. Wharton wrote 'Horrible' beside his name in her diary. ('I have described the encounter between Fitzgerald and Edith Wharton,' notes Mr. Turnbull, 'as it was told me by Theodore Chanler, who was there'.)

I am myself undertaking a brief thesis of one hundred thousand words for the literary department of the University of Spittoon on the great bordello controversy and would welcome any further information on it. What did Lapsley think? What did Mrs. Wharton really say?

Mr. Turnbull writes with understanding about Fitzgerald's rather formidable friends Hemingway, Thomas Wolfe and Edmund Wilson. 'His (Hemingway's) inclination is towards megalomania and mine towards melancholy,' wrote Fitzgerald and perhaps the best cure for the surfeit of slickness which the perusal of so many of his stories engenders is to return to the gloomy letters and notebooks of his last battle against oblivion.

22

THOMAS WOLFE

If the greatest art partakes of the condition of music, then the greatest critic is a musical critic, and his greatness is in his freedom, and his freedom is freedom from autobiography. No one can write his autobiography in music, and if he does we can pretend it is something else; but in literature there is no getting away.

I could inflict on you every word, thought, idea, feeling about myself and the people I have met in the last five years and call it a novel and you would have to read it. This tyrannical egotism, which is really neurosis, can hire the uniform of genius and borrow Joyce's cock-eyed crown. 'Oh boy, you are fine. There is no atom in you that is not fine. A glory and a chrism of bright genius rest upon you. God bless you: the world is yours.'

'I have at last discovered my own America, I believe I have found my language. I think I know my way. And I shall wreak out my vision of this life, this way, this world, and this America, to the top of my bent and to the height of my ability but with an unswerving devotion, integrity and purity of purpose that shall not be menaced, altered or weakened by anyone.'

Admittedly Thomas Wolfe is writing to his publisher, and they are gluttons for verbal beefcake, but the language is strangely like Hitler's. Why bring in America always? And who are these enemies who wish to menace, alter or weaken him? Right first time. The critics.

Not the critics one values, the constructive who praise but the sterile, the dead—the Hemingways, Fadimans, etc., who find fault. Expatriates! Waste-landers! 'Their idea of helping you is to kick you in the face.' 'A writer is an open target for anyone in the world who wants to throw a rotten egg.' 'I have been shy and silent before these liars and fools far too long. I have eaten crow and swallowed my pride for ten years before the waste-landers, the lost generations, the biter-bitters, the futility people, and all other cheap literary fakes—but now I will hold my tongue no longer: I know what I know and I have learned it with blood and sweat. . . .' And so they are all put into the gaschamber of Thomas Wolfe's novels.

I should like to say more about these novels for they belong to my youth and I remember them coming out as one remembers the sullen explosions from a quarry on some long-distant summer noontide as we sat tippling on the lawn: 'It must be twelve o'clock. They're blasting again.'

This time I have really tried to read one and I can say with all my heart: this man is not a novelist; he is an obsessional neurotic with a gift for words who should write only about himself and who cannot create other people. He is the Benjamin Robert Haydon of American literature beside whom Dreiser is a dainty Benvenuto Cellini. He is hypnotised by the growth of his own personality and by the search for a spiritual father, a hormone who will accelerate the manic urge still further.

To be looking for a father is a wonderful excuse for dropping people, and Wolfe took advantage of this to the full. Although the climax in his short life seems to have been the 'break with Scribners' or the shedding of the faithful pilot, Maxwell Perkins, my own experience as a much-dropped, deposed, dethroned, decapitated father figure, a wandering Wotan, is that the father invariably does the dropping first in so far as he senses the mist of total obscurity or the hideous alpine glow of success that is gathering round his prodigy and I think that Maxwell Perkins must have failed to conceal his apprehension, both as a publisher and a friend, about the ponderous, paranoid, turgid flow of the Wolfe novels as the lonely giant, at grips with his enormous task of holding back absolutely nothing, emerged from solitude, every few minutes, to complain about some utterly unimportant word or criticism or well-meant piece of advice. 'I don't think he *consciously* wants me to fail or come to grief,' wrote Wolfe, 'but it's almost as if *unconsciously*, by some kind of *wishful* desire, he wants me to come to grief, as a kind of sop to his pride and his unyielding conviction that he is right in everything.'

Intimate, impressive and exemplary as was his relationship with Perkins, it was thereby doomed, while the tie with Frere of Heinemanns, cooler because there was no compulsion here to justify and explain himself, less love and so less resentment, is an admirable testimony to the unassuming loyalty and understanding which he received from the older man. With Frere he could discuss beer and chophouses, with Perkins he *must* discuss his soul. Frere he called more than a publisher, a friend; Perkins was more than a friend, a father, so that it is typical that after the bitter quarrel the last deeply-moving deathbed letter should have been to him when he looked back on their meeting on a roofgarden after the success of his book—'and all the strangeness and the glory and the power of life and of the city was below.'

The king of father-chasers and prince of autobiographers was Joyce, and this similarity of purpose (fulfilment of genius through finding of father) united Wolfe to the great exile, with fatal detriment to his style. These echoes are apparent throughout *Look Homeward, Angel*,[1] which mews with self-pity and Celtic twilight.

He saw a brief, forgotten gesture, her white broad forehead, a ghost of old grief in her eyes. Ben Gant—their strange lost voices. Their sad laughter. They swam toward him through green walls of fantasy. They caught and twisted at his heart. The green ghost-glimmer of their faces coiled away. Lost. Lost.

'Let's go for a smoke,' said Max Isaacs.

The high spirits, clowning and parodying, the scenes of broken-down family life are Joycean too. I have said I do not think Wolfe was a genius, nor am I sure he was a novelist; but in these *Selected*

[1] *Look Homeward, Angel*, by Thomas Wolfe (Heinemann).

Letters[1] he stands out as a fascinating writer. In his letters he could permit his egotism full rein. He made copies of his best letters or else did not send them or else got them back; he gloried in the fluent medium.

As he was a large and violent young man things were constantly happening to him. There was a terrible beating-up in Munich, an encounter with Joyce on the battlefield of Waterloo. The editor of the letters does not seem aware that the account of the 'musey-room' at Waterloo forms one of the key passages of *Finnegans Wake*, and that Wolfe (chagrined at not being recognised) was present at one of the most fortunate fertilisations of modern literature.

Inexcusable I find the omission, in the edition prepared for this country, of Wolfe's most interesting letter (unsent naturally), in which he describes at great length a devastating encounter with Scott Fitzgerald at the Ritz in Paris in 1930. Here this huge, ramshackle, shy, deep, good, suspicious and resentful young man, who looks like a genius and has nothing but talent, meets the older but not very fatherly little dandy, drunk and at the height of his success, who tries to launch Wolfe on Franco-American society. 'Every writer,' Fitzgerald tells him, 'is a social climber.' Wolfe rebuts the charge splendidly, but it is, all the same, in the little man from Princeton for all his snobbery and air of talent that the genius resides. Their subsequent Zola-Flaubert arguments are all coloured by this episode.

Suppose Wolfe had lived (for his death was inadvertent): at his present age (fifty-seven) he would have been an enormous figure in American literature. His driving energy, his egotism, the basic strength and rightness of his values both as an artist and a man would have seared away the blindness and the rhetoric; he would have come to terms with his persecution mania for he could never have dried up or become a spent ranter.

His prose would have been worthy of the poetical force beneath it, his absurd rocketry about great America, decadent

[1] *Selected Letters of Thomas Wolfe*. Edited by Elizabeth Nowell (Heinemann).

Europe and so on been chastened by failures—the bull blundering about after critics' capes would have learnt wisdom. He would have been the Whitman of the Beat Generation, of course—and of many others—instead of the Thinking Bull. 'Why is it that we are burnt out to an empty shell by the time we are forty. . . . Is it because we take a young man of talent—a young man proud of spirit, and a thirst for glory, and full with the urge to make his life prevail—praise him up to the skies at first, and then press in upon him from all sides with cynics' eyes and scornful faces, asking him if he can *ever do it again* or is done for, finished?'

23

E. E. CUMMINGS

I HAVE lately felt aware of a worry at the back of my mind about the death of the American poet E. E. Cummings who liked to be known as e. e. cummings. It is an added misfortune to die at the end of August or beginning of September when all one's friends are away in the hills or on the beaches; the event appears slightly unreal for there are no critical estimates or personal tributes. That was what was at the back of my mind, the feeling that I had missed something, that at any moment I would open a paper and find the tribute and the estimate I expected. But months have passed and once again the thought arises which all must feel as they grow old, that it is they who are the custodians of the dead, and that if they wish to read something about one of them they will have to write it themselves.

Here is what I expected:

Edward Estlin Cummings was born in October, 1896, in Cambridge, Massachusetts where his father was a Unitarian minister. He was educated at Harvard like his father, went to France in the first world war, wrote an extraordinary war book, *The Enormous Room* (1922), fell in love with Paris for two years, then returned to America and devoted his whole life to painting and poetry.

He was a natural anarchist who made no concessions to authority and remained all his life a poor man, one of the very few poets to have no other jobs. He insisted on making typography part of the structure of his poems; this intrigued some and alienated many. It was not an affectation but part of his preoccupation with language, the heresy, one might call it, of Mallarmé's *Coup de dès*.

He lived most of his life in Patchin Place, New York, which somehow reminded me of Margaretta Terrace, Chelsea. He was a man of very great charm, with a lovely wife, absolutely authentic in all his personal relations because he would not recognise any others. He set a high standard of friendship and perhaps was too easily disappointed. He enjoyed his painting as much as, probably more than, writing poetry. He was built like a rather rangy pelota player with a long Etruscan face which looked very well in a beret. He could metamorphose at will from the Harvard man of letters to the East Side tough, talking venomously out of the side of his mouth. He was one of the people in America I most wanted to get to know and it was worth it; we had some French meals at the Lafayette and I introduced him to Auden whom he had never met, and I published a book of his, *One Times One*, when I got back. It proved quite unsaleable. He was a very isolated figure, but far too happy to be lonely. He began to obtain a lot of recognition in the 'fifties, but I don't think he cared much about it; he was used to feeling indignation and to taking the offensive against all life-haters, from intellectual Marxists to venal critics and the complacent American bourgoisie.

When a young man, in his Paris days, he seems to have undergone a manic visitation from the Muse; his long prose work and five volumes of poetry all came pouring out in two or three years (1922-25) and he could also hold forth all night without pausing, looking like a sophisticated apache. These poems, I think, are his best work, and at this time he had the entrée to *The Dial* through Gilbert Seldes and Scofield Thayer and also won the admiration of Ezra Pound.

He must have been a little like a rougher, uncorrupted Scott Fitzgerald, an American romantic turning realist. His favourite form was the Shakespearean sonnet which he broke up into a violent, almost colloquial medium. His best poems remind me of Catullus; there is a controlled fury about them, an erotic exhilaration. I don't know of anyone who has so caught the excitement and despair of brothels and speakeasies in the Prohibition days, in that New York from which the other expatriates kept away.

The 'thirties was a bad time for him as for so many writers of his generation. Unlike Fitzgerald, he was not almost forgotten, but went off into polemic and had great difficulty in finding a publisher, though he must have been the only poet to have discovered as a patron a tame printer, Mr. S. A. Jacobs, who welcomed his typographical challenge. During the war his poetry picked up again and since then he has been in all the anthologies. I do not feel, however, that his later poetry was his best. He was a lyric poet who continued to celebrate love and spring and young lovers with all his warmth and to hate death and conformity, cowardice and apathy—but who to some extent lacked an intellectual growth within so that his hymns to love and life could appear sentimental and his satirical typographical cryptograms grow wearisome.

Anarchist attitudes age badly, and I think to get the feel of authentic Cummings one must turn back to the earlier poems of *Is 5* (his fifth book, 1925) or the larger revision of his first poems, *Tulips and Chimneys.* There we will find sudden illumination, as if we are watching the lights go on along the Boulevard from the window of some dingy hotel bedroom or waiting for a girl in a New York speakeasy on a winter afternoon.

> *Dick Mid's large bluish face without eyebrows*
> *sits in the kitchen nights and chews a two-bit cigar,*
> *waiting for the bulls to pull his joint. . . .*

The total silence surrounding Cummings's death made me wonder if it were not part of a larger ignorance, if today the two alienated cultures are not art and science but British and American. I began to consider how many people in this country have read, as well as Cummings, Wallace Stevens, William Carlos Williams or Hart Crane.

Hart Crane was a frenzied middle-western alcoholic homosexual whose passion was to write like Rimbaud and who succeeded. He is nearly as important as Dylan Thomas, who greatly admired him, and when he was drowned in his early thirties (1932) was at work on a fascinating group of tropical poems, *Key West,* an adult change from his overloaded but magnificent sequence about Brooklyn Bridge.

He wrote best when drunk, with the gramophone playing the same piece of jazz all night, awaiting some magical *donnée* in the manner of Francis Bacon. And if that seems surprising, how much more surprising is the case of Wallace Stevens, a poet of great intelligence and exquisite fancy who clung all his life to the insurance business and became managing director of a large company from which he refused to retire at seventy-five. And of Dr. Williams, who has been in every *avant-garde* magazine since 1920 and remained a suburban G.P. His last book, *Paterson V*, has some of the best lines on old age since Yeats.

And while we are about it, how many Americans know what a wonderful poet we have in Mr. Arthur Waley, whose translations from the Chinese from 1916 onwards were really the profound answer to both the academic and the Georgian styles and which performed—or could have performed—the same liberating function that Dr. Williams did, with his 'Nantucket' or 'By the Road to the Contagious Hospital'.

And how many English know it either?

24

GEORGE ORWELL

SIR RICHARD REES was a close friend of Orwell and an editor of the *Adelphi* for which he wrote and therefore one of the people best qualified to bring out a book about him. It is a short book[1] and a simple one; Sir Richard does little more than present Orwell's character as it seemed to him and then take us through his books from *Down and Out in London and Paris* to *1984* and the last essays.

But he does this very well; one feels that his conception of Orwell's complicated nature is the right one and makes sense when applied to his books and that Sir Richard could have written three times as much if he had chosen. This is the book on Orwell I have liked the best; and he is someone delightful to read about because his personality generated a certain casual intimacy which was very endearing.

The tragedy of Orwell's life is that when at last he achieved fame and success he was a dying man and knew it. He had fame and was too ill to leave his room, money and nothing to spend it on, love in which he could not participate; he tasted the bitterness of dying. But in his years of hardship he was sustained by a genial stoicism, by his excitement about what was going to happen next and by his affection for other people; and these are the years when Sir Richard was closest to him.

He explains that there were four separate strains in Orwell: the Promethean rebel, 'a profoundly serious and tragic pessimist'; the second 'sympathetic to authority at least as long as it is benign and

[1] *George Orwell: Fugitive from the Camp of Victory*, by Richard Rees (Secker & Warburg).

paternal'; the third an eighteenth-century rationalist 'debunker of spurious idealism and spirituality'; the fourth a romantic, a lover of the past, of 'old-fashioned virtues, old-fashioned customs and old-fashioned people.' Another way to express this would be to say that he suffered from a typically English form of the Oedipus complex by which, having dealt his father's authority a swinging blow, he would rush up to ask 'Have I hurt you?'

I once wrote that he was a revolutionary in love with 1910. This England of 1910, the London of *Riceyman Steps*, the country-side of Henry Ryecroft, the nation of village shopkeepers, of little tobacconists in urban alleys, of decency and individualism was the damsel in distress to be rescued from the dragon of the ruling class, the monster of Church and State, the capitalist oppressor.

Sir Richard draws an interesting parallel between Orwell and Conrad although I do not remember Orwell expressing any early enthusiasm for Conrad so much as for Shaw, Wells and Samuel Butler. Gissing came later.

Both Orwell and I were dominated by the headmistress of our private school; it was this remarkable woman who dished out rewards and punishments, who quoted Kipling and inculcated patriotism, who exalted character and moral courage and Scottish chieftains in kilts. We learnt the father values from a mother, we bit the hand that fed us, that tweaked the short hairs above the ear. But it was a woman's hand whose husband's cane was merely the secular arm. Agonising ambivalence!

Orwell, too, felt bitterly that he was taken on at reduced fees because he might win a scholarship; he saw this as a humiliation, but it was really a compliment.

In any case, I would say that his character was already formed by the time he had arrived at Eton and I regret that the volume of *Collected Essays*[1] still does not include the extraordinary *Such, Such were the Joys* which is the key to his formation and which has only been published in America.

Personally, I think that the secret of Orwell's reduced school-fees (a secret, incidentally, perfectly kept) caused Orwell to adopt

[1] *Collected Essays of George Orwell* (Secker & Warburg).

a prematurely economic explanation of society which does not allow for the many 'grace and favour' apartments of which the Establishment disposes. The real heroes of his preparatory school were not peers and plutocrats but kilted charmers who were good at cricket (perhaps their fees were reduced too) and who sometimes afterwards got into serious trouble.

Another point I would raise with Sir Richard is this assumption:

When one considers how many of the first intellectuals, in this century alone, have died early from consumption—Chekhov, Katherine Mansfield, D. H. Lawrence, Simone Weil, and Orwell, for example—it seems reasonable to ask whether this disease may not sometimes be connected with the strain and effort of swimming against the stream.

I do not think there was anything psychosomatic about Orwell's illness. Although he told me he found the disease interesting, I think he most bitterly longed to be well. As a small boy he was always sneezing; he was big and strong but obviously 'chesty' and a sufferer from one of the two English diseases, bronchitis (rheumatism is the other), inherent in the climate. This was made much worse by the pneumonia which he caught in Paris and by his experiences in the Spanish War, but he was never an incandescent character like Lawrence or like those frail, highly-strung individuals who 'fall into a decline'.

I agree with Sir Richard's interpretation of his character and assessment of his books. *Animal Farm* is the best, *1984* I think fails aesthetically through personal despair. I remember giving a very favourable review to *Burmese Days*, but Sir Richard's favourite is *Coming Up for Air!* I enjoyed every word of this short book and, after that, the pleasure of turning to the admirable *Collected Essays*.

'My starting point is always a feeling of partnership, a sense of injustice', he wrote in 1947: but also 'So long as I remain alive and well I shall continue to feel strongly about prose style, to love the surface of the earth, and to take a pleasure in solid objects and scraps of useless information . . . a good prose is like a window-pane.'

25

LOUIS MACNEICE (1961)

MR. MACNEICE is one of our regular poets, he has been with us now since 1935 (the year of his *Poems* though not of his first book) and has averaged a new book every two years. He is therefore taken for granted in the English way; that is to say, no one ever devotes a whole critical article to him or considers it at all remarkable that he should have maintained such a consistently high level of talent and intelligence for so long.

He is like an ancient catalpa in a London square dazzling with its annual display of blossom the passers-by who are unable to see it. It is time that someone spoke up and said what pleasure his writing has given during the last quarter of a century since he arrived, in full possession of all his gifts, with the first startling lines of 'An Ecologue for Christmas':

> A. I meet you in an evil time
> B. The evil bells
> Put out of our heads, I think,
> the thought of everything else.
> A. The jaded calendar revolves,
> Its nuts need oil, carbon chokes the valves.
> The excess sugar of a diabetic culture
> Rotting the nerve of life and literature . . .

down to some of the extraordinary poems in this volume,[1] such as 'The Bad Dream' or the deceptively simple 'Truisms' or 'Selva

[1] *Solstices*, by Louis Macneice (Faber).

Oscura.' What is the connecting thread? What qualities hold throughout his verse?

To begin with, he is a classical scholar and so we shall always be able to rely on his grammar, on his lucidity, on mental processes which, if not always easy to follow, obey the rules of thought as practised by good minds; and he has also a knowledge of prosody.

On the other hand he is not a don, his philosophy has been tested in a hard school; he is not intellectually arrogant which lends an added beauty to his intellectual images; he is a tough-minded stoic with a soft spot for hedonism. His weakness is a tendency to fall into flatness and banality, the music giving out and the thought disappearing into clever tricks. At such times he seems to be playing the tortoise to Professor Auden's hare, and this perhaps is what Dame Edith Sitwell meant by referring to his 'inelasticity of rhythm, his verse either sticky in texture or disintegrated, gritty and sabulous'. He has a strong vein of journalism and sometimes seems to be putting the *New Statesman's* 'London Diary' into free verse.

But the toughness and energy of the journalist sustains the poet and philosopher who also draws sustenance from love and nature and travel, and from his local inheritance as an Anglo-Irish expatriate, a product of the Oxford of Auden, Spender, Day Lewis and Rex Warner.

Like Dylan Thomas he managed to write some of the best war-poetry; in fact the books which I enjoy the most, besides his first *Poems* are *Plant and Phantom* (1941), which includes one of his best love-poems ('Time was away'), and the Irish poems of *The Last Ditch* and of *Springboard* (1944) which also includes 'Brother Fire', 'The Libertine' and 'Prayer before Birth'. And, of course, *Autumn Journal* (1939), where the journalist has helped the philosopher to preserve for ever the uneasy atmosphere of 'Munich'.

Of his latest book Mr. Macneice writes:

I would say of myself that I have become progressively more humble in face of my material, and therefore less ready to slap poster-paint over it. I have also perhaps found it easier to write poems of acceptance, even of joy. . . . My own position has been aptly expressed by the dying Mrs.

Gradgrind in Dickens' *Hard Times*: 'I think there's a pain somewhere in the room but I couldn't positively say that I have got it'.

If we accept that Mr. Macneice is a Scholar-Journalist in the sense in which Matthew Arnold wrote about the Scholar Gypsy, we can group together some of his new poems as *faits divers*; an album of remembered war-pictures, topical water-colours of Regent's Park, lecturing scenes—in the restaurant car, breakfast at the airport, and so on—many of them delightfully written and including an excellent satire on itinerant culture-diffusionists, 'Old Masters Abroad'.

> Painfully grinning faces like dogs' or
> Inattentive like cats' all over
> The static globe affect to be lectured
> By the singing birds of unknown England . . .
> At Bablockhythe the stripling Ganges
> Burns on her ghats the scholar gypsy
> There's a deathly hush on the rocks of Aden . . .
> Nine bean rows rise in the Kalahari.
> The faces listen or not. The lecturers
> Mop their memories. All over the static
> Globe the needle sticks in the groove.
> It is overtime now for the Old Masters.

The most cunning and apparently effortless of these little word-sketches are the 'Nature Notes', and the 'Indoor Sports' with its eulogy of darts and shove-halfpenny and devastating epigram on crossword puzzles. The scholar also triumphs in the universal 'Dark Age Glosses', four poems which Auden would have crammed into four flawless sonnets but for which our tortoise takes twenty lines each in order to leave an indelible picture.

The love-poems are his best since *Plant and Phantom* and reveal a sensation of unexpected homecoming which is the reward, sometimes, of those who have lived and suffered poetically:

> Perhaps suddenly too I strike a clearing and see
> Some unknown house—or was it mine? But now
> It welcomes whom I miss in welcoming me;

The door swings open and a hand
Beckons to all the life my days allow.

It will be seen that the diction of these poems is very plain; there is a total lack of ornamentation, very little rhyme, and it sometimes seems not poetry but a form of stark prose. The last love-poem has no punctuation and a great many words of one syllable, approaching the line of Dylan Thomas. One poem, 'Country Week-end', he calls a deliberate exercise in simplicity. I am not sure I do not prefer something more sensational such as the 'Bad Dream', for I like Mr. Macneice's verbal fireworks, from 'Bagpipe Music' to the 'Streets of Laredo'. But one cannot prevent middle-aged poets from throwing out a lot of ballast:

So now it is time. Decant the oil,
Turn up the wick. Call it escape
Or what rude name you like—or call it
A good deed, rather a good night:
one good night in a naughty world.

26

DYLAN THOMAS

'PUSHING up theses,' that is the euphemism which men of letters use for being dead; a long littleness of dons lies ahead of us, unless we have been afflicted with the curse of lucidity: now comes a symposium of thirty-eight writers to describe Dylan Thomas as they knew him, or to discuss his work.

Professor Tedlock has reprinted many scattered pieces about Dylan Thomas, not usually giving their dates, so that some of them conclude with the hope that, in the future, he will change his tactics; some even are unaware of the impending war which was to produce his greatest poems.

I myself came across the other day my review of *The Map of Love* for the *New Statesman* in 1939, and was surprised by the patronising tone which I adopted. Three things were to happen to Dylan Thomas after 1939; the poems in *Deaths and Entrances*, the emergence of the actor and reciter and broadcaster, and his early death; and none of this is adumbrated in some of these articles about him.

The biographical glimpses, however, take us right up to the final 'insult to the brain' which is now as familiar to us as the horn-wound which killed Manolete or the rose-bush which pricked Rilke. This publicity aspect of Thomas which links his death to Rupert Brooke and Rudolf Valentino in an apotheosis of the absurd, surely needs a few years to settle, and I am inclined to recommend *The Legend and the Poet*[1] only to those who wish to read everything written about him, not to those who are still ignorant of his 'craft and sullen art'.

1 *The Legend and the Poet*. Edited by E. W. Tedlock (Heinemann).

Since the book is in two halves we must judge them both separately. The first, the reminiscences, contains some fascinating material, by Messrs. Durrell, Davenport and others, including the verbatim report of one of Thomas's lectures on the poetry circuit. One must imagine the exhausted performer facing the usual circle of enlightened students, all of course thesis-minded, and the inevitable 'creative-writing' teacher whose ambivalent attitude to visiting authors has often been analysed. This one took place at the university of Utah:

'Is it ever fair deliberately to confuse the reader?'

Thomas: 'I thought someone would take me up on that. No, it is a deliberate avowal of your own inefficiency. It is impossible to be too clear . . . I am trying for more clarity now. At first, I thought it enough to leave an impression of sound and feeling, and let the meaning seep in later, but since I've been giving these broadcasts, and reading other men's poetry as well as my own, I find it better to have more meaning at first reading.'

'But on the other hand, isn't it possible to narrow and fix a meaning to the exclusion of richer levels of meaning?'

Thomas: 'O God, isn't education wonderful! . . .'

He dealt an even deadlier thrust at the thesis-industry when a student asked, 'How do you tell if a poem is good or not?'

'If I like it.'

'But what do you go by?'

'I like one because it is better than the others.' (Silence.)

The professor had to suppress this heresy. 'Perhaps we should do as you suggest and like a poem because we think it better than others, but students have to pull it apart and analyse why they like it and write it all down for the professor.' (Very long pause.)

And professors have to pull it apart too, in order to contradict other professors, which they do in the second half of this book, where the same lines appear and re-appear to be given quite different interpretations. On the whole, the unfriendly reviews linger longer in the memory because Mr. Grigson and one or two others do show up the truth of the admission that Thomas made in jest, that sound and feeling preceded meaning, and that the famous letter to Henry Treece, on his method of composition, should be taken with a grain of salt. Thomas loved to parody himself and everyone else; his mixture of genius and humility allowed him to by-pass all the usual paraphernalia of poets; about his meaning or method of work he would say whatever he felt you would like to hear. Although he was a most conscientious craftsman and took infinite pains in the writing of his poems, he liked to sell them to editors for cash down and then it was extremely difficult to get him to correct a proof, 'because poets did not go to offices like businessmen'.

An error I should like to correct is that the visits to America (to make money for his English income-tax) were the cause of the alcoholism which led to his death. The closeness of death is present in all his poetry and when I first knew him, soon after he had come to London, he was determined to drink as much as possible and to imagine that he had T.B.

He was already obsessed with the idea that a poet should die young and live in such a way as to risk his own destruction. At an age when many an undergraduate is doing the same thing, it did not seem pernicious that he should aim at the intoxication of a Marlowe, a Baudelaire, a Rimbaud, or a Dowson, because he seemed able to do without drink for his creative country-periods, and because he was still a young poet, not the heavy-drinking Fleet Street character which he afterwards became.

Of course, his detractors are right in that some of his poetry is merely surrealist and consists of heavily-flogged imagery which belies all meaning—but despite this he was a genius and when he could weld his own backward-looking religious and romantic sensibility into the new forms he desired, he created a new poetry: as Hugo said of Baudelaire, a 'frisson nouveau'. That his imitators are so artificial and empty does not prove that his poetry is bad, only that it is inimitable.

So one comes back to Dame Edith Sitwell and the other appraisers of his work in this volume for, despite the limitations of his genius, which could operate only in a narrow range of central ideas—childhood—birth—sex—crucifixion—death, it can carry us into the world of great art, while the critical examinations here gathered together in the end generate only weariness. The author of one of them complains that Thomas could have just as well written 'the synagogue of the water-bead, and the round Zion of the ear of corn', as the reverse. But he didn't (ears of corn are not round), and what he did write was better, and no one else could have thought of it.

The death of a young poet, as Mr. Karl Shapiro writes in the concluding essay, inflicts a psychic wound upon the world and is the cause, among poets themselves, of frightening babbling and soothsaying.

27

DENTON WELCH

THE journal of a sedentary writer is an exercise in fascination. Confined in one place, condemned to a certain monotony, deprived of the resources of dialogue and plot, the writer pits his mind, his privacy, the whole quality of his imagination against the reading public. Will he lose them or hold them? One might see this as the supreme test of a contemporary writer, the mark of the professional rather than the amateur. Denton Welch passes it with flying colours. I have read every word of this long book[1] with increasing delight, I have blotted out wind and rain, age and infirmity, anxiety and want in the recesses of his keen, bright, fresh, sensuous thought-stream and lived happily behind his mischievous observant eye.

A doomed and youthful poet, condemned to a horrible and lingering death by a twist of blind chance (he received a spinal injury when a motorist knocked him off his bicycle in Bromley), he yet manages to exude a quiet happiness as well as courage, intelligence and determination, while our foreknowledge of his death (a few weeks after the journal breaks off in 1948) illuminates many of the trivial entries with a lyrical underglaze as poignant as the becalmed sadness of the exquisite idling creatures in the dying Watteau's 'Halt During the Chase'.

Before his accident Denton Welch was an art student; his illness seconded him to literature.

Disease ever present, and the shadow of death, as if conscious of the meaningless cruelty to which they had condemned him,

[1] *Journals*, by Denton Welch (Hamish Hamilton).

mitigated his fate by sharpening his gifts of clarity, intuition, an unfailing effortless liaison with the right words. One is never conscious of hard work and erasures: his style ripens like an October pear that measures every hour of sunshine against the inevitable frost.

Two books of stories, an autobiography, a novel about his sickness and this journal (nearly half of which, I am distressed to learn, seems to have been omitted) make a most imposing show for a creative period of some five years, from the day in 1942 when the Editor of *Horizon* first saw him into print with an uproarious account of a visit to Sickert.

The description delighted Dame Edith Sitwell who became his guardian angel and opened the way to a series of literary encounters which form a kind of subdued comic relief in the pages of his journal. It is a great pity that some of these were omitted as malicious. Youth ought to judge the middle-aged and successful harshly and even unjustly, for too often they are ridiculous and they get terribly in the way.

Denton Welch had some of the clairvoyance of genius and a little of the terrible malice of the sick, he glimpsed the appalling vulgarity inseparable from rude health except in the bodies of the Housmanesque farm labourers whom he could observe on his walks in their natural surroundings. Otherwise he was a very old-fashioned young man. Born in 1915, the younger son of a successful China merchant from Shanghai, utterly English in outlook and background, a felicitous misfit, he gave his work the atmosphere of the early 'twenties. Mr. Jocelyn Brooke, in his wise introduction, compares him to Firbank. I am also reminded of Barbellion, Katherine Mansfield, Mr. E. M. Forster.

He adored the eighteenth century and writes charmingly about period doll's houses, teapots and teaspoons, china, silver . . . the luxurious warmth and colour of the drawing room as it appears to those who see it from the nursery. Old houses he also loved and the old people who lived in them. Like many artists he was mildly snobbish and thus fortunately aware of the magical and sombre poetry of the Fall of the most haunted of all houses of Usher, the aristocratic civilisation built up by the English over two hundred years of plenty.

This is, however, but one aspect. It is a happy and absorbing book because the writer was happily absorbed by simple things. Mid-Kent, half suburban, half huge romantic park, is delineated in all weathers with careless affection; curious people come and go; we find ourselves in a bright microcosm of childhood as if we were inside a glass ball where it is snowing on red roofs and little painted people. I hope others will make their way inside and enjoy this picture of the happy, wholesome, dedicated monotony of the artistic life.

28

EDITH SITWELL

'My poems are hymns of praise to the glory of life': thus Dame Edith takes up her position with Whitman and Dylan Thomas and the mystics, with Blake and Rimbaud. 'To produce a poetry that is the light of the Great Morning, wherein all beings whom we see passing in the common street are transformed into the epitome of all beauty, or of all joy, or of all sorrow . . .'—this is her aim, and where she differs most from others who have set about it is in the intense and exacting concentration through all her life on the properties of words as sound, on pace, rhythm, the nature of vowels and consonants, their evocative powers:

> While she lies embalmed in the fire's gold sheen
> Like a cross wasp in a ripe nectarine,
> And the golden seed of the fire droops dead
> And ripens not in the heart or head! . . .
> Pomona, lovely gardener's daughter,
> Fruits like ripples on the water
> Soon will fade . . . then leave your fruits,
> Smooth as your cheek or the bird's flutes,
> And in this lovelier, smoother shade
> Listen to my serenade.

A clear twenty years separate the first four lines (from 'Bucolic Comedies') from the last six (from the enchanting 'Sylph's Song'); notice the slightly top-heavy Tennysonian rhythms of the first quotation and the streamlined delicacy of the latter, in which every word may be said to be commonplace yet born again through the musical manipulation of long vowel sounds, of f's and s's. 'I bring you branches green with dew' is another simple-subtle gem from the same poem.

That Dame Edith and Dylan Thomas should have proved our greatest war-poets may seem paradoxical, but the explanation is in Coleridge: 'he prayeth best who loveth best', and in both of them the capacity for horror and compassion was commensurate with their reverence for life.

> All the weight of Death in all the world
> Yet does not equal Love . . .

It is fitting that she should conclude with the elegy on the death of the young poet [Dylan Thomas] whom she had been among the first to encourage.

There are 400 pages of poetry in the *Collected Poems*,[1] of which nearly half belong to Dame Edith's later period, after 1940. It is the period of long lines and long odes, comparable with Mr. Eliot's *Four Quartets* or Yeats's post-Byzantian manner. I remember Logan Pearsall Smith's intoxication with these new poems and how he, who had once been Whitman's youngest visitor, would trumpet out

> I who was once a golden woman like those who walk
> In the dark heavens—but am now grown old
> And sit by the fire, and see the fire grow cold,
> Watch the dark fields for a rebirth of faith and of wonder.

I assume that most readers are familiar with the fine poetry of 'Green Song' and 'Street Songs' or the magnificent elegy on Hiroshima, 'The Shadow of Cain'; but there are two earlier poems or rather groups of poems included here which I would like to recall to their attention: 'The Sleeping Beauty' and 'Gold Coast Customs', which date from 1923 and 1929.

I read 'The Sleeping Beauty' when it first appeared and it became immediately confused with Ravel's music to which the words seemed absolutely to fit themselves:

[1] *Collected Poems of Edith Sitwell* (Macmillan).

Beneath those laden boughs, the gardener sighs,
Dreaming in endlessness, forgotten beauty lies . . .

There is nothing so moving as when we absorb in youth a contemporary work of art hot from the press, and so I put off re-reading 'The Sleeping Beauty' for fear of being disappointed. Yet it now overwhelms me as an astonishing *tour de force*; it has something pre-Raphaelite, as in Tennyson's poems or the Burne-Jones frescoes at Buscot with something of the eighteenth century—yet it is also Verlaine's eighteenth century (there is a Verlaine and Herrick influence in the early verse as strong as the later Donne, Whitman and Rimbaud), and the pattern which runs through the 'Baroque Tapestry' is a threnody for lost youth as in the lovely stanzas

When we were young how beautiful life seemed!

It is the theme, too, of that enchanted autobiographical poem, 'Colonel Fanlock'.

Of 'Façade', which we now associate as much with Constant Lambert's voice and Sir William Walton's music, Dame Edith writes: 'The poems in "Façade" are *abstract* poems, that is, they are patterns in sound. They are, too, in many cases, virtuoso exercises in technique of an extreme difficulty'—and so are dismissed Don Pasquito, black Mrs. Behemoth, Daisy and Lily and Mr. Belaker 'the allegro Negro cocktail-shaker'! But for those who care to read themselves into a poet's garden where

Amid this hot green glowing gloom
A word falls with a rain-drop's boom.

'The Sleeping Beauty', with its wonderful opening phrase, falls like the hair of Mélisande.

It was an article by Sir Kenneth Clark which led me to 'Gold Coast Customs', an allegory on the resemblances between the Mayfair jungle and the cannibal rites of King Munza of Ashanti which reaches a pitch of despair hardly matched by any other work between the wars. It is written with a controlled savagery and a sense of personal betrayal, like *King Lear* or *Troilus and*

Cressida, and the images of death and corruption are alkaline and sinister. Many an artist has taken a London hostess as his symbol of all that is most callous and frivolous and venal in the world; but none is so malignant as Lady Bamburgher, King Munza's Mayfair opposite number, when she gives a party.

> One fantee wave
> Is grave and tall
> As brave Ashantee's
> Thick mud wall. . . .

—and the heavy, thunderous atmosphere of human sacrifice is immediately established. This extraordinary poem with its African rhythms and its Negro-art imagery concludes with a genuine prophecy of the air-raids and then announces the new themes which Dame Edith was to find in them—the gold and the wheat.

> Do we smell and see
> The sick thick smoke from London burning
> Gomorrah turning
> like worms in the grave. . . .
> Bahunda, Banbangala, Barumbe, Bonge
> And London fall . . .
> rolling human skin drums. . . .
>
> Yet the time will come
> To the heart's dark slum
> When the rich man's gold and the rich man's wheat
> Will grow in the street that the starved may eat,
> And the sea of the rich shall give up its dead.

When we come to compare the collected poems of Dame Edith Sitwell with those of Yeats or Mr. Eliot or Professor Auden it will be found that hers have the purest poetic intention of any; the honey may sometimes fail, but is never adulterated.

PART FOUR

PAGING MR. SMARTIBOOTS

z

THE EGGHEAD SHRINKERS

THE sale of Mr. Maugham's collection of modern pictures for half a million pounds set me wondering what he would have received if not his pictures, but all his original manuscripts and first editions had come under the hammer. He would have been lucky, I speculated, if his complete 'oeuvre' brought in one tenth of the sum realised by his paintings, so enormous is the gap today between the value set on pictures and the written word.

Paintings, apart from the satisfaction they give, have both a display interest and an investment value, while rare books must lurk in fire-proof boxes or be put away under glass. No one jumps up in the middle of dinner to get a closer look at them.

But there is more to it than status. Modern painting occupies the preponderant place in the great creative movement of our time; modern literature is also part of the same movement but it has spent its revolutionary momentum. Despite innovations in technique and experiments in language the forms of poetry, biography and the novel remain unchanged; it is only the modern sensibility in them which we can salute and recognise. Writers like Lawrence who exemplified a revolution in sensibility remained conservative in technique, technical innovators like Gertrude Stein whose prose cubism dates from 1909 could obtain an audience only for her pot-boilers. Of twentieth-century writers Joyce alone has welded the force and content of his mind to a perpetual search for original forms.

The written word has not produced its Demoiselles d'Avignon or its Guernica, its Picasso, Braque or Mondrian, and so there is a certain justice in the discrepancy between the value of an author's manuscripts and the wares of his painter-friends.

Yet there are signs the gap is closing. Up to the end of the last war hardly any writer would have expected more than £60 for the manuscript of one of his books, nor more than a pound or two for any of his first editions. In 1939 Mr. Eliot's *Prufrock* fetched one pound fourteen shillings at auction, Yeats's second book, *The Wanderings of Oisin* (a presentation copy to May Morris) went for five pounds ten shillings and one of the hundred signed copies of Joyce's *Ulysses*, bound in morocco with the original covers, for seven.

But times have changed and this may well prove the last year when those three books are still within reach of the private collector. America has redressed the balance of the old world or rather its studied indifference to its own avant-garde. The incomprehensible have powerful friends.

'In the last academic year' (I quote from *Time* Magazine for April 6th) 'twenty-eight campuses had library book-budgets of more than $300,000 . . . most voracious of all is the University of Texas. . . . Last year it acquired perhaps $2,000,000 worth of rarities.' This year (according to *Time*) it can spend $4,000,000. 'Tactically Texas goes in heavily for inviting authors down to lecture and, in the process, winding up with their papers.'

This process, by the way, is largely benevolent. The best American universities will not pay only for what an author has written but for what he has tried to throw away; his notebooks, correspondence, false starts; they will sort it all out for him and accept material which is never to be shown and provide him with copies and even resident facilities for writing his autobiography. His waste-paper basket becomes as precious as the late Aga Khan's bath-water. He can look the milkman in the eye. It is probably the best thing that has happened to writers for many years.

I was discussing this on my last trip with the boyish President of Chincoteague, that small but powerful university with an estimated budget of (approximately) one million pounds a minute. 'You have heard of Victor Galbraith,' he said, 'who wrote the

Bunns of Macaroon?' 'Is he still alive?' 'Well, yes, in a manner of speaking.' We entered a long, low building out of the glare of the immense coppery campus. 'This is his archive. Here are his note-books, the rough drafts, the finished drafts, the typescripts, the carbons, the galleys, the corrected galleys, the page proofs, the corrected page proofs, the seven issues of the first edition with seventy copies of each, the seventy other editions, the paperbacks and translations, the correspondence with his publisher and agent, the Braille edition, the pedigrees of the Bunns—and a model of Macaroon before the fire. And the same for his forty-one other books. And here, behind the barbed wire, is his classified material, some of it, like the letters from his bank-manager, not to be published for one hundred and fifty years.'

'Magnificent.' 'You don't feel there's anything lacking?' 'Well—yes—perhaps it's the man himself.'

The President shook his head. 'No—we've tried that. He is resident Galbraith lecturer and librarian of the archive and we made him a drum-major in the Chesapeake navy as well. But we still don't feel we're getting close to him. Every day an author's here he's a day further from what he was when he provided our material. His condition deteriorates; drink-stains, slight foxing, wear at his edges, spots on his dust-wrapper, sometimes he cheeks the students and won't answer queries. The image is damaged. So we've loaned Galbraith to Seattle. We take in all his mail and send him photostats. He's taped of course.'

'Taped?' 'Bugged. He's got an instrument sewn in that records all his conversation. No cause for Seattle to have that. Those are his rolls in that warehouse over there. Just imagine if we'd been able to do that for Shakespeare!'

We entered the next building. 'Here we are trying another process for authors we have acquired. Something we picked up from the Jivaro Indians.' 'The headshrinkers?' 'Could be.' We passed by a row of what appeared to be open doll's houses in various styles of architecture. In each was being enacted a Lillipu-tian scene—a late Victorian drawing-room with a frilly parlour-maid serving tea—'why there's Gosse and Moore'—there were some ninetyish poets drinking in the Café Royal, a clean Mediterranean kitchen with a tiny man with a red beard washing up, a stormy session at the Abbey Theatre, and suddenly we came to a bookshop in a Paris street, its walls hung with photographs. And there was Ford with his sea-lion face and Pound throwing back his head and Joyce reading from a midget book in the magical voice of his Anna Livia recording. 'Teems of times and happy returns. The seim anew.'

I burst into tears. 'You've bought 12 Rue de l'Odéon!' The President smiled deprecatingly. 'Not just number Twelve—the whole of the Rue de l'Odéon and the Place de l'Odéon and the Rue de Tournon at the back. You see, some of our students are rather shy. They like to walk around the block once before they go in.'

He patted my shoulder, 'I understand we've acquired quite a restaurant in the Place de l'Odéon. Care to try it?'

2

PAGING MR. SMARTIBOOTS

As an Englishman abroad who is accused—quite unjustly —on the jacket of this book[1] of starting 'the myth that the English love travel' I was extremely anxious to get in first with my refutation. But on a Mediterranean island with notoriously bad posts how to do it? On the first Monday of this month I took a taxi to the helicopter station and pressed my review into the pilot's hand even as the blade began to rotate. It would be in Naples within the hour, he promised, and in London that night. Almost a week later I opened the paper and found to my consternation that I was 'on holiday'.

I revisited the helicopter station and found the same pilot. He had put the right stamps—300 lire—on the letter and handed it in at the airport, as he said, an hour later. It has still not arrived and I presume is languishing in the drawer of some official. Had I posted it in the ordinary way it would have been on time. This means that for the rest of my life whenever I go abroad again and promise to mail an article a colleague will say: 'Is that really wise? We don't want another Ischia.'

So with quite new feelings about 'Abroad' since I first opened this book I am reviewing it again. The first time, I complained about the many authors in this anthology who crabbed and carped. They seemed a smug, provincial crowd, egoists in principle, egotists in performance who yammer on about themselves as if they were

[1] *The Englishman Abroad.* Edited by Hugh and Pauline Massingham (Phoenix).

performing a valuable service in belittling anything that might otherwise endanger their vanity.

'The Alps, sir, are tolerable high mountains where they don't know the first thing about hanging meat.' 'I grant you Saint Peter's is very large but I found nothing in the whole city as noble and harmonious as the new crescent at Buxton.'

DAMNED AWKWARD MOMENT

The shadows were now lengthening so I sent out for my usual breakfast of trout's cheeks and pheasant's tongues, half a hundredweight of which are more efficacious against the spleen, I find, than even the Lord Abbot's conversation. I was just unrolling my travelling pedigree to form a kind of *vela* or capacious awning against the sun when a particularly ill-favoured major domo in the Abbot's maroon livery begged to present the English 'Trottagloba' with 'His Beatitude's compliments, milor, and trouts' cheeks is HORF!'

FIRST DAY IN THE TIROL

I immediately inquired the mountain's name. 'It does not deserve to have a name' some wag made answer, 'it is only a mountain'. But a more serious gentleman informed me that it was the Aarshorn, the principal summit of the Bummi Alps. I thanked him appropriately' (Rev. Septimus Stayathome's Journal).

PAGING MR. SMARTIBOOTS

I noticed a plug for an electric razor (like most Wykehamists I still use a cut-throat) and by keeping my finger on another switch I was able to prevent the wireless coming on. A mysterious object beside my bed was presumably a wig-stand for the hotel was very up to date. A shower, a bath, a douche, a bidet, and some kind of spray which might have been a fire hose or worse were provided, all luckily rendered innocuous by the absence of running water whose recent demise was hinted at by an occasional death-rattle from a tap marked C which might stand equally for *Caliente* or cold. The light by my bed, so bright, had it functioned, that it could have come straight from police headquarters had evidently been mistaken by various migrants for a lighthouse and their pretty corpses lay dashed around the base where a flat disc engraved with cuneiform manikins with brooms and pails and suitcases and trolleys reminded me of the sybarite I might yet become if the current were to be reconnected. So this was the Alvarez Hulton!

I feel I could write a whole travel anthology myself in the eighteenth, nineteenth and twentieth-century manner—and this is a tribute to the general good humour and gusto of the Massinghams' compilation. They include only British writers and exclude poetry (but not poets). This proves an axiom—that the greater the writer the better his travel-writing. Genius will out. Byron, Shelley, Lawrence, Hopkins, Doughty, are in a class by themselves. Auden, Beckford, Gertrude Bell, Borrow, E. M. Forster, Gibbon, Aldous Huxley, Isherwood, Horace Walpole also give unfailing pleasure. Dickens and Thackeray hold their own.

Among modern travellers I am delighted to see Robert Byron adequately represented, and William Sansom's two pieces are perfect of their kind. The modern section does not include many living travellers: no Evelyn Waugh, Sacheverell Sitwell, Patrick Leigh-Fermor, Alan Ross, J. R. Ackerley, Geoffrey Gorer, James Pope-Hennessey, Alan Houghton Brodrick, Gerald Brenan, Patrick Kinross, Rose Macaulay or Somerset Maugham, to name but a few; and there is only one quotation from Norman Douglas.

There is room for a whole new anthology of travel considered as a modern art from Gissing and Douglas onwards. Perhaps questions of fee and copyright interfered with the project, perhaps the editors worked through these candidates and dismissed them, but I feel they have not faced up to the vast amount of interesting travel books in the last thirty years, or even read Ford's *Handbook to Spain*, for example, as well as his *Gatherings from Spain* or Douglas's *Fountains in the Sand* or *Together*, or Lawrence's first travel book, *Twilight in Italy*.

I did not find a single entry I wanted to skip, and the Massinghams do not make the mistake of adopting some obscure traveller and working his journals to death. Apart from ease of locomotion (i.e. the helicopter) the two great changes in our time are the removal of vermin (mosquitoes, fleas, bugs) and of drains (smells); only Mr. Sansom, I feel, could tell us now what a country smells like.

3

THOSE GOOD OLD RESTAURANTS

I DEVELOPED an interest in great restaurants at an early age and was fortunate to have known some of them before they were pulled down. A schoolboy dining alone at Voisin's or Frau Sacher's was a vulnerable target, but even so I think the awe which such establishments generated was not entirely in the eye of the beholder. The pale panelled rooms, with their cane-seated armchairs and dim lamplight, their aroma of old claret and fine sauces, of Romanoff and Suvaroff, were decorated in the russet and gold of an autumn beechwood. The only adornment was an ancient bottle pointing at one from its silver basket or a dish of enormous Comice pears. A *maître d'hôtel* who had frightened our grandfathers presided and, after a few formal inquiries, handed one over to the secular arm of the *sommelier* who spread open his list of wines like a dossier.

While I was thus incriminating myself the restaurant would fill up; that is to say, about half a dozen elderly gentlemen would seat themselves in separate corners, their white beards dissolving into their spotless napkins against which the rosette of the Légion d'Honneur gleamed like the eye of a sitting hen. *Sénateurs*!

There was the restaurant of Prosper Montagné, with his rare prints and gastronomic library, a favourite of Valéry and Fargue; Madame Genot, whose two wines came from her own vineyards, who cooked only for two tables of four, and brought people the bill if they smoked while eating; ("I thought you had finished.") the xenophobe Boilève's, with its woodcock and its sawdust-strewn floor; and Foyot's where a little spiral staircase led upstairs to a grave long-windowed suite.

Such temples of taste still represented the culinary orthodoxy of the nineteenth century where 'old men who never cheated, never doubted', served the same rich irreproachable dishes that had given Baudelaire his spleen and Goncourt his liver or officiated over the wine at the table where Tailhade was celebrating when an anarchist's bomb put out his eye.

What has happened to them now? Some have disappeared, like the Degas profiles which frequented them: others have suffered a nightmare transformation and gone the way of giant flowers that have lost their scent, beauties who have had their faces lifted or eighteenth-century houses redecorated by eighteenth-century experts. They have become slaves to the star system.

Success is always dangerous; in our century it is fatal: it is a century in which everybody is a snob about everything, when vast catalogues and inventories take the place of creation. Such an inventory of French restaurants, even of lorry-drivers' 'pull-ups', is now made once a year, and the cooks depend on the number of stars or knives-and-forks allotted to them in the motorists' Debrett. Three stars, four knives-and-forks, their hash is settled!

Once a year, in memory of the sacred *frisson*, I try one out: I might be on Hollywood Boulevard. In a glass case by the door will be one of Sir Winston's half-chewed cigars or a film star's slipper and from the moment we enter the vestibule, or shoot up in the lift, the Show is On!

The staff look normal at first sight but on closer inspection are all actors. The *maître d'hôtel* winks at me roguishly, as if he read in my heart some infamous secret and hides me behind a sideboard stacked with Nebuchadnezzars of Armagnac. The *sommelier*, when at last he arrives in his green apron, won't let us see the wine-list but makes a clucking noise, hugging his missal under one arm and blowing a kiss into the air with the other. 'White wine sweet, red wine dry, you leave it to me,' he barks, as he seals his lips with a stumpy finger. All the waiters are self-conscious, everyone is playing a part.

At one restaurant, which enjoyed a literary celebrity under

Louis-Philippe and then reopened about a hundred years later, I noticed six magnates from the Land of Punt—'*La table Balzac pour ces messieurs*'. At another a Belgian industrialist asks for '*Un petit Beaujolais qui pousse au crime*'. The Senators have vanished, together with every local inhabitant competent to judge. Only Americans can pay the prices, and they do not understand what they pay for. I have seen wines priced at 25,000 francs a bottle.

In the provinces the restaurants with the stars enjoy permanent radio and fluorescent lighting: they are dependent on motorists who come for one meal and demand the local specialities which are always the same—Dutch mussels, Danish trout or Polish crayfish, *Homard au whisky*, langouste from Mauretania, tinned truffles or foie gras.

I dream of a starless restaurant with a plush banquette where the owner wears the chef's white cap, where the young and decorative or the old and talented would eat for nothing and the rich pass a stiff examination and pay an entrance fee.

4

GOOD FOOD

MR. POSTGATE is a gourmet and a man of the Left, a combination not unusual in France, where the Revolution set the great chefs free to start the first good restaurants. Here it is rare to try, like Mr. Postgate, to bring good food and an interest in good food within the reach of all. His sturdy, hopeful little guide[1] now appears every two years, always with more pages. Like *The Boy Friend* and the Espresso Bar, it has become an institution, praiseworthy, for it has done so much to encourage the revival of cooking, yet occasionally maddening, for it reposes on a disastrous fallacy.

Mr. Postgate demands integrity; he refuses all advertisements and tries to discourage such indirect bribes as the ordering of an excessive number of copies by admiring caterers. No one professionally interested in a restaurant may recommend it (there is no check on pseudonyms) but all recommendations are counter-checked by one or two other bona-fide members (anyone who buys the book is a member). The guide is kept right up to date and the restaurants are divided into four groups.

With such admirable precautions, what then is the fallacy? There is no grading of the testers themselves; nothing to suggest that the majority of them know anything about food and drink, and whereas some, like Mr. Philip Harben, are famous judges, others retire behind initials, or manifest enthusiasm without judgment, or even make mistakes (there are no 'giant scampi' in the Adriatic). The jaundiced reader (for I address the choosy and

[1] *The Good Food Guide.* Edited by Raymond Postgate (Cassell).

dyspeptic rather than the iron oesophagus of youth) will notice that Mr. John Betjeman recommends his favourite city chop house and nowhere else, while Mr. X.X. or Mr. W.W. eats all over the place. I suggest that a gastronomic 'driving test' be imposed on all members before their recommendations are accepted and that the initials of gourmets of acknowledged standing be printed in heavier type.

In the only rural area where I know all the eating places well, none deserves inclusion in any guide whatsoever and some which are here mentioned I found the scene of harrowing ordeals. This also applies to many of the London entries from Fitzroy Famagusta to Pimlico Provençal, though Mr. Postgate is alive to the eccentricities of the latter school.

He even includes a new section on railway dining-cars. I wonder if he knows the menu of the seven-fifteen from Station X. This dinner has never once been altered in the last five years, it is as classic and eternal as the menu of la Mère Fillioux. Mushroom soup, tinned but with skim mysteriously added (the chef's secret) or half a small grapefruit with a woollen cherry in the middle; choice of roast mutton divided into small blackened strips like pemmican or grilled turbot, a rough, leathery skin to which a few edible fragments of white matter adhere, both assisted by greasy potatoes and a salvo of grey tinned pea-bullets. The gourmets on this run order a 'mixed grill', the evening name for egg, sausage and bacon, and grab the occasional packages of Ryvita. I believe this meal is delivered ready cooked to the diner from whose windows the prisoners can survey delicious beanfields or laden cherry orchards.

The typical faults of present-day British cooking are the abuse of tinned foods, particularly fruit and vegetables, the bad cooking of vegetables and the over-cooking of meat, the use of bottled mayonnaise, of margarine mixed with butter, of false cream and bad coffee, together with various 'short cuts' such as calling ham with tinned peaches 'Virginia ham'. The personality goes into the staff rather than the cooking and in addition very few restaurants have tables sufficiently far apart, with comfortable chairs and discreet lighting. *The Good Food Guide* pays little attention to décor but lists some outstanding country inns and restaurants which seem to deserve a 'vaut le voyage'; one is in Glen Lyon, Perthshire, one in Anglesey, others perhaps in Scarborough or Cardiff or outside Bath, while nearer home Bray, Aston Clinton and Felpham are remarkable. When given a real but obscure talent to appraise this guide is admirable.

English social history is revealed—at Pulborough are a couple who 'have lived many years in Ceylon', at Northiam they can produce 'a complete Burmese curry', 'Malayan mild susu curry' is served near Bognor, at Exmouth 'lobster Isafu' from Ghana, and Cantonese prawns at both Leeds and Haywards Heath.

'Les Pays Gourmands' would seem between London and Oxford or in South Devon, the worst-nourished counties the South Midlands, Dorset, Suffolk, Essex. Too often the entries are ambivalent and monotonous, running something like this:

'Bilchester. The Sir Roger de Chatterley Hotel. [In the Roger de Chatterley country.] Colonel Stebbings insists on punctuality: if he can be ready, so can you. Pleasant English fare, Roast Beef, Roast Mutton, fricassée and cottage pie but as a speciality the Colonel will knock you up "Scampi Gunga Din" or "Watervole Great Rift Valley". Breakfast nine, lunch one, dinner seven, doors closed when first course is served (other tyrants please copy), no children, no teas, no meals in rooms, dogs welcome. "Short" wine list consisting of some six items of which you will find the Peraquita as good as any. "Good show", writes an enthusiast. "In three years' time, if other members co-operate, the Colonel will have his own asparagus." Recommended: Ben Alder, Paddy Fields, (Mrs.) Gale Warning.'

5

THE BEATS

'ALONG with others I hung around with in the 'twenties, I had indulged in marijuana.' When square egghead Cyril Connolly came to this sentence[1] he nearly flipped his wig. Like this cat Lipton could be as old as him—and if he could make the scene among the beatsters why not me? And soon Connolly had gotten himself a pad in Venice West, the new Thebaid of Los Angeles where all the mad things were happening which made San Francisco's North Shore look like Greenwich Village.

'First thing you got to change,' said the gentle oldster, 'is your name.' We were squatting on a mattress in Itchy Gelden's pad with Mr. Lipton's tape-recorder purring away. 'Like why should the poor square need a name? He's among friends!' Itchy's tolerance was proverbial. Then Angel Dan Davies spoke up with a rattle of his Bongo drums. 'There's only one name a man needs, man, and that name, man, is—man.' 'Like Mortal Man,' said Chuck Bennison, and from that moment Cyril Connolly was dead and Mort Conamore was born, with nothing more to do but play it cool and bring up his wind.

At first it looked like Mort would never 'relate'. He had to forget more than all the rest had ever learnt and that wasn't saying much. He cut down to two shirts and one pair of jeans and let his beard grow. 'The beard,' he will tell you, 'just grew naturally out of not shaving for a few weeks. It's my letter of resignation from

[1] In *The Holy Barbarians*, by Lawrence Lipton (W. H. Allen).

the rat-race.' Angel considered the greying mould. 'Like Mort, that letter took a long time.'

Dostoievski is an all-pervading influence that, for this very reason, no-one thinks of mentioning. Tolstoy, Andreiev, Turgenev and Lermontov are known only by name. Thomas Mann and Marcel Proust are honoured and unread classics. William Saroyan's early short stories are sought out in yellowing paperbacks, and in some quarters he is listed as an 'influence' among beat writers. Henry James is tough going for them.

Mort was quick to throw the whole lot overboard and because he had met Henry Miller, Dylan Thomas and Gregory Corso (in Venice Europe) some of the cats took kindly to him. When offered marijuana, he had a good alibi, 'Like, man, I don't smoke.'

For spiritual satisfaction was what Mort was seeking and he turned to the 'Holy Barbarians' who in his youth would have been called 'anarcho-pacifists' to see if they could provide it. These lemmings, in full flight from the American industrial system, 'a total rejection of the whole society', had stopped on the verge of the Pacific without the know-how to throw themselves in.

'Art is love' says artist Wally Berman, and his words are scrawled on the walls of the Venice West Espresso Café. 'Art is love is jazz is work (sex) is pot (marijuana) = Zen' hazarded Mort one evening and was rewarded with a burst of crazy silence. He was trying hard with his vocabulary by now and forgetting a thousand facts a day. One morning all the Sèvres date letters went, another day it was the Roman Emperors, the Popes and the Kings of England. 'There are no trees in Venice West,' Angel told him —'You can forget your botany and your first editions, man, we don't look for hallmarks on a can of beer.' Alcohol, however, was permitted. 'William Carlos Williams evidently puts no stock in trance or drug-induced hallucination, nor does Kenneth Patchen, although both, and Rexroth as well, have praised wine as a dis-inhabitant' (p. 254).

Unfortunately Mort found that Mr. Lipton's glossary of beat

terms was quite different from Caroline Freud's (in *Encounter*). 'Lay some bread on me' means 'Lend or give me some money' and, when he tried it, Mort agreed with Mr. Lipton that 'the alienation of the hipsters from the squares is now complete.'

'It was the mad season in Venice West. Things were happening and if you were really *with it* you couldn't show it any better than by flipping your wig.'

Things were happening everywhere now; in San Francisco, in New York, in Chicago, New Orleans, Seattle. And people were converging on Venice West from everywhere to tell about them.' 'Like more and more people everywhere are just giving up,' was Mort's comment. 'The squares are breaking.' But he still couldn't quite make it. Like Gide, his drug was lucidity. He couldn't blame reason for all that was wrong in the world.

It seemed to Mort that jazz, sex and marijuana could only afford physical sensations which, however disturbing, would never alleviate his craving for a lightening of his own opacity. He was never 'way out', only just round the corner. The intoxication which this new trinity offered was purely sensual and therefore subject to the law of diminishing returns. There was not enough inspiration to go round.

The art of the beat generation which rejects all technique and criticism and relies on the purely personal statement ('Like Art, Man' was the title of one exhibition) in any handy material is like the private devotions of a mystical sect—incommunicable. Mr. Lipton gives a tape-recorded conversation about a funeral, which no one attended. Angel: 'If a culture has a ritual, a real living ritual, it doesn't matter what you do with the body. The only thing that matters is what the living make out of it—out of the fact of death—and that means the fact of *life*, the meaning of life. Marriage is *one* thing. Mating. Love. I can do something with that. I can understand it. But dying—wow—death. I don't know *what* I'd do with it. Like I don't even know what it is.'

Something stirred among Mort's obliterated memories. 'Dying —wow!' Where had he read that? '*Wa! Wa!* Who is this heavenly ruler who can lay low the great ones of the earth?' The last words of King Wamba. Was this all they could tell him? He looked up one more phrase in Mr. Lipton's glossary: 'Cop out—to settle down—go conventional. In some circles you may be charged with copping out if you shave off your beard.' Next day the British Consul laid some bread on him and he was disinhabited.

6

BOND STRIKES CAMP

SHADOWS of fog were tailing him through the windows of his Chelsea flat; the blonde had left a broken rosette of lipstick on the best Givan's pillowcase—he would have to consult last night's book-matches to find out where he had grabbed her. It was one bitch of a morning. And, of course, it turned out to be the day! For there was always one breakfast in the month when a very simple operation, the boiling of an egg so that the yolk should remain properly soft and the white precisely hard, seemed to defeat his devoted housekeeper, May. As he decapitated the fifth abort on its Wedgwood launching-pad he was tempted to crown her with the sixteen-inch pepper mill. Three minutes and fifty-five seconds later by his stopwatch and the sixth egg came up with all systems go. As he was about to press the thin finger of wholemeal toast into the prepared cavity the telephone rang. It was probably the blonde: 'Don't tell me: it all comes back—you're the new hat-check from "The Moment of Truth",' he snarled into the receiver. But the voice which cut in was that of his secretary, Miss Ponsonby. 'He wants you now, smart pants, so step on the Pogo.'

Swearing pedantically, Bond pulled away from his uneaten egg and hurried from the flat to the wheel of his souped-up Pierce Arrow, a Thirty-one open tourer with two three-piece windscreens. A sulphurous black rain was falling and he nearly took the seat off a Beatnik as he swerved into Milner. It was that kind of a Christmas. Thirteen minutes later his lean body streaked from the tonneau-cover like a conger from its hole and he stood outside M.'s door with Lolita Ponsonby's great spaniel eyes gazing up at him in dog-like devotion.

'Sorry about the crossed line,' he told her. 'I'll sock you a lunch if they don't need you at Crufts.' Then the green lights showed and he entered.

'Sit down, O07.' That was Grade C welcome indicating the gale warning. There had been several lately. But M. did not continue. He surveyed Bond with a cold, glassy stare, cleared his throat and suddenly lowered his eyes. His pipe rested unlit beside the tobacco in the familiar shell-cap. If such a thing had been possible, Bond would have sworn he was embarrassed. When at length he spoke, the voice was dry and impersonal. 'There are many things I have asked you to do, Bond; they have not always been pleasant but they have been in the course of duty. Supposing I were to ask you to do something which I have no right to demand and which I can justify only by appealing to principles outside your service obligations. I refer to your patriotism. You are patriotic, Bond?'

'Don't know, sir, I never read the small print clauses.'

'Forgive the question, I'll put it another way. Do you think the end justifies the means?'

'I can attach no significance of any kind to such expressions.'

M. seemed to reflect. The mood of crisis deepened.

'Well, we must try again. If there were a particularly arduous task—a most distasteful task—and I called for a volunteer—who must have certain qualifications—and only one person had those qualifications—and I asked him to volunteer. What would you say?'

'I'd say stop beating about the bush, sir.'

'I'm afraid we haven't even started.'

'Sir?'

'Do you play chess, Bond?'

'My salary won't run to it.'

'But you are familiar with the game?'

'Tolerably.' As if aware that he was in the stronger position, Bond was edging towards insolence.

'It has, of course, been thoroughly modernised; all the adventure has been taken out of it; the opening gambits in which a piece used to be sacrificed for the sake of early development proved unsound and therefore abandoned. But it is so long since they have been tried that many players are unfamiliar with the pitfalls and it is sometimes possible to obtain an advantage by taking a risk. In our profession, if it be a profession, we keep a record of these forgotten traps. Ever heard of Mata Hari?'

'The beautiful spy?' Bond's voice held derision. The school prefect sulking before his housemaster.

'She was very successful. It was a long time ago.' M. still sounded meek and deprecating.

'I seem to remember reading the other day that a concealed microphone had replaced the *femme fatale*.'

'Precisely. So there is still a chance for the *femme fatale*.'

'I have yet to meet her.'

'You will. You are aware there is a Russian military mission visiting this country?'

Bond let that one go into the net.

'They have sent over among others an elderly general. He looks like a general, he may well have been a general, he is certainly a very high echelon in their K.G.B. Security is his speciality; rocketry, nerve gases, germ warfare—all the usual hobbies.' M. paused. 'And one rather unusual one.'

Bond waited, like an old pike watching the bait come down.

'Yes. He likes to go to night clubs, get drunk, throw his money about and bring people back to his hotel. All rather old-fashioned.'

'And not very unusual.'

'Ah.' M. looked embarrassed again. 'I'm just coming to that. We happen to know quite a bit about this chap, General Count Apraxin. His family were pretty well known under the old dispensation though his father was one of the first to join the party; we think he may be a bit of a throw-back. Not politically, of course. He's tough as they come. I needn't tell you Section A make a study of the kind of greens the big shots go in for. Sometimes we know more about what these people are like between the sheets than they do themselves; it's a dirty business. Well, the General is mad about drag.'

'Drag, sir?'

M. winced. 'I'm sorry about this part, Bond. He's "so"—"uno di quelli"—"one of those"—a sodomite.'

Bond detected a glint of distaste in the cold blue eyes.

'In my young days,' M. went on, 'fellows like that shot themselves. Now their names are up for every club. Particularly in London. Do you know what sort of a reputation this city has abroad?' Bond waited. 'Well, it stinks. These foreigners come here, drop notes of assignation into sentries' top-boots, pin fivers on to guardsmen's bearskins. The Tins are livid.'

'And General Apraxin?' Bond decided to cut short the Wolfenden.

'One of the worst. I told you he likes drag. That's—er—men dressed up as women.'

'Well, you tell me he's found the right place. But I don't quite see where we come in.'

M. cleared his throat. 'There's just a possibility, mind, it's only a possibility, that even a top K.G.B. might be taken off guard—if he found the company congenial—perhaps so congenial that it appealed to some secret wish of his imagination—and if he talked at all (mind you, he is generally absolutely silent), well then anything he said might be of the greatest value—anything—it might be a lead on what he's really here for. You will be drawing a bow at a venture. You will be working in the dark.'

'Me, sir?'

M. rapped out the words like a command. '007, I want you to do this thing. I want you to let our people rig you up as a moppet and send you to a special sort of club and I want you to allow yourself to be approached by General Apraxin and sit at his table and if he asks you back to his hotel I want you to accompany him and any suggestion he makes I request you to fall in with to the limit your conscience permits. And may your patriotism be your conscience, as it is mine.'

It was a very odd speech for M. Bond studied his finger-nails. 'And if the pace gets too hot?'

'Then you must pull out—but remember. T. E. Lawrence put

up with the final indignity. I knew him well, but knowing even that, I never dared call him by his christian name.'

Bond reflected. It was clear that M. was deeply concerned. Besides, the General might never turn up. 'I'll try anything once, sir.'

'Good man.' M. seemed to grow visibly younger.

'As long as I'm not expected to shake a powder into his drink and run away with his wallet.'

'Oh, I don't think it will come to that. If you don't like the look of things, just plead a headache; he'll be terrified of any publicity. It was all Section A could do to slip him a card for this club.'

'What's its name?'

M. pursed his lips. 'The Kitchener. In Lower Belgrave Mews. Be there about eleven o'clock and just sit around. We've signed you in as "Gerda".'

'And my—disguise?'

'We're sending you off to a specialist in that kind of thing—he thinks you want it for some Christmas "do". Here's the address.'

'One more question, sir. I have no wish to weary you with details of my private life but I can assure you I've never dressed up in "drag" as you call it since I played Katisha in "The Mikado" at my prep. school. I shan't look right, I shan't move right, I shan't talk right; I shall feel about as convincing arsing about as a night-club hostess as Randolph Churchill.'

M. gazed at him blankly and again Bond noticed his expression of weariness, even of repulsion. 'Yes, 007, you will do all of those things and I am afraid that is precisely what will get him.'

Bond turned angrily but M.'s face was already buried in his signals. This man who had sent so many to their deaths was still alive and now the dedicated bachelor who had never looked at a woman except to estimate her security risk was packing him off with the same cold indifference into a den of slimy creatures. He walked out of the room and was striding past Miss Ponsonby when she stopped him. 'No time for that lunch, I'm afraid. You're wanted in Armoury.'

The Armoury in the basement held many happy memories for

Bond. It represented the first moments of a new adventure, the excitement of being back on a job. There were the revolvers and the Tommy guns, the Smith and Wessons, Colts, lugers, berettas, killer weapons of every class or nationality; blow-pipes, boomerangs, cyanide fountain-pens, Commando daggers and the familiar heap of aqualungs, now more or less standard equipment. He heard the instructor's caressing voice. 'Grind yer boot down his shin and crush his instep. Wrench off his testicles with yer free hand and with the fingers held stiffly in the V sign gouge out his eyes with the other.'

He felt a wave of home-sickness. 'Ah, Bond, we've got some hardware for you. Check it over and sign the receipt,' said the lieutenant of marines.

'Good God, what's this? It looks to me like a child's water-pistol.'

'You're so right—and here's the water.' He was given a small screw-top ink-bottle full of some transparent liquid. 'Don't spill any on your bib and tucker.'

'What'll it stop?'

'Anything on two legs if you aim at the eyes.'

Bond consulted the address of his next 'armourer'. It was a studio off Kinnerton Street. The musical cough of the Pierce Arrow was hardly silent when the door was opened by a calm young man who looked him quickly up and down. Bond was wearing one of his many pheasant's-eye alpacas which exaggerated the new vertical line—single-breasted, narrow lapels, ton-up trousers with no turn-ups, peccary suède shoes. A short covert-coat in cavalry twill, a black sting-ray tail of a tie, an unexpected width of shoulder above the tapering waist and the casual arrogance of his comma of dark hair low over the forehead under his little green piglet of a hat completed the picture of mid-century masculinity. The young man seemed unimpressed. 'Well, well, how butch can you get? You've left it rather late. But we'll see what we can do.'

He turned Bond towards the lighted north window and studied him carefully, then he gave the comma a tweak. 'I like the spit-curl, Gerda, we'll build up round that. Now go in there and strip.'

When he came out in his pants, the barracuda scars dark against the tan, a plain girl was waiting in a nurse's uniform. 'Lie down, Gerda, and leave it all to Miss Haslip,' said the young man. She stepped forward and began, expertly, to shave his legs and armpits. 'First a shave, then the depilatory—I'm afraid, what with the fittings, you'll be here most of the day.' It was indeed one bitch of a morning. The only consolation was that the young man (his name was Colin Mount) allowed him to keep the hair on his chest. 'After all, nobody wants you *all* sugar.'

After the manicure, pedicure and plucking of the eyebrows it was time to start rebuilding. Bond was given a jock-strap to contain his genitals; the fitting of an elaborate chestnut wig so as to allow the comma to escape under it was another slow process. And then the artificial eye-lashes. Finally what looked like a box of tennis balls was produced from a drawer. 'Ever seen these before?'

'Good God, what *are* they?'

'The very latest in falsies—foam-rubber, with electronic self-erecting nipples—pink for blondes, brown for brunettes. The things they think of! Which will you be? It's an important decision.'

'What the hell do I care?'

'On the whole I think you'd better be a brunette. It goes with the eyes. And with your height we want them rather large. Round or pear-shaped?'

'Round, for Christ's sake.'

'Sure you're not making a mistake?'

The falsies were attached by a rubber strap, like a brassière, which—in black moiré—was then skilfully fitted over them. 'How does that feel? There should be room for a guy to get his hand up under the bra and have a good riffle.' Then came the slinky black lace panties and finally the black satin evening skirt with crimson silk blouse suspended low on the shoulder, a blue mink scarf over all and then the sheerest black stockings and black shoes with red stilettos. Bond surveyed himself in the long glass and experienced an unexpected thrill of excitement; there was no doubt he had a damned good figure.

'Well, you're no Coccinelle,' said the young man, 'but you'll certainly pass. Hip-square! Drag's a lot of fun you'll find. One meets quite a different class of person. Now go and practise walking till you drop. Then get some sleep, and after that, if you're good, we'll make up that pretty face and launch you at the local cinema.'

After practising in high heels for a couple of hours, Bond went back to his couch and lay down exhausted. He dreamed he was swimming under water on a stormy day, the waves breaking angrily above him while, harpoon in hand, he followed a great sea-bass with spaniel eyes that seemed to turn and twist and invite him onward down an ever-narrowing, weed-matted gully.

When he awoke it was dark and he fell avidly on the Blue Mountain coffee and club sandwich Miss Haslip had brought him. 'Now we'll start on the face—and here's your evening bag.' Bond transferred his water-pistol, ink-bottle, Ronson lighter, gun-metal cigarette case and bill-folder and emptied the contents of his wallet; a vintage chart from the Wine and Food Society, an 'Advanced Motorists'' certificate, another from the Subaqua Club, a temporary membership card of the Travellers, Paris, the Caccia, Rome, Puerto de Hierro, Madrid, Brook, Meadowbrook, Knickerbocker and Crazy Horse Saloon, Liguanea, Eagle, Somerset (Boston) and Boston (New Orleans), ending up with a reader's pass for the Black Museum. When he had done, Colin emptied the whole lot into a large envelope, which he told Bond to put in the glove compartment, and handed back the water-pistol and key-ring. 'Try these instead,' and Bond was given a powder-puff, a couple of lipsticks, some Kleenex, a package of cigarettes (Senior Service) with a long cane holder, some costume jewellery and a charm bracelet and a membership card in the name of Miss Gerda Blond for the Kitchener Social Club, Lower Belgrave Mews, S.W.

In a compartment of his evening bag he found a pocket mirror, tortoiseshell comb, enamel compact and a box of eye make-up with a tiny brush. 'When you get mad at someone it's a great relief to take this out and spit on it. The harder you spit, the more of a lady you'll seem.' Mount showed him how to apply the little brush, the mascara and black eye-shadow. 'When you don't know how to answer, just look down for a little—lower those eyelashes, that'll fetch them—and make with the holder. And do be careful in the Loo. That's where nearly all the mistakes are made. Now we're off to the Pictures.'

'What are we going to see?'

'La Dolce Vita.'

In the dark cinema Bond noticed a few interested glances in his direction. A man in the next seat put his hand on his knee. Bond knew the drill; a policewoman in Singapore had shown him. You take the hand tenderly in yours and extend his arm across your knee. Then you bring your other hand down hard and break the fellow's arm at the elbow. He had just got it all set up when the lights went on.

'I wanted you to see that picture, it gives you so many approaches,' said Colin Mount. 'You can try Ekberg—the big child of nature—or one of those sophisticated cats. Now off you go. Better take a taxi, that hearse of yours looks too draughty.'

In Lower Belgrave Mews, Bond rang the bell, showed his card and was immediately admitted.

The Kitchener was discreetly decorated in the style of 1914 with a maze of red plush and some old war posters. The familiar, rather forbidding face with pouchy eyes and drooping moustache and the pointing finger, 'Your King and country need you', recruited him wherever he looked. There were two upstair rooms, in one of which people were dancing. The other held a few divans and tables and a little bar. They had once formed a large double drawing-room. On the landing above, the bathrooms were labelled 'Turks' and 'Virgins'.

Bond sat down at a table, ordered 'Eggs Omdurman' washed down by a 'Sirdar Special'. He noticed several couples dancing sedately to the Cobbler's Song from 'Chu Chin Chow' on a pick-up. There were posters of Doris Keane in *Romance* and Violet Loraine in *The Bing Boys* and of Miss Teddy Gerrard. The subdued lighting from pink lampshades, the roomy banquette, the liver-flicking welcome of his 'Eggs Omdurman' and the silken recoil of the 'Sirdar Special' made him feel for the first time content with his preposterous mission. Had he not worn the kilt at Fettes? He was in it now, up to the sporran. All at once a woman's low voice interrupted his reverie. 'Dance?' He lowered his eyes, as he had been told, and thought furiously. To refuse, in fact to tell her to get the hell out, was his first reaction—but that might arouse suspicion. He had better play along. 'Thanks. I'd love to,' he managed in a husky contralto and looked up past a mannish red waistcoat and tweed jacket into a pair of faintly mocking brown eyes. It was Lolita! Speechless with disaster, Bond wondered how long it would be before the story was all over the office. If only his disguise could last a couple of rounds. And then he remembered. Was he not 007 and licensed to kill with his water-pistol? He tensed himself and let the sweat dry on his forehead. In a moment he was hobbling on to the dance floor, where it was much darker, to the strains of 'Japanese Sandman'. His secretary seemed transformed: capably she manoeuvred him into an obscure corner where they rocked up and down as she began to hold him closer, sliding a leg between his and shifting her hand slowly and expertly down his spine. He began to wonder how the jock-strap would hold. Suddenly she drew back a little and looked him in the eyes. 'What's your name?'

'Gerda'—he croaked—'Gerda Blond.'

'It's your first visit to the Kitch, isn't it?—well, Gerda, I could fall for you in a big way. I bet you could give someone a good butt in the eye with those charleys.' She ran a finger gently up a full, firm breast and gave a start when the nipple shot up trigger-happy as a Sensitive Plant. 'Gerda, I want to ask you a question.' Bond lowered his eyes. 'Have you ever slept with a woman?'

'Well, no, not exactly.'

'Well, you're going to tonight.'

'But I don't even know your name.'

'Just call me Robin.'

'But I'm not sure that I can tonight.'

'Well, I am. And let me tell you; once you've been to bed with me you won't want anyone else. I know what men are like—I work for one. No girl ever wants a man once she's made it with a dike. It's the difference between a bullfight and an egg-and-spoon race.'

'But I can't imagine what you see in me.'

'Well, you've got a pretty good figure and I like that in-between colour, like a Braque still life, and I adore the wizard tits—and then you're not like the other mice, sort of virginal and stand-offish—and I'm crazy about the spit curl.' She gave it a sharp tug.

'That's not a spit curl,' pouted Bond. 'That's my comma.'

'Have it your way. And I like your husky voice and those droopy eyes and right now I'm imagining your little black triangle.'

'Oh, belt up, Robin!'

'Come on, Gerda, we're going back to my place.'

Miss Ponsonby began to lug him off the dance floor. Immediately, out of the corner of his eye, Bond caught sight of a stout figure in a dinner-jacket at another table, a bald head and fishy stare and a pair of enormous moustaches, even as a thick forefinger shot up like an obscene grub and began to beckon to him. A deep voice rumbled: 'Would the two little ladies care to accept a glass of champagne?'

'Certainly not,' snapped Miss Ponsonby. 'Father would turn in his vault.'

'Thanks a lot. No objection,' came Bond's husky contralto. His secretary wheeled round. 'Why, you black bitch—you filthy little tart, I suppose you support a basketful of bastards at home all bleating their bloody heads off. Go along and I hope the old Tirpitz gives you a Lulu.' She gave Bond a ringing slap across the eyes and burst into tears. As she left she turned to the new arrival. 'You watch out with that bint. Mark my words. She'll do you in.'

Bond held his smarting cheek. The foreign gentleman patted his arm and pulled him on to the banquette. 'What a headstrong young lady—she gave me quite a turn. But here comes our champagne. I have ordered a magnum of Taittinger Blanc de blancs, '52—it never departs from a certain "tenu"—independent yet perfectly deferential.' He had a trace of guttural accent but what impressed Bond most were the magnificent whiskers. He had seen them only once before on a Russian, Marshal Budenny, Stalin's cavalry leader. They gave a raffish Eighth Army-turned-innkeeper look to the big-nosed military man and were perhaps symptomatic of the formidable General's atavism.

Bond collapsed on to the alcove divan and raised the paradisal prickle to his lips, remembering Monsieur Georges, the wine waiter at the Casino Royale who had called his attention to the brand in the first of his annual agonies.

'Perhaps I had better introduce myself,' said the General. 'I am a Yugoslav travelling salesman here to make certain business contacts and tonight is my evening of relaxation. All day I have been in conference and tomorrow I have to go down early in the morning to Salisbury Plain. Vladimir Mishitch. Just call me Vladimir; the accent is on the second syllable.'

Bond noticed he had not inquired his own name and finally volunteered with downcast eye, 'My name is Gerda. I like travelling too but I'm afraid I haven't anything to sell.'

'One never knows. "La plus belle fille du monde, ne peut donner que ce qu'elle a." ' The General stuck his hand into Bond's blouse and ran his fingers through the hair on his chest. 'That's a nice rug you've got there, Gerda.' Bond lowered his eyes again. 'And that—that is pretty too. How do you call it?'

'That's my comma.'

'I see. I'm afraid I make more use of the colon. Ha! ha!' Bond did not know whether to seem amused or bored, and said nothing. 'Tell me, Gerda—' the General's voice took on a warmer colour. 'Have you ever slept with a man?'

'Well no, not exactly.'

'I thought not, Gerda—your little girl friend—the paprikahühn—she would not allow it, hein?'

'Well, it's something we've all got to do sooner or later.'

'And I suggest you do it right now—for when you've been to bed with a real man, a man of age and experience, you won't ever want anyone else. It's like the Salle Privée at the Sporting Club after a tea with your P.E.N.'

He inserted a torpedo-shaped Larranaga such as seldom reaches these shores into an amber holder and poured out the ice-cold champagne until Bond unaccountably found himself sitting on his lap in some disarray, while the General broke into stentorian song:

> How you gonna keep them
> Down on the farm
> After they've seen Paree!

Bond broke away.

'Aren't you going to have a dance with me?'

The General roared with laughter. 'I have never learned to dance except our Yugoslav ones and those we dance only with comrades.'

'I expect I could pick them up.'

'Yes. Like I have picked up you. I will play one to you in my hotel and you will dance like an Ustashi.'

'But they were all fascists, weren't they?'

The General laughed again. 'They danced very well at the end of a rope. Like Homer's handmaidens—with twittering feet.'

Bond found the allusion faintly disturbing. 'It's too hot, let's go.'

The General paid the bill from a bundle of fivers and hurried down the stairs; it was only, Bond noticed, a little after midnight. 'We will take a taxi, Gerda, it is less likely to be followed.'

'But why should anyone want to follow you, Vladimir?'

'Business is business; don't worry your pretty little head.'

The taxi turned off St. James's Street and stopped in a cul-de-sac. 'But this is not a hotel.'

'No, Gerda, furnished service flatlets. Mine is in the basement, so we go down these steps and don't have to face your night porters—so puritanical—and so expensive. Though anyone can see you're not an ordinary lady of the town.' He covered a falsie in his large palm and cupped it hard. 'Pip—pip.'

'Leave me alone. I've got a headache.'

'I have just the thing,' said the General and paid off the taxi, almost flinging Bond in his tight skirt and high heels down the steps into the area. For the first time he felt a twinge of fear. To the taxi-driver he was one of London's many thousand fly-by-nights off to earn their lolly—yet no one else in the great indifferent city knew his whereabouts nor what manner of man was preparing to have his way with him. At home in Chelsea his black shantung pyjamas would be laid out, the evening papers and the *Book Collector* spread on his night table, the digestive biscuits and Karlsbad plums, a bottle of San Pellegrino, a jigger of Strathisla. Lately he had taken to spinning himself to sleep with a roulette wheel or some Chopi xylophone music from the Transvaal asbestos mines. . . .

Vladimir opened a Yale and then a mortice-lock and let them into a typical furnished basement flat, a beige sitting-room with a sombre bedroom beyond. The fog was beginning to probe again, like a second day's grilling by Interpol. 'Here, swallow this for the headache—and have a glass of whisky—Teachers, Cutty Sark, Old Grandad or do you prefer vodka or slivovitz?'

'Old Grandad—and what about you?'

'Oh, I'll help myself to some vodka.' It was a tiny error but a revealing one. But perhaps the General argued that a Yugoslav drank slivovitz enough at home.

Bond put a cigarette in his mouth and just remembered in time to let the General light it. He took the yellow pill which he had been given, palmed it and pretended to swallow it with a grimace. 'I hate all these pills and things. I don't believe they're any good AT all.'

The General raised his vodka. 'To Friendship.'

'To Friendship,' chorused Gerda, lifting up her Old-Grandad-on-the-rocks. She was thinking fast. The purpose of the pill she hadn't swallowed must have been to make her sleepy but hardly to put her out. She had better play drowsy.

'Let's have another toast,' said the General. 'Who is your best friend?'

Bond remembered the gambit pawn. 'Guy Burgess.'

The General guffawed. 'I'll tell him. He'll be delighted. He doesn't often get a message from such a pretty girl.'

Bond lowered his eyes. 'He was my lover.'

'One can see that by the way you walk.'

Bond felt a mounting wave of fury. He opened his bag, took out his mascara and spat viciously. The General looked on with approval. Bond produced another cigarette. 'Here, catch.' The General tossed over his lighter. Bond, with the eye-brush in one hand and the pack in the other, brought his legs neatly together as it fell on his lap.

'Where were you at school, Gerda?'

'Westonbirt.'

'And so they teach you to catch like a man—what is a woman's lap for? She widens it to catch, not brings her legs together. And when she drowns she floats upward not downward. Remember that. It may come in useful.'

Bond felt trapped. 'I'm so sleepy,' he muttered. 'I don't understand.'

'Quick, in here.' The General pushed him into the bedroom with its electric fire and dingy satin coverlet. 'Undress and get into bed and then look under the pillow.'

Bond took off his blouse and skirt while the General gallantly turned his back, but kept on his stockings, pants and 'bra', then got out his water-pistol and filled it, dropped the pill behind the bed and finally climbed in and felt under the pillow. The first thing he found was a tube of some oily-looking substance, the next was a shoe-horn with a long cane handle, the last was a piece of paper with 'No one is the worse for a good beating' printed in heavy capitals. 'Ready,' he called and lay quietly until the General in a blue quilted vicuna kimono came simpering in. Bond made a kissy noise and as the General climbed on to the bed and advanced his hairy handlebars reached out with the water-pistol and shot him full in the eye.

The General wiped his face with a silk handkerchief. 'Temper, temper,' he giggled as the liquid ran down his chin. 'What a silly toy for a naughty little girl. Who do we think we are, a black mamba?' He picked up the shoe-horn and dealt Bond a vicious cut across the falsies.

'Help, help, murder,' screamed Bond and once again as the General drew back his mind began to race furiously. Somewhere along the line he had been double-crossed. But when? He lay back drowsily. 'Vladimir—it was only my joke. I'm so sorry. Now let me sleep.'

'Soon you shall sleep—but we have all to earn our sleep. Now shall I beat you first or will you beat me?'

'I will beat you, Vladimir, or I shall certainly drop off before my turn comes. Besides I've never beaten anyone before.'

'Tell that to Guy Burgess.' The General handed over the long shoe-horn and lay down on his stomach. You can kill a man with a short stick, Bond remembered. Get his head forward. Hold the stick in both hands and jab one end up under his Adam's apple. It had all seemed so easy in Armoury. But the General's broad shoulders were in the way. 'How dare you speak to me like that.' Bond jumped up and ran for the bathroom.

As he hoped, the General lumbered after him. 'Come out, you young fool, I can't sit around all night while you play hard to get. I'll miss my train to Porton.'

Porton! The anthrax boys! Bond's nipples stiffened at the name. 'I won't come out till I get my little present.'

'Fifty pounds—if you'll go the limit.'

'I want half now.'

The ends of some five-pound notes protruded under the bathroom door. Bond pulled hard but the General, he guessed, must be standing on them on the other side. That meant he was right by the door which opened inward. Bond would have to fling it open, get Vladimir's head forward and ram his throat in one continuous movement. He was in peak training, his opponent would assume him to be half asleep—it could be done. He counted down from five (the nearest he ever got to a prayer), threw open the door and discovered the smiling General with his hands deep in his kimono pockets and head thrown far back. There was a strong smell of cigar and Floris mouthwash. Still holding the shoe-horn in one hand, Bond lunged forward with the other, got hold of both ends of the handlebars to bring his head down and gave a tremendous tug. There was a screech of rending cardboard and the General gave a yell of pain; a gummy red patch was spreading where the whiskers had been. Bond stared into the cold blue eyes and this time they fell before him.

*

'I'm sorry, James,' said M. 'It was the only way I could get you.'

Bond drew himself up; his eyes flashed fire, his comma glistened, his breasts firmed, the nipples roused and urgent; his long rangy body flared out above his black silk panties, he looked like Judith carving Holofernes. In two seconds of icy concentration he saw everything that had to be done.

'It's been going on so long. I've been through too much. Don't think I haven't fought against it.'

Bond cut him short. 'I thought fellows like you shot themselves.' M. hung his head. 'Have you got a gun—sir—?' M. nodded. Bond looked at his watch. 'It's a quarter past two. You may employ what means you prefer but if I find out you are still alive by nine o'clock I shall alert every newspaper here, Tass and United Press—Moscow, Washington, Interpol and Scotland Yard, *Izvestia* and the *Kingston Gleaner* with the whole story. If it had been anyone else I might have urged you to leave the country but with modern methods of eliciting information you would be blown in a day.'

'You're quite right, James. I've staked all and I've lost. I hope you'll believe me when I say it would have been for the first and last time.'

'I believe you, sir.'

'And now perhaps you'd better leave me, 007; I shall have one or two reports to make.'

Bond flung on his blouse and skirt, worked into his stilettos and snatched up his bag and tippet.

'One last question, James. How did you guess?'

Bond thought of simply confessing that he hadn't guessed, even when the water-pistol had proved a dud. Right down to the Taittinger M.'s arrangements had been perfect. But that might look bad on his file. Then it came back to him. 'You spoke of Homer's handmaidens with "twittering feet" when Ulysses hanged them. That was in Lawrence of Arabia's translation. Robert Graves objected to it. I remembered that you had said Lawrence was your friend. It might have occurred to you that Graves could be mine.'

M.'s face brightened and the sickening love-light shone once more. 'Good lad!'

It made Bond want to spit in his mascara. 'Sir.' It was the guardsman's simple dismissal. Without a backward glance he let himself out and stamped up the area steps into the fog. In a few hours the finest Secret Service in the world would be without a head: Miss Ponsonby and Miss Moneypenny would lack an employer. All over the world transmitters would go silent, quiet men grip their cyanide or burn their cyphers, double agents look around for a publisher.

And he would be home in his black pyjamas, snoring up an alibi in his big double bed. There could be only one successor, one person only immediately fitted to take up all the threads, one alone who could both administrate and execute, plan and command. M., as he said, had played and lost. Come egg-time 007 Bond (James) would no longer be a mere blunt weapon in the hands of government. 'M. est mort! Vive le B.!'

And when all the razzamataz had subsided, he would put on his glad-rags and mosey round to the old Kitch. . . .

'Taxi!' The cab drew up to him in the dim light of St. James's Street. 'King's Road, corner of Milner,' he rasped.

'Jump up in front, lady, and I'll take you for nothing.'

Bond jumped.

[1962]

7

THE DOWNFALL OF JONATHAN EDAX

'AFTER all, Jonathan, you can't take it with you.' At lunch, yesterday—Friday—from Brenda, that hoary old cliché again. It set me thinking. Of course, logistically, one couldn't. There's no point in actually being buried with the loot like Tutankhamen though I would enjoy the sight of my coffin being followed to the vault by a procession of packing-cases and tea-chests. Crated rather than cremated. 'For the present, if nobody minds, I'm quite content to stay here.'

But, come to think of it, there *is* a way of taking it with one, and that is to endow the whole thing as a museum. One preserves one's name and it keeps the collection together. More than one dare expect from one's own family. They shall have front seats at the opening—if they can get away from their jobs. I can picture their faces. I'm certainly not going to take *them* with me:

The Edax Foundation: A small closed collection, museum and library open thrice yearly to the general public with microfilm material available to accredited students. Endowed by Mr. Jonathan Edax, this small closed collection contains some of the choicest examples of etc., etc., illustrating the taste and discrimination of its munificent founder. A fitting memorial to the days when it was still possible for a private individual, etc., etc. . . .

'The human eye deteriorates all it looks at'—whoever wrote that should be my first Curator. Museum. Mausoleum. Except on the three annual viewing days the collection should be kept in permanent darkness. Pharaoh would have approved. But what about tomb-robbers? Photoscopic devices, the most up to date in existence, will give instant warning of the minutest disturbance, such as the flashing of a light.

But these are morbid thoughts. My collections are incomplete. And I am still here to complete them. I shall go round to little Truslove. He's sure to be away.

Thomas Truslove. My oldest friend. Once a most gifted young poet, he is now completely forgotten and spends all his time on television, editorial boards, P.E.N. Club activities, book of the month clubs and American lecture tours. Last week in Buffalo, this week in Bonn—he only comes to England in his sabbatical year. But—and this is the point—he continues to be deluged with every pamphlet, every privately printed book that comes out. You can find anything at Truslove's. When I go round I always take a second edition of something or a second issue or a defective copy, and substitute it, when his back's turned, for the right one. To him that hath shall be given. He never notices; only likes painting anyway. Sometimes he tries most generously to present me with my own rejections, the ignorant booby. Today I took round a second edition of Hopkins. Virginia Truslove opened the door.

'You've come to see Thomas? He's in Borneo. But he'll be back tomorrow morning. We're lunching with the Clarks.' I gave her the gimlet gaze. 'I've come to see *you*.' Virginia was what some people would consider 'still a beautiful woman.' She looked rather flustered. '*Mille grazie!* Do come in.' I put down my coat in the hall and walked straight into the library. 'Would you like some tea?'

'Nothing better. I'd give my soul for a nice cup of tea—the way you always make it.' 'I'll get it myself.'

It always works! Drinks, no—too often they're on the table. But tea!

'I'd give my soul for it'—and down she goes to the basement. Ten clear minutes and always a warning rattle on the way back!

Sure enough, there was the right Hopkins—1918. The exchange was the work of a moment and I dived into the pamphlets: 'Poems written in Discouragement', only fifty copies—'to my young friend Thomas the Rhymer, W. B. Yeats.' 'Prufrock and other observations,'—'To Thomas from Tom.'

I didn't know where to begin. Even in my inside jacket pocket a slim volume might run a slim risk of being detected. 'Dear Thomas, Even you won't dare to print this, Wystan.' Jiminy cricket! Which shall it be—or why not all three?

Oh!

'Wasn't I quick! That's the electric kettle. I hope you haven't been too bored.'

'Just leafing through a few of Thomas's old circulars.'

'Aren't they a nuisance? As soon as he comes back we're going to have a thorough clean-out. Books are bad enough—but manuscripts, letters—he's kept *everything*.'

'Would you like me to go through them for you?'

'How angelic—but why should you do all this for me?'

'For an excellent reason.' And I looked down at her with my gimlet glance.

'There ought to be a law against it. Look at this one—"With some trepidation, Dylan". Why can't all these poets let poor Thomas alone. Nobody can print anything without inflicting a copy on him. He's like the British Museum.'

'I could start right now.'

'We'd better wait till he comes back. We might throw away a drawing by mistake. He won't be long. He's only gone to deliver a message at a conference.'

'In Borneo?'

'He's beamed at the Orient, you know.'

'Fortunate fellow!'

She put the pamphlets back in the glass-fronted bookcase and set the tea-tray on the table. Damned interference.

When I got home with my Hopkins, Brenda was waiting.

'Jonathan—where have you *been*?'

'Went to return a book to old Truslove.'

'Caroline's fallen downstairs.'

'Did she hurt herself?'

'No, thank God. Not this time.'

'Well then, it's not very important.'

'It happens to be important as she fell downstairs because you won't put up a gate, and you won't put up a gate because you're too mean to spend three pounds as all your money goes on teapots and candlesticks and filthy old books and china and glass and furniture and silver and candlesticks and teapots.'

Teapots! It's quite true I had been too busy with that bookcase to have a proper look. The Trusloves were just the kind of people to inherit some Queen Anne. Back to the Trusloves first thing tomorrow!

'Teapots with no tea, decanters with no wine, centrepieces for non-existent dinners—and Caroline could break her neck for all you'd care.'

'Why don't you get the gate yourself?'

'Out of what *you* give me?'

Now I happened to have read that small children have a very good sense of self-preservation even when descending stairs and that if they do fall their little bodies, with so much fat and water content, are extraordinarily resilient. I shut myself into my study and accommodated Hopkins—'I am gall, I am heartburn'—among my 'Recent Acquisitions'.

A few minutes later the telephone rang: 'It's me, Virginia. I'm so worried. Thomas has just cabled he's stopping off at Jakarta to judge some Indonesian Abstracts. He'll be late for the Clarks and miss his Lit. Soc. What shall I do?''

'You'd better take me with you.' 'Oh, what a good idea! Jon, you're so thoughtful for me!'

I remembered that I hadn't quite finished my egg at luncheon and retired to the pantry. The Clarks! *Véritable caveau d'Aladdin.* My luck was in. I found the egg and went back to my study. When I stand up before my largest bookcase I call it 'being at the Controls'. I feel like a captain on the bridge or Sandy Macpherson at his Wurlitzer. I quite expect the whole thing to sink down through the floor at the end of my virtuoso performance.

This evening I took out the keys of the plate-chests, then I inspected the green and yellow Sèvres, the Vincennes, the Chelsea and some of the Meissen and went back to the Controls again. That Yeats, that Eliot, that Auden manuscript perhaps weighed a few ounces between them, occupied the same space as one bad novel, yet were worth several hundred pounds and represented for me the conclusion of years of search and patient effort. Good old Truslove—if he'd only been born a few years earlier and had been given *Mosada* or *A Lume Spento.*

God's most deep decree
Bitter would have me taste. My taste was me.

I couldn't get Hopkins out of my head. 'My taste was me'—what a title for an autobiography! And when one's taste is flawless—near-perfect, and matched by a nose and an eye for a bargain and a bump of curiosity and a righteous ambition to spoil the Philistine, there's no end to what one can pick up. To know what someone else values is to be already on the way to possessing it.

Saturday: Today I woke with a tiny worry. On the landing I heard Brenda and Caroline: 'One two three four, one and two and three and four,' no doubt a charming maternal tableau. Then I remembered. Why hadn't I noticed the teapot? After our lunch we must go back there. And I would take a few old copies of *Horizon* and *Penguin New Writing* to stuff up any gaps I made in the tidying.

With silver and china it's not so easy. One can't 'borrow' somebody's dinner service or pocket a *garniture de cheminée.* One has to learn to carry cash and make unpredictable offers. Carry cash! That hurts. Still, I am a gentleman and a gentleman is someone who can reasonably expect to live in the same style and demand the same treatment as his forefathers in a society which has gone completely haywire. The world owes me a living, says the parasite. No. I owe myself a living, says the gentleman. Let Edax hold what Edax held; and a little bit over for safety.

Telephone! 'It's me, Virginia. Jonathan, I'm so worried. I've rung up the Clarks and they'd rather the lunch was put off till Thomas got back. And now I've no one to lunch with today.' The skinflints. To hell with all of them.

'Well, lunch you know is never very easy for me. But perhaps we can meet afterwards.'

'But if you were free to lunch with the Clarks I thought perhaps you might. . . .'

'And get poisoned in one of those filthy restaurants? I see a man got thrombosis from Scallops Mornay.'

'Well then—you must come and lunch here. I'll have to see what I can do with my own fair fingers. But don't expect the Crown Derby.'

'You have some Crown Derby?'

'Well, I don't know what it is, of course. . . .'

Why do they all say *of course*?

'. . . But I do know it's fearfully old and Granny thought the world of it. It's supposed to be terribly valuable.'

'It sounds like Mason's Ironstone.'

'What's that?'

'I said we'll have to turn it over and look at the marks.'

'No need to be improper.'

'Very well then, one o'clock.'

Silly bitch. The last woman I took out to lunch cost me £12,000 for four words. Well, with her 'Yes' you could say it made five words. I could still hear her in the next room, with her kitchen cough, moving about and making lists of all the things that she and Caroline 'simply had to have'—shoes, shirts, sheets, socks, chocs, each item more perishable than the last—and the Spanish girl with her list, too. Thank God there was one sane person in this household of crazy women.

The Edax Endowment. A Thought at the Controls; some of my books—some of the rarest—have other people's book-plates, coats of arms, country-house libraries (people with country-house libraries are among the biggest suckers in existence). Should I leave the book-plates in? Or steam them off? Or leave it to the executors? But who are my executors? Do I know a single person who isn't a bloody fool? One might choose an heir by examination. My will would be an examination paper. Or a treasure-hunt. But with all these bibliographies flying around they'd be bound to cheat. But to-day I shall put it aside, I feel sound as a Getty—and all a-tingle for the chase.

'Jonathan—where are you *going*?'

'Out to lunch—for a change.'

'But your egg.'

'Stuff it.'

'And the shopping-money.'

'Borrow from the Spanish girl.'

'Jonathan. Do you realize you haven't paid her wages for three weeks. Caroline's shoes are worn out. Do you expect us to live on air—when do you think I last went to the hairdresser?'

'Oh for God's sake. Get a long-playing record of yourself and send it to the Naggers' Club. Best years of your life. Worn your fingers to the bone. Waiting on me hand and foot. All that jazz.'

The usual screams and yowls in which Caroline joins with automatic mimicry. Thank God somebody keeps his head in this bedlam. Luckily I had chosen my cane and so had no further cause to linger. I blessed the Fermier-Général who had selected the perfectly fitting gold pommel with the reassuring *chinoiserie* and I blessed the country-house croquet set where I had annexed it.

The Spanish girl! Once the Trusloves' proudest possession—nothing she wouldn't do—laundry, mending, no evenings out. I soon got my eye on her. Took a bit of winkling, too—I told her that her employers were atheists who would probably poison her. Brenda is a Catholic, you see. Marriage is a life-sentence with her. So I give—and expect—no quarter. I had to go to church myself, just to convince the *chica*, and listen to the sermon. 'Nor his ox nor his ass nor his manservant nor his maidservant.' The whole works. These Spaniards! Eat you out of house and home!

One of my grievances against old Truslove is that he would choose to live halfway between two fare-stages. One either has a goodish walk or has to go on and break into a coin. Luckily it was a fine day.

Virginia opened the door. 'Look at him. Isn't he smart! With the hat and the cane and the Sherlock Holmes profile. Positively satanic.'

Damned impertinence. 'You don't look too bad yourself.' She was what our ancestors called a handsome woman, chivalrously adding 'very fine eyes'. Poor Truslove. Twenty years of marriage, say a pound a week to feed her and another for pin-money—thousands of pounds down the drain. Every woman after forty is a wasting asset.

'I know how you love beautiful things. I've got out all my treasures.' We sat down to a fricassee of chicken and a bottle of rosé. King's Pattern everywhere; all the silver was heavily embossed and the Crown Derby was quite respectable Coalport. 'The place for good china is under lock and key.' I wagged an admonitory finger, 'And now, since you've spoilt me so thoroughly, may I make one more request?'

She gave me a salute of twenty-one gums.

'Granted as soon as asked.'

'Can we have tea instead of coffee?' She looked rather sadly at the Cona machine. 'I'll go and make it myself.' Five minutes to go, with that damned electric kettle. I made a rush at the bookcase. It was locked. It was one of those big mahogany efforts and there, behind the glass, I could see all the presentation copies and the enigmatic untitled backs of the slimmer volumes. It wasn't really locked, I discovered, only jammed, otherwise I should have felt deeply insulted. I gave a good pull and the whole front came away; the hinges had gone. A sheet of glass fell forward and splintered round my head, badly cutting the hand which I raised to protect it. Virginia entered with the tray—'Oh you poor thing—let me bandage it. You must have a tourniquet. Why, you've bled all over the manuscripts.'

It was true. 'Thomas—even you won't dare to print this' had become completely illegible. She thrust a pamphlet in my pocket—'Here, have one of these for luck.' And then I spotted the teapot. It was hexagonal, genuine Queen Anne. I even got it up high enough to see the Britannia standard. One would commit murder for such a piece—or worse. What havoc it would wreak among my Georgian urns and melons! It must be worth thousands.

'Jonathan,' said Virginia, 'I've been wanting to talk to you for a very long time. You're not happy, are you?' I gave her the old gimlet. 'Poor old Jon—you can't deceive me. You see I know all about you and Brenda.' 'There's nothing to know.' 'Yes—that's just what I do know—and I know you only married her because she was engaged to Thomas.' 'Virginia——' 'And when you took Brenda—can't you see, Jonathan—there was nothing left for me to do but marry him.' 'Virginia——'

'Stop—and I too know what a marriage with nothing is like because that's what mine is. Married to a poster, a voice on a dictaphone, an airplane reservation. We can't go on like this, Jonathan. I'm forty now and you must be . . .' 'Virginia!' 'Wait—don't worry—you shall have me. You've been so sweet, so patient, so understanding—coming always to see me when he's out—yet never a word disloyal to him, always his best friend. Don't think I haven't noticed!—Dispelling my loneliness, my emptiness—and you so big, so quiet, so kind.' 'Virginia!' 'Wait—silly. I'm all yours now. Listen. I've cabled: "Don't hurry back. Clark's lunch postponed. All well—Virginia." Now aren't I rather clever!'

'Virginia—the teapot. Whose is it?' 'Mine, you silly-billy. Do you think we would be drinking tea out of it at this moment if it were his. Do you think I wouldn't protect your chivalry. Whither I go, it goes—my dowry—it will be about all I have. There used to be a silly old kettle on a stand as high as myself.' 'Virginia, I feel faint. My wrist. I must see a doctor. No, I can walk, thank you.'

Once in the street I pulled out the pamphlet she had given me. Unbelievable—the ultimate rarity! *The Bourbon Rose and other poems*, by Alberic Chute. Privately printed, Newport Pagnell, 1886. His first book—of which up till now only two copies were known, Hayward's and the Bodleian's. Alberic Chute, that exquisite talent, silenced it was said by some evil tentacle of the Wilde scandal after his third and most remarkable book of poems! He would be nearly ninety now, if this post-Raphaelite pre-Imagist were alive . . .

If he were alive! Why not—and if he is alive then he shall

inscribe *The Bourbon Rose* for me and I will possess a better copy than either of the others. I made for a telephone box. There he was! Alberic Chute, Squire's Mount, Hampstead. Should I ring up to make sure? Often the worst of all methods. First they hang up on you and then they won't let you in. Desperate occasions require desperate remedies. I took a taxi. When I rang the bell there was a commotion. The door was opened by an elderly man. 'Can I see Mr. Chute?' 'Mr. Chute is very ill indeed and can see no one.' 'The matter is extremely urgent.' 'I am afraid any question of urgency is now purely relative.' The last word gave me a clue. 'You see, I am his son.' 'Mr. Chute was unmarried.' 'That is my tragedy, not his.' 'Your name.' 'It would mean nothing. Here are my credentials.' I held up the book to him. 'Newport Pagnell—yes—he did live there, for a very considerable time. Well, you had better come in. I am Doctor Prout.'

He led me through to a room on the ground floor. 'I should warn you it may come at any moment. My patient is in uraemia.'

It was a small sitting-room with no good pieces into which a brass bed had recently been moved. On this was lying a tiny old man with closed eyes and a nose like a tin-opener, his hands milking the coverlet. A nurse was standing by. She held a finger to her lips. With my cane in my bandaged hand and *The Bourbon Rose* in the other I tiptoed over.

I have managed to live more years than I care to consider without any close experience of death. There is nothing in such a phenomenon to appeal to the collector. The foot-hills of Death and Love are, however, hunting-grounds for such of us as lay up treasure on earth and pursue enduring artefacts rather than the illusions of common humanity. I have often found a long face at a memorial service lead to substantial pickings.

I was brooding on certain gaps that still needed closing before my serried ranks of Americana could be brought up to combat strength when the nurse disappeared behind a screen. Almost immediately the sick man opened his eyes and seemed to want to sit up. He favoured me with a penetrating stare. I brandished *The Bourbon Rose* before him and reached for my pen; but to do that I had to lean the cane against the bed and a rash movement of his caused it to slip so that the heavy gold knob with its mandarins and pagodas fell with a clatter on the parquet. With glaring eye the old poet tried to heave himself up and thrust forward, his hand jerking at me as the nurse rushed round. 'You—' he gasped and fell backward. I had enough presence of mind as the doctor entered to retrieve my cane and sink my head on my arms. 'My father. . . .'

I was more than relieved to get away on the pretext that I had to telephone and I had run quite a distance from Squire's Mount, my black felt hat in one hand, my cane in the other before I realized that I had left *The Bourbon Rose* behind. Agony! I felt such a stinging sense of loss that I could almost have wept. The greedy old bastard!

By felicitous combinations of the London Transport system I made my way home for I pined to be at the Controls again. My reference library alone is more extensive than all the books to be found in an ordinary household; it starts in my bedroom and spills all over the upper landing. I can trace the mark on a piece of china, the owners of a crest, the rubric of a goldsmith, the succeeding possessors of a book or manuscript, the vicissitudes of some piece in the saleroom, in a matter of minutes. They are the jig-tools of my occupation.

Before letting myself in I sent off three cables to Truslove: care of P.E.N. Club, Jakarta; British Council, Singapore; and Nehru, Delhi. 'Clarks up-fed threaten off-brush. Hurry!' Then I made a dash for the landing. Great God! At the top of the stairs stood a hideous little gate of white metal, stuck onto the wall at each side by suction-pads. For a household of hurdlers!

'Brenda', I shouted. She came out, smiling. 'I thought you'd be surprised. Now our daughter—for you seem to forget that she is yours as well as mine—can grow up without risking her life every few minutes.' 'How did you pay for it?' 'I charged it.' 'You have no account.' 'I put it down on yours.' 'You PUT IT DOWN!' I felt a lump of rage surge up and choke me, like when Caroline tore the book jackets. 'You filthy extravagant slut, I'll sue you.' 'Miserly old madman.' 'I'll put a notice in the papers. I'll hound you out of my house.'

The telephone rang in my bedroom. (I permit no outgoing calls.) 'It's me, Virginia. Darling. He's on his way back. We must leave at once. I'm desperate.' 'Impossible. I can't ever see you again.' 'Then I shall kill myself. Now.' 'Goodbye.' These crazy women! Suddenly I had a vision of the little hexagonal teapot in all its leaden moonglow perfection. Now was my chance. I ran out of my room and took a flying kick at that bloody gate.

'Aaaaaaaahh. . . .'

A verdict of death by misadventure was returned on Mr. Jonathan Edax, the well-known connoisseur and collector who broke his neck by falling down the stairs at his home in Holland Park on Saturday night. The stairs were exceptionally steep and a gate had recently been installed at the top of them by Mrs. Edax; it had presumably been insecurely attached. The deceased had appeared to be in a disturbed frame of mind at the prospect of making his will. Mr. and Mrs. Thomas Truslove were present at the inquest but were not called upon to give evidence. Jonathan Hagan Edax was born in 1895 at Bedford, where his father was a prosperous solicitor. After completing his studies, he had early made his mark in the correspondence columns of learned periodicals and was soon recognised as a formidable opponent in the auction room at a time when it was still possible for a private individual, etc., etc.

8

FIRST EDITION FEVER

I DON'T know when I discovered the Grand Design that was formulating behind the sporadic intensity with which I collected the authors I loved; perhaps it lay always at the back of my activities; certainly it was present by the time I wrote my last article on collecting first editions in January, 1936. My ambition was no less than to possess in their original form all the books which constituted the modern movement in literature; that is to say in the guise in which they first appeared to their contemporaries. The prime necessity was to have a clear picture of the modern movement so as not to be beguiled into the collector's many backwaters, such as the assembling of expensive books from private presses which specialise in fastidious reprints.

Modern books are not always attractive in themselves but in bulk they make a very agreeable picture, a mosaic of human aspiration. A book collector is like a lighthouse keeper who offers sanctuary to buffeted and exhausted migrants as they home towards the friendly beam. Once behind glass they are safe from pollution. If one loves a writer's work the highest form of appreciation is to protect and enjoy his books in the guise in which they first appeared and which illustrates the growth and variation of his talent. The envy, vanity and competitiveness of collectors are a minor phenomenon compared to the satisfaction with which they contemplate 'the precious life-blood of a master-spirit' in its well-cared-for envelope.

There are many other joys in collecting. It sharpens the historical sense. It enhances our encounters with authors and gears us to the land of the living. It also brings us into contact with booksellers, who are a race apart and one and all delightful company, as befits those in whom the ideal and the practical are so nicely blended, and they lead to booksellers' catalogues, favourite reading surpassed only by a good bibliography; and then follows the excitement of the chase, with much opening of parcels and filling up of gaps. Perhaps the relieving of anxiety is a greater satisfaction than any other, for I notice that once a title is crossed off the 'wanted' list one is apt to forget it.

I do not propose to enumerate my rarities, a dull business or to proclaim my needs, which are really limited to about a dozen books I shall never possess; the earliest works of Joyce, Yeats, Pound and Hemingway, Forster and Lawrence.

I am very lucky however to have backed my own judgment in the 'thirties. For there has been a revolution in favour of the Revolutionaries; the soft-currency minds have been driven out by the hard. Much of the credit for this goes to American critics and professors of literature who have influenced the American university libraries and so created an insatiable demand for the rare books which are seminal to the modern movement and not merely entertaining derivatives. This need has driven up the price of Eliot, Joyce and Yeats to astonishing heights (at least ten times their pre-war value). On the other hand, Pound (all of whose early books were published in this country) has not yet appreciated to the same extent.

The system I advocate is to perceive clearly which are the main peaks in the range, the books by the writers who advance the human spirit further and to go all out for them, afterwards filling in the subsidiaries. Sometimes these books are decorative in themselves, sometimes they are also scarce, occasionally, like *Animal Farm*, they are neither; but in the late 1920's self-consciousness set in and writers began to produce artificial rarities.

Thus Joyce's work opens with two or three almost unobtainable pamphlets, a scarce first book of poems and two expensive but essential works of fiction, *Dubliners* and *The Portrait of the Artist* (New York, 1916), followed by the most important novel of the period (1910-30) *Ulysses*. The first edition of this book

(1922) consisted in all of a thousand numbered copies and it is a 'must,' in my opinion, to have one of these, which now fetch between £20 and £30 (unsigned). After *Ulysses* the artificial rarities began and various fragments of *Finnegans Wake* came out in expensive limited editions. It affords no proportionate pleasure to acquire all of these, many of them in slip cases and this also is true of the later work of Lawrence and Norman Douglas. The end of the 'twenties witnessed in fact the inflation of the privately printed book.

Frivolity and monotony are the two aspects of modern first editions which the collector must try to avoid. Some publications are monotonously presented and the result is the Left Book Club or the poets of the 'thirties whose uniform, excellent for each, is the same for all. Only such writers' first books are unusually designed. Here the two rarities are Auden's *Poems* printed (and how!) by the eighteen-year-old Stephen Spender in 1928, of which about a dozen copies exist and Spender's own *Nine Experiments* (Frognal, 1928) which I believe to be even rarer. Evelyn Waugh's privately printed *P.R.B.*, 1926 (on the pre-Raphaelites), of which there has never been a census is also uncommon. Luckily their second books, Spender's *Twenty Poems* (Blackwell) and Auden's *Poems* (Faber, 1930), both in paper covers, are also decorative and contain much better work.

Is this rising market based on an illusion, like the boom of the late 'twenties? It is an illusion only if the modern movement itself turns out to be a momentary fashion or if the driving force (the acquisitiveness of American colleges) becomes spent or changes direction. Or the universities might go all-American. Already they rightly prefer drafts and manuscripts to the printed word and require, above all, documents which their Eng.-Lit. students can exfoliate, extrapolate or just imbricate and explicate.

But something did happen in that crucial period between 1910 and 1930 which cannot be undone by the vicissitudes of fashion. There was a combination of new outlook and new feeling with a new use of words. The outlook was there in Flaubert's *Bouvard & Pécuchet* (1880), the use of words in Hopkins's poems; the process accelerated when Pound became Yeats's secretary and got Eliot and Joyce published in little magazines. I have a feeling that the movement, even if it ended with Dylan Thomas, will outlast our time.

I have noticed that book-collectors tend to go for the item they associate with their own youth (it used to be *The Wind in the Willows*) and so as each generation is written off and boxed, there is a tendency for its sentimental values to die with it. In that case we who welcomed Lawrence, Joyce and the later Yeats as ennoblers and liberators will be deprived of our verdict and they may go the way of Swinburne and Pater, Flecker and Rupert Brooke.

Nothing can replace the excitement of greeting new work by contemporaries when one is young and impressionable; the appearance in the early 1920's of *The Waste Land*, *Ulysses*, *The Sleeping Beauty*, *The Flower Beneath the Foot*, *Antic Hay*, or the Chinese poems translated by Arthur Waley were for me a form of demoniac possession. How can the young experience the same happy desire to enshrine them? They cannot. But they may still uphold Yeats's *Later Poems* of 1922 as proof that he is the greatest poet of the West since Baudelaire. Collectors can gamble that a man who in his middle seventies could write

> Slim adolescent that a nymph has stripped
>   Peleus on Thetis stares.
> Her limbs are delicate as an eyelid;
>   Love has blinded him with tears. . . .

will not go the way of the other members of the Rhymers Club.

The recent bibliographies of Yeats, Joyce and Eliot are a mine of information. They protect the bookseller against making mistakes and are also an immense help to the collector like those stamp albums which used to have a picture of every stamp in the place for it. Is book-collecting just a deteriorated form of philately? There is that element in it, especially in the filling up of gaps and the emphasis on condition, rarity and such things as dust-wrappers. The Americans are hipped (or should one say squared?) on dust-wrappers, which they regard as an integral part of a book's original appearance. This leads to much painful discrimination and finally to the manufacturing of Cellophane wrappers for the jackets themselves, since these are highly deciduous. Perhaps one should keep the books in the shelves under glass and send the jackets to the bank.

There is no ultimate justification for book-collecting except that it preserves the books for we know deep-down that it is all make-believe; the tenderest inscription, the warmest dedication, the liveliest photograph cannot bring dead authors back to life. The collector has but to fall sick or move house a few times for his possessions to take on a woe-begone appearance. It is his own enthusiasm, anxiety and cupidity which maintain order and keep the arrangements alive; without him his books are like a cellar of rare wines buried under an avalanche. How depressing are those roped-up bundles that we see in the auction rooms, how different they will look when they have found a new master.

Let us suppose, however, that some eager youth who reads these words wishes to start a collection. How should he go about it? He will certainly possess some books already. The first thing is to purchase a work like the *Annals of English Literature* (O.U.P.) which gives the year in which most modern books appeared; this acts as a compass which will guide him through the jungle. Then he should get hold of as many booksellers' catalogues as possible to obtain some idea of the prices. *Book Auction Records*, issued annually by Stevens, Son and Stiles, lists all the principal sales under authors and so indicates the 'highs' which exceptional copies have fetched.

A new collector will find he needs many sources. Here are some:

(1) *Local booksellers:* these are always accessible, reliable and not too expensive. They are the joy of provincial towns and many of them keep a couple of shelves for modern first editions.

(2) *London specialist dealers:* these are not cheap but they know much more than we do and so can give good advice. They will in the end discover nearly every rarity but others will also be waiting

for it. No one can possibly collect without being on at least one of their mailing lists or calling in to inspect their stock. They always keep a surprising number of cheap books.

(3) *Your friends:* every friend has at least one book which you want and a true friend will part with it, unless he be a collector. This may make him dread your visits but it remains a test of friendship which many survive. Women friends are particularly generous and seldom collect. (Every book-collector's wife rates his obsession slightly below compulsive gambling. A wise collector always gets first to the postman.)

(4) *It is essential* to have one helpful friend or dealer in America as so many modern first editions stem from there. On the other hand it is not nearly so difficult as one would expect to find rare American books in England.

(5) *Swapping with other collectors:* this soon involves a superhuman restraint and delicacy.

(6) *Unsolicited gifts:* delightful, but often unsuitable.

(7) *Treasure trove:* bargain boxes, attics, country auctions, books in antique dealers, etc. Disappointing.

Do not hesitate to ask authors you meet to sign their books for you. It is the only way we can improve them. This should never be done by post or without previous acquaintanceship. No book lent, even if only from one room to another, is ever returned in exactly the same condition. It is less disagreeable to refuse to lend ('I wouldn't even lend it to *myself*', as Jonathan Edax used to say) than to have to pester people to return a book and thus lower their opinion of themselves as well as of you. Conversely a collector does not borrow since it would be intolerable to have to return. He quietly notes the title and sets out to acquire it.

Do not buy books you do not really want because they are cheap nor hesitate to spend more than you intend to obtain a rarity. Rare and even scarce books live up to their name and one may have to wait several years, by which time the price will be much higher. It is not just the famous books which are hard to find. Several million books of 1938, 1939 and 1940 perished in the Blitz, particularly in the fire of Simpkin Marshalls, hence the rarity of Beckett's *Murphy*, Macneice's *Yeats*, McAlmon's *Being Geniuses Together* and so many others. Of all headaches for collectors the amassing of the first editions of Anthony Powell's five pre-war novels in my opinion brings on the worst. Beside him even Orwell is relatively easy.

If Yeats, Eliot, Joyce and Dylan Thomas are too expensive, whom should the new addict collect? The Edwardians, for a start, for here are to be found many predecessors. Then there are the first books of poets as listed in John Hayward's famous catalogue. Georgian poets are still in very small demand. Of the major poets Edith Sitwell is still undervalued. Only *The Mothers*, her first book (1915), and *Façade* (1922) are above the £10 limit. All her books are delightfully got up and full of variety, several in signed limited editions. Robert Graves was also prolific of slim volumes, many of which are still easy to obtain.

The 'Thirties, as I have said, are unpalatable to collect because of the uniformity of presentation. Nevertheless they are absurdly underpriced and our addict can obtain all Auden (except his American firsts) all Spender, Day Lewis, Macneice and Isherwood (with a little patience) and most of Waugh and Greene. And now is the time to do it.

All collectors tend to live in the past but they should make an effort to buy new books by new authors before they reach the booksellers' catalogue. This, of course, involves reading them. How far should love for favourite authors be carried? Should it extend to collecting all subsequent editions of their books? No. They take up too much room. Should one collect the prose of poets and the poetry of prose writers? Yes; if in book form. Should one collect their contributions to other books? Yes. To periodicals? Only for poets, I think. The test of our devotion to an author is whether we are prepared to collect his journalism. The test of an author's devotion to his collectors is not to provide us with any.

Lastly, should one collect magazines? Yes: they are the undergrowth out of which tower the forest giants and they are never artificial rarities. Nothing else so conveys the *couleur du temps*, the unselfconscious excitement of a particular period. Moreover they are never reprinted. Even so, compared to the true collector our new devotee will probably remain, like myself, hopelessly superficial, possessing only one copy of one edition and confining himself to what he can enjoy reading, his library a memorial to the kind of writer that he would like to have been.

9

ONE OF MY LONDONS

ONCE or twice a month, like an old trapper clinging to his pelt-less round, I revisit London to correct a proof, drink oysters with a publisher, prospect an auction-room or favourite book-shop. I stay, if at all, but one night for I am usually depressed by the stale air and listless shuffle of the street, the monumental tawdriness of lettering and lighting, the quicksand of vague faces—and nothing, I find, comes up to the moment of arrival, the taxis of Charing Cross, the stucco of King William Street or glitter of Saint Martin's—unless it be the lamplit curve of the river when the train trundles homeward over the bridge.

One blue summer twilight, however, I was passing by a mews flat in Knightsbridge where two window-boxes were in flower above a painted portico. A tall well-dressed young man with a baby in his arms stands on the darkening step; the door is opened by a laughing girl in nothing but a bath-towel, silhouetted against the light in the hall-way. In that moment I have unwillingly lived myself into this couple; I was there when they first met at a cocktail party; I know that weak, longhanded young man, his cruel charm and mannered voice and his incurable unrest: I see this naked girl bubbling with hope in her pale summer frock, keen on the arts, angry with mother, stabbed suddenly by desire and maternal anguish as she accepts her first whisky from him. And I am aware that the Past has yanked me back, that they are one with innumerable couples I have known, with all the trapped young *couche-tard* fathers and honey-headed girls determined, as they pile into the little car at week-ends, to make the best of things while the drink bills and the garage bills and the tailor's bills pile up after them until that terrible quarrel at the night club, when first she wipes her lipstick from another's mouth and his wallet bulges with treason. . . . And another day, while crossing Bedford Square, I am doubled up with nameless and immediate anguish, blackened with fear—and forced to run for sanctuary to some old dusty counter and efface myself among Victorian prints, the collected works of Lamartine or the unsaleable *Picciola*. And then I remember Petronius: 'An old love pinches like a crab.' It is my discarded mistress who has nipped me, the great city reminding one that no indifference, however ingrowing, is proof against a casual jab from her nondescript sting-ray buildings:

> Tout l'affreux passé saute, piaule, miaule, glapit
> Dans le brouillard sale et jaune et rose des Sohos
> Avec des 'all rights', et des 'indeeds', et des 'hos! hos!' . . .

London is the capital of prose, as Paris of art or New York of modern living and most of this good prose is concerned with dandies or with slums or with fog: sometimes the dandy goes slumming and sometimes, taking advantage of the fog, the slum-folk sneak up on the dandy. The London I like best is the one I can find in books where it lies embalmed between 1760 and 1840, the dandies still outnumbering the slums and the fog as yet barely invented.

This London takes shape with Rochester and Etherege; in Congreve, Pope, and the 'Journal to Stella'; it comes into its own with Boswell; Boswell and Casanova who both set out to conquer the city in 1762 and who themselves are conquered by love, if love be the proper term for Louisa and La Charpillon. And now comes the golden age of the dandies, the London of Chesterfield and Horace Walpole, of Selwyn and March, of Fox and Sheridan, of Alvanley and Brummell, of White's and Brook's and Almack's, Devonshire House and Albany. Brummell fled to Calais in 1816, a few hours after his appearance at the opera—when his famous note: 'My dear Scrope, Lend me five hundred pounds for a few days; the funds are shut for the dividends or I would not have made this request. G. Brummell' had received its infamous reply:

'My dear Brummell, All my money is locked up in the funds. Scrope Davies.' The Beau's life was written by Captain Jesse who met him in his old age at Caen and who also edited the Selwyn correspondence; four volumes of absorbing small-talk from the later 18th century. As a cure for anxiety and worry and for that nameless sickness of the inner eye which views the contemporary world in monochrome, I would suggest a prolonged immersion in these irresponsible letter-writers, in the strong, calm flow of London's eighteenth century whose eddies broaden into the Regency, with Harriette Wilson, Greville and Captain Gronow to complete it, and some of Mr. W. S. Lewis' admirable documentation, such as his *Three Tours Through London* to fill in local colour.

The dandy's world is friendly, formal, and heartless, occluding the imagination, and if the cure in that direction should not go deep enough, I would propose a visit to the more spiritual London of the Romantics, to Hampstead and Highgate and Islington in the days of Keats, Coleridge, and Lamb—or a compromise may be sought in the drawing room of Holland House of which we possess such complete descriptions by Greville, Macaulay, and Talfourd.

It is scarcely seven—and you are seated in an oblong room, rich in old gilding, opposite a deep recess, pierced by large old windows through which the rich branches of trees, bathed in golden light, just admit the faint outline of the Surrey Hills. Among the guests are some perhaps of the highest rank, always some of high political importance, about whom the interest of busy life gathers, intermixed with others eminent already in literature or art, or of that dawning promise which the host delights to discover and the hostess to smile on. All are assembled for the purpose of enjoyment, the anxieties of the minister, the feverish struggles of the partisan, the silent toils of the artist or critic, are finished for the week; professional and literary jealousies are hushed; sickness, decrepitude and death are silently voted shadows. . . . Every appliance of physical luxury which the most delicate art can supply, attends on each; every faint wish which luxury creates is anticipated. . . . As the dinner merges into the dessert, and the sunset casts a richer glow on the branches, still, or lightly waving in the evening light, and on the scene within, the harmony of all sensations becomes more perfect; the choicest wines are enhanced in their liberal but temperate use by the vista opened in Lord Holland's tales of bacchanalian evenings at Brook's, with Fox and Sheridan, when potations deeper and more serious rewarded the Statesman's toils, and shortened his days, until at length the serener pleasure of conversation, of the now carelessly scattered groups, is enjoyed in that old, long unrivalled library in which Addison drank and mused and wrote; where every living grace attends; 'And more than echoes talk along the walls'.

It was nourished on such fairy tales (though with appetites more approaching those of Boswell and Casanova) that I came to live in London at the age of twenty-three. I had been taken on as secretary by Logan Pearsall Smith who had the idea of trying to endow a form of literary scholarship for a young writer by giving him a few pounds a week to live on while preparing a masterpiece and while assisting his employer by gleaning for the various anthologies which punctuated his leisure. I still carried some old debts from Oxford and my salary was soon pledged far ahead. I had also a weakness for taking my friends out to dinner at the Ivy, which has hardly changed at all in a quarter of a century; at the Berkeley which has changed considerably; at Boulestin's which was then a small pink paradise in Leicester Square or at the Tour Eiffel (the most expensive) which has quite disappeared, all turtles turned. Desmond MacCarthy gave me the novels to review for the *New Statesman* and I went to live with an Oxford friend who had gone into journalism. We rented an Edwardian cottage studio in Yeoman's Row, Knightsbridge, full of high-backed Italianate furniture and cardboard Spanish ironwork.

Drowsy hour or so in the empty house, sit in my future arm-chair and read idly while somebody strums on a piano and the slum children play outside; a heavy sullen evening of imminent rain. Enjoy the children's voices and the sad thudding of their ball against the high windows. Explore the house and love it. Fondness for the strange furniture and garden outlook. Queer intimacy of possession in the empty house, a feeling of *Childe Roland* and that I would write well here. Take a taxi to the Board of Trade and wait about in the rain for an hour and a half in the hope of seeing A. No sign of her and with a curious sense of dream-like fatality I plunge southward into Lambeth through a green and streaming urban sunset. At last I come to Charnwood Street lapped in obscurity and glaucous twilight with girls who laugh at me from upper windows. There is no answer to the bell and only a baby's crying greets me as I stand by the milk bottle outside the door. . . .

October 3rd, 1927.—Long quiet evening alone. Digestion very bad, dining off tea. Read Maurice Baring's letters from his Russian friend. He writes: 'Any person taking a special interest in me is a frightful burden from which I flee in terror. I had always a disgust for men who want a woman to wash their soul's dirty linen for them and tell them the soul itself is pure. Marivaudage—Looking in woman for something she hasn't got and which you haven't got, begging where you should be giving, which leads to unceasing hesitation, and not knowing which is, after all, the right one. If you want inspiration from a woman, you must change her as you change your buttonhole; if you want to make her satisfied and be satisfied with that, marry her and turn philister. But be clear about what you want'.

More unpleasant than filing one's bills is the effort of facing all the people I have thought I was in love with, permanently, since the summer. N. whom I hate, P. who is a bore, S. whose shares go neither up nor down, A. whom I have forgotten altogether, L. who is only eleven, and now R., but six years older, unawakened, stolid, last of the line of fair-haired, competent Dorian maidens about whom I feel so passionate and poetic.

October 7th.—R.'s mother came to tea on Thursday: Delicious, exquisite, and alarming. She said that she didn't believe that children really began to live till their parents were dead, that she had had a happy childhood because her mother and father were happily married, that all her sisters and she had made happy marriages, and that she was sure happiness in childhood was based entirely on that; she talked of the unhappiness of youth and how unnecessary it seemed, her daughters were not as happy as she. She spoke of the importance of money to marriage and as she was leaving said: 'We must find you a rich wife!'

Philoctetes' farewell to his island is the most Elizabethan thing in Greek. The more I review novels, the more I read the classics, the only literature that is complete, that satisfies every need, and provides a decent privacy where one can understand oneself and be alone. I suppose I have had as much enjoyment from Tibullus this year as from any other author.

October 10th, 1927.—I get happier and happier, autumn intoxicates me, so does London, so does Yeoman's Row and the slum children and the evenings spent *à l'ombre des jeunes filles en fleur*. It becomes harder and harder to read or write. Dinner with the Berensons in Lady Horner's house, which is full of books and pre-Raphaelite portraits, all somehow a little wrong. B. B. looked more pained and beautiful than I have ever seen him, but very old, Isaiah as a French Academician. His temper was bad at the beginning of the meal (soup, fish, partridge, ices, champagne and port). He said life consisted of a double rebellion, tragic and comic, the one a revolt against death and oblivion from which sprang all works of art and love, the other a revolt against the law of averages which made people try to be different from others and discover new forms of old age or marriage or writing. He said 'Bloomsbury' had not got beyond the comic rebellion, Roger Fry had adopted his own early principles and never got beyond them, Eliot was a thin and squeaking Matthew Arnold and 'Bloomsbury' a kind of dandyism only compatible with youth. He said Europe was not decadent, neither was England, the only decadence was that of the Roman world from the first to the fifth centuries A.D., and that decadence could never occur as an isolated intellectual phenomenon as it was primarily physiological and therefore, since physiologically even England was unchanged, there could be no true decadence.

In art also, he went on, people were still looking for new forms, while decadence consisted in doing bad work in old ones. America wasn't decadent either, the real danger to England was not Americanism, but civil servants, Tchinovnik—the spirit which had ruined Russia, the spirit of Keynes in the *Nation*.

Mrs. Berenson said Oscar Wilde was the only person of his time whose eyes did not travel on to look for someone more important when he spoke to you. She met him once five times in a week and the last time he said, 'I can't possibly sit next to you, you have heard all my conversations for this week and I have nothing more prepared. Is there any one of them you would like to hear again?' 'Yes, the one about Evolution,' said Mrs. Berenson, and he went through it but so perfectly that it all seemed to arise from her own replies. B. B. said one could review books for a limit of two years without becoming a hack. I complained of my material happiness, that I enjoyed life so much at present that I had no ideas at all beyond a vague meditation about physical things. He told me not to mind. 'Ideas will come,' he said, 'but youth will go'.

Wednesday.—Bob Boothby, his mother, and Nina Seafield to luncheon. I like her and she asked me to a cocktail party. Boothby asks me to dinner. Write an offensive letter to R. which may do some good and go round to Nina's. She has red hair, blue eyes, an attractive stubby figure, a lovely stammer and gasping kind of speech. Bob is there, and offers me a job; exciting. Back and dine out with Patrick at his club. Ring up R. to hear her voice and write to her again. Mrs. Fitz's, and a lovely girl called Lola; French, very young and attractive. Back, still desperately in love with R., to a late bed.

Thursday.—Dinner with Bob Boothby and Gladwyn Jebb at the House of Commons, excellent dinner, liked them both. We hear the new Prayer Book thrown out, most exciting. Walked back with Gladwyn, it was agreed that henceforth I should be a cad and a careerist.

Thought of R. glows like an electric toaster.

Friday.—Lovely letter from R., hope springs again. Walked round to Elm Park Gardens but the house was dark. Hours and hours of watching but never a light. Thought of Swann and Odette and felt like my own ghost.

Κὰγῶ γαρ προθύροις νίσσομαι ὑόμενος.

Saturday.—Failed to ride with Nina owing to the snow. Lunch with Logan and we go afterwards to Battersea Park. See a good 18th century church with tomb of Bolingbroke. Logan said Holland House must have been terribly dull. He had met in his youth one of the old survivors of that world where the conversation used to consist of long monologues which displayed your general knowledge and reading (in the case of the survivor, Aberdare, his topic was the route of Alexander's Indian expedition) while all the other old gentlemen sat around like croquet-players, waiting to cut in at the first cough.

He said there were three illusions everybody passed through: falling in love, starting a magazine, and thinking they could make money out of keeping chickens. Back and wait ages for R., go in and out into the snow again and change and re-change my tie. At last she comes and we discuss our situation, not arriving at any settlement beyond the general relief of being able to discuss it. R. very lovely and boyish, wearing a yellow skirt that matched my cushions; brown-faced, green-eyed, tender and jovial. Her sister came to fetch her and we all went to Westminster in the tube and walked to South Kensington through the snow. Feel infinitely happier after seeing her. On to Nina's for dinner. N. very attractive and Gilberte-like. On after to the Café Anglais, drink R.'s health several times, back late and write to her in the small hours.

Tuesday, *December 20th*.—Wrote my article in the morning. Very cold day. Lunch at the Traveller's with Gladwyn. Send off article. Go on to tea with Hilda Trevelyan. George Moore comes, impressive and fussy. He said no good literature had ever come out of a salon. Logan said, 'What about Proust?' George Moore (triumphantly) 'Who wrote that?'

Home to dress, then dine with Leigh at the Ivy. He is charming, and afterwards I go to North Street to fetch Nina. Thrill in the drawing room, the candles, the log fire, the dull light on my top hat, the taxi waiting outside in the snow, then Nina's footfall on the stair and delicious roucoulement of greeting. On to Lady Cunard's, carol-singers drear, dance with Nina and talk to Patrick and Brian Guinness. Snobbish thrill at sight of the Prince of Wales walking alone up the wide staircase and shaking hands at the top with Maurice Baring and Diana Duff Cooper. Enjoy the rich patina of the evening, the lovely women and vacant faces of the extroverts, the expression of envy on Clarence Marjoribanks' face as he asked me to introduce him to Nina, and the fatuous air of luxurious abandon on Lady Cunard's as she danced with the Prince. We sat next to him at supper.

The storm brewed over the week-end and the main fact out of a mass of complication and rumour is that R. and I are at all costs not to meet or write again.

*

March, 1928.—General sense of depression and discontent, with usual horror of literature and hopeless uncertainty over R.

> . . . 'clene out of your minde
> Ye han me cast, and I ne can nor may
> For al this world, with-in myn herte finde
> T'unloven you a quarter of a day' . . .

The *soif* for life has greatly intensified so that to dine out every evening is not enough and has to be contrasted in a sequel among the centres of vitality; nearly every day I street-prowl. Cultivated people are shrimps in a rock-pool from whom I can learn nothing.

Rotherhithe.—Good docks and bridges but very little life, a few pubs, some wooden houses, continuous smell of lice which makes one feel abroad.

Limehouse.—Gambling dens suppressed. Met a Chinaman in Pennyfields who offered to show me round, he was reading a book on psychology. Touching to see the English waitress writing out Chinese ideograms on bits of paper and learning fresh ones from the proprietor. When she got one right, she smiled foolishly and threw it on the fire.

Shadwell.—Love Lane disappointing. Ratcliffe Highway, where there were a thousand brothels in 1890, is no more. Good market in Watney Street, best in evenings. Embankment lovely.

Wapping.—Good high street, wharves and water stairs. Here I saw that strange, nocturnal goatish clergyman stoop around an alley, blinking at the unaccustomed light from the bonfires (Guy Fawkes Day) that crimsoned his long white beard.

Whitechapel.—Much the best part of East End, especially side streets off Commercial Road (markets) and Leman Street, Wentworth, Old Montague streets, on the Stepney side. Here is Latin gaiety, crowds and music and colour, rows of cars standing outside obscure cafés, and an excellent band and a tiny dance-hall. The Jewesses are amazingly attractive, a mass bloom seems to emanate from them in large quantities and they appear to walk up and down the street all night. Men dingy and undersized. Even when English themselves, these girls all deeply dislike the English, and the foreigners' good manners and capacity for passion are everywhere well-spoken of.

Soho.—New Compton Street. Café opposite Greek restaurant entirely full of Negroes. Very crowded, good grenadine.

Wardour Street.—Chinese restaurant with marvellous waitress, seventeen, father West Indian, mother German, name Lydia.

Hopkins Street.—Café apparently always full of crooks, sinister, open all night.

Desperate anxiety to get abroad, away from R.'s world; deepening passion for low life. Live in Green Dragon Court, Hop market, Southwark.

Lily: 'Oh! I do like Piccadilly, don't you? I could never stay away from it long. Once I went to live with a man, a nice man he was, too, he had a flat in Earl's Court and I stayed down there three months. Well, one day he sent me up West to get some things and I got to Piccadilly about six o'clock. When I saw the lights and everything I was happier than I'd ever been. "I am not going to lose this again," I said, and so I never went back. I left all my clothes down there, and everything else, too. I don't know what he must have thought. Well, I got a fiver that night and I walked into Maxim's with it and when the waiter came up I ordered two bottles of champagne. Well, when I'd drunk them I noticed a woman with a red dress on, sitting with a man opposite me, so I said, "You ought to give me that red dress, it would suit me much better". I suppose I was a bit tight but I just said it to make conversation and she flew into a tearing rage. "Take this woman out, she is drunk," she said to the manager. "I'll show you whether I'm drunk," I said, "I've paid for this and I've a right to have it", and I hit him on the head with a champagne bottle. Oh! there was an awful row. The band stopped and all the dancing and a detective came and threw me out and they said I'd be arrested if I ever put my head in there again. But I don't mind, I never cared for Chinamen. Well, goodbye; they say the first man you meet after midnight on Hallowe'en means something to you—not that you're quite the first.'

*

Palette for 1927. *Autumn.*—Brown and gold—brown curtains and chairs of Yeoman's Row, gold tiles in the fire, the green leaves through the lattice windows, then yellow leaves, then black stems of trees. The lights of Brompton Road, the news-boys outside the tube station as I come back from the *New Statesman* to the gramophone, the warm light, the evening paper and a late tea. Drinking with Patrick on idle Sunday mornings, going to the Film Society, dinners alone at the Ivy, theatres alone in the yellow fog. When I say suddenly, 'autumn', I first see nothing but brown and gold, then I see three pictures rolled into one, the brown fur rug on my sofa, the two gold cushions, R.'s brown dress against them, her golden face and hair, a glimpse of the trees through the drawn curtains, a wild excitement in the air—still brown and gold the picture changes, a cold wet afternoon by Battersea bridge, R., slim, golden, slant-eyed, in boy's felt hat and brown jumper, looking down the road and tapping with one foot on the kerb—the swirl of the grey autumnal river, the wet embankment, the waiting figure against the trees of the park, her marsh-green eyes and yellow hair. Windy twilight in the Fulham Road, the roar of buses, the November dusk, walking away from Elm Park Gardens in the eddy of fast-falling leaves from plane and elm crushed close on the rain-swept pavement: swirl of the Debussy quartet matching the wide curve of the road and the depression in my heart: walking on this windy evening, the lamps just lit and wet with rain, alone along the broad street, brown street with lights of gold.

*

Except for poverty, incompatibility, opposition of parents, absence of love on one side and of desire to marry on both, nothing would appear to stand in the way of our union.

*

Even after twenty-five years I cannot read the jottings of this vanished youth who bears my name without discomfort. Insecurity and the only-child's imagined need for love have stamped him and I remember every detail of his unhappy courtship; the two lovely sisters who captivated the two newly installed young bachelors, the marvellous promise of that autumn, the mischief-making false friend, the apprehensive mother and the furious father who so easily separated us.

And this mined area round the Brompton Road is but one of my Londons, even as Chelsea and Bloomsbury and Regent's Park have other danger zones and trip wires. When the last war broke out, I happened to rent the same studio in Yeoman's Row and to sleep in the room where twelve years before I had experienced so many emotions, such maiming of heart and pride, where I had discovered London and the blessing of mixed society and had fallen in love and been frustrated—but never was the Past recalled to mind—for it is too subtle to operate in such a fashion, and we may haunt the scene of our triumph or disappointment with perfect impunity until—in one split second—the sky darkens; the figure in the bath-towel who could have been R. opens the door to the young man that might have been me; there is a moment of recollection, and the Past strikes; the long-buried voice or gesture loom, adumbrating relentlessly the pangs of human loss—apprehension of beauty and awareness of loss—which constitute the sour-sweet juice of Time: 'Darkness and lights: tempest and human faces,' as De Quincey dreamt, 'and at last, with the sense that all was lost, female forms—and clasped hands and heart-breaking partings and then—everlasting farewells, and again and yet again reverberated—everlasting farewells.'

The best attitude to such London apparitions used to be a visit to the Sherlock Holmes Museum which has been withdrawn, for too long a time, to America. The reproduction of Holmes' study with his unfinished breakfast waiting, the invisible gramophone playing street music, with the sound of a hansom cab arriving, of a newsboy crying the victory of Omdurman, dismantle our personal time-bomb and carry us back into a male society which protected us even before we were born. If such a mystical experience be not available, then let us visit some splendid tradesman of the old school; a tailor, a wine merchant, a bootmaker, a vendor of fine silver, of old china, fishing rods or saddles. If we owe them all money, it won't work, and we must try a good barber. I know of one who used to shave the Aga Khan in his bed without waking him. But best of all is the interior of a club, with a copy of *Country Life*, an arm-chair and some anchovy toast since clubs were designed expressly to keep the demon at bay, and so here again we are back with the dandies whose leathery faces sneer down at us from their engravings. But even clubs have their perils, such as electric fires and waitresses; some careless old members have a habit of dying in them and one can be stricken down in a sullen moment while contemplating the accumulated selfishness of so many elderly lonely people. London is dangerous; it is a place for the strong and methodical, for the brute and the bank manager; but for the sensitive who are allergic to social sheen and waste, to apathy and ugliness, who have lived so long and behaved so badly, who used to think once of all the fabulous houses that they might be lucky enough to enter and now, with Samuel Rogers (last ornament of Holland House) 'find a walk through the London streets like a walk in a cemetery'—for us, there is nothing to beat the 7.15 from Charing Cross, the thundering girders of the bridge and the funeral bake-meats on the diner.

10

BEYOND BELIEVING

I HAVE reached an age at which I am sometimes asked what I believe. The question invariably confounds me. Before I can reply the mind panics as when, in a free association test, it is given the word 'lake'—lake, hake, fake, crimson-lake, '*Delacroix, lac de sang hanté des mauvaises anges*'—deep sleep: and at the thought of that eternal sleep (better lake than never) I linger delectably over the word: reaction time twenty-five seconds. So, like La Fontaine, I believe in sleep: the time spent in sleep (the time when we are out of trouble) is not charged to our account but is handed back to us in later life to use as we please: sleep and its stealthy approaches: daydream, doze, siesta, garlic's blackjack; wine's persuasion; the phrase dimming on the page, the book falling from the hand; these are reservoirs of perennial youth and therefore all but sacred. 'Death will come on swift wings to him who disturbs the sleep of the Pharaoh' (Inscription on Tutankhamen's tomb).

Sleep first then, and secondly—Irresponsibility. And by irresponsibility I mean the refusal to accept any obligations as a social animal, as well as a mere European, Englishman, or good citizen.

Hippocleides, a young Athenian chosen by Cleisthenes of Sicyon as husband for his daughter. At the final banquet Hippocleides not only insisted on dancing, but even stood on his head on the table and waved his legs in the air. Cleisthenes was disgusted and cried, 'O son of Pisander, you have danced away your marriage'. The young man smiled and said, 'Hippocleides don't care', which became a proverb. (Lemprière's Classical Dictionary.)

A proverb which we too seldom hear when all the talk is of Atlas;

of shouldering burdens and responsibilities, of fulfilling trusts and missions, carrying out our obligations as a great power, great debtor, etc., and meeting new crises, sternly facing facts. What are these facts? That modern man, and in particular, Western man, and above all, European man has become mortally involved in a web of duties and sanctions, of social, emotional, and intellectual obligations. Knowledge desires to be known and the task of the living is to acquire it. The past refuses to let itself be obliterated at the old pace. Consider the London Record Office, the newspaper files of the British Museum, the wills and codicils of Somerset House, the multiplication of microfilm: then compare for one moment the life of man with that of an African elephant, which lives for about the same span. How much knowledge will the elephant, wisest of beasts, require in its eighty years? Of what to eat, what not to eat, of where to go, where not to go.

Consider the savages who surround such elephants—pygmies, Azande, and the like—they need to learn only a little more, a few crafts and skills, hunting methods, songs and dances, tribal traditions, witch doctors' beliefs. But an educated Western European begins to be crammed at the age of three; he must go to school, learn to read and write, acquire Latin and French, history, science, economics, mathematics, draw a map of the kingdoms of Israel and Judah, know the purchasing power of the mark in the reign of King John or the logistics of a Roman legion; his I.Q. is graded at four-and-a-half, endless examinations and probably two years of military service await him, then a lifetime of ferocious competition and financial liabilities, until, at rest in the tax-free grave (though even graves must be kept up), he hands on the burden to his loved ones in the form of posthumous debts and death-duties. I have left out the particular responsibilities of each country as the custodian of its national glories or protector of other people's; I remark only on my travels that ignorance is bliss and that the happiest people would be the least organised, except that no one will let them alone. I think Freud in his *Civilisation and its Discontents* understood the root of the trouble when he remarked that the State is more anal-erotic (mean, tidy, obstinate, and grasping) than the individuals who compose it. We inherit the passions of bygone bureaucracy, we have created even in our least corrupt institutions (inland revenue, customs and excise, probate, etc.) non-human cancerous growths, benignant tumours which oppress our society. The living cannot breathe because the dead refuse to die. A packet of old love-letters turns up in the attic—a delicious theme for a novel. But I have seen such attics slope downstairs; I have watched a fine dinner party ruined as a coprolithic flow of old stamp catalogues, imperfect collections of mosses and minerals, of pedigrees of racehorses, time-tables, bus tickets, score-cards, or boxes of brass cowbells, Welsh postcards and legless Swiss bears, piles up against the door and pelts like a rain of lapilli on stricken host and guests, dispelling the aroma of cigars and brandy, of roses and red wine, in a dusty fæcal miasma of hereditary hoarding. It is to early Christian art, according to Malraux, that we owe the first wonderful portraits of old men; the Jeromes, Augustines and Gregorys no longer merely serene, their wise old faces furrowed with the consciousness of sin and suffering. Hippocleides must dance them away.

*

The universe spells death with a small 'd'
Disdains proud 'I' yet sanctions little me. . . .

The natural condition of created things I hold to be one of undiluted ecstasy. Self-consciousness is the consequence of some imperceptible deviation in biological process, a deviation spreading like a ladder in a stocking which cannot now be halted.

Very small organisms have no fear or knowledge of death which, in a cell, is synonymous with parturition, and quite large organisms have no feeling of pain. It was not obligatory that there should be any disturbance of the primal ecstasy according to whether one ate or was eaten. The plankton barges into the Whale's open jaws as the Tunnel of Love. The indifference to death of some large creatures like turkeys and camels remains otherwise inexplicable. 'Man has created death' because he has watched man die. Even so, assuming that natural, even violent death could be part of our ecstasy as human beings or that our awareness of it can add meaning and poetry to life, such noble exits can be the reward only of a Sophocles or Goethe for in our time and place so full a life—the slow, simultaneous ripening and ultimate rotting of mind with body—is seldom attainable. The happiest creatures are those which live out their brief existence in instinctive harmony with the universe, unconscious of their role in it. But since self-consciousness has arisen, we must stake all on developing it to the ultimate moment when we shall have completely understood our environment, for to understand may be to change it, to find a way of reducing death (so nearly a blessing, and the source of all our dignity and tragedy) to something we can bear. Self-consciousness, which begins with the awareness of death, may end with its elimination. And here we have certain indications that we are on a likely path.

I believe in two wholly admirable human activities, guilt-free, unpunished, two ends in themselves rewarding: the satisfaction of curiosity (acquirement of knowledge) and the mating of like minds (friendship and mutual attraction) with the apprehension of beauty in so far as it be not included in the other two. It is impossible to undertake any kind of research without being perpetually made aware that the truth is plying us with suggestions, the past prodding us with hints and that if no benefits result from such assistance, it is not the fault of our heavenly helpers but of our all too human obtuseness. Who wrote *Kubla Khan*? We now know what books Coleridge had read; everything that was in his mind—but we know also how completely incapable he was, in normal conditions, of making use of such knowledge. Setting this impotent polymath to a constructive task, forcing an entrance into his cranium, the divine ecstasy (inspiration) flowed in, reassembled the metaphysical jigsaw into the greatest poetry to which the sodden organism could be attuned, then broke the reverie. With all the help of inspiration we can do only a little better than our best.

The mating of like minds is often expressed by the meeting of bodies and I would like to include both under the heading of mutual attraction—but with full physical union on the one hand or long-standing friendship on the other a whole new set of obligations arise. I refer only to the phenomenon of 'getting off' with someone, to the magical moment when we are neither hurt nor bored, when the letters in a name spin its anagram, when a handshake proclaims the return of Ulysses and a look can awaken the hyacinth of unborn springs. Sometimes these two profound and unpunished sensations are blended, especially when we are studying the past lives of old artists and writers for then knowledge and love coincide and the dead whom we have exhumed are reincarnated by the imagination.

Here one is greatly helped by such things as association copies and if an attachment to these be sentimental, there is no greater sentimentalist than I, for I believe that communication with dead writers becomes particularly intense when one is reading their marginal annotations, their note-books or letters. Good criticism is a form of spiritualism but the medium must possess the facts, not a lock of hair. The living denigrate the dead; they must or else they would be dominated by them but the handwriting of a dead man still retains something of his bygone arrogance. The Past, of course, is the natural subject of literature, though many writers ignore this or, to put it another way, it is what Time does to Action that is our particular province. Homer, Dante, Shakespeare, Milton, Flaubert, Proust, they all climbed under the tent. At five, ten, twenty, fifty, one hundred, or one thousand years ago, according to each writer, a point of maximum intensity was reached on which imagination could focus and so marinate people and events to perfection.

Do I believe in Art? If life be ecstasy there is nothing to say but 'Alleluia', if that ecstasy be lost then what can Art do to re-live it? And here we discover the weakness of any such word as belief. In the last analysis, at the moment when the bullet sears the flesh, when the plane plummets or the anæsthetic counts me out, can I really claim to believe in anything but panic and self-pity? No. Then how can I believe in Art? Or Liberty?

'Give me liberty or give me death'—does it mean any more than 'give me Leamington or give me Bath'? In the ultimate crisis, to those without religious faith, surely all belief seems equally absurd? In moments of acute sea-sickness or in that extraordinary onset of semi-consciousness known as being 'taken ill' there is simply nothing or nobody but seems ridiculous and sinister, indifferent or hostile. I still suffer from occasional attacks of claustrophobia in lifts or crowded theatres and before the invisible hand starts throttling me—'fugitive from some just doom'—I receive an alarming impression of having walked into an enemy ambush. In those seconds on the edge of panic all my values collapse and crumble into common absurdity. One might argue that these are moments of irrational fear and that one might feel differently at the long-expected onset of death when resignation replaces anxiety. 'On some fond breast the parting soul relies', and I hope that it is true, but I still think there should be one word for believing in art as I believe in it, in the sense in which we say, 'I believe in colonic irrigation', and another for the faith of patriots and martyrs.

'Would you die for your country?'

'I have so many countries.'

'Would you die for Queen and country?'

'Not if I could help it. I regard it as my duty to cling to consciousness until the last possible moment.'

'Duty to yourself?'

'Duty to my consciousness.'

'As an artist?'

'Certainly.'

'As an artist, forgive me, you don't write much?'

'And I compose, paint, sculpt even less, but I am an artist all the same.'

'What then is Art?'

'Art is the conscious apprehension of the unconscious ecstasy of all created things.'

It is one process to perceive this ecstasy, another to be able to communicate it. Once perceived in terms of human consciousness, we set this ecstasy against man's knowledge of his fate and engender an attitude either of acceptance or rebellion, realist or romantic. I believe in the supreme importance, virtue, and necessity of this process for the history of Art is the chronicle of such human achievements as have approached nearest to perfection, of the elixir of humanity. This, I think, explains the homogeneity of genius; constantly, when we read of the childhood and adolescence of men of genius we are struck by how alike they are, by their effortless technical mastery of their medium at an early age, their precocious feats of memory, of understanding of adult states, above all, by the immense richness of imagery in a writer like Keats, of melody in a composer like Mozart which reveal their immediate insight into this blissful universal harmony.

I do not believe in original sin but as a mythological statement of the human condition it seems painfully true. The fall, and the likelihood of going on falling, explains far more to me than the idea of progress and perfectibility; we have a bias to ruin, an itch for self-destruction; our moments of ecstasy are sometimes intolerable and must be blotted out. The heart rusts, the soul silts up. I cannot accept this back-sliding as a theological fact, but I feel it may be biologically or physically correct, that in bodies the process of ageing may instigate cruelty, lethargy, betrayal quite automatically; and I have remarked that any physical rejuvenation in myself—a slimming cure, a ski-ing holiday, a walking tour, even high altitudes in an aeroplane, induces a corresponding re-adaptation of belief, an impulse to universal love which endures till former conditions, over-eating, over-talking, over-competing, 'flu and fatigue, reassert themselves and the concept of love as the key and purpose to everything, the condition of the upper atmosphere, is once more enfeebled by the terrestrial envelope and the struggle for existence.

Even the lightness and brightness of all the materials connected with aeroplanes seem to point to a more light-hearted and light-headed way of life. The smiling air hostess is the archaic Greek *Κορη* in the Temple courtyard, the reassuring captain is the young bearded Zeus. In the air books seem inappropriate, the ectoplasm of the earthbound.

I have always been fascinated by the study of climate and in particular by its relationship to art. On the whole, art is a sun-substitute—perpetual sunshine casts out art. Where are the art centres of the world? New York, Boston, Chicago, London, Paris, Brussels, Amsterdam, Munich, and Berlin, all with long winters. There is hardly any great painting south of Rome or Madrid, and an interesting map could be made of the concentration of genius, of the southern limit of antique shops, of easel painting (at what point does it become too hot to have pictures on the walls?), of good bookshops even. I noticed in the Tropics that European poetry only became significant just before it was going to rain and that incidentally it was no longer possible, owing to humidity or white ants, to enjoy fine bindings or first editions. Air-conditioning may increase the yield from warm places even as central heating has pushed the creative limit northward but the fact remains that if I were to say 'I believe in Art', I would really mean, 'I believe that in certain physical states (not extremes of pain, fear, lust, or ecstasy) the literature, painting, music, architecture, sculpture produced between latitudes 40 and 60 in the last two thousand years under seasonal conditions can justify existence to me while I also live between latitudes 40 and 60, and am subject to a similar awareness of the seasons.'

I have noticed that Indians and Africans who spend some time in Europe very quickly assimilate European art which is not a racial but a geographical product; they take to it like umbrellas. All art, then, is relative, but the artist is eternal and if I could only be sure I were one it would not matter what else I believed. But only one part is an artist; another wishes to be remembered as lover, friend, sage or scholar, or simply an endurer, one who stayed to the end.

What Yeats wrote of Wilde, that 'because of all that half-civilised blood in his veins he could not endure the sedentary toil of creative art' is true of most of us. Flaubert's day or indeed any other day spent between library and desk will often be felt a day wasted even as the sensation of movement, the most pointless journey will always seem valid by its combination of thought and action, of mobility with the indulgence of curiosity. An archæologist's life seems to me among the most admirable. I believe that it is still possible for him to make discoveries of such significance that they may serve to put humanity back on the right path, discoveries about primitive Christianity or the nature of Egyptian and Greek religion, the lost books of Sappho and the Greek dramatists, Petronius, Tacitus, Livy, the *catalogue raisonné* of the Alexandrian library (I regard the burning of the Alexandrian library as an inconsolable private grief) or of buried works of art which will come to light in our time because we are so desperately in need of them.

Another profession I particularly admire is the Doctor's, above all the specialist in mental diseases who works on the frontier between psychology and the physiology of the brain and I also envy diplomats and Special Correspondents, for they are nomads without guilt. The capitalist, I mean the true capitalist, who lives by and through the manipulation of his capital, is also a free man after my own heart and when he combines great undertakings with a passion for the arts I feel he is to be ranked only a little lower than the artist himself, with Maecenas or the Medici, the princely builders, like the Popes and *Fermiers Généraux*. And yet what a miserable man is the artist with his vanity and envy, servility and egotism—and how much more miserable the capitalist who so seldom does anything for the living and competes for the prestige of the Past with rival collectors. If I were asked to name some characteristics typical of the mid-20th century, I would put first the uncritical worship of money, the spread of nationalism, the tyranny of the orgasm, the homosexual protest and the apotheosis of snobbery. Money, sex and social climbing motivate society.

Never have the rich lived so inconspicuously for themselves or done so little for other people—or been so rich for that matter, for I do not count the various altruistic tax-evasion schemes, the trusts, foundations and municipal galleries which are now the rage, a form of giving away money that the state has already earmarked, which permits the minimum human contact and plants on other shoulders the onus of discrimination. The ideal rich man of today is ideally mean, saving every sixpence for his posthumous trust rather than personally rewarding a poet or a painter, and purchasing only an occasional farm or a piece of Cromwellian silver or an Impressionist like Sisley who is dead yet not altogether in the museums. Often he is homosexual and a snob about everything as well (though seldom a nationalist), and invariably an amateur painter or writer who is jealous of his colleagues, though eager to pick their brains. He paints best in winter, at Nassau, when all the other painters are in bed with 'flu, and writes most in summer, in his beach house. He no longer is privately printed but obtains very good terms. For money has emerged twin victor from the 20th-century wars—money for the Haves and Nationalism for the Have-nots. Never has wealth held so many attractions or provided such a sanction for the good life since the whole texture of living is altered for those who possess it. Money need no longer clog the mind and coarsen the sensibility. It provides an extra dimension. The rich can travel light, at last, airborne from one æsthetic experience to another; they dodge the winter, the wear and tear of sedentary toil, of families and fidelity, they are as remote from us as the cuckoo during the seven months when he is away. Only people engrossed in their work or who are perpetually in love can ignore this mobility.

So an alternative way of putting the question would be to say, is there anything you yourself believe in more than money, sex, or social climbing? Or nationalism? Any belief which enables you to contemplate without envy or inferiority the masters of life in this most luxurious of possible worlds? Here again I turn to my well-worn trumps (1) the artist (and I would add the saint and the mystic if I knew more about them), (2) the lover, and (3) the joker, Hippocleides. Them and only them the capitalist cannot buy, the nationalist inflame or the snob deflate. They remain what the ancient Egyptians called 'true of voice'.

But there must be something else! Looking out of my garden window at the tall poplars and the Down beyond, listening to the confident squawk of an autumnal pheasant, the *fin-de-saison* stridency of the lawn-mower, I am linked by my consciousness to the world of natural living of which for more than fifty years I have formed a part. Has this half-century of self-speculation given me nothing to affirm, nothing to render my leaving of the world of more consequence than the mowing of the grass, the shooting of a pheasant, the felling of a tree? '*Un homme au rêve habitué*' he died while still uncertain of the divinity of Jesus or the identity of Shakespeare, a sceptic of whom we can proudly write: '*Mort sur le champ d'ennui!*'

'We must live this life,' answer Hippocleides and Voltaire, 'as if every minute were precious except the last—a bad quarter of an hour about which we can do nothing.' '*Supportons la vie qui n'est pas grand'chose et méprisons la mort qui n'est rien de tout.*'

'Every third thought shall be my grave,' counters Prospero, 'you have perhaps ten, perhaps twenty years to prepare. Let every activity be subject to that end! Make a good death!'

'Consider a child,' says Hippocleides. 'What does everyone require of a baby? That it should eat well, sleep well and laugh. Who wants to tell it of sorrow or fear, of death and disease, of sin and suffering? Children are our guests in the world and we must entertain them as well as we can and spare them the inconvenience of our mortal condition as we would a visitor from another planet. And what we would for them is surely right for us?'

I have left out one phenomenon besides the search for truth and the obsession with the form and shaping of a work of art—the devotion which is distilled, after years, from all the possessive kinds of love; which may have originated in boredom, unhappiness, habit, or lust, from an accident of fusion that creates something profound and selfless ('the giving which plays us least false') like the love of a parent for a child which yet keeps something of the child about it—a positive permanent illusion, a projection of lost early loves on to one person. In the field of discovery and the world of love miracles still happen. The presence of one of these long-suffering accomplices in our last act of existence may help to ease us out of it, or, when all those whom we have truly loved are dead, they may suffice to tip the scales for death, until dying becomes a renewal of communication with them. The rest is mineral emptiness.